By Any Media Necessary

CONNECTED YOUTH AND DIGITAL FUTURES
Series Editor: Julian Sefton-Green

This series explores young people's day-to-day lives and futures. The volumes consider changes at the intersection of civil and political reform, transformations in employment and education, and the growing presence of digital technologies in all aspects of social, cultural and political life. The John D. and Catherine T. MacArthur Foundation's Digital Media and Learning (DML) Initiative has supported two research networks that have helped launch this series: the Youth and Participatory Politics Research Network and the Connected Learning Research Network. The DML Initiative and the DML Hub at the University of California, Irvine, also support production and open access for this series.

connectedyouth.nyupress.org

By Any Media Necessary: The New Youth Activism
Henry Jenkins, Sangita Shresthova, Liana Gamber-Thompson, Neta Kligler-Vilenchik, and Arely M. Zimmerman

By Any Media Necessary

The New Youth Activism

Henry Jenkins

Sangita Shresthova

Liana Gamber-Thompson

Neta Kligler-Vilenchik

Arely M. Zimmerman

With an Afterword by Elisabeth Soep

NEW YORK UNIVERSITY PRESS

New York

NEW YORK UNIVERSITY PRESS
New York
www.nyupress.org

References to Internet websites (URLs) were accurate at the time of writing. Neither the author nor New York University Press is responsible for URLs that may have expired or changed since the manuscript was prepared.

ISBN: 978-1-4798-9998-2

For Library of Congress Cataloging-in-Publication data, please contact the Library of Congress.

New York University Press books are printed on acid-free paper, and their binding materials are chosen for strength and durability. We strive to use environmentally responsible suppliers and materials to the greatest extent possible in publishing our books.

Manufactured in the United States of America

10 9 8 7 6 5 4 3 2 1

Also available as an ebook

Contents

Acknowledgments   vii

1 Youth Voice, Media, and Political Engagement:
Introducing the Core Concepts   1
   Henry Jenkins

2 "Watch 30 Minute Video on Internet, Become Social
Activist"? *Kony 2012*, Invisible Children, and the
Paradoxes of Participatory Politics   61
   Sangita Shresthova

3 "Decreasing World Suck": Harnessing Popular Culture for
Fan Activism   102
   Neta Kligler-Vilenchik

4 Between Storytelling and Surveillance: The Precarious
Public of American Muslim Youth   149
   Sangita Shresthova

5 DREAMing Citizenship: Undocumented Youth, Coming
Out, and Pathways to Participation   186
   Liana Gamber-Thompson and Arely M. Zimmerman

6 Bypassing the Ballot Box: How Libertarian Youth Are
Reimagining the Political   219
   Liana Gamber-Thompson

7 "It's Called Giving a Shit!": What Counts as "Politics"?   253
   Henry Jenkins and Sangita Shresthova

Afterword: Necessary Learning   290
   Elisabeth Soep

Notes   309

Bibliography   311

Index   335

About the Authors   347

Acknowledgments

We would like to collectively acknowledge those who have critically engaged with this work and offered constructive suggestions about how to improve it, including Nico Carpentier, Nick Couldry, Mimi Ito, Joseph Kahne, Peter Kramer, Diana Lee, Sonia Livingstone, Lissa Soep, S. Craig Watkins, and Ethan Zuckerman. Each of you have helped us to clarify core concepts, frame central arguments, rethink wrong-headed assumptions, and otherwise brought greater nuance to this work.

This book would not have been possible without the support of Connie Yowell and others at the John D. and Catherine T. MacArthur Foundation, who have had the vision over the past decade to support so many initiatives in the space of connected learning and participatory politics. As we discuss throughout, this work emerged from our collaboration with the larger Youth and Participatory Politics (YPP) Research Network. So we want to acknowledge here the network's fearless leader, Joseph Kahne, his capable team (among them, Chris Evans, Erica Hodgin, Ellen Middaugh, and Sandra Mistretti), and the network members (Danielle Allen, Cathy Cohen, Jennifer Earl, Elyse Eidman-Aadahl, Howard Gardner, Mimi Ito, Lissa Soep, and Ethan Zuckerman). Many of the ideas here—far too many to acknowledge individually—emerged from our regular brainstorms and administrative meetings. We also want to acknowledge YPP's sibling network, the Connected Learning Network (Dalton Conley, Kris Gutierrez, Mimi Ito, Sonia Livingstone, Vera Michalchik, Bill Penuel, Jean Rhodes, Juliet Schor, and S. Craig Watkins) with whom we have maintained close and cordial relations throughout this process.

At USC we are deeply grateful to Gabriel Peters-Lazaro, Holly Willis, and others at the USC School of Cinematic Arts Media Arts + Practice Division. We also acknowledge Alexandra Margolin for her ongoing work on our project.

We want to signal our deep appreciation for the research assistants who worked on this project (Raffi Sarkissian, Karl Baumann, Samantha

Close, Diana Lee, Ritesh Mehta, Kevin Driscoll, Rhea Vichot, Alex Leavitt, Zhan Li, Yomna Elsayed, and Lana Swartz)—each of you have made significant contributions to the evolution of this manuscript. We have also benefited through the years by being able to bounce ideas and get feedback from Mike Ananny, Kjerstin Thorson, and several generations of members of the Civic Paths research group at USC (Melissa Brough, Kevin Driscoll, Alex Leavitt, Zhan Li, Lori Kido Lopez, Joshua McVeigh-Schultz, Andrew Schrock, Benjamin Stokes, Chris Tokuhama, Rhea Vichot, Christine Weitbrecht, Samantha Close, Raffi Sarkissian, Michelle Forelle, Nathalie Marechal, Nicholas Busalacchi, Kate Miltner, Carla Mendonca, Kari Storla, and Neha Kumar) and more recently, from those who have participated on the Civics and Social Media collaboration grant, especially Paul Lichterman and Nina Eliasoph.

We want to thank Eric Gordon and Paul Mihailidis from the Civic Media Reader project, who have been important thinking partners as we have sought to better understand how to design and deploy the digital extension of this book; we thank the fine folks at Pivot TV, Participant Media, and HitReCord for their help in developing materials that contribute to that resource; and we thank educators at the National Writing Project (Faye Peitzman, Paul Oh, Katie Kline, Linda Christensen, Christina Cantrill, Nicole Mirra, Kathleen Hicks, and Albert Vazquez-Mejia) and the National Association for Media Literacy Education (Michelle Ciulla Lipkin) who have helped to test and share these materials.

And of course, we want to acknowledge the ongoing support of Eric Zinner (the best editor a writer can work with), Alicia Nadkarni, and the others at New York University Press, and we wish to thank Julian Sefton-Green and the editorial board of the Connected Learning Book Series.

Chapter Specific

Chapter 1: The ideas contained within this chapter and the conclusion evolved over several years in response to rigorous and generous feedback received from a range of different audiences, including those provided by events hosted by the Alliance for Peacebuilding; American Academy of Religion; Aspen Ideas Festival; Babes-Bolyai University; Bocconi University; Central European University; Charles University; Concordia University; the Digital Media and Learning Conference;

Emory University; European Institute of Design; Georgia State University; International Communications Association Latin American Conference at Pontifical Catholic University of Chile; Library Foundation of Los Angeles; London School of Economics; Loyola Marymount University MIT; Pomona College; Shoah Foundation; Stanford University; University of California, Davis; University of California, Irvine; University of California, Los Angeles; University of South Florida Humanities Institute; and University of Sunderland. The ideas were also shaped in conversation with several crops of students who took Henry Jenkins's classes on Civic Media and Participatory Politics.

Chapter 2: We thank everyone at Invisible Children who made our research there possible. This was a case study that spanned many years and changes within the organization and we are deeply indebted to IC staff and supporters who continued to make us feel welcome through it all. Specifically, we thank Jason Russell, Jedidiah Jenkins, Ben Keesey, and Zach Burrows for the ongoing conversations about IC's directions and plans. We are also so grateful to Talitha Baker, Laura Weldy, Lauren Henke, Hailey Mitsui-Davis, Cameron Woodward, Ananda Robie, Andrea Ramsay, Jessica Morris, and Maggie Leahy for helping us attend specific events, coordinate interviews, and just generally for their support with the details of our research. We are grateful to Beth Karlin, who became an ongoing conversation partner as this research developed. Finally, we thank Jon Chu and Harry Shum for providing an insider-outsider perspective on IC through their involvement with the Legion of Extraordinary Dancers. As always, our biggest thank you goes out to the many young IC supporters who took the time to speak with us over the years.

Chapter 3: The Harry Potter Alliance has, in many ways, inspired our work and prompted us to think about how popular culture and fan enthusiasms inspire youth civic engagement. Throughout this project, we continued to look to this group for both insights and inspiration. We are deeply indebted to Andrew Slack for openly sharing his vision with us. Our deepest thanks goes also to Jackson Bird, who was always willing to read drafts, discuss aspects of the research, and provide us with valuable insights, and to Paul DeGeorge and Matt Maggiacomo, who supported this research as executive directors of the HPA. Thank you to the local HPA chapters, on both the West and East Coast, who invited us to their events—the Los Angeles Auror Brigade, the HPA of Pasadena, and the New York Dumbledore Army (NYDA). Thank you also to Melissa Anelli for her help with attending LeakyCon. On the Nerdfighter front, we are hugely indebted to Hank and John Green for supporting this research, and particularly thank John for giving his time in interview. A huge thank you to Valerie Barr for providing assistance and feedback on drafts, as well as to all members of Catitude. Thank you to the local CalNerdCon Nerdfighters for inviting us to your events. And thank you to Lori Krake Earl—your daughter has been an inspiration for so many, and you have in many ways inspired our research on this unique group. Our biggest gratitude goes to all Nerdfighters, HPA members, and Imagine Better supporters, who have talked to us in interviews, during quidditch games, while waiting in line in fan conventions, or while strolling through the Occupy Los Angeles encampments—we hope to have captured your experiences.

Chapter 4: Our research on American Muslim youth would not have been possible without the support of the Muslim Youth Group at the Islamic Center of Southern California and the Muslim Public Affairs Council. At a time when issues of privacy and unwanted surveillance continue to weigh heavily on our minds, we are particularly grateful to the leadership at these organizations who opened their doors to us as researchers. In particular, we thank Soha Yassine, Mariam Mohiuddin Edina Lekovic, Yasmin Hussein, Susu Attar, Aman Ali, Bassam Tariq, Akifa Khan, and members of the Elev8 collective for their support and insights. We also owe a huge thank you to the MPAC Young Leaders Participants and MYG youth who participated in the research. And finally, this case study would not have happened without the initial advice from Brie Loskota and Sumaya Abubaker at the USC Center for Religion and Civic Culture.

Chapter 5: Our research on immigrants' rights activism would not have been possible without the support of DREAM Team Los Angeles, DREAM Team Orange County, IDEAS at UCLA, Dream Activist.org, the National Immigrant Youth Alliance, the California Dream Network, the staff and students at Santa Ana College, especially Cecilia Arriaza, and Hop Tarrant and the Bell High School Gay Student Alliance. We also want to thank Manuel Pastor and the USC Program for Environmental and

Regional Equity. We also owe a huge thank you to Veronica Terriquez at the USC Department of Sociology for her insight and collaboration. Finally, none of this work could have happened without the participation and leadership from undocumented youth activists across the country.

Chapter 6: We wish to sincerely thank the staff, members, and supporters of Students for Liberty, which we have been thrilled to see grow tremendously in the years since we embarked on this case study. We especially thank SFL co-founder Alexander McCobin and Vice President Clark Ruper for their enthusiasm and openness about our work. We also thank the scholars, friends and activists who helped us with our exploratory research, including Paul Gamber III, Zhan Li, L. Paul Strait, Wes Benedict, Robert Butler, Norman Horn of Libertarian Longhorns, and members of Young Americans for Liberty. Thanks also to Kaja Tretjak and Amy Binder for their expertise and thoughtful advice on libertarian and conservative youth organizations. Lastly, we can't underscore enough the valuable insights and contributions of all the interviewees who participated in this project. Their passion and determination is an inspiration.

Personal

Henry: I would like to personally thank Cynthia Jenkins, who has always been the most important sounding board and thinking partner for everything I produce; Charlie Jenkins, who also has become a key editor and collaborator on my work; and Amanda Ford, whose careful management of all aspects of my professional life enable me to achieve ten times what I could have otherwise.

Sangita: I thank my family for their inspiration and support. Amish Desai, Marek Desai, Miroslava Shresthova, and Rajendra Shrestha, I would be nothing without you.

Liana: Liana sincerely thanks John Gamber-Thompson and Lisa Gamber for their unwavering support as she pursued a long path of reading and writing things. She also thanks the winsome Wesley Gamber-Thompson, of whom she can only hope to be as supportive. She dedicates this work to Paul Gamber, who taught her that you're never too old to find what you love.

Neta: Neta would like to thank her family for their continuous love, support, and encouragement, and for accommodating her research travel, even when it is to a fan conference. Yasha, Daniel, and Mattan, you are my endless source of strength and happiness.

Arely: Arely thanks her family for their support: Luis Andres and J. Angelina Zimmerman, Veronica, Andres, Gabriel and Christian Garcia, Ivelise Morales, Margarita and Ernie Castellanos, and Camilo and Carola Zimmerman. I dedicate this work to Graciela and Miguel Angel Claros, my guiding lights.

* * *

Lastly, we thank and acknowledge each other. Over the course of five years, the MAPP team coalesced in an extraordinary way, and our personal and professional camaraderie runs deep. While writing this book together, our thinking around participatory politics grew, as did some of our bellies as three of the authors added three healthy baby boys (and future scholars?) to the team. Every chapter has been made stronger by the input from each of the individual authors, and we truly see this book as the result of a collective conversation. We know the friendships will last, and we hope the conversation does, too, with many more contributors.

1

Youth Voice, Media, and Political Engagement

Introducing the Core Concepts

Henry Jenkins

Zombies/Activists/Fans

Fall 2011. An army of people dressed as zombies—many of them from Zombiecon—a New York City horror fan convention—had just disembarked from a big yellow school bus at Washington Square Park, then the home base for Occupy Wall Street. The zombie had emerged as one of many key symbols of the Occupy movement—standing in for "undead corporations" that were sucking the lifeblood of the 99 percent, soulless executives who had lost their humanity in pursuit of capital. Elderly tourists (mostly little old ladies) with cell phone cameras were stopping the zombies to pose for selfies and attempt to better understand their strange costumes, resulting in a series of exchanges that would further spread awareness of the protests. You could see the seniors (not to mention the zombies themselves and other protesters) texting, tweeting, and sending photos or videos. Passing the word was the point; Occupy was less a movement than a provocation (Trope and Swartz 2011). Its goals were primarily discursive; Occupy sought to shift how the American public thought about inequalities of wealth. Occupy's goals were also spatial: to reclaim public spaces for public purposes. And the little old ladies questioning the zombies were part of the process, spreading the word via each of their social networks.

This is what democracy looks like in the 21st century—yet another shift in the evolving image-bank through which Americans collectively imagine the prospects of social change. The Cultural Front in the 1930s sought to influence the development of popular culture, giving rise to Aaron Copland, Norman Rockwell, Frank Capra, and many others (Denning 1998). The most traditional (and now often banal) images of American democracy draw on symbols that took shape during this period.

1

The protest movements of the 1960s also tried to tap into the languages of popular culture—especially those of rock and comics—to create a counterculture, one which was implicitly and often explicitly critical of corporately owned media. As Fred Turner (2008) and Aaron Delwiche (2013) suggest, our current cyberculture built on the foundations of the 1960s counterculture, giving rise to the rhetoric of digital revolution. The protest movements of the early 1990s embraced a DIY aesthetic, inspired the indie media movement, and employed culture jamming as a way of "blocking the flow" of concentrated media. Adbusters, a key culture jamming organization, begat Occupy, but Occupy pushed beyond their rhetorical practices.

Even painted in such broad strokes, one can see an ongoing process through which young people have refreshed and renewed the public's symbolic power as they fight for social justice; they often push back against inherited forms and search for new mechanisms for asserting their voice. Occupy, like other recent protest movements, tapped pop culture to express participants' collective identities and frame their critiques. Thus a more playful style of activism is emerging through this appropriative and transformative dimension of participatory culture. Images and stories from superhero comics or cult television series are not only a shared reference among participants but also will be understood by a larger public. So the activists dressed up, created their own videos, and shared those videos on YouTube, where they were seen by many who were not going to Washington Square, Los Angeles City Hall, or any other Occupation site. These various activities offer examples of what this book is calling participatory politics. Participatory politics might be described as that point where participatory culture meets political and civic participation, where political change is promoted through social and cultural mechanisms rather than through established political institutions, and where citizens see themselves as capable of expressing their political concerns—often through the production and circulation of media. Throughout this book, we will be considering examples of innovative organizations and networks that have deployed mechanisms of participatory practice to help young people enter the political process. And we will identify alternative models for the political process that respond to or suggest a way to move past what some have described as a crisis in American democracy.

By Any Media Necessary seeks to address a core contradiction. On the one hand, there is a widespread perception that: the institutions historically associated with American democracy are dysfunctional, public trust in core institutions is eroding, civic organizations no longer bring us together, elected representatives are more beholden to big contributors than to voters, electoral processes have been rigged to protect incumbents and to disqualify minority and youth participants, periodic government shutdowns and budget crisis reflect a core impasse between the two parties in Washington, the mass media is increasingly concentrated in the hands of a dwindling number of conglomerates, the news we are receiving is sharply biased by those same partisan interests, surveillance invades our privacy and intimidates would-be political participants, and very little is likely to emerge at the level of institutional politics that is going to shift those conditions very much. Whew! On the other hand, we have seen an expansion of the communicative and organizational resources available to everyday people (and grassroots organizations) as we become more and more accustomed to using networked communications toward our collective interests. You will not understand this book unless you see both of these two claims as largely true, with grassroots media being deployed as the tool by which to challenge the failed mechanisms of institutional politics.

In *Networks of Outrage and Hope: Social Movements in the Internet Age*, Manuel Castells (2012) describes a range of political movements from the *indignadas* in Spain to the "Arab Spring" uprisings to Occupy Wall Street that deployed grassroots expression and networked communication to construct a new political imaginary. Castells writes, "Since the institutional public space, the institutionally designated space for deliberation, is occupied by the interests of the dominant elites and their networks, social movements need to carve out a new public space that is not limited to the Internet, but makes itself visible in the spaces of public life" (10). Castells makes three core claims. First, such spaces create a strong sense of community, forging social bonds and collective identities between participants. Second, such occupied spaces become sites for imagining alternatives, generating new symbols, reconnecting with historical memories, and testing and refining new rhetorics, often in a highly accelerated fashion. And, third, these encampments became "spaces of deliberation," testing new models for debate, collaboration, and collective

decision making. Such sites enable rapid innovation on the level of social formations, personal and collective identities, rhetorics and symbols,
and deliberative mechanisms and processes. And networked communication empowers the rapid diffusion of those innovations.[1]

The American public desperately needs to find ways to make the government work on its behalf, since many of the core issues—such as citizenship rights for undocumented youth or an end to racialized police
violence—are questions that involve the relationship between citizens
and the state. But many of today's grassroots organizations believe that
the most effective way to put pressure on the government is through
the exercise of expressive and discursive power—through education
and cultural change—rather than necessarily through the ballot box. In
Counter-Democracy, Pierre Rosanvallon (2008) describes the various
mechanisms by which citizens in Western democratic countries have
sought to hold their governments accountable for working within and
preserving the infrastructure of democracy. He argues that new political practices have expanded in response to growing skepticism toward
governments and disengagement with institutional forms of politics:

> For some time now, political scientists have tried to identify unconven-
> tional forms of participation, which may have increased in number as the
> rate of participation in elections declined. The number of people partici-
> pating in strikes or demonstrations, signing petitions and expressing col-
> lective solidarity in other ways suggests that the age is not one of political
> apathy and that the notion that people are increasingly withdrawing into
> the private sphere is not correct. It is better to say that citizenship has
> changed in nature rather than declined. There has been a simultaneous
> diversification of the range, forms, and targets of political expression. As
> political parties eroded, various types of advocacy groups and associa-
> tions developed. Major institutions of representation and bargaining saw
> their roles diminish as ad hoc organizations proliferated. Citizens now
> have many more ways of expressing their grievances and complaints
> other than voting. (19)

Understanding these new mechanisms of political participation is central to this book's project.

Ethan Zuckerman (forthcoming) has asked his readers to take a long, hard look at these new mechanisms of political participation in order to better understand their underlying models of change and to assess which may be the most effective means of achieving particular goals: "If I care about racial justice, should I work to elect candidates from a particular political party, run for local office, participate in a march, write an op-ed or a blog post? Given my skills, capabilities and time, am I likely to be effective in bringing about the changes I wish to see through a given civic act?" To address these questions, Zuckerman contrasts the different tactics protestors used in the immediate aftermath of the police shooting of unarmed black teen Michael Brown in Ferguson, Missouri, in August 2014. Zuckerman notes the complex interplay between traditional forms of street protest and social media responses designed to direct greater attention onto what had happened: "The protests in the streets documented online, and the online protests calling attention to events in the streets represent some of the ways in which civic media—the use of participatory media technologies for civic participation, political engagement or social change—has become a routine part of protest movements, opening participation in protests far beyond those physically present."

Much like Occupy, Ferguson and subsequent protests against racialized police violence have generated new political symbols, tactics, and frames. Anusha Kedhar (2014), for example, has described the ways that the "Hands Up! Don't Shoot" gesture has been performed not only in the streets of Ferguson but around the world as an expression of solidarity and as a means of embodying a particular subjectivity: "The hands up don't shoot slogan implores the protestor not only to stand in solidarity with Michael Brown by re-enacting his last movements, but also to *empathize* by embodying his final corporeal act of agency. As a collective gesture, it compels us to take note of and publicly acknowledge the bodily proof of Michael Brown's innocence." Under the hashtag #ifthey-gunnedmedown, African Americans were encouraged to share contrasting photographs of themselves in different personas—dressed for work or graduation or military service as opposed to more casual street clothes—as a means of calling out how the news media's selection of such images for publication can dramatically shape the public's perception of

Brown or others involved in police violence. This campaign allowed dispersed supporters to feel connected to the protest, offering a template for what meaningful participation might look like and identifying others who shared a similar worldview. The use of such tactics also reflects a growing awareness of the ways protestors have been able to coalesce and mobilize quickly via social media.[2]

Zuckerman argues that such social media campaigns often seek to change media representations as a means of shaping public perceptions and social norms. Such a model of change, Zuckerman argues, underlies many efforts to deploy social media because this approach builds upon the social affiliations and cultural practices many young people use on a daily basis. Such campaigns, he suggests, are easy to execute but hard to assess: "It's one thing to measure how many millions of Facebook users changed their profile photo to the logo of an equality campaign, and another to determine whether those profile changes led to a change in public acceptance of equal marriage rights." Moreover, such messages risk adding more clutter to an already vast media landscape, as citizens are pulled and tugged by many such efforts.

As we are writing, protests around the U.S. and around the world are escalating amid a growing awareness of a pattern of similar incidents in which black bodies have been subjected to brutal and discriminatory police force. We still do not know how effective these various tactics will be in sustaining an ongoing social justice movement; we also do not know by what criteria we should appraise their effectiveness. Rather than burning out, there are some signs that each of these campaigns has fueled the next (with the #BlackLivesMatter campaign following from the Trayvon Martin death helping to inspire the responses in Ferguson), adding new symbols and gestures to the mix (such as the choking "I can't breathe" imagery associated with the death of Eric Garner, another black man, caught in a lethal police chokehold), and tapping mounting public frustration and rage. Whether this effort alters police practices or not will depend both on the ability of the mostly young civil rights leaders to transform a series of local causes into the basis for an ongoing movement, and on whether government officials are prepared to acknowledge and respond to these protestors. How do we weigh the impact of public awareness campaigns against the refusal of multiple grand juries to take legal action?

Throughout this book, we will be exploring in what senses these kinds of expressive practices might be politically meaningful, both for those who participate (for whom benefits might include developing their voices and skills as citizens) and for those who receive such messages (for whom benefits might include gaining access to alternative perspectives to those represented through more mainstream media channels). We also will call attention to some of the risks and limits of these particular tactics, and the model of change that inform them, as we sort through this underlying tension among an increasingly unresponsive government, a public with an expanded communicative capacity, and an emerging generation seeking to change the world.

A Crisis in Youth Participation?

In this book, the term "youth" refers to people in their teens or twenties. It defines not simply a stage of physiological or psychological development, but also a stage in the process of acquiring the skills necessary for political participation at an age where there is less than complete access to the rights of citizenship. This group includes high school students, who may not yet be eligible to vote, and college students and young adults, who do not yet have the right to run for many elective offices. That said, we regard the political work these young people are doing not simply as preparatory for adult roles but also meaningful on its own terms as an intervention into core debates of our time. We find that young people sometimes begin getting involved with these causes in their high school years and may be providing organizational leadership by their late twenties, suggesting a kind of ecology of participation that was important to capture through our research. The idea that people in this category have a distinct political identity is evoked by the popular 1960s slogan "Don't trust anyone over 30." But it is also signaled by various other political discourses about youth that dismiss young people for not embracing what older people see as appropriate forms of civic and political participation.

While our focus here is on youth, keep in mind that some of the organizations we study allow for cross-generational participation around shared interests and common goals. Also, we are looking at networks of young people who are coming of age at a particular historical, cultural, and technological juncture, and our analysis deals with their current political and civic lives, rather than some universalized notion of child development or idea of a generational identity that will remain fixed throughout the rest of their lives. We do not know what kinds of political lives these people will lead as they grow older, so our focus is on what they are doing now and not what kind of people they are becoming.

Youth are often seen as emblematic of the crisis in democracy—represented as apathetic about institutional politics, ill-informed about current affairs, and unwilling to register and vote. Peter Levine (2006) identifies a number of flaws in this narrative:

> The narrative of decline overlooks creative developments, often led by youth, that may be building the foundations of civil society in the twenty-first century. . . . The decline story overlooks that various subpopulations engage on issues of special concern to them. . . . It overlooks certain positive trends in youth engagement, such as a steep rise in volunteering rate in the United States. . . . It treats a withdrawal from major institutions (such as elections and the press) as a decline, when these trends may actually reflect growing sophistication. Perhaps youth are deliberately and wisely choosing not to endorse forms of participation that are flawed. (15)

In short, Levine suggests, youth may be pursuing politics through different means than have historically been acknowledged within research on institutional politics or social movements. Scholars need new approaches for studying American public life, approaches that acknowledge and work past the core contradiction between dysfunctional governance and the public's expanded expressive capacity. Melissa Brough and Sangita Shresthova (2012) explain this point of view:

> Over the last several decades, younger generations in particular have become civically and politically engaged in new and different ways, related less to electoral politics or government or civic organizations and more to personal interests, social networks, and cultural or commodity activism (a form of protest that is typically levied against private companies rather than governments). These modes of political participation are often enacted through informal, noninstitutionalized, nonhierarchical networks in and around the Internet (Bennett 2008[b]; Ito et al. 2009;

Jenkins et al. 2006; Kahne, [Lee, and Feezell] 2011). They are political insofar as they aim to influence or change existing power relations.

Many American youth are making calculated choices that they may be more effective at bringing about change through educational or cultural mechanisms than through electoral or institutional means and through a consensus rather than partisan approach—addressing social problems on levels where voluntary actions can make a difference. Such a response is not irrational. Over the last two presidential cycles, there have been dramatic increases in voting by youth, African Americans, Latinos, Asian Americans, American Muslims, and a range of other groups, which is often cited as a key factor in Obama's victories. However, these shifts in political engagement have not translated into much congressional action on behalf of the issues that matter most to these constituencies. What progress has been made has occurred through executive decree, court decisions, or shifting public attitudes.

W. Lance Bennett (2008a) talks about some of these shifts in terms of "the empowerment of youth as expressive individuals" (2). Here, though, we want to stress their collective—rather than individual—dimensions. As Castells (2012) suggests, political change is being forged through social and political networks that come together online and in physical space to explore new possibilities. We discuss those shifts from a perspective of cautious optimism. We want to document these new cultural mechanisms for political change: how they are working in practice for particular youth involved within specific organizations and how these practices may be forcing us to rethink what "counts" as politics. While we are skeptical of change occurring in the short term through the mechanisms of institutional politics, we are intrigued by political, social, and cultural changes occurring around the edges of the dominant institutions, as young people work together to address issues that matter to them.

Mainstream journalism has tended to dismiss these new kinds of tactics as "clicktivism," but the central thesis of this book is that there is something bigger going on here that cannot be described in relation to a single platform. These young people are seeking to change the world *through any media necessary.* For Occupy, for instance, this meant connecting their struggle to everything from *V for Vendetta* (Guy Fawkes

Meme from Occupy Wall Street movement.

masks) to *Sesame Street* ("99 percent of the world's cookies go to 1 percent of the monsters") and translating those messages into "memes," documentary videos, public projections, street theater, and body art, among many other media practices. But the highly visible activities of Occupy are simply the tip of the iceberg, reflecting a much broader array of youth-driven movements actively promoting political change.

We do not mean to imply that all young people are a uniform group of so-called digital natives, equally comfortable with the possibilities of using networked communications to spread their messages. We share the concerns danah boyd (2012) raises when she writes that the *Kony 2012* campaign illustrates inequalities in the current communication context: "The fact that privileged folks—including white American youth—can spread messages like this is wonderful, but my hunch is that they're structurally positioned to spread information farther and wider than those who are socially marginalized." Such systemic and structural inequalities remain a real limit to this emerging style of politics, even as new media tactics are also deployed by American Muslims or undocumented immigrants, youth who are more "socially marginalized." In our work, we've discovered young activists who have overcome enormous difficulties in gaining access to the means of cultural production and circulation: from bloggers who did not own their own computers to filmmakers who did not own their own cameras and who relied on community centers and public libraries for digital access. Some groups have easy access to the skills, knowledge, resources, and social connections that enable them to exert their voice into public affairs in a way that is meaningful and effective. Others—especially many of those economically deprived, socially marginalized, historically disempowered—do not.

Who We Are

In 2009 the John D. and Catherine T. MacArthur Foundation established the multidisciplinary Youth and Participatory Politics (YPP) Research Network, focused on better understanding these issues. This YPP network, led by Joseph Kahne (Mills College), was part of the foundation's digital media and learning initiatives, which have resulted in a wide array of white papers, reports, and book-length publications—as well as an international conference, launched in 2010, which annually attracts more than 1,200 participants. The YPP network's efforts includes a large-scale quantitative survey, conducted by Joseph Kahne and Cathy J. Cohen, documenting the political lives of American youth with a strong emphasis on the quantity, quality, and equality of their new media practices, as well as more qualitative efforts to understand different forms of political participation. Network participants also include Danielle Allen (who has edited a collection of essays reexamining the ways the internet has impacted classic understandings of publics and counterpublics), Howard Gardner (whose Good Participation project has been interviewing young people who are involved in traditional political organizations and volunteer service organizations), Jennifer Earl (who has been documenting new forms of protests and online petitions), Lissa Soep (who has been exploring the platforms and practices that might help young people become more involved in participatory politics), Elyse Eidman-Aadahl (who has been engaging educators as they think through new forms of civics and writing instruction that may help young people discover their political voice), and Ethan Zuckerman (who has been developing case studies exploring best practices drawn from social movements from around the world).

A subset of this larger research network, the Media, Activism, and Participatory Politics (MAPP) research team at the University of Southern California, has developed case studies of innovative networks and organizations that have deployed participatory politics to get young people involved in efforts to heighten public awareness and promote social change. Altogether, we've interviewed several hundred young activists drawn from the following efforts:

- Invisible Children (IC), an organization founded in 2005 and dedicated to ending the human rights violations perpetrated by warlord Joseph Kony and his Lord's Resistance Army. IC stumbled into the global limelight when they released *Kony 2012*, a 30-minute film that broke YouTube's viewership records.
- The Harry Potter Alliance, a nonprofit organization also established in 2005, which encourages civic and political engagement by using metaphors from J. K. Rowling's best-selling fantasy series. The name Imagine Better is used for HPA's efforts to expand its outreach to engage with a range of other fan communities, including those around *The Hunger Games* and Superman. HPA exists in a loose affiliation with Nerdfighters, a YouTube community that initially formed through videos exchanged between vlogging brothers Hank and John Green.
- The youth networks connected to the Muslim Public Affairs Council and Muslim Youth Group based at the Islamic Center of Southern California, which engage American Muslim identities by encouraging expression and community-focused civic identity formation in a post-9/11 climate.
- The network-based, undocumented youth commonly referred to as DREAMers who engage in immigrant rights organizing and activism to achieve legislative reform.
- Students for Liberty (SFL), a group based in libertarian economic and social theories that has recently advocated for an expansion of "second-wave libertarianism."

Research for this book was conducted over a period of six years and included interviews, participant observation, and media content analysis. Our selection of the cases referenced above reflected an initial desire to look at groups defined around brands (Invisible Children), fan interests (Harry Potter Alliance, Imagine Better, and the Nerdfighters), faith-based communities (American Muslims), identity politics (DREAMers), and shared ideological and philosophical commitments (Students for Liberty). Yet, these frames broke down as we discovered each of these groups was more diverse in its background, goals, and beliefs than anticipated. While Invisible Children does use many sophisticated branding techniques to rally its supporters, we rarely heard IC members speaking of the group in those terms; many of them saw their involvement with the group as part of a much larger commitment to human rights advocacy. While Harry Potter Alliance, Imagine Better, and the Nerdfighters do build on the infrastructure and shared cultural knowledge of fandom, we also found participants who had joined because of their political commitments and who were not particularly fans of the media content being discussed. We found that American Muslim youth were seeking to change their shared cultural identity. We saw that that both American Muslim youth and DREAMers are, as groups, much more ethnically and racially diverse than many might have anticipated, and thus that both are committed to forging coalitions across different identity categories, rather than speaking from within a single demographic. Meanwhile, we had sought out the Students for Liberty in hopes of expanding beyond the progressive focus of our cases. While SFL does offer an ideological alternative, we found that these libertarians do not identify in any simple way with any given political party, that many of them do not define their identities on a progressive-conservative axis, and that at least some regard themselves to be left-libertarians, a concept that does not arise in mainstream discussions of the movement. In sum, the categories that led to the selection of these cases were shown to be not fully adequate upon our prolonged examination of these groups.

Also, while these groups clearly (and intentionally) span a broad ideological, geographical, and community spectrum, they also share important similarities. Though they differ in the degrees to which they rely on formal structures, hierarchical leadership, and centralized messaging and the extent to which they are connected with institutional politics, they all place a strong emphasis on personal and collective storytelling. These stories often depend on grassroots media production and circulation, as well as on the deployment of content worlds, often drawn from popular culture. In each case, as well, young people actively influence the practices and rhetorics of these movements. They are helping to frame the agenda. They are helping to shape the media and the messages through which they are pursuing their causes. And they are making active decisions at every stage of the process. Our cases emphasize various dimensions of participatory culture and politics. These groups involve different populations, working toward distinctive causes, and deploying varied tactics. Yet as we have been conducting this research, we have consistently been struck by these groups' ongoing attention to the cultural and social dimensions of participation, even as they work alongside political institutions and nonprofit organizations with more conventional approaches.

Our examples here are all U.S.-based, and we locate their activities within debates about American politics. However, these same tactics are being deployed by youth-centered movements all over the world, and we are eager to see other scholars explore what it means to do participatory politics in other cultural, political, and economic contexts. As we've selected these cases, we are aware of the much broader range of contemporary youth movements that are applying creative approaches to shifting the political debates around the environment, public health, poverty, antimilitarism, prison reform, campaign finance and media ownership reform, labor rights, gender and sexuality issues, racism, and countless other concerns. No book could cover the full scope of youth political participation, but we explore some key organizations working on these other issues as part of the digital archive (byanymedia.org) we have built as a resource for those reading and teaching this book.

Each of the five core chapters focuses on a specific case study while exploring key aspects of a broader theory of participatory politics. This includes notions of circulation and the paradoxes of participatory politics in relation to Invisible Children (Chapter 2); cultural activism, fannish civics, and content worlds in relation to the Harry Potter Alliance, Imagine Better, and Nerdfighters (Chapter 3); the tension between publicity and privacy, storytelling and surveillance among American Muslims (Chapter 4); the value of confessional storytelling and the risks of "coming out" online in the example of the DREAMers (Chapter 5); and the relationship between participatory and institutional politics, as well as the value of educational as opposed to electoral approaches, in the case of Students for Liberty (Chapter 6).

Each of the book's authors has been an active contributor to the MAPP research, and, while the chapters are identified with individual authors, this book reflects multiple years of conversations among us. The designated writers for each chapter oversaw the field work for that case and also did the core of the writing, though each member of the team has had input into the other chapters. Because we want to emphasize the collaborative nature of our work, the collective term "we" is used throughout to refer to the research team as a whole.

Our Book Title

Tani Ikeda, the co-founder and executive director of ImMEDIAte Justice, was one of more than 20 young activists—representing different organizations or networks—who participated in a webinar on storytelling and digital civics we organized in January 2014. Ikeda's organization uses media training for young women to promote "a world where individuals have the freedom to make their own choices about their bodies and sexualities." The group's first "About Us" page on its website places an emphasis on fostering youths' voice: "Our mission is to encourage girls to imagine a just world by telling their untold stories of gender and sexuality through film. We believe young women can have a strong and positive impact on their communities if given the tools to amplify their voice" (ImMEDIAte Justice n.d.). The group sees making informed, conscious decisions about which media to use as central to such efforts.

During the webinar, Ikeda described the ways ImMEDIAte Justice encourages participants to inventory the symbolic resources at their disposal as they consider channels for sharing their messages:

> So if you have a camera, use that to tell your story. If you don't have that, if you've got a pen and a pad, write your story. If you don't have that, you can literally speak your story. . . . It is something we always talk about because constantly, constantly, there's a lack of resources in our communities, so it is really about figuring out how to tell our own stories by any means necessary.

Our team glanced at each other knowingly when Ikeda made this comment, since it echoed ideas we had already formulated through our ongoing conversations. We've found that the most highly motivated youth—those most eager to change the world—are taking advantage of any and every available media channel to tell their stories. This is what we mean by our book's title, *By Any Media Necessary*, which plays on a phrase coined by the French philosopher Jean-Paul Sartre (in reference to struggling against class structures and economic inequalities) but made famous through a similar vow by Malcolm X (1964a): "That's our motto. We want justice by any means necessary. We want freedom by any means necessary." As he described the emergence of a new movement, Malcolm X specifically saw media as a key part of this effort, discussing in the same speech the development of a speakers bureau, a cultural organization, and a newspaper to get the word out, and perhaps, most interestingly, a space where "youth can play an active part."

Then as now, the key word is "necessary." Malcolm X was willing to accept violent protest only when and if it became necessary; contemporary protesters use whatever medium is most likely to produce their desired impact. As Ikeda suggests, these young activists lack access to the resources required to tell their stories through mass media and so they are looking for alternative means to communicate their most urgent messages. Certainly the most dramatic changes have occurred around digital and mobile media in terms of the speed and scope with which messages travel across a dispersed population. Such new media tools will get most of our focus here, yet these so-called new media have not so much displaced more established forms of political speech as supplemented them. Because they are responding to different issues, different communities, and different circumstances, our case study groups make different choices about what media to use. So we will see groups here using smart mobs, comics, posters, and even chocolate frogs to spread their messages. More than that, the same organization may deploy different media and tactics at different moments in its campaigns and may embrace having different community members delivering different narratives through whatever means are most readily available.

For us, the phrase "by any media necessary" captures five important aspects of contemporary civic culture, developed over the next five sections of this chapter. First, we look at how new hybrid systems of media-content circulation can bring unprecedented power to the voices of individuals and groups without access to mainstream forms of distribution. Second, we push back against recent accounts that have focused primarily on the political effects of singular platforms—Twitter or Facebook—in favor of a model that sees young activists as deploying any and all available media channels to share their messages (transmedia mobilization). Third, we make an argument for the importance of the civic imagination as a set of practices designed to inspire participants to change the world. Fourth, we trace the ways that the public's expanded communication capacities are enabling a transfer of skills and practices from participatory culture toward participatory politics. And finally, we consider the ways that participating in these networks provides opportunities for informal, peer-to-peer civic education, a process that we link to larger considerations of connected learning.

Beyond Culture Jamming: The Politics of Circulation

Confronting a world dominated by broadcast media, owned by corporate monopolies and largely closed to grassroots messaging, Mark Dery (1993) urged activists to disrupt the flow, block the signal, and hijack the signs coming from Hollywood and Madison Avenue—an approach known as culture jamming. Dery projected that an alternative form of politics might emerge as networked communications became more widely accessible, one he hoped would be "interactive rather than passive, nomadic and atomized rather than resident and centralized, egalitarian rather than elitist." As Jenkins, Ford, and Green (2013) note in *Spreadable Media*, the past few decades have seen dramatic increases in grassroots access to resources for cultural production and circulation and improvements to the infrastructure required for collective action. *Spreadable Media* draws a distinction between distribution (corporately controlled flows of media) and circulation (a hybrid system where content flows at least partially on the basis of decisions by individuals and groups, even as it is still responding to a context created through the agenda setting and content production of media industries). Today, rather than jam the signal, activist groups surf media flows. Rather than seeing themselves as saboteurs who seek to destroy the power of popular culture, they regard popular narratives as shared resources that facilitate their conversations (Jenkins forthcoming).

Let's consider a powerful example of how the circulation of media content through social media can significantly amplify the voices of politically active youth. University of Oregon undergraduate Samantha Stendal was outraged by the media coverage around the 2013 Steubenville rape trial, which involved two Ohio high school football stars who were arrested, tried, and convicted of raping a 16-year-old girl after she got drunk at a party. The mainstream media, Stendal felt, paid more attention to how these accusations would adversely affect the high school athletes than to how the rape would impact the life of the young woman. She and some classmates produced a short (25-second) video entitled "A Needed Response," which modeled how "real men" might react in a similar situation—showing care for a drunken female coed, rather than violating her. Stendal posted the video on YouTube as a contribution to the larger conversation: "The message I hope that people can get from this video is that we need to treat one another with respect. No matter what gender, we should be listening to each other and making sure there is consent" ("'A Needed Response'" 2013). The video spread fast, reaching more than a million views within a few months and provoking editorial responses from mainstream news outlets. Ultimately, the purple-haired filmmaker and her collaborators received a Peabody Award, the first ever given for a YouTube video. The publicity around the Peabody Award, presented in May 2014, pushed its viewership even higher; as of April 2015, it had surpassed 10 million views. This is a spectacular success by any account, but success does not necessarily require such massive viewership or such national impact. By lowering transaction costs, digital processes of circulation make it possible for communication to occur at various levels; consider how many student-produced videos might reach 1,000 or 10,000 viewers, and compare that to the communication environment of a few decades ago. We might understand this award-winning video as simply one text—one communication act among many—that has led to a greater public focus on "rape culture" and the failure of administrative responses to rape on American college campuses in recent years.

Networked Practices

In many cases, media tactics move fluidly between online and offline spaces, and messages circulate in both tangible and virtual forms. "Yarn bombing" represents an emerging tactic for feminist interventions in public spaces, with knitters (most often women) taking over the streets through the spontaneous and unauthorized creation of yarn installations that might wrap around or cover over a public eyesore or otherwise seek to convert the ways we engage with our everyday surroundings (Close forthcoming). Yarn bombing is a material practice; while the specifics are new, it resembles graffiti, street theater, and a range of other ways that protest groups have occupied the streets. Yet yarn bombing is also a networked practice. Participants find each other online; they use social media to facilitate their planning or to share techniques with other collectives; and they capture and transmit photographs of their work.

And in many cases, social movement participants are also using networked communication practices to respond to content produced and distributed through broadcast media, again altering processes of circulation. In 2010, TLC (formerly The Learning Channel) launched a reality television series, *All-American Muslim*, which followed the daily lives of Muslim families in Dearborn, Michigan. In early December 2011, the Florida Family Association (FFA), a conservative group dedicated to defending "traditional American Biblical values," argued that *All-American Muslim* dangerously "misrepresented" American Muslims by focusing on everyday suburban families. According to the FFA, this focus on the ordinariness of American Muslim lives would "lull" Americans into thinking that Islam posed no threat to the American "way of life." The group was able to pressure Lowe's (the home improvement store chain) and other sponsors to withdraw their advertisements. But then American Muslims engaged on social networking sites, using the hashtag #LOWEsboycott to fight back.

Kadir, an American Muslim digital media consultant, recalled how he helped organize the Lowe's boycott on Facebook. His and others' initial Facebook posts led to a series of conference calls to discuss next steps. More than 40 activists participated in one of those calls. They started a Google group for the "steering committee." They put up a website. They created a petition on signon.org. Then they volunteered to organize protests in Virginia, New York, New Jersey, Michigan, and California. Their activities ranged from online petitions and circulated videos to a Hijabi Flashmob staged in a Lowe's store in the Bay Area. Soon, prominent and established American Muslim advocacy organizations like the Muslim Public Affairs Council (MPAC) and the Council on American-Islamic Relations (CAIR) gave their support, and news outlets like CNN, the *New York Times*, and the *Huffington Post* reported the Lowe's boycott story.

By December 14, the controversy reached *The Daily Show*, where host Jon Stewart voiced his dismay "that some group in Florida complain[ed] that the Muslims on *All-American Muslim* [were] too normal." Speaking from a Lowe's parking lot during that same comedy segment, "Senior Muslim Correspondent" Aasif Mandvi reported that he was "disappointed" because Lowe's should be shut down completely: "If we are serious about fighting terror, we have to shut down their supply chain, i.e. Lowe's, aka the one stop jihadi-superstore." The company did not ultimately reverse its decision; *All-American Muslim* was canceled after one season due to low ratings. But the networked activists were able to galvanize popular awareness, as other Muslim and non-Muslim institutions, celebrities, and public figures voiced their support.

Stories That Matter

In *Why Voice Matters*, Nick Couldry (2010) defines voice as the capacity of people to "give an account of themselves and of their place in the world" in terms that are not only personally meaningful but can also be heard and acted on by others. Couldry makes clear that serious work on the politics of "voice" requires us to go beyond "a celebration of people speaking or telling stories," but rather must be placed in a larger "political context," one describing the forces that enable or block certain voices from being taken seriously as part of ongoing struggles over power (130). The borders of the political are fluid; different theorists may draw the line at various places. Throughout this book, though, we return many times to the issue of what makes certain practices political and what factors may constrain their potential impact.

Couldry ends his book with a call to reconsider what conditions need to be in place for voice to meaningfully enter public life; the rise of new media platforms has not guaranteed a political outcome, especially when those tools are controlled by corporations more interested in making money than expanding civic participation. Yet the availability of networked communications has given more people access to the means of expressing their voice, increased public and governmental awareness of the diversity of voices that are seeking to be heard, led to new consideration of what kinds of spaces and platforms are needed for effective political exchanges, and fostered what he calls "new intensities of listening" (140) as more participants feel an ethical need to try to process the emerging conversation. More and more, politics requires soliciting participation, getting people to tell their own stories, and also working together to amplify voices that might once have gone unheard. The Peabody Awards, referenced above, describe their mission as recognizing "stories that matter." In a networked era, more of us have the capacity to produce and circulate stories that matter to us both personally and politically, but this does not insure that all of those stories are equally likely to be heard by those people who have the power and authority to act upon them.

While telling one's personal story as a means of political consciousness-raising may have been a central aspect of earlier forms of identity politics, such storytelling takes on new significance when that story may be captured on video and circulated through online platforms and social network tools to reach many whom one might never encounter face to face. Many youth are deploying personal storytelling—through, for example, spoken word poetry—in order to link their stories to larger concerns within their communities, speaking for those who are not in a position to speak for themselves. In a MAPP-hosted webinar, spoken word poet Joshua Merchant described how he prepared emotionally to share his own story:

> When I started to write about myself as far as my identity of being a queer black male of color from East Oakland, that was terrifying, and it's something that's still terrifying. I am also very aware that if I don't [share my story], hell of a lot of people are still being muted, a heck of a lot of people from my community are not being heard. . . . You realize that you have a responsibility. Something that started off as just me needing to express myself because I didn't have nobody to talk to, or I didn't think anyone would listen to me, becomes "other people need to hear this

because I know they're from somewhere else than where I am from or from a similar place where this can change something for them."

We will examine many other examples where looking straight into a camera and sharing one's lived experience contributes to a larger political process—IC supporters sharing how they became concerned about genocide, DREAMers coming out as undocumented, or American Muslims challenging dominant images of what it means to be Muslim.

However, the confessional video—almost the emblematic example of Couldry's idea of "giving an account of yourself" in the digital age— represents only one genre of political storytelling. Consider, for example, the case of Jonathan McIntosh, a 20-something political remix artist. McIntosh's "Buffy vs. Edward" video depicts a confrontation between the pale, glittering young *Twilight* heartthrob and the empowered demon hunter from *Buffy the Vampire Slayer*. McIntosh created "Buffy vs. Edward" as an expression of his own frustration with the romanticization of "stalking" across the *Twilight* series. McIntosh uses Buffy to challenge Edward's misogynistic and patriarchal attitudes, rebuffing his repeated advances and, ultimately, staking him. The video sparked discussion on *Twilight* fan forums around the series' gender politics. Speaking at a Transmedia Hollywood event at UCLA in 2013, McIntosh explained:

> I think what was most exciting about it for me was that it did create conversations about what was abusive behavior and what was romantic behavior . . . how the media [is] sort of framing these very problematic male behaviors as romantic. What was exciting about it is that it happened primarily on blogs devoted to *Twilight* . . . . For me, it was trying to create a dialogue about something that is quite serious—you know, stalking and abusive relationships through a lens of something people are already talking about.

A subsequent production, "Right Wing Radio Duck," adopted a more overtly oppositional stance, though still expressed through playful appropriation of images. In it, McIntosh juxtaposed Glenn Beck's anti-immigrant rants with vintage Donald Duck cartoons. McIntosh (2011) explains:

I felt that Donald Duck would make an ideal pop culture character with which to explore Beck's messages and impact. Donald seemed an especially appropriate choice for this remix because he was originally created by Disney to represent a frustrated down-on-their-luck "anybody" character during the great depression. The current economic recession many Americans are struggling with today seem to parallel the struggles Donald faced in the old shorts from the 1930s and 1940s. I hoped that through Donald's situation, viewers of this remix might understand why people are drawn to the Tea Party. They are often very legitimately frustrated and angry people looking for answers. And most of the time they are not getting any real answers from the corporate mass media or from either political party. In the remix Donald turns to Beck in desperation and is offered answers—crazy answers, but answers none-the-less.

This video drew national attention when "Right Wing Radio Duck" was denounced by Beck, Bill O'Reilly, and other Fox News commentators who refused to accept the idea that it was produced by a young media maker and circulated by grassroots networks, rather than being secretly funded and distributed by the Obama campaign.

There Are No Twitter Revolutions: Understanding Transmedia Mobilization

Malcolm Gladwell (2010) claims so-called Twitter revolutions build on weak social ties and do not motivate participants to put their lives on the line. Make no mistake—what we are describing here is *not* a Twitter revolution. Gladwell's historical analysis rests on the unfair comparison between platforms (Twitter or Facebook) and social movements (whether the civil rights movements of the 1950s or today's Arab Spring and Occupy movements). A fairer comparison might have been between today's Twitter revolution and the telephone revolution of the 1960s, since we know that Martin Luther King, Malcolm X, and other black leaders used the telephone as a key tool for coordinating activities among other black church leaders, freedom riders, and a range of other dispersed sets of supporters. Yet few readers would reduce the civil rights movement to the effects of long-distance phone calls. Rather, the telephone was one tool among many this movement deployed toward its aims. Aniko Bodgroghkozy (2013) documents the various strategies the civil rights movement's leaders deployed to get their messages onto network television, often by staging protests in sites they felt would be most likely to provoke aggressive responses so that they could force racists to reveal their true faces to the public watching CBS, NBC, and ABC. And, of course, these civil rights leaders translated their cause into cultural references they felt would touch those who did not speak the languages of establishment politics—including even publishing comic books to translate nonviolent resistance into a youthful vernacular (Fellowship of Reconciliation 1955)—while using the communication infrastructure provided by the historically black press to address more focused messages to their supporters.

Similarly, today's civil rights leaders—for example, the undocumented youth who have rallied in support of the DREAM Act—act across diverse media platforms as well as through face-to-face conversations and street protests. Like many previous generations of civil rights activists, they use conference calls to connect and coordinate among various groups, but they also use social media to coordinate action across a more dispersed network and circulate online video or internet memes to dramatize their political narratives for not just current but also potential supporters (Zimmerman 2012).[3] Sometimes, they bypass broadcast media, other times, they seek mainstream coverage.

Whatever inequalities remain in terms of access to technologies, skills, and other social resources, we have found many instances where new media has provided tools and infrastructures by which marginal groups engage and participate in the public sphere. By claiming such space, subordinate groups can use networked media to expand the civic domain, even as elite groups seek to constrain the definition of what is "legitimate" in the public arena. For subordinate groups, these spaces of "everyday talk" are crucial for the development of political consciousness, for reinforcing shared cultural norms, and for working out alternatives to the dominant culture's views of their identities and interests (Harris-Lacewell 2006 4).

Our focus on fostering change "by any media necessary" is informed by current discussions of transmedia activism and mobilization. Lina

Srivastava (n.d.), who originated the concept, defines "transmedia activism" as "a framework that creates social impact by using storytelling by a number of authors who share assets and create content for distribution across multiple forms of media to influence social action." The Transmedia Activism website argues that transmedia practices may deepen the public discussion over topics of shared concern: "Multiple entry points allow donors, activists, partners and audiences to have a comprehensive and coordinated experience of a complex issue, and co-creation allows increased engagement with an issue and greater movement toward action."

Writing in regard to the immigrant rights movement in Los Angeles, Sasha Costanza-Chock (2010) notes important generational differences between older activists who seek to centralize the production and flow of messages and younger activists—including the DREAMers—who want to multiply and diversify both the messages and the channels through which they flow: "Transmedia mobilization thus marks a transition in the role of movement communication from content creation to aggregation, curation, remix and recirculation of rich media texts through networked movement formations" (114). Throughout the book, we will use Costanza-Chock's term "transmedia mobilization" as more or less interchangeable with the concept of transmedia activism discussed above.

Transmedia mobilization expands what counts as participation. Because digital media practices can be participatory, transmedia mobilization requires co-creation and collaboration by different actors. Because it is open to participation by the social base of the movement, transmedia mobilization is the key strategic media form for an era of networked social movements. The theory of transmedia mobilization does not view media as apart from, but rather *a part of* social movement formation. Media, Costanza-Chock argues, is no longer solely serving the purpose of messaging; it also involves "strengthening movement identity formation and outcomes" (115).

Some forms of media production and participation are designed to help cement bonds within an emerging social movement, creating a context for shared identities or mythologies which, as we will discuss, enables participants to act collectively to achieve their shared social agenda. Drawing on ideas from Robert Putnam and Francis Fukuyama, Sabina Panth (2010) explains:

> *Bonding* in social capital is referred to as social networks between homogenous groups. Bonding can be valuable for oppressed and marginalized members of the society to band together in groups and networks and support their collective needs. . . . The shared social norms and cooperative spirit from *bonding* also provide social safety nets to individuals and groups to protect themselves from external invasion.

So in the case of undocumented youth, media production helped to connect together a group of dispersed participants who had been forced to hide their common identities and experiences; we will discuss this in terms of the creation of "coming out" videos in Chapter 6. Other media production is designed to reach beyond the counterpublic to identify and educate potential supporters as part of an attempt to shape public opinion, a set of practices more closely associated with Putnam's "bridging social capital." As Panth continues, "Bridging allows different groups to share and exchange information, ideas and innovation and builds consensus among the groups representing diverse interests."

Historically, social movement players might have chosen different strategies and communication channels to achieve bonding and bridging functions, but the current media environment is increasingly porous. Content produced for one audience and one purpose can easily be accessed in a networked environment by quite different groups, including those hostile to the original intent. danah boyd (2014) and Michael Wesch (2008) describe such occurrences as "context collapse." Writing about video sharing in the age of YouTube, Wesch explains what happens when a video reaches unintended audiences: "The problem is not lack of context. It is context collapse: an infinite number of contexts collapsing upon one another into that single moment of recording. The images, actions, and words captured by the lens at any moment can be transported to anywhere on the planet and preserved (the performer must assume) for all time."

As a consequence of context collapse, language crafted in order to speak to the shared assumptions and norms inside a group are made public to those outside the critical counterpublic, both potential supporters and potential haters. All of the groups we've studied grapple with this reality, that an expanded communication capacity can also result in expanding conditions of exposure and vulnerability. Context collapse recurs across the book, but especially in relation to *Kony 2012* in Chapter 2 and the play between publicity and privacy as experienced by American Muslim youth in Chapter 4.

Many groups are now experimenting with what alternative media strategies that empower their supporters to take a more active role in shaping communication flows might look like. Transmedia mobilization is unstable and fluid, shifting tactically in response to changing conditions on the ground. It is highly responsive to the uneven access that participants have to different media platforms, tools, and channels.

The groups we discuss are differentially situated in terms of their embrace of different media tactics and strategies and of their openness to bottom-up participation in shaping their messages and their circulation. Invisible Children, for example, has a fairly rigidly structured organization; authorized leaders make many key decisions that define IC's vision and its core tactics. IC actively recruits new members into local chapters that maintain some autonomy from the parent organization. IC actively trains youth leadership to support their activities through summer camps, internships, and local events. And many of these local chapters are affiliated with schools and universities, on the one hand, or churches, on the other (Brough 2012). IC's media production remains tightly controlled, though there has sometimes been a limited interest in encouraging DIY videomaking practices. IC represents transmedia mobilization with a limited model of youth participation but with stronger emphasis on the cultural and social dimensions of politics than a traditional nonprofit might have. IC's *Kony 2012* video circulated via the dispersed network of supporters it had built up over almost ten years of organizing on the ground.

IC also demonstrates some of the challenges of maintaining a networked organization. As the organization received pushback from other human rights groups, it faced a leadership crisis. IC spokesperson Jason Russell had a highly publicized breakdown and the other national leaders—his longtime friends—circled the wagons. A new generation of leaders stepped up behind the scenes and shaped IC's response, but it took them a few days to regroup. This delayed response left the more loosely affiliated network members exposed. IC was too centralized and not sufficiently participatory, and knowledge was not adequately dispersed across the network. Ironically—as we discuss in Chapter 2—in the wake of *Kony 2012*, the organization became more centralized to maximize control over its messaging rather than maximize participation.

Compare IC with the DREAMer movement (see Chapter 5). The traditional U.S. immigrant rights movement has had elements of both grassroots and institutional mobilization, but it has largely been tied to institutions like labor unions, the Democratic Party, and a range of non-profit organizations. The traditional movement tends to break down according to ethnic or national boundaries, to be geographically localized, to maintain tight control over its messaging, and to rely on the ethnic media—radio personalities in the case of the Spanish-language communities in Los Angeles (Costanza-Chock 2010). The DREAMer movement marks a shift away from many of these formalized structures. Youth are connecting across nationality and across geographic location through their capacity to mobilize via social media. DREAMers have a dispersed capacity for media production: any participant can—in theory—create and share videos, and, as a consequence, there is much less control over messaging. These less hierarchical structures allow the DREAMer network enormous flexibility to respond to changing conditions (Zimmerman 2012), especially when the struggle shifted from passing a proposed federal law to supporting a series of local and state initiatives. The DREAMers' network could spread knowledge from any point to any other point. Leaders emerged organically, and there was not a fixed or hierarchical structure that might overrule local innovation. Critics, on the other hand, of such networked organizations often stress the fragmentation or incoherence of their messaging, suggesting that such tactics make it hard for institutional players to identify and respond to their collective concerns. At the same time, the DREAMers still benefited from training and support from more formal organizations.

Dreaming Alternative Tomorrows: The Civic Imagination

Speaking at the 2008 Harvard graduation, J. K. Rowling told a generation of young students who had come of age reading her books, "We do not need magic to change the world, we carry all the power we need inside ourselves already: we have the power to imagine better." Neither a generic celebration of the human creative capacity nor a simple defense of bedtime stories, Rowling's talk described how her earlier experiences working with Amnesty International shaped the Harry Potter books. Linking imagination to empathy, she called out those who refuse to expand their vision: "They choose to remain comfortably within the bounds of their own experience, never troubling to wonder how it would feel to have been born other than they are. They can refuse to hear screams or to peer inside cages; they can close their minds and hearts to any suffering that does not touch them personally; they can refuse to know" (Rowling 2008). As Chapter 3 discusses, Rowling's "Imagine Better" concept inspired the Harry Potter Alliance's efforts to forge common cause with various other fandoms.

Rowling's call to "imagine better" could describe a range of movements that are embracing "a politics that understands desire and speaks to the irrational; a politics that employs symbols and associations; a politics that tells good stories" (Duncombe 2007, 9). Liesbet van Zoonen (2005) has similarly questioned the divide between the affective commitments of fans and the cognitive processes associated with active citizenship: "Pleasure, fantasy, love, immersion, play, or impersonations are not concepts easily reconciled with civic virtues such as knowledge, rationality, detachment, learnedness, or leadership" (63). As a consequence, there has historically been a tendency to devalue the role of imagination within the sphere of politics.

As we've pursued this work, we've increasingly been drawn toward the concept of the "civic imagination," which we define as the capacity to imagine alternatives to current social, political, or economic institutions or problems. Put bluntly, one cannot change the world unless one can imagine what a better world might look like. Too often, our focus on contemporary problems makes it impossible to see beyond immediate constraints and develop a clearer sense of what might be achieved. One also can't change the world until one can imagine oneself as an active political agent. For many of the young people we spoke with, the message they received on a daily basis was that what they had to say didn't matter. These social change organizations work hard to help them learn to trust their own voice. And for some of these young activists—especially those who come from privileged backgrounds—the development of the ability to imagine and feel empathy for others who are living under different conditions is a key stage in their political awakening.

There is no doubt a utopian dimension of this civic imagination—some of what these youth imagine is impossible to achieve. But, as with other utopian models of the past, there is a value in articulating one's goals and ideals, using them as a yardstick against which to measure current conditions and identifying factors that might block the realization of those "dreams." Of course, not everyone's dreams come true, and there is a negative flipside to the civic imagination, which has to do with disappointment, frustration, disillusionment, and rage that may also spark political protest. Here, too, critical discourses—even at their most dystopian moments—often depend on an implicit set of ideals about how power should be distributed. Writing about the "Hands up! Don't Shoot!" gesture, Kedhar (2014) describes the ways that such street theater or as she prefers, street dancing "can transform a space of control, in which their movements are restricted, into a space of freedom, in which their movements are defiant, bold, and empowered, a space in which they have the ability to move freely."

We are not unique in emphasizing the place of imagination in fomenting social and political change. The term "political imagination" often refers to the ways individuals perceive and understand the political world (Adelson 1971). "Imagination" is used here in the sense of forming a mental image of something that is abstract. But such theories of the "political imagination" may have overlooked the potential role of "imagination" in its additional sense: contemplating things that are not real, or forming a picture in your mind of something you have not seen or experienced. For youth, this focus on potential civic roles is important since, as writers like Shakuntala Banaji and David Buckingham (2013) suggest, young people are often excluded from playing an "actual" or "meaningful" role in the processes associated with institutionalized politics. Their agendas are marginalized, and often, as with the current voter suppression efforts that make it harder for American youth to register to vote through their schools, they are disenfranchised. Yet our cases show that young people are learning to identify and frame political issues in language that speaks to themselves and their peers.

The Institute for the Future reached a similar conclusion about the value of imaginative citizenship when participants at the inaugural ReConstitutional Convention, held in 2013, penned a manifesto for what they call the "public imagination":

Any democracy requires a thriving public imagination, in order to make visible, sharable, and understandable to all the people new ideas, new models, new potential policies. We cannot make any kind of collective decision unless the collective can understand what is at stake, and envision where it may lead. . . . We must strive to understand the private imaginations of others, whose reality is defined by different lived experiences, and assumptions. ("Framework: Public Imagination" 2013)

Their document describes a movement from private imagination toward its realization in forms that can be shared with a wider public. That process often depends on images already familiar to participants from other contexts—images drawn not from political rhetoric but popular fantasy. Many of the youth we interviewed feel ownership over these popular myths but struggle to make connection with symbols associated with traditional civic life.

Civic Agency and Ethical Spectacles

Andrew Slack, the young community organizer who has been a key leader of the Harry Potter Alliance, explained the price of falling back on alienating and stagnant rhetoric as a means of teaching the emerging generation about democratic values: "It affects how people feel regarding their civic agency, civic engagement, and civic education—all of these falter and contribute to a systemic empathy deficit that has a destructive effect on every aspect of the democratic process including our collective ability to get beyond political blind spots through imagining new possibilities to effectively respond to our most stubborn problems around inequality, environmental crisis, etc." (personal correspondence, 2014).

For Slack and other fan activists, the solution comes through mobilizing popular stories as an entry point for political conversations, which brings us back to the zombies at the Occupy Wall Street encampment, the ways Jonathan McIntosh allowed Donald Duck to take down anti-immigration rhetoric, and the use of Harry Potter references to explain the stakes in human rights struggles. Chapter 3 discusses such practices in terms of fannish civics, in which they depend on a deep understanding and emotional commitment to a content world, and cultural acupuncture, in which these remixes tap into broadly shared knowledge about current popular culture trends that might be accessible to a larger audience.

As we have presented our research, some skeptics have expressed concern that "empowerment fantasies" may be displacing empathy for real-world problems; others have suggested that for these young fans—who often come from privileged backgrounds—it is easier to access human rights concerns through allusions to popular culture than through traditional mechanisms of consciousness raising and identity politics. Yet such mechanisms play vital functions even in those groups where people are directly advocating for their own rights and dignity. For instance, to explain his undocumented experiences, in a post on his blog, Erick Huerta—an immigrant rights advocate —explained how he turned to Superman, who was "from another planet . . . and grew up in the United States, just like me." Superman, a character created in the 1930s by two Jewish high school students—both second-generation immigrants from Eastern Europe—has become a key vehicle by which another wave of immigrants has sought to understand their place in American society (Engle 1987; Andrae 1987). If ever there was an illegal alien, it is Kal-El from the planet Krypton, whose parents sent him from his native world in search of a new life and who slipped across the border (via spaceship) in the middle of the night, got adopted by an Anglo family, has had to hide his true identity and remain silent about how he got here, and yet has been deeply dedicated to promoting and defending American values.

Retelling Superman's narrative in this way offers an empowering fantasy for other undocumented youth. Across her research on the DREAMer movement, Arely M. Zimmerman found several examples of the deployment of superhero imagery. One respondent described the experience of discovering other undocumented youth online as like "finding other X-Men." Another compared their campaign, which involved youth from many different backgrounds, to the Justice League. A third suggested that posting a video on YouTube in which he proclaimed himself "proud" and "undocumented" had parallels to the experience of Spider-Man, who removed his mask on national television during Marvel's *Civil Wars* storyline. A graphic created for an online recruitment campaign used the image of Wolverine to suggest what kind of hero youth volunteers might aspire to become. These images also provided a means by

SUPERMAN WAS AN ILLEGAL IMMIGRANT

Dreamers use Superman to explain the immigration experience.

which the debates about immigration rights might be discussed from new perspectives, reaching many who had never considered their experiences in this way before. Subsequently, the shared use of the superhero mythology allowed Imagine Better to partner with immigrant rights groups for a campaign that accompanied the release of *Man of Steel*, discussed in more detail in Chapter 3.

It is not surprising that Huerta uses superhero comics as a means to explain his lived experiences of being undocumented. His Superman saga exists alongside a range of other efforts to mobilize the superhero as a kind of technology for sparking the civic imagination, including uses of Wonder Woman for feminist politics (Yockey 2012) and Captain America as a symbol for both reactionary and progressive organizations (F. Phillips 2013).

As Stephen Duncombe (2012a), one of the authors of the manifesto for the public imagination, explains:

Scratch an activist and you're apt to find a fan. It's no mystery why: fandom provides a space to explore fabricated worlds that operate according to different norms, laws, and structures than those we experience in our "real" lives. Fandom also necessitates relationships with others: fellow fans with whom to share interests, develop networks and institutions, and create a common culture. This ability to imagine alternatives and build community, not coincidentally, is a basic prerequisite for political activism.

Our concept of the civic imagination is closely related to the set of practices Duncombe (2007) has identified as "ethical spectacle." Duncombe documents tactics that command public attention, often by dramatizing the stakes of a political struggle, and often in a language that is playful, even comic, rather than sober and literal-minded. These ethical spectacles work best, he tells us, when they emerge from participants' collective imaginations, when they are flexible enough to adapt to changing situations, when they are transparent enough that spectators understand them as constructed, and when they have utopian dimensions—because they allow us to think beyond the range of current possibilities.

So far, our discussion of the civic imagination has identified examples that deploy fantastical elements from popular culture to make their political points. Such examples are often the most surprising, since they look so different from the forms of political speech we associate with earlier generations. But the civic imagination is also at play as young people share their own real-world experiences, as in, for example, Joshua Merchant's spoken-word pieces. Consider another example. On December 11, 2012, Noor Tagouri, a 19-year-old American Muslim woman, posted a video, "My Dream: First American Hijabi Anchorwoman #LetNoorShine," on YouTube. In it, she recalled how a photo of her sitting behind an ABC news desk took on a life of its own on Facebook and garnered 20,000 likes in one week. Noor then asked various media celebrities—including Oprah Winfrey, Lisa Ling, and Anderson Cooper—to let her shadow or intern with them to help fulfill her dream of becoming the first hijabi (scarf-wearing) news anchor on an American primetime news network: "It is the people from every corner of the globe who have liked and shared my photo and sent me thousands of letters and messages of their support, who gave me the confidence to ask . . . [for] this." The video was both an expression of Noor's dreams and an encouragement to imagine a different status for Muslims in American media.

Photo from Noor Tagouri's campaign to become a hijab-wearing anchor on commercial television.

Writing about a 1957 news photograph showing white citizens jeering at black students as they attempted to enter a once segregated school, Danielle Allen (2006) tells us:

> The photo forced a choice on its U.S. viewers, and its power to engage the imagination lay in this. The picture simultaneously recorded a nightmarish version of a town meeting and, by presenting to a broad public the visible structure of segregation, elicited throughout the citizenry an epiphantic awareness of the inner workings of public life and made those mechanics the subject of debate. (5)

Noor's video does similar work, enabling us to envision, discuss, debate, and struggle to achieve other possibilities. Allen argues, "As democracy develops an explanation of how its citizenry is a coherent body, 'the people,' and makes this body imaginable, it also invents customs and practices of citizenly interaction that accord with that explanation" (17). In short, changing how the American public imagines democracy may be a key first step toward altering how Americans perceive and treat each other, essential if undocumented or American Muslim youth are going to be embraced within "we the people." The photograph of Noor in her hijab sitting in a network anchor's chair called attention to the absence of American Muslims within the mainstream media, while also promoting the young woman's aspiration to someday enter the media on a more equal basis. The photograph Allen discusses became part of the shared political culture through its circulation via mass media; other young activists have similarly used social networking platforms to heighten the visibility of their own creative works.

Imagining Communities

Benedict Anderson (1983) used the term "imagined community" to describe one of the core mechanisms shaping strong nationalist movements in the 19th and 20th centuries; people across the British empire read the *Times* of London, and through this shared experience and through the ways that the newspaper articulated a common agenda, they were able to connect diverse everyday experiences to a larger project of empire building. Today, the term "imagining communities" might be more productive. Young people are not simply accepting an agenda constructed by mass media for their consumption, rather they are actively co-constructing the contents of the civic imagination through networked communications. They are building a group identity that might fuel their campaigns and, within those campaigns, they are developing ways of expressing their shared visions for what a better society might look like. Such exchanges may occur at all levels—from the hyperlocal to the transnational, from friendship circles to social movements and formal organizations—yet imagining is an activity, something produced and not simply consumed.

In Anderson's classic formulation, these communities were imagined because they consisted of massive numbers of people who would never meet each other face to face but somehow felt connected to each other; the same would be true for today's imagining communities, except that in the context of a many-to-many networked communications system, the potential for direct contact between participants is different from what could have been achieved among the readers of the *Times*. Ethan Zuckerman (2013c) has noted the many ways that contemporary participants in the online world fail to realize its more cosmopolitan potentials, and fail to reach out to people from different backgrounds than their own, yet there is still a greater opportunity for such interactions than could be facilitated through print culture.

We are speaking here of the civic imagination rather than the public imagination or the political imagination for several reasons. The public imagination emphasizes the social structure—envisioned as a public or counterpublic—from which these acts of imagining arise, while we see these young people involved in something more fluid, a good deal less rationalized than the way the public sphere has traditionally been conceived. Peter Dahlgren (2009) tells us:

> The civic resonates with the notion of public, in the sense of being visible, relevant for, and in some ways accessible to many people that is, situated outside the private, intimate domain. "Civic" carries the implication of engagement in public life—a cornerstone of democracy. Interestingly, the civic also signifies the public good. It conveys a sense of the altruistic, a

WAIT!
BEING CUTE
— *isn't a* —
PRE-EXISTING
CONDITION
ANYMORE?

Thanks, Adorable Care Act!

Adorable Care Act meme.

kind of "service," doing good for others, such as volunteer work. . . . The civic is thus a precondition for the political, in the sense that it situates us within the realm of the public. (58)

We are describing as "civic" those practices that are designed to improve the quality of life and strengthen social ties within a community, whether defined in geographically local or dispersed terms. Some of these acts of imagining are closely linked to various forms of institutional politics, seeking to advocate changes that can be achieved only through governmental action.

For example, the Adorable Care Act was an effort to educate the public about the national healthcare policy often called "Obamacare" through the creation of memes that linked policy concerns with images of cute animals, designed to be circulated through social media platforms. In other cases (as we've already suggested) activist groups have sought change through different means—for example, fighting back over terms of service on Web 2.0 platforms that restrict their expressive freedom or promoting change through education (as will be discussed in relation to the "second-wave" libertarians).

Christina Evans (2015), another member of the YPP network team, has been using the term "digital civic imagination" in a somewhat different but closely related sense—to refer to the ways that young people are (or are not) able to reconceptualize the social media practices they use in their everyday lives into tactics they might deploy as citizens. Through interviews with young people in Oakland, Chicago, and rural North Carolina, Evans found that young people often need help to translate skills they acquired in their social and recreational use of media toward political ends, and she considers what roles educators might play in that process. Our work can be understood as helping to map the trajectory from participatory culture to participatory politics.

Making the Leap: From Participatory Culture to Participatory Politics

Our book's focus is not on new technologies per se, but on the possibilities (real and imagined) that we might use these tools to achieve greater political participation. Many initially acquired the skills and accessed infrastructures supporting this activism through cultural, rather than overtly political, activities that have become more widespread in the everyday experiences of American youth. To be clear, the cultural is always already (at least implicitly) political, but our focus here is on the ways that cultural practices are being deployed toward explicitly political ends. We are not walking away from decade-long debates about whether appropriation and remix practices may have political effects in terms of allowing us to reimagine gender and sexual identities in the case of slash fan fiction, allowing us a momentary escape from the control of regulatory structures (as in for example, discussions of Beatlemania in Ehrenreich et al. 1997), or inspiring struggles over intellectual property law constraints on political speech (as in the case of the Organization for Transformative Works.) Yet there have always been those who argued that such practices did not constitute "real politics," which—in their eyes—involved mobilization, voting, petitioning, protest, and labor organizing. This book is thus taking up the challenge of mapping some of the points of contact between cultural and institutional models of politics and we are starting by charting the interplay between participatory culture and participatory politics.

Participatory culture describes a diverse set of shared activities and social engagements, ranging from fan fiction writing and crafting to gaming, through which people collectively carve out a space for expression and learning. Describing the educational dimensions of participatory culture, Henry Jenkins et al. (2006) stress that groups involved in such activities are characterized by "relatively low" barriers to artistic expression and civic engagement, strong social support for creating and sharing and for the development of "voice," informal practices providing mentorship and training for would-be participants, and contributors' sense that what they share matters. Young men and women who learned how to use their cameras recording skateboarding stunts, to mash up images to make cute cat pictures, or to edit fan videos are now turning their skills toward political speech and grassroots mobilization. These "creative activists" often speak to each other through images borrowed from commercial entertainment but remixed to communicate their own messages; they are often deploying social media platforms, sometimes in ways that challenge corporate interests; and they are forging communities through acts of media circulation.

By Any Media Necessary responds to recent analyses by writers such as Nico Carpentier (2011), Peter Dahlgren (2011), Christopher M. Kelty (2013), and Aaron Delwiche and Jennifer Henderson (2013), who have called for more precise distinctions between different models of participation. Delwiche (2013), for example, draws strong links between the kinds of participatory democracy advocated by the counterculture of the 1960s and the forms of participatory culture that emerged in reaction to networked computing. Today's participatory culture and politics reflects decades of struggles to gain greater control of the means of cultural production and circulation, to free the communication environment from powerful gatekeepers. Yet a range of interests have attached themselves to a rhetoric of participation, which may mask the continuation of old inequalities in how wealth and power are distributed. Kelty writes:

> "Participating" in Facebook is not the same thing as participating in a Free Software project, to say nothing of participating in the democratic governance of a state. If there are indeed different "participatory cultures" then the work of explaining their differences must be done by thinking

concretely about the practices, tools, ideologies, and technologies that make them up. Participation is about power, and, no matter how "open" a platform is, participation will reach a limit circumscribing power and its distribution. (29)

As we seek to deepen our understanding of participatory politics, we need to be more precise in describing the forms participation takes. Critics of participatory politics often see participation as simply another term for co-optation, implying that participating in a neoliberal economy only empowers corporate forces controlling the pipelines through which these new messages flow (Dean 2005). Rather, we describe participation in terms of the ability to forge a sense of collective voice and efficacy through larger networks that work together to bring about change.

A More Participatory Culture

Participation, as Nico Carpentier (Jenkins and Carpentier 2013) suggests, is a utopian ideal: "There is no end point. It will never be achieved . . . There will always be struggle, there will always be contestation. There will always be elitist forces trying to make things go back to the old ways" (266). Drawing from Carpentier, we see participation as an aspiration as much as it is a reality, something groups such as those we survey are striving to achieve. Carpentier (2011) makes a productive distinction between what he calls minimalist models of participation where participation is limited in scope and what he calls maximalist models that see participation as playing "a more substantial and continuous role and does not remain restricted to the 'mere' election of representatives" (16–17). Here, participation is understood as a matter of degree—few situations match his ideal of maximalist participation.

While Jenkins's original white paper (Jenkins et al. 2006) used the term "participatory culture," we will refer to "a more participatory culture" to call attention to those who have not yet acquired the skills and access and who lack the power and status needed to meaningfully participate. A more participatory culture is one where more people have access to the means of cultural production and circulation and one where more key decisions are made with the active and expanded participation of community members. A more participatory culture is not an inevitable outgrowth of technological change; to achieve it will require struggles to broaden access to technological infrastructures and participatory skills, struggles against the corporate ownership and government regulation of communication channels, struggles to retain our collective rights to privacy and to free expression, struggles to be heard and respected by institutional power brokers, and struggles against various forms of segregation and marginalization.

Our research is helping to identify many ways that activist networks have "empowered" young people, especially those who are already culturally engaged, to embrace more active roles as citizens. Many youth are finding their civic voices through projects that encourage them to produce and circulate media. While we see much to celebrate here, we are also concerned about the precariousness of some of these publics, which contend with the same pressures that have disempowered other young people in the past. In a review of the existing literature, Jennifer S. Light (2015) concludes:

> Time and again, it seems, when the cost has fallen young people have turned to new media as tools for political expression among themselves and to the broader community of adults. Yet, in keeping with the history of alternative media more generally—for adults, too, have been enthusiastic users—the youth who used media technologies but did not control media systems found traditional gatekeeping authorities—all adults—eager to assert control over and restrict technologies' future use. (33)

Throughout the book, we consider a range of factors that limit the capacity for participatory politics, including issues of media literacy and civic skills (in the case of *Kony 2012*), digital access (in the case of the DREAMers), surveillance (in the case of American Muslims), and institutional entanglements (in the case of Students for Liberty). Perhaps most powerfully, we address the range of institutional constraints and ideological blinders—the larger power dynamics around race, gender, sexuality, legal status, or generation that make it hard for young people to meaningfully participate in the political process.

What Does Participatory Politics Look Like?

In a white paper for the MacArthur Youth and Participatory Politics Research Network, Cathy J. Cohen and Joseph Kahne (2012) define participatory politics as "interactive, peer-based acts through which individuals and groups seek to exert both voice and influence on issues of public concern" (vi). This report identified various forms of participatory politics, including the sharing of information through social media, engaging in online conversations through digital forums or blogs and podcasts, creating original content in the form of online videos or photoshopped memes to comment on a current issue, using Twitter and other microblogging tools to rally a community toward collective action, or deploying databases in order to investigate an ongoing concern. Participatory politics represent forms of political participation that are embedded in the everyday life practices of young political agents. Cohen and Kahne explain:

> The participatory skills, norms, and networks that develop when social media is used to socialize with friends or to engage with those who share one's interests can and are being transferred to the political realm. . . . What makes participatory culture unique is not the existence of these individual acts, but that the shift in the relative prevalence of circulation, collaboration, creation, and connection is changing the cultural context in which people operate. (3)

Joe Kahne, Ellen Middaugh, and Danielle Allen (2014) stress that their "notion of the political extends beyond the electoral focus" to include a "broad array of efforts" that range from "electoral" activities to "lifestyle politics" (1). More specifically, they propose the following activity types as characteristic of participatory politics:

Circulation. In participatory politics, the flow of information is shaped by many in the broader community rather than by a small group of elites. . . .

Dialogue and feedback. There is a high degree of dialogue among community members, as well as a practice of weighing in on issues of public concern and on the decisions of civic and political leaders. . . .

Production. Members not only circulate information but also create original content (such as a blog or video that has political intent or impact) that allows them to advance their perspectives. . . .

Mobilization. Members of a community rally others to help accomplish civic or political goals. . . .

Investigation. Members of a community actively pursue information about issues of public concern. . . . (41)

Cohen and Kahne have overseen two national surveys, each collecting data from roughly 3,000 survey respondents aged 15–25. The bad news is that despite the publicity around Obama's courting of the youth vote, more than half (56 percent) of those contacted had not been involved in politics in any form over the 12 months prior to being queried. Somewhat more reassuring was that what they are calling participatory politics does not "distract" youth from forms of institutional political practices (such as voting, petitioning, street protest, or writing letters to the editor). On the contrary, Cohen and Kahne found that those who engaged in participatory politics (roughly 40–45 percent across all racial categories) were almost twice as likely to vote as those who did not.

Seeking to better understand how these various sets of practices entered the lives of American youth, the Good Participation team at Harvard University (Rundle, James, and Weinstein forthcoming), conducted in-depth interviews with 70 civically and politically active youth between the ages of 15 and 25. The youth they interviewed were more likely to engage, on a regular basis, with some of these practices (especially circulation, production, and investigation) than others (dialogue, feedback, and mobilization), while there was a wide range in the depth and degree of sophistication with which they were applying these practices.

Ben Bowyer, a member of the YPP survey team, also analyzed data from the Pew Internet and American Life Project that was collected following the 2008 and 2012 elections (Smith 2013). He found substantial increases in these participatory practices over this four-year period. For example, the number of youth posting pictures or videos related to social and political concerns increased from 10 percent to 21 percent; the number sharing political news through social media went from 13 percent to 32 percent; and the percentage who had started a group online supporting a cause went from 14 to 26 percent. By almost every measure, the percentage of youth engaged in participatory politics is growing at a rapid rate. Keep in mind that these practices often involved deeper commitments of time, energy, social capital, and other resources than many of the mechanisms of institutional politics (voting, for example), supporting our argument that at least some young people are not "disengaged" but rather are conducting politics through other means.

Reflecting what we've described as the participation gap, these skills and experiences are unevenly distributed among American youth. The good news is that these sets of participatory politics practices may be more broadly accessible across race than those practices associated with institutionalized politics. Cohen and Kahne found that 43 percent of white, 41 percent of black, 38 percent of Latino, and 36 percent of Asian-American youth participated in at least one act of participatory politics during the prior 12 months. By contrast, the difference in voting in 2008 between the group with the highest rate of turnout according to the U.S. Census Bureau—African American youth (52 percent)—and the group with the lowest rate of turnout—Latino youth (27 percent)—is 25 percentage points. These findings offer hope for forms of political participation that more fully reflect the demographic diversity of contemporary American society. However, there is still heavy stratification on the basis of educational background and some of the more "advanced" practices are much more likely to be performed by those with high educational, economic, cultural, and social capital than by those who are more disadvantaged. So while participatory politics does raise hope for fostering a more democratic culture, it can not in and of itself overcome some of the structural inequalities that have historically blocked many from participating in civic and political life.

In a critique of the concept of participatory politics, James Hay (2011) writes, "It would be too simplistic to generalize blogging, photoshopping and social networking (media revolution) as the condition for an enhanced democracy" (666). Hay cites the Tea Party as an example of a more participatory—yet reactionary—approach to politics, a debatable proposition given how much this right-wing group relies on traditional hierarchies, established media channels, funding from conservative think tanks, and established political framing practices, and how little room it has for youth participation. But Hay is correct in stressing that participatory politics may be just as likely to generate reactionary as progressive politics, and we have debated where Invisible Children and second-wave libertarianism fall on this spectrum. As we will see in Chapter 6, the young libertarians have sought to negotiate for themselves a space between party politics and more participatory forms of engagement. These new platforms and practices potentially enable forms of collective action that are difficult to launch and sustain under a broadcast model, yet these platforms and practices do not guarantee any particular outcome, do not necessarily inculcate democratic values or develop shared ethical norms, do not necessarily respect and value diversity, do not necessarily provide key educational resources, and do not ensure that anyone will listen when groups speak out about injustices they encounter.

Forging New Links: Civic Paths and Connected Learning

A key challenge is to identify the mechanisms that help young people move from being socially and culturally active to being politically and civically engaged. Linda Herrera (2012), for example, interviewed young Egyptian activists to map the trajectory of their involvement with digital media prior to becoming revolutionaries. For many, their point of entry was through recreational use—downloading popular music—trading Hollywood movies, gaming, or sharing ideas through online discussion forums and social networking sites. Mundane involvements in participatory culture exposed them to a much broader range of ideas and experiences than allowed within the official culture of this Islamic nation, encouraged them to acquire digital skills and discover their personal voice, and enabled them to forge collective identities and articulate their hopes for the future. As Herrera concludes, "Their exposure to, and interaction with, ideas, people, images, virtual spaces, and cultural products outside their everyday environments led to a substantial change in their mentality and worldview" (343). Such practices involved transgression against government and religious authorities who sought to restrict their engagement in popular culture; such shared experiences led them to understand themselves as a generation that has developed distinctive cultural and political identities through their engagement with each other via an ever evolving array of digital platforms. We have seen similar patterns throughout our interviews with American youth who have become involved in these various activist movements.

Many "traditional" civic organizations enable youth to participate based on an apprenticeship model, where they learn through subordinating themselves to a powerful adult mentor. By contrast, our case study groups adopt a more participatory model, in which young people are taking control of and shaping their own modes of engagement. In this model, learning takes place not only vertically, from expert to newcomer, but also horizontally, from peer to peer. Such sites often blur the distinction between interest-based and friendship-based networks that have informed other work in the connected learning tradition described below. Young people may enter a given network based on shared interests and with the intention of working toward collective goals; in the process, they become integrated into rich social communities that often motivate and reward their continued participation. Some of this mentorship is built into the group's formal activities, while other forms emerge organically as participants learn through practice (Kligler-Vilenchik and Shresthova 2012).

Current scholarship (Gibson 2003; Bennett 2008b; Wattenberg 2008; Buckingham 2000; P. Levine 2007) suggests that young people are rarely addressed as political agents, that they are not invited into the political process, and that they are not consulted in the political decision-making process, whether local, state, national, or global. According to these studies, young people are most apt to become politically involved if they come from families with a history of citizen participation and political activism, if they encounter civics teachers who encourage them to reflect on and respond to current events, if they attend schools where they are allowed a voice in core decisions, and if they participate in extracurricular activities and volunteerism that gives back to their community. Most forms of activism reach the same core group of participants, who already are politically engaged, and redirect them toward new issues. But the Harry Potter Alliance and the Nerdfighters, for example, often target young people who are engaged culturally, who may already be producing and sharing fan art, and help them to extend their engagement into politics, often by deploying existing skills and capacities in new ways. Kahne, Lee, and Feezell (2011) discovered that involvement in online networks organized around shared interests (fandom, for example) also shapes political identities: "online, nonpolitical, interest-driven activities serve as a gateway to participation in important aspects of civic and, at times, political life, including volunteering, engagement in community problem-solving, protest activities, and political voice" (2).

The Carnegie Corporation's report on the Civic Mission of Schools (Gibson 2003) argues that educational institutions play a crucial role in allowing students to rehearse civic skills by participating in decision-making processes directly impacting their lives, yet many schools are backing away from this historic mission because they fear controversy with parents or loss of control over school governance in what is seen as a risky time for American education. Lauren Bird, the 20-something-year-old communications director for the Harry Potter Alliance, represents the kind of youth who might have fallen through the cracks under these conditions. Across a series of interviews, Bird shared a personal story about how schools fail to engage students with the political process:

> I wasn't terribly civically engaged when I was younger. I had some teachers who told us of the importance of watching the news and being responsible citizens and I followed that advice as best I could, but the contents of the news or just what being a "responsible citizen" meant, was rarely discussed. I grew up in a suburb in Texas during the War on Terrorism. You can guess the kind of ideologies most of my educators held. As I started realizing that I didn't agree with most of the things the culture around me preached, I quickly learned to stay silent and pretend I did. . . . I wish I had had more grown up examples of diverse and critical thinking. I wish there had been more teachers who were talking about current events or about how to get involved in our communities. . . . That would've gotten my feet wet to want to be more proactive and involved.

We first interviewed Bird as a comparative literature student at New York University, who had just starting to become more actively involved as a video blogger for the Harry Potter Alliance. Bird recounted having been invested in the Harry Potter books since the age of eight and doing video projects since high school. Bird was drawn into the social media around fandom and participated online but never "IRL" (in real life). In high school, an encounter with the videos created by John and Hank Green led to a discovery of the Nerdfighter community. But Bird developed interest in the civic aspect when the Harry Potter Alliance was involved in Help Haiti Heal (a campaign that raised enough money to fund five cargo planes full of disaster relief supplies) in 2010—and was amazed by the ways fans used their power to help. A few months later, Bird applied to a video editor position with the HPA and is now a paid staff member; Bird will resurface later in the book as a participant in some of the group's Hunger Games and Not in Harry's Name campaigns. Today, Bird remains more engaged by the fannish aspects—rather than the specifically political dimensions—of the organization's mission.

This moment when Bird was able to put all of these pieces together—linking creative skills, fannish ties, and the desire to make a difference—represents an example of what Mimi Ito, Lissa Soep, and their collaborators (Ito et al. 2015) describe as "consequential connections," a concept that has emerged from the MacArthur Foundation's Connected Learning Initiative. Connected learning research (Ito et al., 2012) seeks to identify and map "the constructed features of the cultural and social environment that support connections, brokering, and translations across spheres of activity," primarily in terms of the ways young people's interests and activities within their homes or their peer culture relate to what gets valued by schools and other powerful institutions in their lives. Ito et al. (2015) argue, "Learning is most resilient and meaningful when it brings together multiple spheres of a young person's life." For Bird, school-based civics education failed to motivate civic action, whereas fan activism brought increased awareness and encouraged deploying recreational skills toward political ends.

A white paper on connected learning (Ito et al. 2012) describes some underlying assumptions:

Connected learning is socially embedded, interest-driven, and oriented toward expanding educational, economic or political opportunity. It is realized when a young person is able to pursue a personal interest or passion with the support of friends and caring adults, and is in turn able to link this learning and interest to academic achievement, career success or civic engagement. (42)

Young people often take more chances and invest more of themselves in their recreational lives than they do in the school environment, especially given today's constant pressure to prepare for standardized testing. Such connections, the connected learning researchers conclude, are fluid as young people try out identities and explore interests, drilling deeper into those they find meaningful and moving on to others that look rewarding.

What these young people do for fun may move swiftly into forms of social and political engagement if, say, outside forces threaten the worlds they have built for themselves. For example, Rachel Cody Pfister (2014) shares a case study involving Hogwarts at Ravelry, a community of young knitters who came together as a consequence of their shared interests in all things Harry Potter. Through this community, participants articulated a "shared purpose, culture, identity" that empowered their civic actions. When the group sought to organize the "Ravelympic Games" in parallel with the official 2012 Olympics, they received a threatening letter from the U.S. Olympic Committee. The community used its social network to educate members about the stakes in this conflict, to brainstorm possible responses, to reach appropriate allies, and to shift public opinion. The parallels between the struggles of this crafting community in the Harry Potter fan realm and the kinds of civic activities that drew Lauren Bird to the Harry Potter Alliance should be clear enough; in both instances, fandom provided the conceptual resources, the shared identity, and the sense of collective empowerment required for political participation.

One of the key ways that networked communication has mattered (especially when coupled with the outreach efforts of the kinds of organizations we are studying) is in creating opportunities for youth to enter new kinds of communities and, through them, to open themselves to "consequential connections." Another case in point is 15-year-old Enzo from Students for Liberty. Enzo attended a California high school where a majority of liberal-leaning students supported President Obama in the 2012 election; he knew of no other students who shared his budding interest in libertarian ideology: "There aren't really any high school groups per se, and I'm probably the only libertarian at my high school because either everyone is gung ho about Barack Obama because it's the fad or is just a Republican because their parents are. And so, I don't really have a group or membership or anything. I'm just kind of there." What's more, at 15, he did not have a driver's license, access to transportation, or the financial means to contact like-minded young people in his community. Instead, Enzo formed friendships with a group of young libertarians he met on Tumblr, using the space to learn more about the movement and to "try on" a new identity that diverged from his parents' more conservative beliefs. Enzo, whose views on social issues like gay marriage led him to explore libertarianism, said, "There's the generation gap; like the older generations aren't as accepting of libertarianism as the newer ones are," and explained that pursuing his interests online helped him steer around obstacles to participation:

> Tumblr is a very good place to find like-minded stuff and discuss, so that's where I met most of my libertarian friends. That's where we mostly converse. They have invited me to some places but my parents won't take me because they can't afford it or it's too late or it's on a weeknight or something like that. It's kind of hard, so it's mostly online and stuff like that, and just talking to my friends at school and trying to convert them.

Enzo's explanation reveals not only the possibilities of participating online but also the concrete limits around civic and political participation for young people, particularly those who have not reached voting age; many potentially meaningful connections are not fully realized because young people need adult support to fully pursue their emerging interests.

Participating in What?

Across this book, our focus is primarily on new and innovative political networks, which are choosing tactics and rhetorics that respond to the popular desire for meaningful participation. We are describing the mechanisms through which participants are struggling to achieve greater equality in their capacity to exert voice and influence within decision-making processes that will determine our collective futures. When critical theory is framed in a language of resistance, readers pretty much know what it is "the people" are resisting—neoliberalism, racism, homophobia, patriarchy, militarism, and so on. When the conversation turns to participation, theorists are forced to think about what is being built, what a more ideal society might look like, and the real-world roadblocks that make it difficult to achieve maximized forms of participation. Again and again, such discussions must return to the core question: Participating in what?

As researchers debate what kinds of spaces offer opportunities for meaningful participation, Carpentier (Jenkins and Carpentier 2013) proposes a productive distinction between "participating in" and "participating through" media. So, for example, while one is free to submit a wide array of videos through YouTube, the governance of that platform is controlled by its corporate owner, Google. No one can claim to be a citizen of YouTube, which is run for profit and not for the collective welfare. Unlike, for example, Hogwarts at Ravelry, the comments section on YouTube is notoriously uncivic, a space known for harsh and hateful posts, often directed by dominant groups against any and all forms of minority expression. Yet one study (Thorson et al. 2013) identifies thousands of videos posted by the Occupy movement on YouTube, videos that often challenged corporate interests and circulated at a range of scales from the hyperlocal to the global. Groups such as those involved in Occupy have forged strong political movements in part as a consequence of the ways they communicate with each other through YouTube, but they have remained at the mercy of the corporate interests that decide how free expression will be limited within this platform.

A distinction similar to the one just described can be drawn between participation within grassroots organizations that advocate for change and participation within the governance of the society. Young people are experimenting within participatory structures within their social and recreational lives, bringing some of those structures to the work they are doing as political agents. But these structures are not necessarily accepted within established political institutions and thus do not always influence public policy. We return to this question of what counts as politics in the book's conclusion. Some young people are ambivalent about whether some of the projects we will discuss should be understood as political as opposed to purely cultural and educational. We wanted to flag the issue here as it is important to recognize that more work must be done before American democratic structures are going to be as fully and meaningfully participatory as many might desire.

Carpentier (Jenkins and Carpentier 2013) insists that for processes to be truly participatory, there must be equality and reciprocity between participants, a standard not fully met by every organization we discuss, let alone by the commercial platforms they use to pursue their goals. Yet the rhetoric of participation raises expectations about how power should be distributed—expectations that are expressed through struggles over terms of service—but also through the formation of alternative media networks that allow participants greater control over what happens to their materials. And we will see in Chapter 6, some groups opt out of traditional civic practices, such as voting, because they see them as less effective at promoting desired political changes than approaches emphasizing educational outreach and cultural change.

We will be especially interested in the roles organizations and networks play in fostering participatory politics. Young people often describe the language within which Americans conduct institutionalized politics as exclusive (in that you have to already be immersed in the system to understand what's being said) and repulsive (in that the sharply partisan tone of current discourse turns politics into something that is divisive and disgusting). Ethan Zuckerman (2013b) argues that young people are turning to participatory politics because they see a failure in more traditional civic institutions and practices: "Here's an ugly, but plausible, explanation for the shifting engagement in civics: It's not that people aren't interested in civics. They're simply not interested in feeling ineffectual or helpless." By contrast, the groups we study invite participation. They have strong incentives to recruit new members and to maintain the continued involvement of existing members. Members "care" about the issues, they "care" about their communities, and they "care" about their own identities as citizens. Such networks offer participants collective frames that can intensify individual members' desires to make a difference (Kligler-Vilenchik et al. 2012).

These groups map ways in which individual participation can add up to something larger. They direct attention to specific issues and propose ways that people can work together to bring about change. They train members to produce their own media and tell their own stories. They offer networks through which this media can circulate and reach an engaged and appreciative audience. Above all, they create a context where "talking politics" is a normal, ongoing part of the group's social interactions. Ethan Zuckerman (2013b) asks, "If civics is driven by passionate participation, how do we create a deliberative public space?" The answer may be to make civic and political discussions part of our everyday interactions with our friends and family, something sociologist Nina Eliasoph (1998) suggests is relatively rare; typically, people avoid discussing politics with people that matter to them because they seek to avoid conflict.

Robert Putnam (2000) famously described civic organizations—in his example, bowling leagues—as providing such a context for civic and political exchanges in midcentury America. Insofar as these new forms of participatory politics interject political messages into the same platforms young people use to share cute cat pictures, they also open a space where political deliberation becomes normative. Some may dismiss the idea that new political discourse might, for example, emerge from fan communities or gaming guilds, but keep in mind that Putnam's bowling leagues were themselves sites of play—not serious in their goals, but nevertheless constituting shared spaces where publics could be formed, ties could be strengthened, and political values could be articulated. The YPP network's large national survey has found that those people who engage in interest-driven networks online are five times as likely as those who aren't involved to engage in participatory politics practices and nearly four times as likely to participate in forms of institutional practices. Such online communities may be as much a predictor of civic participation as traditional afterschool clubs such as newspaper, debate, or student government or service learning and community volunteering.

That said, if such groups are helping to facilitate the transition from participatory culture to participatory politics, they still are not as fully democratic as their participants might imagine. Neta Kligler-Vilenchik (2014) argues that not every kind of political conversation can occur within every cultural space: she has shown, for example, that the Nerdfighters have not been nearly as comfortable or as open with discussions of racial diversity and inequality as they have been in fostering discussions around sexual and gender identity politics, often falling back on the much-disputed idea of a "post-racial society" as a way of shutting out rather than opening up discussions about the role race plays in the lives of its participants. When social affiliation is less constrained by physical geography, participants may be drawn to different communities because of what they allow them to talk about. So while the civic imagination may perform some bridging functions in enabling messages to travel from one community to another, it may also enable some forms of exclusion, given that some popular representations are more accessible and more transparent to particular groups.

Peter Dahlgren (2003) has proposed a set of criteria by which we might assess the viability of civic culture. For democratic models of participation to be achieved, there need to be "minimal shared commitments to the vision and procedures of democracy, which in turn entails a capacity to see beyond the immediate interests of one's own group" (156). The organizations and networks we discuss—to varying degrees—provide the preconditions for this kind of civic culture. These groups achieve this kind of political potential by fostering a shared set of *values* regarding what an ideal society might look like, encouraging a sense of *affinity* among members, enabling access to greater *knowledge* about the world and the issues they confront, modeling a set of democratic and participatory *practices*, helping youth to develop their *identities* as civic agents, and providing a context for meaningful political *discussions*. Dahlgren models these traits as a circuit; each builds upon the other, reinforcing the group's progress toward supporting democratic participation. Even where all of these conditions are met, there still often needs to be some kind of catalyst that inspires this civic culture to take action around a particular concern. What we are calling participatory politics involves activities that foster one or another attribute of Dahlgren's civic culture but also efforts to inspire and organize civic action. We will revisit these criteria in Chapter 3 as we discuss how fan organizations like the Harry Potter Alliance and Nerdfighters provide the preconditions for civic and political participation.

Across this opening chapter, we have introduced five foundational concepts (as well as a range of related vocabulary) that will inform the chapters that follow. First, we described how individuals and groups outside the dominant political structures are making use of emergent systems of narrative circulation to give their voices a strength and scope often unavailable to earlier generations. Second, we described the concept of transmedia mobilization/activism to stress ways young people are seeking to shape public opinion across a broad range of different platforms. Third, we discussed the civic imagination as opening up possibilities to envision alternatives and through them, to think about what kinds of change might be possible. Fourth, we talked about participatory politics as a set of practices that allow young people to deploy the skills they acquired through their everyday engagements with social media and participatory culture to change the world. And finally, we discussed connected learning in terms of the ways these organizations enhance their participants' civic education, often by connecting the political realm to other activities they care about. We see close relationships between these core concepts, which suggest something about the media strategies, creative vision, organizational activities, and informal learning practices through which American youth are conducting politics in the early 21st century.

What Comes Next?

In the next five chapters, we examine each of our case study organizations. As we do so, we will expand the analytic vocabulary we use to discuss participatory politics. Chapter 2 considers Invisible Children as a group that struggles to reconcile its attempts to control the framing of its message and its dispersed network of young participants who help spread that message. Here we identify paradoxes that shape this and many other organizations that are trying to embrace participatory politics. Among the tensions we consider are those between goals and process, comprehensible and complex stories, activism and entertainment, consensus and contention, spreadable and drillable messages, and top-down and bottom-up approaches. We explore the ways that Invisible Children, in ramping up to *Kony 2012*, placed more emphasis on empowering youth to tell their own stories, yet following the backlash against the video, became progressively more centralized—ultimately disbanding its participatory activities, and finally announcing plans to shut down. At the same time, we rebut some of the criticisms directed against IC, showing how it was not exclusively reliant on a politics based on digital circulation but rather sought to prepare participants for more in-depth engagement with its mission through on-the-ground, face-to-face activities as well as the use of social media.

Chapter 3 considers the Harry Potter Alliance, Imagine Better, and the Nerdfighters as examples of fan activism. Over the years, these groups have addressed a range of different causes, rather than define themselves around a single mission, and they have relied on the larger infrastructures that have grown up around fan communities. Here we deepen our concept of the civic imagination, exploring how these groups harness the power of popular culture as an alternative, shared language through which to talk about politics. References to shared content worlds carry affective attachments for their members, offering more empowering fantasies about what it might mean to fight for social justice. We consider two different models—fannish civics and cultural acupuncture—that these groups deploy to mobilize public support. The difference between the two has to do with the depth of knowledge of the original content world each assumes. Fannish civics inspires fans *as fans* through their shared mastery of shared texts, whereas cultural acupuncture seeks to gain greater circulation by attaching a group's messages to larger public conversations, often inspired by the release of a new entertainment product. This chapter also considers how shared tastes may provide the basis for the creation of "public spheres of the imagination," places where people discuss shared values, hopes, and dreams. But the chapter also considers how a taste-based politics may exclude some would-be participants, insofar as taste is shaped by factors of class or race.

Chapter 4 explores the processes by which American Muslim youth are defining their identities and asserting their voices in the face of the political and social realities of post-9/11 America. If our work on the fan activists stresses that their shared interests in popular culture could provide a bridge into greater civic engagement, contrast that with the fact that speaking as an American Muslim is always already marked as a political stance, even if these youth see themselves as primarily speaking to shared cultural or spiritual interests. We consider a range of expressive projects that involve asserting the diversity of American Muslims identities in relation to the concept of a precarious public—that is, one where there is a considerable gap between voice and influence. What makes the groups and networks we look at especially precarious is the tension between their members' desires to insure that their life stories get told and the fear that they are going to become the focus of surveillance by various government agencies or suffer the consequences of "social surveillance" by conservative parents and religious leaders, or online "haters." For American Muslim youth, constructing their own, alternative narratives involves considerable risks and understandable anxieties, and we take a look at the important role humor plays in easing some of those strains.

Chapter 5 explores the nature of political storytelling from a different perspective—that of undocumented youth raised in America who are supporting the DREAM Act, which they hope will offer them a path to citizenship and, more immediately, reliable access to higher education. A spectacular example of transmedia mobilization, this loose network has sustained its efforts over many years via creative, evolving uses of social media and networked communication, in concert with on-the-ground activities. Here our primary focus is on the production of "coming out" videos, through which these young people share stories of their own experience of risk and vulnerability as a means of forging a stronger, collective voice. Throughout this chapter, we identify a range of both personal and collective reasons why coming out online was an important and effective tactic during the formation of this movement. We also highlight the risks DREAMers confront in acknowledging their immigration status in such a public fashion.

With Chapter 6, we return to the question of how the mechanisms of participatory politics relate to institutional politics (the source of some of the paradoxes we discuss in Chapter 2). Our focus is on Students for Liberty, one wing of what has been described as "second-wave libertarianism." Unlike first-wave libertarians, this movement is more invested in bringing about change through educational and cultural activities than through party politics. On the one hand, these young libertarians receive financial resources and other support from conservative think tanks and individual funders, whose influence on many right-of-center movements in the United States raises questions about whether any such movements can be described as grassroots. Yet these youth are also tapping YouTube and social media to assert their own voices, much like the other groups we have discussed. And many of them are "strategic nonvoters." Despite being well informed and deeply engaged in political debates, they do not see voting as the appropriate mechanism for promoting their causes given the corrupt nature of the current governmental system. Here, again, we see the tension between narrowing opportunities for participation in institutional politics and an expanded capacity for voice via new media.

Chapter 7 pulls together many insights about participatory politics from across the book, exploring what these case study groups share and how they differ. We revisit some core concepts established in this opening chapter, including participatory politics, transmedia mobilization, and the civic imagination. We start the chapter with a story that illustrates the ambivalence many young people feel about being activists, their uncertain position somewhere between participatory culture and institutional politics, and the messages they have internalized from adult commentators that their characteristic forms of political action don't count. We end the chapter with another story—this one illuminating the generational divide between historic civil rights leaders and their contemporary counterparts—and some criteria by which we might determine which forms of participatory politics are effective, for whom, and toward what ends.

An Afterword, contributed by Lissa Soep from Youth Radio—a national youth-driven production company based in Oakland, California—returns us to this chapter's discussion of connected learning. Soep also compares and contrasts the core case studies, outlining which theories of learning might help us to understand how these groups are recruiting and empowering American youth as civic and political agents. Her observations here are primarily aimed at educators, but understanding the underlying pedagogical assumptions shaping these organizations is key to understanding the role they play in the lives of American youth.

Beyond this, we have also developed digital resources you can use to learn more about participatory politics. Check out our By Any Media Necessary website at byanymedia.org. This site assembles an archive of activist videos, including those described in the book and those produced by a range of other networks and organizations, which sample the range of genres and rhetorical practices through which today's young citizens promote their causes. This archive also includes videos produced for the project by Participant Media and Joseph Gordon-Levitt's HitRecord project, which we hope will generate discussions in classes and within civic organizations around digital citizenship. We also include lesson plans for exemplary workshops to help students better understand the core principles and practices of participatory politics.

Educators from the National Writing Project and the National Association for Media Literacy Education have been working with us to share and test this site and its materials in the classroom. We hope this resource provides readers, especially educators but also activists, a chance to extend this book's analysis to explore a broader array of contemporary political and civic practices.

2

"Watch 30 Minute Video on Internet, Become Social Activist"?

Kony 2012, *Invisible Children, and the Paradoxes of Participatory Politics*

Sangita Shresthova

Right now, there are more people on Facebook than there were on the planet 200 years ago. Humanity's greatest desire is to belong and connect. And now we see each other. We hear each other. We share what we love and it reminds us of what we all have in common. And this connection is changing the way the world works. Governments are trying to keep up. The older generations are concerned. The game has new rules.

—*Kony 2012*

In spring 2012, Invisible Children (IC), a San Diego–based human rights organization, released *Kony 2012*, a 30-minute video about child soldiering in Uganda. In a central feature of the film, Jason Russell, one of the group's founders and longtime leaders, speaks as a father to his young son about the evils perpetrated by the warlord Joseph Kony and his Lord's Resistance Army (LRA). The film ends with a call for supporters to help circulate the video in order to make Kony "famous," criticizing the lack of Western media coverage of his atrocities and demanding that the U.S. government take action to end his reign of terror. IC anticipated that the well-crafted video might reach half a million viewers by the end of the year, based on its extensive experience deploying online videos. Instead, *Kony 2012* spread to more than 70 million viewers over the first four days of its release and over 100 million during its first week in March 2012. By comparison, *Modern Family*, then the highest rated non-sports and non-reality program on U.S. television, was attracting a little over 7 million average weekly viewers (based on published Nielsen ratings), and *The Hunger Games*, the Hollywood blockbuster released on March 23 of that year, drew an audience of approximately 15–19 million during its first weekend (based on ticket sales reported by boxofficemojo. com). Inspired by the video's celebration of the power of social media, IC's young supporters demonstrated how grassroots networks might shift the national agenda.

The speed and scope of the pushback against *Kony 2012* was almost as dramatic as its initial spread. IC and its supporters were ill prepared for the video's movement from a relatively tight-knit network of people who knew about the organization and its mission to a much larger population learning about Kony for the first time as someone they knew posted the video on Facebook, forwarded it by email, or blasted it via Twitter. *Kony 2012* drew sharp criticism from many established human rights groups and Africa experts, who questioned everything from IC's finances to what they characterized as its "white man's burden" rhetoric. IC was especially challenged for being out of sync with current Ugandan realities and promoting responses some argued might do more harm than good. Critics saw *Kony 2012* as illustrating institutional filters and ideological blinders that have long shaped communication between the global North and South.

Kony 2012 became emblematic of a larger debate concerning attention-driven activism. In a blog post written in *Kony 2012*'s immediate aftermath, Ethan Zuckerman (2012a) surveys the critiques leveled against the video, stressing that it gained broad and rapid circulation by grossly oversimplifying the complexities of the conditions in Africa and creating heroic roles for Western activists while denying the agency of Africans working to change their own circumstances. Zuckerman explained: "I'm starting to wonder if this [exemplifies] a fundamental limit to attention-based advocacy. If we need simple narratives so people can amplify and spread them, are we forced to engage only with the simplest of problems? Or to propose only the simplest of solutions?" This question haunts not only IC supporters, but leaders of many other activist groups.

By the time *Kony 2012* hit, our team at USC had been studying Invisible Children for three years. We first learned about IC through one of its early, and still controversial, media artifacts, a short dance film entitled *Invisible Children Musical* (2006), which was a takeoff of Disney's *High*

School Musical. In this film, IC's founders turned to popular culture, song, and dance to reach and inspire young people to take part in the Global Night Commute, a multisited live event. The *Invisible Children Musical* polarized our research group when we watched it during our weekly meeting. Some members were intrigued, even excited, by its unabashed appropriation of popular culture. Others literally pushed themselves away from the conference table to express their negative reaction to the film's extravagantly celebratory and admittedly simplistic messaging.

As we learned more about the organization's media and activities, we quickly understood that pushing the boundaries of youth activism was an integral, though not always completely intentional, part of IC's efforts. Through a series of research projects focused on various facets of IC—including learning, transmedia storytelling, and performativity—we delved deeper into understanding the group's media, staff, and supporters. Over the years, we observed many IC events in Southern California. We attended film screenings and watched many hours of IC media. We were invited to attend events that the group organized and visited its headquarters in San Diego many times. We interviewed 45 young people involved with IC and had regular interactions with the group's leadership.

Our ongoing contact gave us a unique vantage point from which to observe IC as it moved from a relatively obscure initiative to an extremely visible (and overly scrutinized) organization that was asked to publicly account for all its decisions. We were also privy to the profound personal and organizational challenges IC faced as the situation around *Kony 2012* escalated. And, we were part of a small group of researchers IC continued to trust after 2012. As one staff member observed in 2013, *Kony 2012* had forced IC to "grow up" overnight; we were able to observe this change firsthand.

Nick Couldry (2010) begins his book *Why Voice Matters* by identifying the many different ways voices get denied or undermined within today's neoliberal society. IC's supporters were mostly drawn from the ranks of more affluent and politically influential sectors of society (see Karlin et al. forthcoming.) Surely, these youth have access to many of the levers (Zuckerman 2013a) needed to make their voices heard. Yet many of them had not been involved in civic life before and would not have become politically active without IC's supportive community. In this book's later chapters, we will see more dramatic examples of marginalized groups seeking collective power through participatory politics, but it's worth stressing that political engagement is not guaranteed even among those who come from more privileged backgrounds. Supporting this perspective, Kligler-Vilenchik and Thorson (forthcoming) show how memes critical of *Kony 2012* exploited stereotypes that young people are ignorant, irrational, duped, or apathetic. Couldry (2010) reminds us, "People's voices only count if their bodies matter," noting that existing forms of discrimination based on race, gender, sexuality, and so forth ensure that some voices go unheard (130), and we must surely add to that list the marginalization which has historically occurred as children and youth first assert themselves into political debates. Couldry also reminds us that "an unequal distribution of narrative resources" may also serve to limit which voices can be heard, since some forms of political speech are more readily recognized than others within institutional politics or journalism (9). The groups we are studying are seeking to expand the languages through which politics can be expressed, finding new vocabularies that make sense in the life contexts of young citizens; as they do so, however, they may often express their messages in ways that make them less likely to be heard by key decision makers.

In this chapter, we use IC and *Kony 2012* to explore the potentials and challenges of participatory politics. Three years after the film's release, we remain distinctly ambivalent about whether the film's immense spreadability translated into a net success for the organization and the youth movement it inspired. We thus use IC and *Kony 2012* to identify some of the paradoxes that must be addressed if we are going to understand whether and in what ways the mechanisms of participatory politics might promote meaningful political change and foster greater civic engagement. The paradoxes we identify here reflect recurring questions the organization faced during this period of crisis and success: How much should IC focus on expanding the youth movement it had built up through the years via its focused anti-LRA efforts? Could IC accept its members' desire for a more participatory organizational model or should it try to retain control over their messaging? Could the story IC told be both simple enough to be easily graspable and complex enough to do justice to the nuances of the LRA conflict? How could IC make its humanitarian and social justice work fun without compromising its acceptance by policy makers and NGOs? And why didn't IC work harder to balance the friendship and cordiality it so treasured with training that equipped its supporters to deal with contentious situations related to its cause? Above all, should this innovative organization be judged based on the results it achieved in pursuit of its policy goals or based on the ways it recruited and empowered a generation of young activists who might have an impact on a broader range of issues?

We watched IC's leaders and supporters twist and turn as they experimented with different responses to these core paradoxes; we saw the group move between models that were more top-down or goal focused and others that were more participatory and process focused. The enormous success of *Kony 2012* brought all of these tensions to a crisis point from which the organization never fully recovered. Each of the groups in our other case studies confront some of these same tensions; each represents a somewhat different model for how successful organizations might solicit and support the participation of their members in an age of networked communication; each group made its own choices, and, yes, its own mistakes, as they sought to address these defining challenges around civic culture in the early 21st century. Few of the cases, though, illustrate these paradoxes as fully as IC does and that's why we are starting here.

Moving beyond the Clicktivism Critique

On August 8, 2013, Jason Russell addressed an auditorium full of young IC supporters. After some initial lighthearted comments, his demeanor changed. "I want to give you a little glimpse into what was going on inside of me," he said. He then recounted the days following *Kony 2012*'s release that led up to his public mental breakdown. "I wrote down all the things that we were pissing off, that we were disrupting, that we were questioning," he recalled. "The list looked like this: Hollywood, social networking, online media, movies, activism, United Nations, America, millennials, journalism, nonprofits, fashion, advertising, and international justice." He explained that's when he realized "why they're so pissed off." In his words, it was "because it's . . . the whole world that is going, 'Who is this? Who are you? How dare you load a 29-minute 59-second video online? And how dare you reach 120 million people in five days? That's not allowed. Something must be fishy. You must be a scam.'" At this point, his usually enthusiastic audience fell silent. Russell's recounting of his personal experiences took everyone back to the moment when the initial excitement about *Kony 2012*'s phenomenal spread gave way to the backlash against Russell, Invisible Children, and the group's young supporters. In *Move*, a film IC released in the fall of 2012, IC communication director Noelle West described her experience:

> My cloud nine quickly dissolved. . . . Our website wasn't built to maintain 35,000 concurrent viewers at one time. So our website's crashing intermittently. The only thing we could communicate through was Tumblr. So you're not going to see information about every single thing that we do from a Tumblr. And that was, I think, the beginning of the conversation turn from "this was the greatest thing on the planet" to "what the hell is this?"

In the same film, Russell described the criticism as a "tsunami" that IC "didn't see coming." In his words, "We turned around, and we were all under water."

Something of the vicious tone of the critiques is captured in comments from Ugandan activist, social media strategist, and blogger TMS Ruge (2012a), who defined *Kony 2012* as "another travesty in shepherd's clothing befalling my country and my continent." To Ruge, the film was "so devoid of nuance, utility and respect for agency that it is appallingly hard to contextualize." Ruge, along with other critics, also questioned the effectiveness of purchasing "a T-shirt and bracelet" as acts that would somehow end a two-decade-long conflict. Other critics accused IC of exploiting the naiveté and ignorance of its young supporters, who they feared would confuse the feel-good process of spreading a YouTube video with the hard work involved in changing a complex international situation.

One internet meme summed up the phenomenon: "Watch 30 Minute Video on Internet, Become Social Activist." This meme is, in many ways, emblematic of a larger critique of so-called clicktivism, defined as the application of the metrics and methods of the marketplace (number of clicks) to measure the success of (arguably) activist efforts. As one critic explains, "The end result is the degradation of activism into a series of petition drives that capitalise on current events. Political engage-

A meme that critiqued and ridiculed the *Kony 2012* campaign.

ment becomes a matter of clicking a few links. In promoting the illusion that surfing the web can change the world, clicktivism is to activism as McDonald's is to a slow-cooked meal. It may look like food, but the life-giving nutrients are long gone" (White 2010). The clicktivist critique often describes online campaigns as involving limited risk or exertion and having limited impact on institutional politics.

The *New York Times'* Room for Debate introduced its discussion of *Kony 2012*, tellingly titled "Fight War Crimes, without Leaving the Couch?" (2012), with this provocation: "Social media definitely have the power to bring attention to terrible problems—but is there a downside, if the 'call to action' is wrong-headed or if these campaigns give young people a false sense of what it really takes to create change?" While networked communications has made it easier for citizens to access and act upon information, making it possible for movements like *Kony 2012* to achieve remarkable speed and scope, we must keep in mind these developments have not always been seen as a positive thing.

Indeed, the most persistent skepticism centers around whether these new platforms and practices make it too easy to take action without ensuring that people have time to reflect. Writing in the midst of the boom and bust surrounding the video, Mark A. Drumbl (2012) concluded: "The *Kony 2012* campaign—and clicktivism generally—have short attention spans and limited shelf life" (484). Some speak about compassion fatigue in a world where political messages get carried by dramatic and simplified videos and then diminish as participants feel the tug of yet another story and another appeal for action. The premise that IC's supporters could achieve dramatic results by mobilizing massive numbers of people online was resoundingly ridiculed by memes, ironically generated and circulated by other internet users, such as one that announced, "You shared *Kony 2012*? Congratulations—you saved Africa." Malcom Gladwell's (2010) critique that Twitter revolutions involved lower risks than previous political movements was expressed by another widely circulated cartoon depicting an exchange between activists of two different generations. The older one, wearing an eye patch, explains, "I lost my eye in a five day student protest in 1970," while the younger one explains, "I just sprained my clicking finger joining a Facebook protest group."

Neta Kligler-Vilenchik and Kjerstin Thorson (forthcoming) identified and tracked 135 such memes circulated in response to the *Kony 2012* campaign, almost all of which were negative in their characterization of IC and its efforts. They saw such memes as part of a struggle over what constitutes good citizenship, with the memes mostly referring back to classic conceptions of the informed citizen some felt were under threat from *Kony 2012*'s more networked model of participation. Michael Schudson (1999) and Roger Hurwitz (2004) have discussed a shift from the older model of the informed citizen toward an emerging model of the monitorial citizen. Under the informed citizen model, people need to possess full knowledge of an issue before they can act politically. Given the complexity of many contemporary issues, this standard is often impossible to achieve and the failure to meet expectations based on it can result in a sense of disempowerment. By contrast, in a networked society, people can monitor specific concerns and then use social media to alert each other to issues requiring greater attention or collective action. We can see the circulation of these political videos

A meme created by Peter Ajtai of insert-joke-here.com pitted generations against each other in the slacktivism debate.

as one mechanism through which monitorial citizenship works. Kligler-Vilenchik and Thorson conclude that the anti–*Kony 2012* memes "may suppress budding political interest and engagement" by dismissing both a political cause that engaged many young people and ridiculing the forms of political participation they chose to make their voices heard: "young networked citizens may be experimenting with new ways not only to become informed, but to act on that information."

If all that happens is the spread of a video, then the system of monitorial citizenship will have failed. However, our research shows that this is not what happened with *Kony 2012*, nor was it what IC intended when it released the film. On the contrary, IC saw such circulations as a point of entry into more intense kinds of political engagement. A high percentage of those reached by such social awareness campaigns may well shift their attention elsewhere, but some research (Andresen 2011) suggests that the act of passing along a video increases the likelihood that participants will take other kinds of action in support of the cause, including contributing time and money. A large part of IC's argument for "making Kony famous" was that, for many years, his atrocities received relatively little media coverage and escaped intense scrutiny from the international community. The group hoped that increased awareness would result in shifts in media coverage and public policy that would hinder the LRA's mobility.

Echoing this, the IC supporters we interviewed post–*Kony 2012* made very realistic claims about the effectiveness of online advocacy campaigns. Nineteen-year-old Johnny discussed writing a class essay critiquing Gladwell's "The Revolution Will Not Be Tweeted." He explained his perspective: "[Facebook and Twitter] definitely can be used as a medium to gather people, to get attention, but it can't be the only thing. At the end of the day, you need bills to be passed. You need money to be raised, but if that [social media] can be used to spread awareness and get the word out and help these things be achieved, that's great. *Kony 2012* proved that." Johnny described the video as a catalyst setting other things into motion, creating the awareness and support that enabled Congress to pass laws impacting what was happening in Africa. In his model, participatory and institutionalized politics worked together to achieve the desired results.

IC offered its members varying degrees of participation, including involvement in large-scale mass gatherings and attendance at training sessions, while it also worked more directly with elite institutions and political power brokers. In fact, many of the supporters we met saw the range of participation IC offered and the "hip" tone of these engagements as crucial to the group's appeal to youth. Stephanie, an IC college club member, confirmed this when she observed that the organization "is really good about having different campaigns" that offer multiple ways to participate and many points for potential engagement that might begin, for instance, with attending an IC screening and grow over time. The bucket list of IC-related activities the youth described included organizing local IC events (often designed to be celebratory in tone), creating their own media to recruit members for local clubs, using social media to maintain support, setting up information tables at their local school or college, designing T-shirts, fundraising toward specific IC goals, and even interning or touring with IC. To Janelle, who was interning with IC at the time of her interview, the key to IC's success with young people is their "youthful, hip vibe," which she attributed to the fact that "everyone in the boardroom is 30 years and younger." As Stephanie reflected on her IC experience, she also appreciated the support and advice she received in running her local club as IC's responsive staff helped her navigate various logistical and organizational challenges.

Over time, IC supported more explicit political lobbying efforts. For example Jack, a college sophomore, described the ways that IC had enabled him to directly contact Senate staffers during a visit to Washington:

> The fact that the staff members of a senator could actually listen to a 17-year-old was pretty amazing. . . . [IC does] a very good job of preparing us. . . . The lobbying meetings I've attended in the last few years have been based around specific legislation or resolutions that they're seeking to pass or, you know, stuff like that. So you get a point of contact from the office and then they send us—they put together, you know, guides, very detailed guides, for both the lobby people leaders and, then, if you have first-time lobby members in your group, they have specific guides for them. And they detail everything from what you should wear to a meeting to what you should talk about.

Jillian, a 22-year-old from Pennsylvania, similarly described the ways that IC provided her and her classmates with the scaffolding they needed to deal directly with their elected officials. She noted that the IC staff members would often call to debrief with her team on what worked or didn't after a meeting took place. The tendency to reduce Invisible Children to a 30-minute video undervalues the much broader array of media tactics the group deploys. Similarly, the idea that this movement depends primarily on short-term reactions to rapidly spreading content underestimates the number of young people who have participated in afterschool organizations, been trained by the roadies who travel the country showing IC films and leading workshops with supporters, gathered for massive scale public protests, attended one of the Fourth Estate conferences, or flown to Washington to lobby government officials.

Clicktivist critiques simplify our understanding of the political life of American youth. Right now, young people are significantly more likely to participate in cultural activities than engage with institutional politics. As a consequence, those activist groups that have been most successful at helping youth find their civic voice often tap into participants' interests in popular and participatory cultures, frequently blurring the distinction between what Mizuko Ito and her colleagues (Ito et al. 2009) categorized as friendship-driven and interest-driven modes of participation online. Ito et al. define friendship-driven modes as "dominant and mainstream practices of youth as they go about their day-to-day negotiations with friends and peers" (15). Such friendship-driven networks are often a "primary source of affiliation, friendship, and romantic partners" for youth. In contrast, interest-driven practices are rooted in "specialized activities, interests, or niche and marginalized identities." Ito et al. clarify that the interest-driven activities often reside within the "domain of the geeks, freaks, musicians, artists, and dorks" (16). Kahne, Lee, and Feezell (2011) closed the circle between interest-driven activities and civic engagement when they examined how young people's interest-driven online activities may "serve as a gateway to participation in important aspects of civic and, at times, political life" (15) and found a correlation between young people's interest-driven participation online and increased civic behavior, including volunteering, group membership, and political expression.

Our research found significant overlap between friendship and interest-driven engagement among IC participants. In their analysis of IC interviews, Neta Kligler-Vilenchik and her colleagues (2012) identified "shared media experiences" (gathering around texts that have a shared resonance), sense of community (identifying with a collective or network), and a wish to help (a desire to achieve positive change) as three key components of participants' IC experiences. For a vast majority of the youth interviewed, all three components intersected with their "friendships" and "interests" as they chose to take action with their friends around issues they cared about. Ruth, who was an intern at IC's offices in 2010, described her experience: "Invisible Children is a lot about relationships. . . . You work together, you play together, you eat together." To Janelle, another intern, this approach results in a "complete great intertwining" of work and fun at IC, making it hard to separate the two. Like Ruth and Janelle, many other IC supporters felt that the group's social elements were crucial to their sustained participation.

Similarly, many interviewees felt that "shared media experiences" significantly contributed to this sense of connection between IC youth.

Melissa Brough (2012) traced the early history and tactics of Invisible Children, stressing that the group has long placed a high priority on media production as a means of creating awareness but also recruiting and training a movement of American young people determined to impact human rights concerns in Africa. Jason Russell and Bobby Bailey, recent graduates of the University of Southern California School of Cinematic Arts, along with Lauren Poole, who was enrolled at the University of California, San Diego, established Invisible Children in 2006 as an outgrowth of their documentary film *Invisible Children: Rough Cut* (2006), which called for the capture of Joseph Kony and fundraised for on-the-ground recovery efforts. The organization grew rapidly: Brough recounts that within six years, they had built an organization with 90 staff on the ground in Uganda running development programs, 30 paid U.S. staff managing outreach, a fundraising apparatus that brought in almost $32 million in 2012, and a network of more than 2,000 clubs in schools and churches. The group's commitment of more than 9 percent of its budget to media making and another 35 percent to mobilization of youth in the United States became yet another site of controversy as *Kony 2012* brought new scrutiny of the organization. Lana Swartz (2012) has similarly noted the diverse range of different media practices the group deploys:

> "The Movement," as Invisible Children calls its U.S.-facing work, includes visually arresting films, spectacular event-oriented campaigns, provocative graphic t-shirts and other apparel, music mixes, print media, blogs and more. To be a member of Invisible Children means to be a viewer, participant, wearer, reader, listener, commenter of and in the various activities, many mediated, that make up the Movement. It is a massive, open-ended, evolving documentary "story" unfurling across an expanding number of media forms.

Brian explained in an interview how IC's media moves people to action: "There is just no way that if you have a beating heart and a pulse in you, that you can watch any of their films and not be moved into action afterwards. . . . [T]here is always something that resonates within you, just, wow, this is powerful." IC youth we met were proud of the group's media, which they saw as central tools in spreading its message.

Spreading *Kony 2012*

There has been a tendency to deal with *Kony 2012* in isolation from the much longer history of IC efforts to rally public opinion against the African warlord. By the time IC released *Kony 2012*, the group had produced and circulated ten previous features and many shorts; helped get legislation passed in 2010; formed local clubs through high schools, colleges, and churches; recruited and trained thousands of young activists through intern programs, summer camps, and conventions; demonstrated the capacity to mobilize those supporters through local gatherings and demonstrations across the country; developed a large-scale operation on the ground in Africa and brought Ugandans to the United States to interface with American recruits; set up a Ugandan and American teacher exchange program; and run national conventions designed to train young activists so that they could explain what was happening in their own words. *Kony 2012* did not simply "go viral" out of the blue; rather, IC had sustained a community and tested strategies of grassroots circulation that reached diverse participants and laid the groundwork for the film's extraordinarily rapid dissemination.

Supported both through top-down distribution efforts and bottom-up, peer-driven media circulation, the film's release relied on what Jenkins et al. (2013) call "spreadability" or an "emerging hybrid model of circulation, where a mix of top-down and bottom-up forces determine how material is shared across and among cultures in far more participatory (and messier) ways" (3). As we think about this spread of *Kony 2012*, we might consider different moments of participation as an alternative to the clicktivism model.

A core group of young supporters who had been recruited and trained over many years through clubs at churches, schools, and colleges took the first steps in sharing the film with their peers. The video then circulated via friends, families, and others within their social networks. Gilad Lotan (2012), a researcher for Social Flow, discovered that the earliest and most active retweeters of *Kony 2012* came from midsized cities in the Bible Belt and Middle America (including Birmingham, Indianapolis, Dayton, Oklahoma City, and Pittsburgh), cities where there were already many active IC chapters. He also discovered, looking at the personal profiles of those early supporters, that many of them displayed

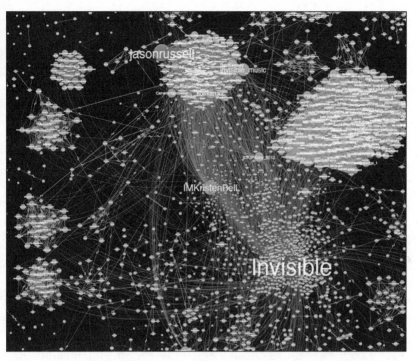

A visualization created by Gilad Lotan mapped the initial spread of the *Kony 2012* film.

signs of strong religious commitments, as well strong ties to their former (or current) high schools and colleges. Part of the group's tactics involved getting fans to target high-profile policy makers and "culture makers," often celebrities known to have strong online followings, in hopes that they would retweet and thus further amplify the message, precipitating greater coverage through mainstream media outlets. Finally, the video provoked responses from concerned others including critics in public policy centers in the United States, critics from the global South who also use digital media to engage within political debates across geographic distances, and other young people who challenged their friends' grasp of what they were circulating.

Each of these sets of participants had a different relationship to the organization and its message. As the video traveled outward from the initial cadre of hardcore supporters, there was a greater risk of what danah boyd (2014) calls "context collapse." For the hardcore supporters, *Kony 2012* was understood in relation to the larger IC story: for example, while critics saw something patronizing in the way Russell was explaining the human rights issues to his young son, longtime supporters saw the video as a moment of maturation, having first seen Russell as a hapless college student in the *Rough Cut*, in contrast to his now stepping into a different—more adult and responsible—role. Meanwhile, the context critics felt was missing from this particular video, including the inclusion of a substantial number of African voices, was more fully developed in other videos the organization had produced. *Tony* (2011), for instance, the film IC released prior to *Kony 2012*, focused specifically on the long-term relationships the group's founders had developed with Ugandan youth and auto-critiqued the culturally naive blunders they had made along the way.

IC's deployment of social media as a channel for circulating *Kony 2012* allowed it to gain much greater visibility than if the nonprofit had been forced to rely exclusively on broadcast media, whether through public service announcements or "earned" media coverage. Yet at the same time, this strategy meant that the group could not fully control where or how the video spread. IC underestimated what Lissa Soep (2012) has described as the "digital afterlife" of the film, in which "the original intentions of media producers are reinterpreted, remixed and sometimes distorted by users and emerge into a recontextualized form" (94). This is a problem encountered by many groups that have sought to deploy such practices. One could argue that even the pushback from African political leaders and commentators reflected the new openness that could be achieved in a system where there was more grassroots control over the means of production and circulation; a traditional public service announcement might never have been seen by these Africa-based critics and, similarly, American supporters of *Kony 2012* would never have heard these critiques in a more localized media ecology.

Kony 2012 is now often held up as the extreme example of a message that was widely circulated, but which did not result in meaningful change. More than three years after the film, Joseph Kony remains at large, a fact that is often cited as the ultimate proof of *Kony 2012*'s failure. Some of IC's critics also find evidence for the meaninglessness of the film's popularity in the subsequent Cover the Night initiative, which asked young people to hang *Kony 2012* posters in their neighborhoods on April 20, a little more than a month after the film's release. Writing for *Policy Mic*, Shanoor Servai (2012) called Cover the Night "the anti-climax to the online brawl" over *Kony 2012*. To her (as to others), Cover the Night proved that a "movement that begins without face-to-face contact between its supporters is unsustainable." While they certainly raise some valid points, these critics fail to acknowledge the turmoil into which the controversy surrounding *Kony 2012* threw IC's staff and supporters—undermining their ability to make the most of the film's extraordinary reception—not to mention the extensive work the organization has nonetheless done to move online contacts into more extended face-to-face interactions among participants. More than that, such critiques ignore the actual policy changes the organization was able to achieve. *Kony 2012* and IC directly contributed to the bipartisan passage of an expansion to the federal Rewards for Justice program, authorizing a reward of up to $5 million for information "that leads to the arrest of Joseph Kony." Indeed, IC leadership was invited to the White House ceremony where President Obama signed the bill into law. Despite such policy accomplishments, however, Invisible Children has had to cut back on its budget and staff and faces ongoing institutional pressures even as it has moved to prioritize its activities on the ground in Africa post–*Kony 2012*.

Paradoxes of Participatory Politics

Invisible Children's attempts to reinvent itself post–*Kony 2012* give us a starting point from which to consider the contradictions and paradoxes associated with participatory politics. We do not necessarily see IC as an exemplar, and this discussion is not intended to endorse the group's choices. But we hope to better understand some of the challenges youth-centered networks confront as they promote social change through participatory politics. In particular, we are pointing toward fault lines within the organization that have surfaced as different segments of the group's leadership lobby for greater or less commitment to these competing principles and as different mixes of these traits dominate various films IC produces and various campaigns it launches.

Goals <—> Process

The tension between IC's primary policy goals, to have Joseph Kony captured and to end the LRA's atrocities, and its main activism objective, to expand the civic capacities of its young U.S. supporters, is the central paradox within the organization. In our first meetings with IC staff in 2009, they openly admitted to being "surprised" when they first recognized that their supporters numbered in the hundreds of thousands. At that time, IC also did not have any formal structures in place to organize and direct these young people's desire to participate. Rather they relied on peer-to-peer personal connections between clubs and specific staff members to transfer knowledge that fell outside immediate IC-determined fundraising strategies. To IC's leadership, the youth movement they had built was an unexpected outcome of their efforts to bring about the capture of Joseph Kony and support the rehabilitation of forcibly recruited child soldiers in the region.

A few months before the release of *Kony 2012*, IC assembled more than 650 of its most dedicated supporters for a gathering at the University of San Diego and announced that the event marked the launch of what they called Fourth Estate. While the term "fourth estate" has long been applied to the role of the press in a democratic society, IC used it to convey something different: the role of citizens in holding governments accountable. Between 2010 and 2014, IC organized three Fourth Estates. While they differed significantly in scope and size, they all took place over several days and included speeches and workshops designed to help "hardcore" IC supporters develop skills required to help the organization achieve its goals at that given moment. Here, IC shared plans with their most trusted supporters. As such, each conference provided unique insights into the organization's shifting priorities and helped us track IC's evolving relationship to participatory politics.

IC's dawning realization about the broader generational implications of its youth base became fully apparent at the first Fourth Estate gathering, which featured both IC-specific programming and more general youth activist sessions. Presenters gave lectures on Uganda's complex colonial and postcolonial history, latest troop movements, and details of IC's plans for the upcoming year, not to mention an overview of ethical issues in international development and a history of colonialism and postcolonial nation-states in the so-called developing world. Given IC's ongoing need to raise funds, the youth spent a significant amount of time generating possible fundraising ideas for the group's upcoming campaign as they shared success stories with each other. They also explored their own motivations for getting involved with IC, and what that might mean in their longer youth activist trajectory. They were even encouraged to write or otherwise document their own "IC story." For the first time, IC acknowledged them as more than "just" enthusiastic fundraisers rallying behind the group's operations in the U.S. and abroad.

In 2011, IC still believed that its paramount goals, to capture Kony and disarm the LRA, could coexist with and drive its expanding youth movement work. As Jedidiah Jenkins observed, IC's specific mission, after all, initially attracted youth. If IC hadn't had a very specific stated goal, what would inspire their young supporters to get involved? The IC we observed in 2011 embraced an approach that our team (Kligler-Vilenchik and Shresthova 2012) identified as "learning through practice," which valued participation and process. Many "traditional" civic organizations enable youth to participate based on an apprenticeship model, in which they work under the guidance of trained experts (see, e.g., Kirshner 2006, 2008). In 2011, IC exhibited a more participatory model, allowing young people to take control of their own activities while still supporting IC's organizational goals.

A little over a year after *Kony 2012*, IC hosted a second, and scaled-up, Fourth Estate conference at UCLA. Focused predominantly on larger-format sessions, the tone and structure of this gathering were dramatically different from the initial event. The second Fourth Estate was much more scripted, giving young participants fewer opportunities to shape activities. Programs focused less on grassroots media production and more on showcasing IC's filmmaking prowess; less on social media circulation and more on formal fundraising; less on participation and more on spectacle; and less on peer-to-peer connections and more on top-down and celebrity-focused messaging. While IC staff attributed some of these shifts to organizational limitations they faced in pulling together a much larger event that included more than 1,400 participants, the changes are also symptomatic of an organization still struggling to regain control and sense of direction after *Kony 2012*. In particular, the second Fourth Estate revealed continuing tensions in IC's vision of new and social media, which may have surprised those who knew IC only through *Kony 2012*. On one hand, IC staff realized that their supporters are "online"—that this sense of connectivity is a vital aspect of what politics means for the millennial generation they see as their core constituency. On the other hand, they privileged "in person" interactions as more substantive and meaningful.

The theater stage was framed with Fourth Estate–branded logos, which served as a constant reminder of who had organized the event and why. While long-term celebrity supporters like Kristen Bell and Jon Chu made an appearance at both Fourth Estates, the second one included a red carpet reception after which the selected celebrities and other invitees were escorted to the upper balcony of UCLA's Royce Auditorium to hear U.S. Ambassador to the United Nations Samantha Power speak and witness IC's ability to engage young people first hand (and from above). Through this impressive display, IC worked to inspire its youth base with motivational speeches and success stories, while largely denying them the chance to directly impact the political narratives being constructed. To some degree, the organization, under attack for most of the previous year, used the second Fourth Estate to "circle the wagons," seeking to protect itself from further missteps and reframe its messages for the campaign's next stage.

Those who criticized IC for its shallow engagement with underlying social justice issues may have been surprised to see the organization make much more overt gestures toward embracing an expanded "millennial youth" identity at the second Fourth Estate. This pivot was apparent in a future-oriented exhibit of real and imagined *Time* magazine covers that IC created for the VIP event. The first three covers were real and focused on actual debates around war, millennials, and the spread of *Kony 2012*. Six fictional covers then portrayed events that IC imagined as possible outcomes. The first imagined cover, dated March 5, 2013 (a year after *Kony 2012* was released), announced Joseph Kony's arrest under the title "#KONYCAPTURED." The following five covers shifted toward imagined visions of global justice and culminated with the victorious headline "How Fourth Estate United One Billion Youth and Changed Earth," clearly establishing IC's investment in the generational debates around millennials. In many ways, IC's second Fourth Estate was a visible display of this investment.

As these real and imagined *Time* covers reveal, post–*Kony 2012*, IC embraced its role as speaking to, for, and with, millennials. In fact, all the youth we interviewed at IC's second Fourth Estate explicitly saw themselves as members of the millennial generation, a generation that they felt had been unfairly criticized for its apathy regarding civic life. Generally identified as those born between 1982 and 2004, millennials have indeed been front and center in debates focused on attitudinal and sociocultural shifts. As a *Time* magazine headline from May 20, 2013—"Me, Me, Me Generation: Millennials Are Lazy, Entitled Narcissists Who Still Live with Their Parents"—suggests, much of the negative commentary around this generation has centered on the premise that they are self-centered, rely on external support, and do not care about the world around them. By contrast, IC used fictional *Time* covers to imagine a future defined by millennials, who, in its vision, will ultimately make the world more "humane" and "united."

In *Millennials Rising: The Next Great Generation* (2000), Neil Howe and William Strauss also argue for a much more optimistic view on millennials, whom they see as a generation that "is going to rebel by behaving not worse, but *better*" (7). More specifically, the authors predict that

[t]he coming of age of the Millennial Generation is likely to take place in the midst of a profound shift in America's social mood, a shift that will match and reflect the new generation's persona. For Millennials, this shift will focus on the needs of the community more than the individual, it is likely to induce large-scale institutional change. Thus, the word *rebellion* is not entirely appropriate. The word *revolution* might better capture the spirit of what lies ahead. (67)

Through the second Fourth Estate, IC explicitly aligned itself with the possibility of a millennial-led *revolution* marked by a shift toward a worldview that sees personal connections between human beings as the foundation for a new sense of social justice and community.

Through its embrace of millennials, IC responded to many of the criticisms leveled at the organization and its most famous media production. It also publicly acknowledged that its ability to connect with young people was, in fact, a key strength. This pro-millennial stance resonated with the young people we interviewed, who saw their involvement with

IC as crucial to countering negative perspectives about their generation. Several speakers at the second Fourth Estate picked up on the millennial theme. Luis Moreno Ocampo, head of the International Criminal Court, expressed his admiration for the youth at the Fourth Estate several times during his speech. On the last day, Samantha Power, the newly appointed ambassador to the U.N., drove this message home once more. Responding to the standing ovation she received when she came onto the stage, she opened her speech with "OMG." Power explained that when she thought about where she should make her first public speech in her new role, there was only one answer—to "spend this time with the people who are determined to promote human rights and human dignity, the next generation who are going to make a profound difference. I was determined to spend my first official weekend with you."

Over time, our continued engagement with the organization revealed the challenges IC has faced in maintaining this balance between its Africa-facing goals and its youth-driven process. Even before *Kony 2012*, the organization's leadership often brought our discussions back to clarifying IC's primary goals, capturing Kony and disarming the LRA. At the same time, many of the young supporters we interviewed felt that IC would continue to exist post-Kony, though they often disagreed on how the scope and focus of the organization would transform. Some felt IC could take on different specific humanitarian issues. Others wanted it to form partnerships with groups that could benefit from its experience in mobilizing youth. They saw a value in fostering greater youth agency and voice and encouraging more participation in core public debates whether or not the organization ever achieved its explicit goals on the ground in Africa. Ironically, when IC was criticized for spending too much of the funds it raised in the United States, this focus on building youth capacity was the core subtext: fostering young activists was becoming a central part of its mission, while the group's critics saw those young people as much like the staff of any other nonprofit organization—a means to an end.

Comprehensible <—> Complex Stories

One key characteristic of participatory politics has been a renewed emphasis on political storytelling and the civic imagination. IC continually negotiates between the recognition that the LRA conflict is complex and stretches far back into colonial history and the perceived need to communicate with its supporters through simple, graspable, and engaging storytelling. Ethan Zuckerman (2012a) argues that this focus on storytelling was central to *Kony 2012*'s success:

> The campaign Invisible Children is running is so compelling because it offers an extremely simple narrative: Kony is a uniquely bad actor, a horrific human being, whose capture will end suffering for the people of Northern Uganda. If each of us does our part, influences powerful people, the world's most powerful military force will take action and Kony will be captured. . . . We are asked to join the campaign against Kony literally by being spoken to as a five year old. It's not surprising that a five year old vision of a problem—a single bad guy, a single threat to eliminate—leads to an unworkable solution. Nor is it a surprise that this extremely simple narrative is compelling and easily disseminated.

Zuckerman notes that this narrative might push the United States toward a closer alliance with other African leaders who are not necessarily more democratic or have no better records on human rights. He describes some of what would need to be included if the group was to move beyond a good-and-evil framing of the situation: "A more complex narrative of northern Uganda would look at the odd, codependent relationship between Museveni and Kony, Uganda's systematic failure to protect the Acholi people of northern Uganda. It would look at the numerous community efforts, often led by women, to mediate conflicts and increase stability." Zuckerman worries that simplified narratives like IC's may lead to a public response that is closer to a moral panic than to collective deliberation over important policy concerns. Yet he also acknowledges that the debate provoked by *Kony 2012*—the editorials, blogs, and podcasts that responded to and complicated its narrative—resulted in a more robust exchange about America's policy toward Uganda.

Staunch supporters often see IC's compelling stories and content world as crucial to their success. As Meg, a young woman featured in a short film that screened during the second Fourth Estate, observed, "I think the reason that Invisible Children spoke so powerfully to me is because they believe . . . that every single person is unique and has their own powerful story. I think that if more people could connect to those individual stories there would be a lot more empathy and compassion in the world." Though IC has told many stories over the years, two narratives remain fairly constant: IC's origin story and the call-to-action story that presents Joseph Kony as an unquestionably evil force that needs to be stopped. IC's origin story starts with its founders' first trip to Africa in search of subject matter for a film project. As Jason Russell recounted during the first Fourth Estate, when he met the night commuters—Ugandan children who traveled to safer locations every night to avoid abductions by the LRA—he knew they had found that story. In an emotional and pivotal moment in *Invisible Children: Rough Cut*, IC's first film, Tony—one of these night commuters—asks the filmmakers whether they will forget him when they return to the United States. Jason made a promise to not only remember, but also to help end the conflict and bring Joseph Kony to justice. In IC films, capturing Kony, as an individual, remains key to resolving the conflict in Uganda and ending the suffering it causes.

There is some truth to Zuckerman's "simple narrative" critique: IC media generally shies away from a deeper, more complex discussion of the LRA, contemporary Ugandan politics, and postcolonial histories. As Swartz (2012) observes, IC's U.S.-based stories (that is, stories of its founders and youth supporters) remain much more fleshed out than the stories of their Ugandan staff and beneficiaries.

That said, the group made efforts to change this situation over time. When we first started our research, the Ugandan staff did not even appear on IC's website, something the group's leaders addressed very soon after we presented our first research findings to them in 2010. As the founders' initial contact in Uganda and now IC's regional ambassador, Jolie Grace Okot has figured as a key validating figure in the organization's African narrative. IC also brought program staff and youth beneficiaries to the United States to join its roadie teams. As one participant observed, the Ugandan roadies were always a very important part of IC's U.S. awareness raising campaigns and post–*Kony 2012*, they became absolutely essential in establishing a more authentic IC narrative.

Outside of more in-depth sessions at the Fourth Estate, IC's presentation of the cause and solution of the conflict remains fairly simple. Specifically, the organization sees Joseph Kony as the problem, raising awareness about him and eventually capturing him as the solution. IC's continued commitment to this simple story and clear call to action obfuscates much more complex pieces in the group's sprawling media output, which includes stories where the founders question their motivations and qualifications, stories of Ugandans affected by the conflict, accounts of IC's rehabilitation programs for former child soldiers, and recently, more technically complex narratives of partnering with other NGOs in the region to create media (flyers and radio broadcasts) that encourage LRA defections. While these more complex narratives are readily available to those who dig deeper, IC's outward-facing media rarely invites such investigation as it still privileges sharing its simple, graspable, powerful, and therefore easily actionable story.

Activism <—> Entertainment

When we asked IC staff what events inspired their plans for the second Fourth Estate, the leaders mentioned Comic-Con, South by Southwest, and Lady Gaga concerts. They said that they wanted to create an event "they would want to go to," and the final result included spectacular dance performances by the Legion of Extraordinary Dancers (LXD) on the first and last days, music concerts that lasted late into the night, and appearances by celebrities from the worlds of entertainment and activism, whose ranks included Harry Shum Jr., Sophia Bush, Rachel Bilson, The Buried Life, and South African activist Jay Naidoo. When IC launched a new campaign, ZeroLRA, in 2013, Jason Russell, in an interview with *Time*, described the initiative as "Netflix meets the Peace Corps meets Comic-Con." For IC, navigating between more traditional, tonally more serious modes of activism and a more playful, entertaining, and youthful approach involves a constant balancing act.

This focus on the ties between entertainment value and activism was part of what initially drew our team's attention to Invisible Children. When we screened *Invisible Children: Rough Cut*, many of us felt that the media it most closely resembled was the MTV practical-joke program *Jackass*, as the hapless young activists stumble their way through Uganda before being politically awakened by discovering the LRA's night raids to abduct children, especially young boys, to become forced participants in their paramilitary organization. Many of the IC members we interviewed stressed how the rough-hewn quality of that early video created an instant identification with the organization's leaders, allowing them to imagine themselves as part of the movement. Beth, an IC intern, explained, "The movie is just very raw, and it's—even though they were older than me—they were kids, and you see these kids just go, they see something, they run into a problem and they're like, OK, now we have to fix this problem." Jade, another intern, shared that the media IC produces "has a lot of a younger feel to it . . . you can definitely tell that the people who work here are a lot younger, they are a lot more media-savvy than a lot of the orgs. They draw in a different crowd than a lot of organizations; other orgs draw large donors and we are staffed by young people, we focus on young people and we realize that young people can make a difference if they're really passionate about it."

Melissa Brough (2012) notes a narcissistic tone in IC's initial appeals that feels more rooted in the realm of consumerism and self-help than in philanthropy and social change movements as we might imagine them historically:

> In IC's media, emphasis is placed on the American donor/activist as much as, if not more than, IC's beneficiaries. Invisible Children's videos unapologetically embrace the opportunity for personal growth offered by entrepreneurial participation in the humanitarian adventure. IC sends the winners of high school fundraising competitions, organized through an online social networking site, to Uganda to visit the schools and camps of internally displaced communities that their funds support." (181–182)

And this may be what got under the skin of the organization's critics. In an article that examines *Kony 2012*'s impact on portrayals of child soldiers, Mark Drumbl (2012) asks, "Is it sensible for international law and policy to be based upon stylized content deliberately airbrushed just to increase attention-worthiness?" (485). In a similar, even more critical, vein, Patricia Daley (2013) introduces *Kony 2012* as "a celebrity-supported geopolitical campaign, masquerading as humanitarian" (384) and concludes that

> *Kony2012* and other celebrity-supported advocacy, such as United to End Genocide, promote a form of global citizenship under neoliberal gover-

nance that seeks to mobilise global youth on international issues from a narrow militaristic, corporate and politically conservative perspective, whilst claiming to be transcending politics. (387)

As IC continues to blend entertainment and social justice through its media and activities, it remains vulnerable to such critiques. And yet this ability to make social justice entertaining is what supporters and staff see as crucial to the organization's continued appeal to youth. Cathy, an IC supporter who first got involved when she was in high school, feels it belongs to a group of organizations that strive to "make charity and humanitarian work attractive" by creating media and events that engage and entertain as much as they educate.

Drawing comparisons between case studies of fan cultures around entertainment media and social movements that have grown around democratic struggles, Liesbet van Zoonen (2005) argues that the walls between the two are breaking down. She writes about *American Idol*, for example, that "the discussion, participation, creativity, interventions, judgments and votes that take place around reality television are all activities that would qualify as civic competencies if they were performed in the context of the political realm." Not only are popular television shows modeling for their viewers what democracy looks and feels like through what John Hartley (2006) has called "plebiscite entertainment," but activist groups are also actively modeling themselves after fan communities. As discussed in Chapter 1, such interactions might once have taken the form of culture jamming—turning mass entertainment against itself—but today they operate under a different valence.

Writing about détournement in *Beautiful Trouble*, a print and online guide for contemporary activists, Zack Malitz (2012) talks about the importance of cultural "fluency." "The better you know a culture, the easier it is to shift, repurpose, or disrupt it," he argues. "To be successful, the media artifact chosen for détournement must be recognizable to its intended audience. Further, the saboteur must be familiar with the subtleties of the artifact's original meaning in order to effectively create a new, critical meaning" (30). Stephen Duncombe (2012b), another contributor to *Beautiful Trouble*, takes this idea of cultural fluency further: "You may not like or be familiar with Nascar, professional sports, reality TV and superheroes, but they are all fertile arenas of culture to work with. It may take an open mind and a bit of personal courage, but it behooves us to immerse ourselves in, learn about and respect the world of the cultural 'Other'—which, for many of us counter-culture types, ironically, is mass culture" (144). He warns that activists cannot afford to ignore the reactionary dimensions of popular texts lest they reproduce them in the process of circulating their counternarratives, yet they also must not remain aloof from the desires and fantasies that motivate fan investments. Duncombe argues that political truths must be "communicated in new and compelling ways that can be passed from person to person, even if this requires flights of fancy and new mythologies" (231). For him, that involves learning from Hollywood, Las Vegas, the games industry, and Madison Avenue.

Yet IC's commitment to the use of popular culture goes beyond the "hold your nose and try not to go native" advice given in *Beautiful Trouble*. The group's leaders do not see the genres they use to construct their media as forays into "the world of the cultural 'Other.'" Rather, they see these uses of popular media as fundamental to the organization's approach. Reflecting on the *Invisible Children Musical* in an interview with this chapter's author, Jason Russell explained why he sees popular culture—and specifically music and dance—as important to what IC does:

> When you're nonprofit, you always compromise on the quality of the content that you're putting out. And so no one opens the email. No one watches the movie. No one buys the T-shirts, because they're ugly and no one spent any time creating them. We were really drawn to Bono and Apple's conviction of always making beautiful things. That musical really just came out of the love for *Captain EO* and Michael Jackson. My brother said, "Listen to the lyrics of the song: 'We are here to change the world.' Isn't that what you are trying to do?" And I said, "We should just do that because it's unorthodox." The academic community will get pissed off, and it will get young people to say, "Wow, you can actually have fun and celebrate and dance and sing while you're changing the world. What a cool concept."

Colin, who had gotten involved with the cause in high school and has become even more active in college, stressed the importance of design aesthetics in shaping public perception of IC's messaging. Many other members stressed the ways that they first learned about Kony through IC's videos and noted that what had attracted them in the first place was that the organization's media did not feel too "causy" when read against other social advocacy materials they had encountered. IC does not simply translate its messages into the language of pop culture; the group's leaders—and their youth supporters—are natural speakers of these languages, with Hollywood genres and pop culture remixes a central part of their experiences since childhood. These issues surface much more dramatically for fan activism groups like the Harry Potter Alliance and the Nerdfighters, which are discussed in the next chapter. Critics such as Sarah Banet-Weiser (2013) fear that efforts like IC's videos amount to the commodification of collective desires for social change and an extension of entertainment values into the political realm. Yet the opposite could also be true—that these efforts involve a hijacking of the vast publicity apparatus to spread political messages that might not otherwise be heard.

Consensus <—> Contention

That groups such as Invisible Children work more through consensus than conflict has been central to their success and reflects the value they place on what Jeff Weintraub (1997) characterizes as "sociability" (17). This more sociable style of civic participation can be enormously appealing to a generation often sickened by today's harsh partisanship. IC provided a supportive environment for young participants to take their first tentative steps into activism, gain greater confidence in their efficacy, and prepare to take action on issues they cared about. Yet, for this very reason, IC's young supporters seemed remarkably unprepared for criticisms of *Kony 2012*. Members of traditional party-based and advocacy groups ready themselves to confront oppositional perspectives. Most of the first 13 Freedom Riders in the civil rights movement (see Carson 1995, 31–38), for example, were seasoned activist members of the Congress of Racial Equality (CORE). As a part of this organization, they had experience and training that prepared them to react appropriately when they were called names, spat upon, and physically assaulted as they confronted the defenders of Southern segregation on the ground. The PBS documentary *Freedom Riders* (2010) includes archival footage of such training and shows activists enacting situations they were likely to encounter. For example, there is a scene set in a diner in which activists are slandered and asked to leave because of their skin color when they try to order coffee. As CORE staff member Gordon Carey recalls in the film, "The training we did . . . prior to the time the Riders got on buses was largely devoted to trying to see how the person's gonna react." In contrast, when IC's core leadership turned inward to deal with Russell's personal tragedy, the group's young supporters were left alone to rebut the mounting attacks against *Kony 2012*. In some cases, they rose to the occasion, demonstrating a great capacity to seek out and deploy information. But, in others, they lacked the critical skills needed to address skeptical classmates or family members.

Sanyu Lobogo, a young Ugandan American, became one of the most visible faces of the anti–Invisible Children movement when she posted a YouTube video insisting that Kony had been dead and his organization ineffective for five years: "The *Kony 2012* Video is not the only information you should rely on. Research. I am all for the cause, just not the video that was made. Do your own research and come back with more info!" Her perspective became increasingly more militant as she, in turn, had to deal with aggressive pushback from IC supporters. One of the IC roadies described what happened when the group screened *Kony 2012* at Lobogo's school: "She [Lobogo] had tweeted out to everyone, 'The Invisible scam are coming in today. Don't go.' It was the most unsuccessful screening we had, eight people there or something. It was awful."

In other cases, though, the group was able to create a context where critics could be engaged in a more constructive manner. Grant Oyston, a college sophomore, had posted some critiques of IC on his blog visiblechildren.tumblr.com, intending to express his distrust to a close circle of friends. However, in a matter of days, his post had been read more than 2 million times. While Oyston's original post was later widely deployed by IC critics, in a later post he argued that he was simply trying to counterbalance the video's framing: "My purpose was simply to show other elements of the story, things that weren't included in the video—obviously there are constraints to what you can fit into a video, but to show things that weren't discussed in the video. To talk about other organizations, to talk about—as I understand it, what Invisible Children does and where the money goes. I raised some concerns about it certainly, but my end goal was always to have people understand more and learn more, get a better sense and then do whatever they think is the right thing to do, with the best information possible . . . but by no means was this an attack on the great work that Invisible Children has done and continues to do." When Oyston encountered a group of IC roadies on his campus, he ended up talking with them for more than an hour, and ultimately granting an interview for the Invisible Children blog on March 21, 2013, in which he told readers: "You're telling a story that's been going on for multiple decades and involves thousands of people. . . . No one person is ever going to understand everything about the story. That's impossible. But if it's something you care about you owe it to yourself to do your best to learn what you can as a reasonable person and get a decent understanding of what's going on."

Many of the youth we interviewed experienced the pushback against *Kony 2012* as a repudiation of their values and beliefs. One of them, Molly, reported, "I think after *Kony 2012* we were kind of walking on eggshells with what we posted online and what we said. . . . I feel like we were bullied. People were picking at every little thing and we were nervous and we were kind of just like we had been around for so long and people stuck with us and we're going to keep our voice. . . . We're not going to stop because somebody is posting on our Facebook that we're a scam or liars." As *Kony 2012* spread, it also reached youth who were not directly involved with IC. For example, 15-year-old Theo, a member of the Nerdfighter community discussed in the next chapter, mentioned his encounter with *Kony 2012* when interviewed about his experience with Nerdfighteria. At first, he found the film "very moving" but later had "second thoughts" about getting involved as he encountered critiques of IC's finances. Kevin, another Nerdfighter we interviewed, felt that the critiques leveraged against *Kony 2012* actually applied to online activism more generally as it became clear that many people who may have shared the film "didn't investigate the issue at all."

While some of the young IC supporters felt that they experienced most of the pushback online, even as they received support from classmates and family at the local level, others found that the online controversy brought the issues into their everyday interactions within their school communities. Natalie, a recent high school graduate, reported, "I think the reason I'm afraid of criticism is because the kids at my school were already criticizing me about it, and I didn't know what to do. . . . The more popular it got, the worse the criticism is going to be." In some cases, the youth were driven away from political engagement as a result of their inability to adequately address these critiques. Natalie did not leave IC—in fact, she took a year off from school to intern in Uganda—but she did describe her growing frustration over her inability to combat what she saw as misperceptions of the group and its agenda: "I'm really going to fight back. I really want to make sure that these people at the end of this argument are on my side. And then they will support Invisible Children. At the same time, I realized that no matter how many facts we threw their way . . . no matter how many conversations we had, there was nothing that I can do to persuade them. . . . Sometimes you have to take the criticism, and you just have to walk away." Molly left these sorts of exchanges more determined than ever to get her message out: "We're going to take those criticisms and we're going to look at them. But we're not going to ignore them. When we see something like, 'You need more information on your website,' so we're going to buff up our website. So we're going to put more information on the website. We're going to put more videos. We're going to put more information out there."

Molly frames the problem as a lack of information—which was partially the case, as the IC website, which the organization had failed to fully update prior to the video's launch because it anticipated a much slower spread of the message, crashed during the early days of the controversy. Yet our research suggests a much deeper problem: the group had done little to help its supporters to acquire skills in formulating and articulating their own opinions, and it had neither reviewed potential counterarguments nor provided its network with the resources needed to rebut them. This failure is consistent with a core finding of the MacArthur survey on youth and participatory politics (Cohen and Kahne 2012): 84 percent of the young people interviewed said that they would "benefit from learning more about how to tell if news and information you find online is trustworthy" (viii).

More recently, IC has placed a stronger emphasis on fostering these critical literacy skills. During interviews conducted following the second Fourth Estate conference, IC roadies and staff mentioned that they hadn't previously felt it urgent to model responses for and provide debating skills to their youth supporters but that they definitely did so now.

As one informal step, IC created "trolling Thursday" on its Facebook page, taking on criticism received that week through social media, sharing it with committed supporters, and publishing the information needed to respond to the critiques. Some of our other case study networks have done much more to foster critical deliberation and prepare their members to defend their positions.

Spreadable <—> Drillable

Jenkins, Ford, and Green (2013) use the term "spreadable" to describe ways that content may be circulated actively via social media through a process that is partially shaped by top-down actions taken by professional media producers and partially by bottom-up choices made by individuals and grassroots communities pursuing their own goals. The *Kony 2012* campaign, which depends on the interplay of a nonprofit organization and its loosely connected supporters, is a classic example of spreadable content. Jason Mittell (2013), however, introduced a second concept—drillability—to refer to the ways that new media's database structures sometimes make it possible to drill deeper and develop a fuller understanding of media content and context. As Swartz (2012) notes in relation to IC, "The extent to which the group 'raises awareness' is largely dependent on how spreadable their message is. Drillability, on the other hand, describes the learning opportunities that exist beyond initial contact with the message. Both features are necessary for newcomers to become advocates of the cause" (11). The traits of a highly spreadable message may be different from those that ensure its drillability, though a coordinated transmedia campaign can achieve both.

Swartz not only finds that IC had been much more effective at achieving spreadability than drillability, but also warns that anyone who drilled deep into the IC site would find materials that could damage the organization; this proved to be the case when critics investigating the group dug up old photographs of the founders waving guns in Africa, learned more about the group's ties to religious organizations (a theme never denied but not overtly raised in much of IC's public-facing materials), and unearthed information that prompted questions about how the group raised and budgeted its money. Meanwhile, what they had difficulty finding was in-depth discussions of the complexities of the current political situation in Uganda and the Congo. While the IC-affiliated youth we spoke with generally defended the group as providing information sufficient to support their efforts, they also alluded to moments when they had to seek out information to defend the *Kony 2012* campaign. In most cases, they argued the information was there if they looked deep enough. That said, IC did not necessarily invite such investigative practices. Rather it focused on brief, easily graspable messages useful for raising awareness and funds for the cause.

Amirah, a young British woman with Pakistani roots, discovered IC through the *Kony 2012* campaign but was frustrated by the shutdown of the group's website and by the ways that her usual news sources like the *Guardian* and the BBC were focusing almost entirely on critiques of the nonprofit rather than the issues IC was calling to the public's attention. Watching the video with her father opened her eyes to a problem she had not known existed and provoked her to use her investigative skills to learn more about the situation online. Johnny, 19, had found *Kony 2012* an effective starting point for discussions, and he became a point person inside his high school for the campaign as he tried to educate his cohort about the issues. He was frustrated, however, that many of them would allow a "rumor heard on Facebook" to color their whole perception of the movement, refusing to listen to the information he was painstakingly gathering.

After the fallout from *Kony 2012*, IC tried to address some of these issues by reorganizing and updating its website. Most of the updates focused on making the group's guiding principles and activities more transparent. For example, IC's "unconventional four-part model"—made up of media, mobilization, protection, and recovery activities—is now described in some detail. Visitors can also easily see how much of IC's budget goes toward each of these areas. Clicking on the "LRA Crisis Tracker" tab takes the visitor to an interactive site that collates LRA updates from various sources to provide real-time information about defections, abductions, and other activities. Despite all these improvements, IC still provides few resources on the history of the conflict. Clicking on the "Conflict Overview" tab takes the visitor to a one-pager that contextualizes the conflict through brief introductions to Joseph Kony, displacement camps, the International Criminal Court, Juba Peace Talks, and Christmas Massacres, before ending with a update on the "LRA Today." Those who want to "Dive Deeper" are then redirected to the "LRA Crisis Tracker." (Meanwhile, IC's robust and frequently updated blog is a crucial, but less easily searchable, repository for information on the violence in Uganda.) The lack of a more carefully curated repository of in-depth information and connections to other sources on the "Conflict Overview" page is quite telling. The page provides visitors with the sort of information they would need to quickly and accurately respond to basic questions but does virtually nothing to help them gain a deeper and more nuanced understanding of the conflict.

Top-Down <—> Bottom-Up

One consequence of IC's focus on entertainment values has been a tendency to emphasize professional media making and top-down celebrity-supported efforts over the kinds of grassroots efforts we will see emerging from our other case studies. A vast majority of creative media production is handled by IC's small, professional, and—in some ways—exclusive team. This centralized control over the production and circulation of media fits hand in glove with an organizational culture that is more hierarchical than that of most of the other groups we examine here. The IC leadership shifts back and forth between its desire to retain control over the group's brand, messaging, and activities and its aim to incorporate diverse and participatory elements (which are to some degree responsible for IC's appeal among young people). Over the years that we have studied IC, we have seen this balance tip in either direction.

On one side might be the "My IC story" initiative, which the organization created during the first Fourth Estate in 2011. "My IC Story" asked participants to craft a narrative of what IC means to them and why this personal connection is important. During breakout sessions, participants shared their own personal stories of how they became involved. The stories then went through several rounds of review and editing to fashion compelling versions the participants could share to help garner support (and raise funds) for IC. Usually, the group focused on finding the most emotionally compelling moment (e.g., "then my mother was diagnosed with cancer") and asking the participant to get to it earlier or consider how it could be used more effectively. Peers then also suggested what parts of a story might be omitted if time was short (e.g., "if you only had one minute maybe you could open with talking about how much the film moved you when you first saw it"). After this feedback, the participants retold their stories, this time standing up to do so. After receiving at least one more round of comments, they took a few minutes to write their stories down in the journals they received at registration.

"My IC Story" was inspired by an unsolicited exchange on the Fourth Estate Facebook group page, where more than a hundred participants decided to introduce themselves in the weeks leading up to the event. In the end, youth were encouraged to record their stories and post them to their fundraising pages hosted on Invisible Children's website. Leading up to the second Fourth Estate in 2013, the youth again introduced themselves prior to the event and were encouraged to create their own videos. But IC exerted more control over the process. They guided the discussion on the Facebook page, and, at times, the staff stepped in to censor discussions.

This focus on smoothing out the rough edges of the grassroots storytelling and media making reflects the organization's desire to gain greater control over its messaging in the wake of the *Kony 2012* firestorm, but the shift struck our team as ironic since, for us, what happened to IC during *Kony 2012* was a product of the group's long-standing tendency toward centralization. Having launched a campaign focused around grassroots efforts to circulate the video, the group's leaders hunkered down when controversy struck. They lacked the capacity to communicate effectively with their dispersed supporters, who often had to confront local controversies on their own. Some of the other groups we study are much better prepared to deal with emergent responses, much more open to innovation from the edges, and much better able to regroup following a disruption of their communications infrastructure.

We observed a similar top-down versus bottom-up tension when we examined how IC tapped celebrity fandom to further its cause. IC has long recognized the visibility that celebrities can bring and has continued to add to its roster of prominent supporters over the years. At the time of writing, this list includes Oprah Winfrey, Harry Shum, Sophia Bush, Tom Shadyac, Jon Chu, and Kristen Bell, among others. IC celebrity supporters express their support for the group in various ways: they help spread IC campaigns through social media (according to Lotan's chart, Bell was instrumental in spreading *Kony 2012*); they make appearances at IC events; they make sizeable donations and encourage others to do the same; and they also seek "product-placement" opportunities for the organization. In return, IC places its celebrity supporters on a pedestal that separates them from their less well-known supporters.

Our distinction here between top-down spectacle and participatory politics echoes another classic distinction in the literature around civic and political engagement—that between a public and an audience. Daniel Dayan (2005), for example, tells us that audiences are produced by acts of measurement, by the number of eyeballs attracted (as in the constant celebration of the number of people who watched *Kony 2012*) or in terms of the amount of money raised (another measure by which IC appraises its success). Publics, on the other hand, actively direct attention onto messages they value: "A public not only offers attention, it calls for attention" (44). A group cannot be meaningfully described as a public—or for that matter—participatory, if it lacks the ability to put issues on the table or if it lacks the collective capacity to deliberate and reach its own conclusions about the topics being considered. Publics, Sonia Livingstone (2005) argues, are "held to be collectivities, more than the sum of their parts, while audiences by contrast are merely aggregates of individuals" (25). From the start, IC has sought to build a strong sense of social connection between its members and increasingly, between U.S.-based participants and their counterparts in Africa. Yet, as the group adopts more spectator-driven models for its rallies, there is some risk that the affective ties will be stronger between individual members and the group's leaders and celebrities than among dispersed members.

Lessons Learned from *Kony 2012*

One key assumption behind this book is that more participatory structures create a sense of belonging and solidarity within groups that are brought together less by geographic proximity than by shared interests and commitments. We see IC as an organization that seeks to tap the participatory impulses of its supporters to foster deeper commitments. Yet, as we've argued, for IC, maintaining and nurturing such participation has been, and continues to be, a struggle. On one hand, IC's leaders recognize, and identify with, the participatory modes of engagement that drew many young people into the organization. They embrace innovative popular culture-inflected modes of civic engagement. In fact, most of IC's leaders are only one or two steps removed from their millennial generation supporters. On the other hand, IC leaders now feel obligated to focus on achieving their goals in Africa, a priority that steers the organization away from actively supporting and encouraging meaningful youth participation. If *Kony 2012* forced IC to "grow up," then growing up for IC has meant a deepening tension between its participatory modes of engaging youth and more traditional top-down approaches. Youth are becoming audiences for rather than participants in creating IC media.

While there is much about IC that still encourages a sense of participation, including a reliance on grassroots circulation and an emphasis on the language of remix culture, IC increasingly operates more like a traditional political organization. However, our interviews with IC supporters also confirmed that the young people involved with the group did (at least at one point in its history) feel a significant sense of ownership over its messages and saw themselves as belonging to the community that formed around its media production and circulation. IC is best understood through the lens of paradoxes that emerge out of these negotiations. Though particular to IC in many ways, we can learn much about participatory politics by grappling with these paradoxes. For one, they point to generational shifts in what politics looks like and how it is practiced. These paradoxes also prompt us to recognize the important role that popular culture and entertainment can play in mobilizing youth.

At the time of this writing, IC's future direction remains unclear as it undergoes a series of very substantial organizational changes. In January 2014, confronting a large shortfall in its fundraising (ironically attributable to the public perception that the group had become rich and powerful in the wake of *Kony 2012*), IC announced that it was cutting back many of the community-building activities we discuss here, including outreach to youth through schools. Instead, as some of their critics had advocated, IC would focus its efforts on ending the LRA conflict. As Noelle West explained in an interview with BuzzFeed (Testa 2014), "We don't need the masses, the gigantic grassroots movement, as much as we have in the past." In its messaging, IC expressed an ongoing commitment to supporting its youth, but on a much less dedicated level. For the many IC staffers who joined the group because of its appeal to youth, the decision to refocus on institutional efforts has been painful. As a consequence of the shift, IC's grassroots youth base has substantially diminished. There was a much scaled-back Fourth Estate in August 2014, which brought together 40 of the group's most committed youth supporters. As in previous years, this Fourth Estate also focused on sharing information about IC programs, but in a much more intimate and low-key setting that felt more like a gathering of friends and family than a formal event.

In December 2014, after continued downsizing at the San Diego headquarters, IC made another, this time more decisive, announcement, declaring that it would shut down all of its U.S. operations at the end of the year. In an open letter addressed to supporters on the group's website, IC's leadership explained:

> So based on our current financial projections, we have decided that the best decision is to shut down the media and mass-awareness efforts in the U.S. and to focus all remaining funds (and future fundraising) on the execution of our most essential programs. We will also be handing off ownership of our Ugandan programs and offices to regional partners. Because of this decision, things are going to look a lot different. We won't be visiting your school in vans, and we won't be making new videos or selling T-shirts. We won't be hosting major awareness events, benefit concerts, or grassroots fundraisers. Invisible Children will be moving out of our San Diego office and the majority of our staff will be let go, including our current executive staff.

In its youth-facing messaging, IC struck a less final note, stressing that there would still be ways for young people to stay involved, particularly if they wanted to be part of IC's Washington, D.C., efforts through Resolve (resolve.org), IC's long-term lobbying partner. Still, the announcement signaled that an era of Invisible Children was ending. Russell encouraged young supporters to sustain their commitment to "changing the world" and to continue to use the skills, friendships, networks, and experiences acquired through IC to achieve their goals.

Within a few hours of IC's announcement, a flurry of youth-generated blog posts, YouTube videos, and Tumblr posts reacted to the news, with many of the posters reflecting about what involvement with IC and its community had meant to their lives. An article published in *Medium* by

Matt Scott Crum (2014), a self-identified IC millennial, exemplified the tone of most of these expressions:

> IC has contributed an important part to the rising of a new generation of activists and leaders; people that were not loyal to just Invisible Children but awoke to a variety of types of injustices and became inspired and dedicated to do *something about something.* On my college campus alone, I can personally name a sizable group of students who altered their careers to be able to fight injustice in some way who got their start, their original passion, from Invisible Children's content.

As if to confirm this sentiment, a core group of Fourth Estate alumni quickly launched "Fourth Estate—The Next Chapter," a Facebook group dedicated to finding ways to harness IC's youth energy into networked activities that would sustain the movement after IC shuts down. As the group continues to brainstorm next steps, it is also actively fundraising for IC's final (and, by previous standards, modest) campaign to raise $150,000 to support its "most vital programs in the counter-LRA mission through 2015." At the time of writing, it is unclear whether and how this fledgling participatory post-IC movement will evolve. But if the fact that they managed to meet and exceed their fundraising goal within a matter of days is an indicator of momentum, then we might be seeing interesting developments among IC supporters in the months to come.

Regardless of whether a clearly defined post-IC youth movement emerges, the organization's approach to mobilizing youth will likely live on as supporter and staff alumni continue to apply skills they acquired through IC to other contexts. We already see IC staff moving into positions at other nonprofits (like Giving Keys and To Write Love on Her Arms), corporate startups, and educational initiatives. We also see them applying IC's approach to storytelling as a catalyst for social change to other causes. As these individuals continue to connect to each other through social media, we expect to see an increasingly more self-aware, loosely networked IC-inspired community of youth leaders take shape.

IC's decision in 2014 to prioritize its overseas goals over supporting its youth base—and its ultimate decision to let young supporters move on—distinguishes it from the groups in our other case studies, for whom youth engagement is central, not tangential, to their existence. Chapter

3 will reveal how a multiple-issue-based approach—rather than a narrow, single-mission focus—can strengthen and sustain grassroots support. As IC's senior leadership readily admits, IC's youth-engagement strategy was an unintended byproduct of its efforts to end the plight of the night commuters that Jason Russell, Bobby Bailey, and Laren Poole met during their first trip to Uganda. Over a decade, IC struggled and experimented with different approaches to achieve this. Along the way, they inspired tens of thousands of young people to participate. As he reflects on IC's early days, Russell laughs, "We were naive. We were stupid. We thought we could end a war." Elaborating on this sentiment, a former IC staff member posted this comment on her Facebook page in response to the news IC shared in December 2014:

> You know how people ask "how are you feeling?" And you're like "I'm fine." But you're really not fine? It's a heartbreaking feeling to watch a beautiful thing you poured your blood sweat and tears into sail off into the sunset. I could rattle off stats about the natural life cycle of a business or that all good things must come to an end, but for some reason this article got me. Sure, mistakes were made at IC. Sure, we "got lucky" far more times than we deserved. But we also gathered together the most generous and idealistic and incredible humans for a genuinely important cause. We weren't scammers or slacktivists or white saviors or getting rich. We just REALLY were that genuine and REALLY trying that hard.

With the organization now likely closing its doors for good within the year, it will be up to its young supporters to decide what defines IC's long-term legacy for youth and participatory politics.

3

"Decreasing World Suck"

Harnessing Popular Culture for Fan Activism

Neta Kligler-Vilenchik

A young fan masquerades as Harry Potter in a YouTube video blog encouraging young people to donate books to libraries and communities in need. In a downtown bar, fans gathered for a "Wizard Rock concert," dancing to songs based on the world of Harry Potter, are approached by volunteers encouraging them to register to vote. In a local library, a group of fans meets every week to discuss how the Harry Potter stories can be linked to real-world issues. All of these unlikely examples mirror ways that a popular cultural phenomenon can be employed toward participatory politics.

Established in 2005 by community organizer and stand-up comedian Andrew Slack, together with co-founder Seth Soulstein, the Harry Potter Alliance (HPA)—whose members are responsible for all the activities mentioned above—is a nonprofit organization promoting literacy, equality, and human rights. The HPA leadership includes a handful of paid staff members and a network of young volunteers, dispersed around the nation, conducting most of their communication online via laptops. The local face-to-face component of the HPA involves a network of over 300 chapters in high schools, colleges, and communities nationwide, and on six continents. The mostly youth-led chapters engage in national campaigns but also promote local projects based on their members' interests. Unlike Invisible Children, described in Chapter 2, the HPA is not defined around a single mission; rather, it addresses a diverse set of causes loosely inspired by J. K. Rowling's content world. For the HPA, the Harry Potter universe is so rich and diverse that almost any real-world cause could be linked to it, allowing the organization to respond quickly to current events as well as to pressing issues raised by its members.

The HPA operates within the structures of the Harry Potter fan community, using its creative tools to encourage civic action. One example is the House Cup competition. Hogwarts, the school of magic in the Harry Potter universe, is organized around four houses, Gryffindor, Slytherin, Ravenclaw, and Hufflepuff, each of which embodies different ideals and virtues. Harry Potter fans deploy many different sorting mechanisms to place members into appropriate houses, and many feel a strong sense of identification and affiliation with their house. This identification is then employed to rally fans, as in the Wrock4Equality campaign, in which members earned points for their respective houses for each person they contacted in the effort to rally Maine voters against an anti–gay marriage proposition. Such structures respect things fans value, and employ them to encourage budding activists to go further than they might have otherwise. In 2011, the HPA established the Imagine Better Network to extend its approach of "harnessing the power of popular stories" to other fan communities, as well as to nonprofits, schools, activist organizations, philanthropists, and Hollywood.

This chapter revolves around the HPA, Imagine Better, and the online Nerdfighter community. While the most unconventional of our case study organizations in terms of their language and civic style, the groups described in this chapter have also been some of the most successful in harnessing the enthusiasm many people have for popular culture and directing it toward engagement with real-world issues. At a time when young people increasingly pull away from membership in traditional civic associations (Putnam 2000; Wuthnow 2002), and are often depicted by the media as uninterested in their communities and disconnected from the political world, we will see here examples of groups that have translated young people's passion for popular culture into participatory politics.

What do we mean when we describe the groups depicted here as "successful"? As we've discussed in Chapter 2 regarding Invisible Children, for nonprofit organizations that mobilize young people, success can be judged on several levels. On the one hand, there is their ability to achieve their civic goals. On the other hand, these groups—some more explicitly than others—seek to encourage their young members to see themselves as civic agents and to feel empowered to make positive change in the world. In Peter Dahlgren's (2009) model of the civic culture circuit, "civic agency is premised on people being able to see themselves as participants, that they find engagement meaningful, and that they experience motivation via the interplay of reason and passion" (102). Such agency is one of the conditions necessary for civic engagement. In the conclusion of this chapter, we will return to Dahlgren to show how these groups link different components of the civic culture circuit model.

In the case of the HPA, since 2005 this group has shown time and again its capacity to empower its young members to engage in actions with real-world impact. Some of the group's most visible campaigns have been charity based. For example, after the 2010 earthquake, the HPA's Helping Haiti Heal campaign raised $123,000 in two weeks from small donations, enabling it to send five cargo planes full of supplies. Every year, the organization runs book drives for communities in need and has donated over 200,000 books to libraries and communities from Brooklyn to Rwanda. Campaigns such as these, which have drawn mainstream media attention, have been instrumental in encouraging the participation of many in the Harry Potter fan community and beyond it as well.

The HPA also works to further its members' understanding of global issues, including ones that get little attention from mainstream media. In July 2007, the group worked with The Leaky Cauldron, one of the most popular fan news sites, to organize house parties around the country focused on increasing awareness of the Sudanese genocide. Participants listened to and discussed a podcast that featured political experts such as Joseph C. Wilson, former U.S. ambassador to Gabon, and John Prendergast, senior advisor to the International Crisis Group, alongside performances by Wizard Rock bands.

The HPA leadership is adamant about going beyond consensual civic engagement and charity to seek more systemic and structural changes, even as it pushes members beyond their comfort zones. As Slack explains, "We do want people to both volunteer with people at a local AIDS clinic as well as advocate for better treatment of AIDS victims in Africa. We want our young people tutoring underprivileged kids and helping them read, getting them engaged in the Internet and learning those things, but then also challenging the rules of the game that are making it possible for kids to go without food" (Jenkins 2009). HPA has also worked toward change through institutional politics—its members have registered over 5,000 young people as voters, and during the marriage-equality campaign in Maine, they called more than 3,500 state residents in a single day.

The HPA and Imagine Better often collaborate with the Nerdfighters, which represent a different model for mobilizing popular culture fans. The Nerdfighters are an informal online community of young people that took shape around the YouTube channel of the VlogBrothers, John and Hank Green. John Green is a best-selling young adult author and Hank Green is a musician and entrepreneur; both now engage in a wide variety of educational projects that they produce for YouTube, such as SciShow and Crash Course, channels dedicated to teaching science, history, and a range of other topics including U.S. government and politics. On their VlogBrothers channel, the Greens upload two videos a week, about "nothing in particular," in their signature style, which involves high-speed talking, multiple jump cuts, and various inside jokes and jargon. Nerdfighters connect not around a fictional content world, but rather around their affiliation with the VlogBrothers and a broader "nerd" identity. As part of this shared identity, the group pursues a shared social agenda, which they call "decreasing world suck."

As the VlogBrothers enigmatically define it in their YouTube video "How to Be a Nerdfighter: A VlogBrothers FAQ," "World suck is kind of exactly what world suck sounds like. It's hard to quantify exactly, but, you know, it's like, the amount of suck in the world." This broad definition leaves much space for individual Nerdfighters to interpret what "world suck" and decreasing it means to them. Examples range from personal acts, such as being a good person or cheering up a friend, to collective acts that fit within our definition of participatory politics. Nerdfighters are one of the largest communities of lenders on Kiva.org, a nonprofit organization that grants loans to people without access to traditional banking systems. Every year, they promote charities and other nonprofit organizations through YouTube videos and encourage small donations from individual Nerdfighters. In 2013, such endeavors raised more than $850,000 for the Foundation to Decrease World Suck, a nonprofit created by the VlogBrothers, benefiting a variety of causes and organizations selected by Nerdfighters.

The HPA and the Nerdfighters have many similarities. Membership between the two groups overlaps often. The groups also have comparable civic goals (though they are articulated differently) and have collaborated on multiple campaigns and projects, often involving the VlogBrothers promoting HPA campaigns in their videos, thus significantly increasing their reach. The size of the Nerdfighters community has been key to the success of its outreach and fundraising efforts; the HPA, while much smaller in membership, has been successful at sustaining members' civic participation over time and supporting their development as civic actors (Kligler-Vilenchik 2013a). Unlike the HPA, Nerdfighters have generally focused their attention on charity and civic engagement, refraining from initiating campaigns with a clear political stance. Yet to the Green brothers, as John Green told us in 2013, a central objective is to encourage young people "to see themselves as people who matter and as people who can shape policy."

Building on case studies of the HPA, Imagine Better, and the Nerdfighters, this chapter explores how these groups deploy popular culture engagement toward political ends and how they both cultivate and activate their members' civic imagination. In Chapter 1, we introduced the concept of the civic imagination, the capacity to imagine alternatives to current social, political, or economic institutions or problems. The groups in this chapter are the ones that focus most on "imagination" and use fictional narratives and imaginary worlds in order to make sense of, relate to, and act upon issues in our real world. We identify different mechanisms through which this deployment works, describing the intersections between fan communities, content worlds, and participatory politics, and the paradoxes that sometimes result. At the same time, we also consider ways in which these practices are applied and adopted beyond the context of fan communities. Using the concepts *fan activism* and *content worlds*, we explore how these groups engage young people through popular culture, and what the strengths and limitations are of such a model.

This chapter is based on three years of research conducted by Neta Kligler-Vilenchik. Building off of previous work conducted by the author and members of the Civic Paths group at USC (Kligler-Vilenchik et al. 2012; Kligler-Vilenchik and Shresthova 2014), the research included in-depth interviews with 15 members of HPA and/or Imagine Better and 15 Nerdfighters, mostly between the ages of 15 and 25, as well as seven expert interviews and ongoing conversations with people in leadership positions in the groups. The research also draws on an analysis of a range of texts and artifacts produced by the groups and their members. An ethnographic component included participant observation at events both large scale (e.g., national fan conferences) and intimate (e.g., meet-ups for local groups).

Fan Activism: Fan Enthusiasm Gone Civic

Participation in informal and formal civic organizations has been regarded as a cornerstone of American democracy at least as far back as Alexis de Tocqueville's visit to the United States in the 1830s. As mentioned in Chapter 1, Robert Putnam's *Bowling Alone: The Collapse and Revival of American Community* (2000) argues that such affiliations have been in decline, citing the disappearance of community bowling leagues as emblematic. While *Bowling Alone* paints a complex picture, pointing to economic distress, long daily commutes, and generational change as possible culprits for this decline, Putnam places much of the blame (about 25 percent of it, to be precise) on media consumption, and specifically on television. As he asked in an earlier work, "How might television destroy social capital?" (Putnam 1995, 678). The claims made in *Bowling Alone* spurred more than a decade's worth of scholarly and public conversations around the forms of social bonds that might restore civic engagement.

The examples discussed in this chapter—and much of this book—make an opposite claim: that popular culture, rather than leading to a disengagement from public life, is being used as a resource around which young people are making connections to civic and political worlds. Putnam understands television viewing as an individual experience, seeing time spent with entertainment content as time away from social experiences. Yet fan communities, this chapter's focus, are by their nature collectives, much like the bowling leagues Putnam longingly describes. Bowling leagues were above all a way to bring people together, to use common activities to create a context where a range of other conversations and actions could take place. We see fan communities as performing similar functions today, with the added value that they provide shared mythologies that can inspire acts of civic imagination and thus represent potential bridges between participatory culture and participatory politics.

Fan communities have long been early adopters of various tools and platforms, which they use for purposes of creative production and circulation (Jenkins, Ford, and Green 2013). Similarly, they have been at the forefront of experimenting with the connections between popular culture and civic engagement—laying the early seeds for many of the ideas in this book. We have come to term this engagement "fan activism":

> Forms of civic engagement and political participation that emerge from within fan culture itself, often in response to the shared interests of fans, often conducted through the infrastructure of existing fan practices and relationships, and often framed through metaphors drawn from popular and participatory culture. (Jenkins 2012a)

As the definition points out, we use "fan activism" to refer both to political participation and to forms of more consensual civic engagement, including charity—though at times we also make distinctions between these forms of participation. At a time when many young people are renegotiating their relationship with the traditional political process, often seen as ineffective, out of touch, or—ironically—uncivil (see, e.g., Zuckerman 2013a), fan activism offers a powerfully resonant means to connect and mobilize young people toward collective concerns. Fandom provides them with a space to gather, talk, imagine, debate, and engage with each other, and much like bowling leagues, it is a space where other kinds of conversations emerge.

We see fan experiences as valuable on their own terms. As a source of pleasure and social outreach, fan creativity matters in a world where many people lack means of creative expression in their schools or in their work lives. Some fan communities are increasingly seeking ways to help their young members become more active citizens. In Chapter 1, we encountered the example of Lauren Bird, who later became the communications director for the HPA. As Bird explained, civic education in school did not leave much room for discussion or expression, while online fandom provided an outlet for creativity and connectivity. Bird's encounter with the HPA during its Helping Haiti Heal campaign served as what is known in the connected learning framework as a "consequential connection," helping to redirect what Bird did for fun toward other goals. The groups discussed in this chapter succeed in making such connections for many who, like Bird, have not previously thought of themselves as civic actors.

The three case studies described here are distinctive in that the groups explicitly promote fan activism through "mechanisms of translation" between participatory culture and participatory politics. Mechanisms of translation (Kligler-Vilenchik 2013b) are practices through which the same activities and social ties that bring fan participants together are deployed to support participatory politics. These groups foster and activate members' and supporters' civic imaginations in different ways: they deploy elements of their content worlds as analogies for thinking about political issues; they encourage supporters to actively produce and circulate media content that often borrows from pop culture imagery; and they provide a social environment that encourages people to reflect on politics and discuss different perspectives.

This chapter's three case studies document fan activism as a practice, but also raise questions about its boundaries, its strengths and limitations. How is fan activism grounded in fan practice, and how does it extend it? When and how are practices of fan activism adopted beyond the realm of fans? Does fan activism have the capacity to shift how a broader public imagines the process of political change? To answer these questions, we elaborate on the concept of fan activism, chart its roots and progression, and describe it as a continuum between two modes: fannish civics, which allows devoted fans to connect their deep knowledge of a beloved text to social concerns, and cultural acupuncture, which builds on sometimes more superficial references to resonant popular culture texts to gain widespread public attention for issues.

Prefiguring Fan Activism

> The teenage girl fan of Madonna who fantasizes her own empowerment can translate this fantasy into behavior, and can act in a more empowered way socially, thus winning more social territory for herself. When she meets others who share her fantasies and freedom there is the beginning of a sense of solidarity, of a shared resistance, that can support and encourage progressive action on the microsocial level. (Fiske 1989a, 136)

In his description of the Madonna fan, John Fiske describes a trajectory from pop culture consumption to potential political action. The young fan's engagement with the text starts individually, when her recognition of Madonna as an empowered woman inspires her own sense of empowerment. The next step is subcultural participation: the fan meets others who share her fantasies and freedom, developing a sense of shared solidarity and shared resistance. This collective identity, in turn, is hypothesized to "support and encourage progressive action on the micro-social level" (Fiske 1989b, 104), the level of politics of everyday life.

Today, one might say that Fiske was hinting at an early iteration of "third-wave feminism," especially as embodied by the Riot Grrrls, but he would have lacked access to that vocabulary in 1989. At the time, his claims were met with overwhelming resistance, as he was criticized for celebrating meaning making over the sphere of material politics (McGuigan 1992) and for having an inflated sense of the power of what he called "semiotic democracy." Self-empowered social behavior, critics argued, does not equal political action. Moreover, he was rebuked for not being able to provide empirical grounding for the behavioral trajectory he was theorizing. Indeed, he struggled to find evidence for the connections he claimed between fandom and social awareness, arguing that "the products of this tactical consumption are difficult to study—they have no place, only the space of their moments of being" (Fiske 1989a, 35). While Fiske's argument was very controversial when he first made it, given current examples of fan activism we may ask if he didn't take his notion far enough—he never envisioned that fan identities would give birth to collective action on the macropolitical level, the politics of societies. When HPA members, for example, connect J. K. Rowling's "outing" of Dumbledore as gay (Smith 2007) to participation in phone banking to promote marriage equality laws, they are clearly engaging in macropolitical fan action.

Fiske believed that popular culture was inspiring political thought and action constantly—but in the confines of people's private conversations, their interactions in front of the home television set, and in their own consciousness, none of which were subject to outside observation. Today's new media environment, on the other hand, brings many of these once-hidden meaning-making processes into much greater visibility. In the context of an increasingly participatory culture, fans and other audience members publicly express their interpretations of cultural texts online, circulating their subcultural creations to friends and family through social networking sites. As online culture has brought

"Harry Potter for Marriage Equality." Fan art by David Roman.

fan communities further into the mainstream, making them more accessible to wider audiences, it also provides tools and platforms through which fans can forge connections between their cultural passions and engagement in social issues. The groups described in this chapter represent some of the most visible and clear manifestations of these connections—and they may be only the tip of the iceberg.

As Michael Saler (2012) notes, fans have drawn connections between fictional worlds and real-world issues since the beginning of fan discussions. Saler examines early-20th-century genre authors, such as Arthur Conan Doyle, J.R.R. Tolkien, and H. P. Lovecraft, whose followings paved the way for the emergence of modern fan culture. He describes how these early fans conversed through letter pages of pulp magazines, or in direct correspondence with each other, allowing them to collectively but playfully inhabit the imaginary worlds that inspired their passions and curiosity. Saler terms these conversations "public spheres of the imagination," spaces where people came together to discuss ideas, hopes, dreams, and fears by mapping them onto shared fictions. These imaginary worlds proved to be powerful touchstones for the real world, precisely because they were so evocative. Imaginary worlds enabled fans to experience strong sensations and identifications that could open their minds to new experiences beyond their everyday lives. Yet these works' fictional status generally allowed participants to avoid the exclusiveness and violence that often mark, for example, nationally based affiliations. Instead, fans of different faiths conversed with each other, creating a public sphere more heterogeneous than those found in many other social contexts.

The function of fan affinities in bridging differences surfaced often in our research, and represents one of the strengths of fan communities as a productive space for participatory politics. Nerdfighters, for example, described how their shared identity as fans creates an environment where heterogeneous discussion and disagreement can be achieved in a civil manner. Jacob, a 20-year-old Nerdfighter, talked about having discussions with people he disagrees with, either because of their strong religious or political views: "Nerdfighters are very—we're very passionate about things but we're also very respecting of other people's opinions. . . . I think most of the Nerdfighters if they're approached by somebody who disagrees with them, they would be able to respond in a more rational way. . . . Most of the Nerdfighters seem to react in an intelligent discussion as opposed to insults."

As Saler's historical examples suggest, establishing a civic imagination by connecting fictional worlds with real-world issues is not a new phenomenon. Andrew Ross (1991) describes science fiction fan organizations of the 1930s and 1940s that served as spaces in which to debate radical political ideas. Helen Merrick (2009) explores a feminist science fiction culture that goes back to the 1960s. Contemporary fan studies have likewise paid quite a bit of attention to ways that fans discuss gender (e.g., Wills 2013), race (e.g., Gatson and Reid 2012), sexuality (e.g., Hunting 2012), and other politically relevant issues through their favorite texts. However, the forging of such political connections was usually aimed at expression, education, and conscience raising—it generally did not lead fans to "march out in the streets" in pursuit of activist goals. Groups like the HPA, Imagine Better, and Nerdfighters differ from these earlier examples in that their civic goals are explicit and they use connections between fictional and real-world issues to motivate real-world action.

Politicizing Fan Activism

Fans have historically organized to protect their collective interests as fans, defending their cultural productions from claims of copyright infringement or other forms of censorship, for instance, or rallying to keep favorite programs on the air, and these actions have provided templates for other activist efforts, helping them to learn how to identify targets, develop tactics, and educate and mobilize supporters in ways that could be directed toward real-world causes. Such efforts may already be civic insofar as we think of efforts to shape the cultural environment—such as promoting funding for the arts or protecting a local landmark from demolition—as civic activities, but the kinds of fan activism we are discussing here uses these skills and infrastructures toward more explicitly political goals. In *Entertaining the Citizen*, Liesbet van Zoonen (2005) concludes that fan practices help hone, "in abstract terms, the customs that have been laid out as essential for democratic politics: information, discussion, and activism" (63). In this sense, fandom may represent a particularly powerful training ground for future activists and community organizers.

In 2012, members of the Civic Paths group at USC edited a special issue of the journal *Transformative Works and Cultures* dedicated to fan activism, which elicited dozens of examples from around the world. The special issue features a diverse set of case studies, ranging from fans of *The Colbert Report* engaging in collective action initiated by the political satirist (Schulzke 2012) to the engagement of Korean popular music (K-pop) fans in charitable fundraising and volunteering (Jung 2012). The range of submissions we received underscored the resonance of this new and emerging concept as a powerful mobilizer for young people today, and motivated us to continue elaborating and refining it.

Most of the examples of fan activism discussed so far focus on members of fandoms. Yet, as Gray, Sandvoss, and Harrington (2007) claim, our current media moment, characterized by increasing technological possibilities to engage in fan activities, has contributed to "the increasing entrenchment of fan consumption in the structure of our everyday life" (8). Consequently, it may be helpful to consider the wider spectrum, from those engaging in "emotionally involved consumption of a given popular narrative or text" (Sandvoss 2005, 8) to the participants in complex, organized social communities of fans. Some of the challenges faced by our case study groups involve whether or not to broaden their target audience beyond the fan community to a wider public—a question we will address through the distinction between two modes of fan activism: fannish civics and cultural acupuncture.

Fannish Civics: Translating Fannish Practice to Civic Talk and Action

Within the HPA, members engage not only in national campaigns, but also in local, member-initiated actions. One such local initiative, which took place within a new, small Southern California chapter of the HPA during 2012, was a workshop dubbed Harry Potter as a Tool for Social Change (Kligler-Vilenchik 2015). The workshop was described by its founder as "an informal study group on how Harry Potter relates to current sociopolitical and personal identity issues." Ranging from six to eight members, the group held six weekly meetings, with each week's discussion devoted to a certain book from the Harry Potter series. While the books served as the discussion's starting points—and as the main hook for most of the younger participants—the group held in-depth discussions around subjects as diverse as Walmart's labor practices, racism, slavery, and the presidential election.

The idea for the group, which can be seen as an almost literal application of our concept of the civic imagination, came from the chapter organizer, 20-year-old Erin. An activist from an early age, Erin works with multiple civic organizations, including the local city hall and a liberal local church. Erin saw the HPA as having unique capacities:

> The Harry Potter Alliance I think can be used to build those strong connections between people and to build those personal commitments to different issues, because they can connect to that story.

Erin is a "die-hard" activist, one who was civically active before the HPA and would almost certainly continue to be so even in its absence. This isn't true for all the group's members. Maura, a dreamy-eyed 21-year-old, is quite far from your average political junkie. In her interview, she explained that she's much more connected to the worlds of fantasy and magic: "With magic, anything is possible . . . our world is kind of boring. You get a job, you grow up and you start a family, that's all there really is to life."

What made Harry Potter as a Tool for Social Change work as a political discussion group? What made it different from other politically minded groups that enabled dreamy Maura to feel just as comfortable in it as activist-minded Erin? We would argue that the group's activities constituted fan activism in the form of *fannish civics*: participatory political practices that directly build on existing fannish practices.

Fannish practices are activities conducted by members of fan communities in relation to their object of affection, either collectively or on their own. Fans use the term "fannish" to refer to practices of their community. Some well-researched fannish practices include writing fan fiction (e.g., Hellekson and Busse 2006), creating fan art, vidding (e.g., Coppa 2008), and engaging in fan discussions. Benjamin Woo (2012) characterizes fannish practices as ones that involve forms of criticism and connoisseurship, and that are charged with affection, pleasure, and commitment or loyalty (183).

The experience of reading, debating, performing, and rewriting Harry Potter has been shared by many in the millennial generation (Anelli 2008). Rowling's stories of the boy wizard, the remarkable school Hogwarts, and the battle against the Dark Lord became global best sellers. Emerging alongside the popular embrace of the web, Harry Potter fandom has developed new media platforms and practices (Scott 2010). The community was among the first to use podcasting and blogs, to develop beta reading practices to improve fan fiction, to distribute MP3 files (such as those of Wizard Rock) through social networking sites, and to use machinima production practices to construct fan vids. Today's Harry Potter fans engage in activities ranging from real-life quidditch (an adaptation of the sport from the books—with brooms but without flying) to operas based on the young wizard's tales. As some of our earlier work (Kligler-Vilenchik et al. 2012) has described, the HPA has thrived by tapping the preexisting infrastructures of the prolific Harry Potter fan community, including fan sites, podcasts, and conventions. Through these practices, fans experience their fictional worlds in new ways, while sharing them with like-minded others.

Engaging in fannish civics is for some another manifestation of their fan enthusiasm. For example, some members' entry into the HPA was directly connected to the void that was left when Rowling stopped writing new books and Warner Brothers completed its series of screen adaptations. HPA member Kathy explained:

> I was so invested in these characters . . . when the books were finally over, there was nothing to do, I couldn't give that up yet. I wasn't ready. So I joined this community [the HPA] that was also just as invested and wanted to really use that investment towards good things. I was like, good, I can be part of this at least. It was still Harry Potter.

Fannish civics is strongly rooted within the practices of a preexisting fan community, which includes not only a connection to a primary text, but a strong social bond between community members. Stephen Duncombe (2012a) stresses community building as one of the practices of fandom that most facilitates its connection to political activism. Indeed, one of the most common themes in the interviews we conducted was the centrality of the "sense of community"—the connections and friendships forged between participants (Kligler-Vilenchik et al. 2012)—precisely what Putnam said was cemented for previous generations through their involvement in various civic organizations.

The content world serves as a first step to forging such social connections, as Becca described: "If I know someone is a Harry Potter fan, I can talk to them all day. We can talk about Harry Potter, no problem. It brings us together." Yet many members are quick to exclaim that it's "about so much more than Harry Potter." Lisa explains that for her, the fan practices and the friendships are the key element of her enjoyment:

> A lot of the people I know in this fandom have only read *Deathly Hallows* one time and they don't particularly like the movies. But the Wizard Rock, the conferences, the podcasts, all of that, that's what they're into and it's the community, like the friends that they've made and stuff like that.

Fannish civics succeeds most when it taps practices that fans already enjoy engaging in, such as talking about the books and films, dissecting the characters, and imagining alternative scenarios, as well as when it builds on the strong social bonds between members. Through such means, the Harry Potter as a Tool for Social Change discussion group was able to harness the interest of even those who, like Maura, are usually disinterested politically, and thus represents a form of "consequential connection" for individual participants. The group's most vibrant discussions deployed fans' mastery of the content world to explain abstract ideas—like inequality, discrimination, and disenfranchisement—and to create an activist commitment. For example, the story of Sirius Black, who in the series we first meet as a dangerous convicted murderer, only to later find out that he was framed, served as an introduction to a group discussion of capital punishment. The political discussion was in turn connected to the opportunity to influence policy: the group talked about the upcoming vote on California's Proposition 34, which would have replaced the state's death penalty with life sentence without parole (the proposition failed).

HPA co-founder Andrew Slack argues that the Harry Potter books take young people seriously as political agents and thus can inspire youth to change the world:

> Young people are depicted in the books as often smarter, more aware of what's happening in the world, than their elders, though there are also some great examples where very wise adults have mentored and supported young people as they have taken action in the world. . . . We are essentially asking young people the same question that Harry poses to his fellow members of Dumbledore's Army in the fifth movie, "Every great Wizard in history has started off as nothing more than we are now. If they can do it, why not us?" This is a question that we not only pose to our members, we show them how right now they can start working to be those "great Wizards" that can make a real difference in this world. (quoted in Jenkins 2009)

Against this backdrop of Death Eater terrorists, bungling or manipulative government officials, a deceptive press, and repressive school authorities, Rowling tells how one young man organized his classmates into

Sirius Black as a prisoner, posted on therpf.com.

Dumbledore's Army, a loosely organized activist group, to go out and fight evil—sometimes working alone, sometimes collaborating with adult groups such as the Order of the Phoenix, but always carrying much of the burden of confronting Voldemort. In our world, young people are likewise confronted not only with social and political problems that often seem simply unsolvable, but also with the consistent message that, as young people, they are too naive, uninformed, and powerless to do anything about those problems. The HPA, by contrast, invites them to use their civic imaginations, to ask what it might mean for Dumbledore's Army to tackle the problems of the real world, and to collectively identify the core sites where such struggles would take place: "What if we gave our teenagers the opportunity to imagine themselves as the heroes that they have grown up watching, rather than treating their precious minds as nothing more than a way to line the pockets of some CEO?" (Slack 2010).

Fan Activism as a Continuum: From Fannish Civics to Cultural Acupuncture

Fannish civics is at its best when it builds on practices that fans engage in anyway, when it rewards fans' mastery and deep engagement, and when it connects fan enthusiasm not only to real-world issues but also to action. At the same time, this means that the main pool of potential participants in fannish civics consists of fans with deep levels of engagement and those who are already embedded within a fan community. If the goal is to encourage participatory politics among broader populations of young people, fannish civics can only go so far.

We can distinguish fannish civics from another mode of fan activism—that of "cultural acupuncture." The term was introduced by Andrew Slack (2010) to describe his broader model of change:

> Finding where the psychological energy is in the culture, and moving that energy towards creating a healthier world. . . . We activists may not have the same money as Nike and McDonald's but we have a message that actually means something. . . . What we do not have is the luxury of keeping the issues we cover seemingly boring, technocratic, and inaccessible. With cultural acupuncture, we will usher in an era of activism that is fun, imaginative, and sexy, yet truly effective.

Recognizing that the news media was more apt to cover the launch of the next Harry Potter film than the genocide in Darfur, the HPA took the approach of identifying key cultural "pressure points," and redirecting the attention they received toward real-world problems. In this way, the group sought to inspire the civic imagination on a more expansive scale, among the broad audiences familiar with Rowling's extraordinarily popular stories. Pinning political and social causes to Harry Potter works not just with fans but more broadly because this content world has a large following, has its own built-in mechanisms for generating publicity, and has demonstrated its capacity to attract repeated waves of media interest. Harry Potter constitutes a form of cultural currency that can carry the group's messages to many who would not otherwise hear them and that channels emotional investments. Often, cultural acupuncture works through grassroots production of new paratexts—such as fan videos—which attach themselves to the larger transmedia campaigns that emerge around major entertainment franchises, potentially redirecting—through what we might call a form of conceptual judo—the strength of the Hollywood publicity machine toward a range of other causes.

Slack came up with his model of "cultural acupuncture" back when the HPA was working with the Harry Potter books and films as its sole reference text. However, over time the real testing ground for cultural acupuncture became the Imagine Better Network.

Originally, Imagine Better was conceived as a way to preempt the predicted disappearance of the Harry Potter fan community. In July 2011, the last movie in the Harry Potter series was released. At LeakyCon 2011, a grassroots fan convention, young fans were talking about "the end of an era," linking the series' conclusion to the end of their own childhoods. As one HPA member, Daniela, expressed it, "so obviously Harry Potter is over, sadly." Fans feared that their beloved community would turn into an example of "zombie fandom," a fan community that has "entered into a state of atrophy, decline or impending demise" (Whiteman and Metivier 2013, 270). Imagine Better was launched at that LeakyCon with the idea of applying the approach that had proven successful for the HPA to other fictional texts and collaborations with other fandoms.

The concern that sparked Imagine Better can be easily understood. The HPA was very successful with Harry Potter fans, but the closure of the primary text with the final film's release left the fan community in a state of uncertainty. When a civic organization—one that plans to be around for a while—is tied to the constantly evolving flow of popular culture texts, this may present a challenge. But while some fan communities die out with the closure of their primary text, this is not always the case. Rebecca Williams (2011) discusses ways that fans of the TV series *The West Wing* reacted to that program's cancellation. Using the concept of "post-object fandom," she shows how they were able to sustain their fannish involvement even after the series' "death." Harry Potter now constitutes a "post-object fandom"—while Rowling releases new content, even in relation to the same universe, the scale is much more minimal.

Still, the fan community lives on—while some fan conventions like HPEF (Harry Potter Education Fanon), which had been held since 2003, have shut down, others such as LeakyCon were still taking place as of 2014. So the HPA still has more life than its organizers might have projected.

While much of the HPA's work falls under the rubric of fannish civics, Imagine Better has been experimenting more with cultural acupuncture, marking a shift in focus from preexisting fan communities to reaching a broader public. To further understand fannish civics and cultural acupuncture as different modes, we examine two large-scale national campaigns that Imagine Better conducted around the release of the first two movies in the Hunger Games series. Whereas the first campaign uses fannish civics, the second moves further on the continuum toward cultural acupuncture.

Hunger Is Not a Game: A Lesson in Extending Fannish Civics

The Hunger Is Not a Game campaign, launched around the release of the movie *The Hunger Games* (2012), based on the bestselling series of novels by Suzanne Collins, was Imagine Better's first effort to reach beyond the Harry Potter content world. The Hunger Games series is set in the fictional country of Panem, which consists of a wealthy Capitol that thrives through its control of 12 districts in varying states of poverty. Every year, two children from each district are chosen to participate in a compulsory televised event called "The Hunger Games," where they battle each other to death until only one winner emerges—the series focuses on the tales of one such participant, Katniss Everdeen.

The Hunger Is Not a Game campaign sought to connect the release of the movie to the cause of world hunger. In this campaign, Imagine Better partnered with an established nonprofit organization—Oxfam— which brought to the table its on-the-ground experience. The campaign planned through this partnership included food donations, fundraising, and awareness raising around the systemic causes of world hunger.

Based on the HPA's previous experiences with Harry Potter fans, the campaign was designed as what we have termed fannish civics, meaning its imagined audience consisted of dedicated Hunger Games fans. While many Imagine Better members identified as Hunger Games fans, they were not necessarily actively involved in the Hunger Games

Hunger Is Not a Game campaign logo, from hungergameslessons.com.

fan community. Thus an early step in the campaign's planning was reaching out to committed Hunger Games fans, including members of several key fan websites, and eliciting their cooperation. Slack appeared as a guest on a popular Hunger Games podcast and even the name for the campaign was taken from a suggestion by a Hunger Games fan. Following the model of fannish civics, the campaign attempted to reach these fans through spaces where they were already engaged.

However, if we've seen that fannish civics works best when it rewards fan mastery, it is not clear that Hunger Is Not a Game met this standard. The campaign's broad references to the movie and its themes did not build on fans' deep engagement with the text. Despite the attempts to involve those within Hunger Games fandom, Madison, a Hunger

Games fan who collaborated with Imagine Better, felt that the campaign resonated only with some segments:

> There is a group who thinks about these things and who understands sort of the deeper underlying message of the book and who want to take that and use it to do some good. But then, you have the fans who like the love triangle. They like the fact that she [Katniss, the protagonist] uses a bow and arrow and they don't really think any deeper than that. And I would love to be able to do more to sort of make these people think more about the subtext and stuff, but I know that it's difficult. I think a lot of that has to come with age and maturity. So I'm hoping in the future, we can do more to reach that segment of the fandom.

Madison's description of some Hunger Games fans' reservations about fannish civics should not be too surprising. In fact, when the HPA was launched within Harry Potter fandom in 2005 it was met with much skepticism from those who believed that real-world politics detract from the magic of the Wizarding World. Slack was seen by some as an outside agitator, trying to manipulate the fan community to benefit his own agenda.

Over time, however, Slack demonstrated his own mastery of the text, and thus his status as a fan, an insider. As he explained: "one of the reasons why I was successful in beginning the Harry Potter Alliance is because I'm such a hardcore Harry Potter fan. Had I not been such a passionate Harry Potter fan, had I not been caring about this myth so much myself, I wouldn't have been able to translate the message as well" (quoted in Jenkins 2009). Jenni, an HPA chapter organizer, shares her memory of seeing Slack's well-worn copies of the books—evidence of his fan mastery:

> Andrew is definitely much better at making links and metaphors between real world issues and the events of the novels, he is great with coming up with very specific links. He has very banged up and marked-up copies of the books. Most of it is in his head, he recalls a lot of stuff on the spot which is unbelievable and for which I applaud him. I have good recall but not as good as him, or maybe I don't reread the books as often as he does.

On the other hand, when Imagine Better started the Hunger Is Not a Game campaign, it was clear that the organizers were not "insider" fans—at least not to the same extent. Underscoring that in the campaign's aftermath, Slack shared the following with his more than 3,000 Facebook followers:

> Just talked with a reporter who asked me what I thought of Katniss being cast as someone who is white—when in fact, Katniss is mixed race. So maybe I was projecting my white privilege or something on to this, but I had always thought that Jennifer Lawrence's complexion matched Katniss pretty well to what I had imagined. Is Katniss, in fact, mixed race? *This is what I get for only reading the books a handful of times instead of being able to recite them from memory like I can with Harry Potter* [our emphasis]. (Facebook post, December 7, 2013)

When mastery of the content world is valued as social currency, such an admission may position Slack as an outsider in the eyes of more hardcore fans.

Moreover, a surprising turn of events raised added tension around who the "real" Hunger Games fans were. When the Hunger Is Not a Game campaign received media attention, notably coverage in the *New York Times* (Martin 2012a), lawyers for Lionsgate, the distributor of the movie, contacted Oxfam and requested that they remove mentions of the campaign as it was "causing damage to Lionsgate and our marketing efforts" (Martin 2012b). Appalled, a member of Imagine Better created a petition calling on Lionsgate to "stop bullying its fans into complacency." After the fans' protest drew attention on both social and mainstream news media, Lionsgate quickly retracted its demands. In the wake of this victory, Imagine Better's organizers celebrated the power of fan activists over corporations. In an interview with the *New York Times* (Martin 2012b), Slack proclaimed:

> Hollywood was not sending an olive branch to the youth demographic that they depend on; they were attempting to whack us over the head with a large branch, rendering us unconscious consumers. It's simply not going to work this way anymore.

The HPA had some history of taking a confrontational approach toward the movie studio responsible for the cinematic texts central to its own fan universe—for several years, the group petitioned Warner Brothers to transition their Harry Potter–themed chocolate frogs into fair-trade chocolate (finally achieving success in early 2015, as we describe in the chapter's conclusion). At the time, the HPA's struggle with Warner Brothers was at an impasse and so the "win" over Lionsgate was especially meaningful to its fan activists. But the confrontational approach toward Lionsgate discomforted some within the Hunger Games fan community. Some fans extended to the studio the same adoration and respect they felt for the Hunger Games narrative and its author. Lionsgate had courted and collaborated with Hunger Games fan community leaders, and those fans felt it ungrateful to confront the corporation. Thus, while Imagine Better worked closely with Hunger Games fans in the planning stages of the campaign, this incident exposed frictions between the groups.

The Hunger Is Not a Game campaign points to some challenges in using fannish civics to engage multiple fan communities. Due to its embeddedness in fannish practices, fannish civics requires deep knowledge of the specifics of each involved fan community and mastery of its content world. These aspects are not easily learned—they are the product of years of being an "insider." Moreover, the fans need to be prepared to take action, often by learning to read their touchstone text through a political lens—as this observation suggests, employing the civic imagination may be a learned skill. So, while *The Hunger Games* is on the surface a more overt political allegory than the Harry Potter saga, using it as a blueprint for taking real-world political action was not necessarily consistent with what dedicated fans were taking from the series. The Hunger Is Not a Game campaign taught Imagine Better's organizers about the difficulty in mobilizing others into fannish civics without being embedded community members.

The Odds in Our Favor: Engaging through Cultural Acupuncture

In 2013, with the release of *Catching Fire*, the second installment in the Hunger Games film franchise, Imagine Better took a different approach that leaned more toward cultural acupuncture. It attempted to engage supporters not by connecting to an existing fan community, but rather by tapping the general public's attention. The Odds in Our Favor campaign, whose goal was raising awareness around economic inequality, began by encouraging participants to upload photos where they show the "three-finger salute," a gesture symbolizing the resistance of the impoverished districts against the prosperous Capitol and its tyrannical leader, President Snow. Here Imagine Better built on popular social media practices: it was 2013 when "selfie"—"a photograph that one has taken of oneself, typically one taken with a smartphone or webcam and uploaded to a social media website"—was chosen as the Oxford Dictionaries' word of the year.

The next stage of the campaign was triggered by some of Lionsgate's marketing decisions, most significantly a tie-in with CoverGirl, which launched a makeup line called the Capitol Collection. Imagine Better criticized Lionsgate for celebrating the oppressive Capitol instead of highlighting solidarity with the oppressed districts, and "turning an anti-classist epic into a platform for the novels' villains" (Slack 2013). Imagine Better then launched a campaign linking the Hunger Games to what they saw as its real message—social inequality—through the release of a YouTube video called "The Hunger Games Are Real."

The video starts with a quote from Haymitch, who advises Katniss and Peeta, contestants in the fictional Hunger Games: "From now on, your job is to be a distraction, so people forget what the real problems are." The video then shows some of the marketing efforts for *Catching Fire*, highlighting the "hot guys" in the cast, only to interrupt the scene with static and a disruptive black-and-white "rebel message." Lauren Bird, the spokesperson for the HPA, dressed in an austere black outfit like that of a rebel leader in the film, proclaims:

> Enough with the distraction, the Hunger Games are real.
> Check it out: In The Hunger Games a small portion of the population controls a majority of the wealth. People have full time jobs and still go hungry.
> Think it's fiction? Think again.

While the audio details the economic disparities in Hunger Games' dystopian country of Panem, the visual shows statistics of real-world economic inequality. For example, the death of Katniss' father in a mining accident is linked to the decline of unionization in the United States; the corrupt justice system in Panem is connected to the fact that African

Americans are incarcerated at six times the rate of whites in the U.S. Bird concludes:

> Does the Hunger Games have hot guys in it? Big fucking deal. It also has something else. Us. People who want justice. President Snows of the world, your reign is coming to the end. You can try and distract us but it's too late–the fire has started and we will not stop. Not until the odds are in everyone's favor.

The video ends with a call to "join the resistance" and links to odds-inourfavor.org, where viewers can participate in a range of real-world actions. The video powerfully succeeds in linking the fictional world to the real one, not only through words but through sound and imagery as well. The dramatic "rebel message" interrupting the Capitol signal gives it a particular resonance and, indeed, it came to be the group's most widely shared video.

In contrast with Invisible Children (Chapter 2), producing videos of professional or near-professional quality had not previously been one of the HPA's strengths. In fact, "The Hunger Games Are Real" is the first video the group made with grant money that enabled the organization to employ a professional video production crew. Early Harry Potter fandom was more focused on text-based modes of expression, such as the writing of fan fiction and the creation of fan websites like The Leaky Cauldron. Accordingly, the HPA at first communicated mostly via text, such as through the group's blog and email list, as well as audio podcasts, which were very popular with the Harry Potter fan community. The videos the group sporadically created to launch campaigns or publicize success stories were generally of modest production quality, intentionally designed with a DIY aesthetic similar to that of other fan-made videos. Yet increasingly, younger Harry Potter fans were embedded in the YouTube community, for whom video production is a key form of expression and communication (Lange 2014). In 2011, the HPA created a regular vlog channel, marking a shift in the amount of video the group produced, as well as the greater attention it began to pay to quality and style. The vloggers were sometimes disappointed by their view count (averaging a few hundred per video) and the fact that they were mostly reaching already-dedicated HPA members. At the same time, relative to the number of views, the videos had a high number of "likes" and, in the comments sections, viewers often engaged in conversation and discussion around the issues raised. As Burgess and Green (2009) discuss, YouTube's different "popularity measures" assess different logics of audience engagement; whereas the view count is a way of "counting eyeballs," high numbers of comments point at a very engaged viewership—which relates to the difference between audiences and publics we discuss in Chapter 2.

In comparison to the modest views of the HPA vlogs, "The Hunger Games Are Real" reached the largest-ever viewership for an HPA video—over 450,000 views. Most of these viewers, it seemed, hadn't heard of the group before. Accordingly, however, the video's associated comments section was characterized less by discussion and conversation as in the intimate HPA vlogs, and more by one-sided and often extreme views, as is often the case with YouTube videos with a large viewership (e.g., the comment by YouTube user richardparadox163: "Does anyone else think this video is trying to incite a Communist Revolution?").

In terms of its strategy and outcomes, the campaign is closer on the continuum to cultural acupuncture than fannish civics, successfully riding on the wave of Hunger Games–related attention through its resonant audiovisual style. Some of the detailed references to specific characters and events from the stories did allow hardcore fans to go deeper than they could with the first campaign, but the video is also accessible to anyone who had watched the movies and is familiar with the storyline, enabling the campaign to broaden its reach beyond the fan community.

One could question to what extent cultural acupuncture is still a mode of "fan activism" if the audiences it seeks to mobilize aren't just fans. We would argue that cultural acupuncture should be understood as a mode of fan activism when it is created *by* fans and develops out of fannish ways of engaging with a text. True, cultural acupuncture constitutes a strategic form of connecting popular culture to social issues— but to be considered as fan activism, as opposed to the kind of culture jamming practices discussed in Chapter 1, it needs to come from a passionate engagement with the original text. And fan activism needs to be bottom-up, emerging from a grassroots movement, unlike the forms of celebrity-based activism that we saw Invisible Children sometimes deploy in Chapter 2; the difference between *Veronica Mars* star Kristen

Bell soliciting support from her followers, and *Veronica Mars* fans taking action on their own in opposition to child soldiering or domestic violence is crucial. Some uses of cultural acupuncture may not constitute fan activism, if they are initiated purely as a way to garner attention. For example, Melissa Brough and Sangita Shresthova (2012) describe how protesters in the West Bank village Bil'in engaged in *Avatar* activism: they covered their bodies with blue paint to resemble the colonized Na'vi race in James Cameron's blockbuster movie and approached an Israeli military barricade, chanting "Sky people, you can't take our land." Photographs and videos of the protest were circulated online, garnering news media attention. We see this video as a case of activists reconfiguring pop culture content and using fanlike tactics to provoke attention, dialogue, and mobilization. In our terminology, this use of pop culture content for specific political goals is a form of cultural acupuncture, but not fan activism. At times, however, activists—through their more strategic use of popular culture—may find themselves becoming fans, as we will discuss briefly in the conclusion to this chapter.

The relationship between fan activism and cultural acupuncture can be linked to the distinction described in Chapter 2 between drillable and spreadable media (Mittell 2013); to recast that distinction, drillable media is characterized by narrative complexity, encouraging die-hard fans to dig deep into the story world to mine new insights, while spreadable media (Jenkins, Ford, and Green 2013) is characterized by "horizontal ripples," often aiming more at the accumulation of views than at long-term engagement. Accordingly, we can think of fannish civics as a "drillable" mode that addresses the most highly engaged fans as its imagined audience. The connections between the story world and real-world issues are often based on an in-depth knowledge of the fictional narrative, rewarding fan mastery and dedication. Based on these characteristics, fannish civics will mostly activate those already engaged in fannish practices. Cultural acupuncture, on the other hand, builds on the "attraction model" of spreadable media. While still connected to the story world, it requires minimal depth of story-world knowledge. With cultural acupuncture, the aim is to reach wide audiences, and the campaign may occupy participants' attention for a shorter span.

While making the spreadable/drillable distinction, Jason Mittell wishes to discourage the normative stance that prefers drillability over spreadability as a mode of audience engagement. Similarly, both cultural acupuncture and fannish civics should be seen as viable models of fan activism, though they may be best suited to different civic goals. We may consider these goals through the lens of what Zuckerman (2013a) terms thick versus thin engagement. Zuckerman defines thin engagement as "actions that require little thought on your part: sign a petition, give a contribution." Thick engagement, on the other hand, asks "for your creativity, your strategic sensibilities, your ability to make media, research, deliberate or find solutions."

Fannish civics worked well for the Harry Potter Alliance in engaging motivated members who were integrated into the fan community and had been taught to read the touchstone texts through a particular lens. Many of these fan activists were inspired to take actions requiring "thick engagement," such as opening local chapters, volunteering as HPA staff members, organizing local book drives, or taking part in creative projects to spread the word. Their participation in the HPA built on their pre-existing embeddedness in the Harry Potter fan community. Arguably, cultural acupuncture may be a more productive avenue for Imagine Better as it seeks to reach out to other audiences and other texts, as this mode of activism requires less familiarity with the practices and structures of each different fan community and may resonate with a wider public. Cultural acupuncture may also be particularly appropriate for efforts that require "thinner" engagement, such as awareness raising, where reach itself is a measure of success (see Kligler-Vilenchik and Shresthova 2012). The spreadability of cultural acupuncture may create entry points, inviting some participants into "thicker" modes of fan activism; it may also inspire young fans, who see the texts they are passionate about and the activist work they're doing spreading to wider, and different, communities.

The Glue That Holds a Community Together: Content Worlds and Taste Communities

As we've seen, while fannish civics and cultural acupuncture differ in the depth in which they drill into a text, both employ civic imagination by connecting fictional worlds to real-world concerns. We now consider how the three groups discussed in this chapter use content worlds and shared tastes as the glue that holds a community together, and we will address the challenges these groups face when attempting to broaden their base of support.

The chapter's three case studies represent different uses of content worlds: while the HPA focuses on one content world, Imagine Better attempts to resonate with fans of different content worlds and to engage broader audiences. Nerdfighters, as we will see, unite fans toward civic goals around broader cultural affiliations. What roles do content worlds serve for fan activists? Do some content worlds better lend themselves to the pursuit of political goals than others? How may content worlds limit the range of issues and audiences these groups can address? We'll begin by examining the HPA's use of the Harry Potter world, before examining ways to broaden out beyond a single content world.

Public Spheres of the Imagination in Action

"Literature creates a whole new world in our minds. It allows us to experience things we've never experienced before." As Becca, a member of the HPA, explained, fan activist organizations tap the rich imaginary worlds created by fictional texts. These texts serve the organization as _content worlds_: "the network of characters, settings, situations, and values that forms the basis for the generation of a range of stories, in the hands of either a commercial producer or a grassroots community" (Jenkins 2012a). In the hands of fan activists, content worlds serve as a form of cultural currency (Fiske 1992). Much as these rich worlds inspire a range of fan expressions such as writing fan fiction, recording a Wizard Rock song, or engaging in fan discussion, they serve as fertile ground for connections to various social issues. These worlds are based in texts that fans not only love, but which they get to know intimately through rereading, rewatching, and discussing with others. Fans' sense of ownership—and mastery—of these texts is what helps them use them as resources in their civic imagination.

In fact, young fans' deep engagement with fictional content worlds most likely surpasses their familiarity with the kinds of civic and political knowledge traditionally valued by scholars of youth engagement (such as familiarity with the workings of government). Within the ideals of the "informed citizen" model, a particular model of citizenship that grew in the progressive era (Schudson 1999), young people are "required"—by others, as well as in their own perception—to have in-depth knowledge of all facets of an issue before they're "allowed" to form and express an opinion. Yet, particularly in an information-rich environment, this ideal may create a standard that is impossible to meet (Thorson 2010), causing some young people to avoid all news content. Instead of admonishing young people for being more interested in entertainment than in the news, fan activism uses the one sphere to deepen engagement with the other—for example, using the hardships faced by werewolves in the magical world to inspire consideration of the discriminatory treatment of minority groups. Satya explains:

> I learned more about myself and more about the world around me, because I think it's a lot easier to understand Harry's world than it is to understand our own.

The HPA's use of fictional worlds to help young people make sense of real-world issues constitutes what Ashley Hinck (2012) calls a "public engagement keystone": "a touch point, worldview, or philosophy that makes other people, actions, and institutions intelligible." Connecting the work of several scholars of democracy, Hinck explains that a public engagement keystone serves multiple goals for the activist group: it creates an anchoring at the level of citizens' lived experiences, it helps identify and bring together people with shared beliefs and interests, and it forges strong ties between activists.

The HPA's use of the fictional Harry Potter world as a "public engagement keystone" extends from the macro-level of the organization to the micro-level of individual participants' interactions and conversations. The richness of this content world, along with fans' deep relationship with it, allows individual HPA members to hone their own civic imaginations, to build their own connections to real-world issues that are most pertinent to them, while enjoying the institutional support of a larger organization that holds out the opportunity for them to initiate collective actions. This is evidenced in the example of the discussion group mentioned before, or in the work of individual chapter organizers like Davia:

> We like to link everything back to Harry Potter. We have to get a little creative sometimes, but we can still link. We were trying to get involved

in some environmental issues so we called it herbology, and with animal things we call it "care of magical creatures."

On the micro-level of individuals, connecting the fictional text to real-world issues may be a learned skill. We encountered before the example of Hunger Games fans who had a hard time seeing the fictional world's relevance to social and political issues in our world. Astera, a 17-year-old HPA member, explained how her experience with the HPA has sensitized her to making such connections:

> A lot of it, I only started to think about once I found the Harry Potter Alliance and all of that. The first time [I read Harry Potter] it was just a really good and surprisingly intricate story. But now that I've thought about it that way for the first time, I realize that there actually are a lot of parallels that aren't even that far of a stretch, and I'm trying to think about all books I read more like that. I'm making them more real and applicable.

For Astera and other HPA members, linking the Harry Potter narratives to real-world issues has served as a consequential connection that encouraged them to read other fictional texts as political allegories as well. But can this work with any text?

If we consider the texts that Imagine Better has worked with, such as Harry Potter, the Hunger Games, and Superman, they have a factor in common, besides having new content released when the group was first organizing campaigns. These are all texts that take place in an immersive "world" of their own, one that is both related to and yet different from the real world. Mark J. P. Wolf (2012) characterizes such fictional worlds as "secondary worlds," which use materials from our "primary world" yet reshape and recombine its elements, creating a world that's at the same time recognizable and different. Such worlds encourage fan creativity by allowing fans to imagine alternative characters, subplots, and scenarios beyond the canonic text, but still within its logic. When fans use these worlds to discuss, reimagine, and seek to change the primary world, they are participating in what Saler (2012) calls "public spheres of the imagination."

Matt Hills (2002) uses the term "hyperdiegesis" to describe "the creation of a vast and detailed narrative space, only a fraction of which is ever directly seen or encountered within the text, but which nonetheless appears to operate according to principles of internal logic and extension" (104). This characteristic of fictional worlds enables fan activism to work not only with the existing characters and story plots, but to create countless connections, even ones that don't exist within the text, as long as they fit in the world's internal logic. We may see a distinction here between the different modes of fan activism: while fannish civics may venture into such creative additions, cultural acupuncture typically sticks to the canonic plot, and even more specifically to ideas familiar to a wide audience.

There are many potential strengths to using fantasy worlds to make sense of the real world. Saler (2012) claims that due to their fantastical elements—what he calls their "as if" status—fictional worlds may help challenge one-sided convictions people hold about the real world. Van Zoonen (2005) discusses how interpreting fictional political narratives can facilitate people's performance of citizenship, for example by helping them imagine a perfect society and an ideal political process that surpasses partisan differences. As Diana Mutz (2006) explains, in many of our life contexts people are surrounded by those similar to themselves, and only rarely do they engage in discussions with people whose political views differ from theirs. The characteristics of fan communities may create a different climate: when discussions begin around fictional content worlds, slowly forming into friendships, people may find ways beyond the "echo chambers" that inhibit more conventional kinds of political communication. This was the experience of HPA member Kevin and one of his closest friends:

> Ron, he is probably the farthest person in comparison of who I am as a person. The only thing that really connects us is Harry Potter, and our political views are completely different, our social views are completely different. You know there are some overlaps—the fight for the equality of people and some of the general things there, but who we are as people is completely different. But we're best friends, because we don't look down on each other because that was a kind of different view.

When done right, fictional content worlds can bridge ideological differences, helping people to see a social issue in a different light and to reach some shared understanding around it. But employing content worlds for activist goals can also be fraught with challenges.

One such challenge is finding the right balance between the content world and the civic goal. While the HPA has been very successful at creating real-world links to the world of Harry Potter, its attempts to base political campaigns around other fictional universes have varied in terms of their depth of engagement with those different content worlds. In Chapter 1, we discussed the rich symbolism of Superman, who was born on the planet Krypton but raised by American parents, having to hide his true identity. Imagine Better attempted to tap this connection in its Superman Is an Immigrant campaign, launched around the release of the 2013 movie *Man of Steel*. Through a video blog for the HPA a year earlier, Julian Gomez, a member of the HPA and one of the campaign's organizers, had publicly come out as undocumented (videos of young people "coming out" as undocumented are dealt with in more detail in Chapter 5). In an op-ed for the *Huffington Post*, Julian (Gomez 2013) described his personal connection to the campaign and to the story of Superman :

> In the summer blockbuster *Man of Steel*, Superman struggles with his identity as an immigrant, terrified that if he tells the American people that he's from another place, they will reject him. I felt that same fear when I was old enough to understand what it meant to be undocumented. Last year, I finally found the courage to publicly speak about my undocumented status in a video blog that has now been watched over 16,000 times.

For this campaign, Imagine Better partnered with Define American, a project led by immigrant rights activist Jose Antonio Vargas, with the aim of "using the power of story to transcend politics and shift conversation around immigration, identity, and citizenship in America." Imagine Better and Define American encouraged people to share their stories of heritage and identity, sparking a conversation around immigration reform. On the Tumblr page wearetheamericanway.tumblr.com, young people uploaded pictures with descriptions of their family heritage, signing with "I am the American way" and Superman's signature S, branded with the colors of the American flag. While the Tumblr page elicited participation, some fans felt that the campaign did not tap the potentially rich symbolism of the Superman content world. This also relates to our fannish civics/cultural acupuncture distinction—the campaign could speak to and be comprehended by a wider audience, but did not engage the in-depth passion of fans. At the same time, the introduction of the "Superman is an immigrant" metaphor brought a fresh perspective into the conversation around immigrant reform.

Beyond a too-shallow depth of engagement, there are other potential pitfalls in connecting secondary worlds to participatory politics. The "internal logics" that make these worlds function, after all, don't necessarily apply to our world, and making direct comparisons may be problematic. A careful balance must be struck between which elements of the story world are taken up and which are left behind, and in some ways, this task may be easier with a world involving fantastical elements such as magic than with a more realistic one. For example, when the HPA calls its members "a Dumbledore's Army for the real world," this metaphor works to convey the idea that these are young people coming together to fight for what they believe in. Naturally enough, it leaves out the parts about practicing magic in order to do so. But when Imagine Better uses the rebellion of the districts in the dystopian world of the Hunger Games as a template for action, one wonders if a revolution seeking to overthrow an oppressive government is really the form of action the group is advocating. While the rebellion metaphor is resonant, it may carry meanings the activist organization does not wish to embrace.

This potential problem manifested around Imagine Better's use of the three-finger salute from the Hunger Games. In Suzanne Collins's dystopian world, the three-finger salute is originally a symbol of solidarity with and respect for others, but over time it acquires a more militaristic meaning of defiance against an oppressive government. In The Odds in Our Favor campaign, Imagine Better asked participants to submit selfies with the three-finger salute to symbolize their resistance against economic inequality. Yet the organization was taken aback when global news media reported that the three-finger salute was being used by protesters in Thailand, opposing the country's 2014 military coup. On the one hand, this was a powerful example of cultural acupuncture happening spontaneously; on the other, the group was worried by the fact that the symbol it had adopted and promoted was being used in a situation involving violent confrontations. Metaphoric resistance—in the context of U.S. democracy—is playful, but resistance to an oppressive dictatorship carries a very different weight of risk and responsibility.

Beyond the challenges of connecting to specific content worlds one at a time, Imagine Better faces the challenge of finding a common ground among fans of different texts. In this model, fans are drawn toward civic action not so much through a single content world, but rather through their shared identity as "fans" (see Jenkins 2011). When fans move from one text to another, that is not a sign of their disloyalty or fickleness, rather, it is a characteristic of fans as nomadic (Jenkins 1992). They are not just "fans of" a certain text—instead, "fan" should be understood as a subcultural identity, which shares certain traditions and practices of the wider fan culture. When it seeks to move beyond a single content world, Imagine Better attempts to build on the practices shared by fans regardless of their primary texts.

In a talk entitled "Orphans vs. Empires," delivered at the TEDx-Youth conference in San Diego in 2013, Slack sought to construct a composite mythology that stitched together images from a diverse set of popular narratives, including *The Wizard of Oz, The Hunger Games, Doctor Who, Star Wars, Superman, Batman, Once Upon a Time,* and *The Lion King,* each of which, he suggested, depicts how people who feel powerless can nevertheless overcome powerful foes and change the world. Stitching together these mythic struggles with real-world conflicts around the globe, Slack asked his enthralled audience (which by this point was engaging him in a call-and-response) to join him in creating "a Dumbledore's army for our world, a Fellowship of the Ring, a Rebel Alliance" that might fight for social justice and human rights, wherever and whenever these core values were thrown into crisis. Here, Slack was not simply speaking to multiple fan audiences, but also looking for the shared values and experiences that linked them together into a larger subculture.

Beyond Content Worlds: Fan Activism Emerging from a Taste Community

Nerdfighters represent another model for broadening fan engagement with civic issues, one that does not center around a specific content world. The informal online community of Nerdfighters consists of mostly young people, who can be primarily characterized as fans of vloggers John and Hank Green. The VlogBrothers' YouTube channel is the centerpiece of the Nerdfighter community's shared universe. This is exemplified in the shared ritual for novice Nerdfighters—watching all the vlogs dating from 2007, comprising over 72 hours of video. As Nerdfighter Adrian explained:

> In order to be a really serious Nerdfighter, what do you do? You watch every single video in a chronological order. At this point, it's been so long that I think it's basically impossible.

Yet while the vlogs are the centerpiece, there is a much wider universe of content that Nerdfighters share, extending far beyond the Green brothers. Nerdfighters see themselves as having "shared interests," liking the same content, and being "nerds." In Nerdfighter Julie's words,

> That's the reason why we're there. We're all Nerdfighters who have some shared interests, with Doctor Who and Harry Potter, Star Wars and whatever other things. But also like we're all nerds, we've always been nerds who just like to think a lot. I mean, I don't know, it's like you can have honestly intellectual conversations.

Nerdfighters generally say that they share an interest in "everything nerdy"—a term that is very broadly defined. Nerdfighters referenced a range of examples of "nerdy stuff," including YouTube celebrities, the musical *Cats*, stop motion Lego animation, and the American Museum of Natural History. This may allow for more inclusivity than the example of the HPA, which generally attracts fans of a particular franchise. Moreover, beyond their identification around "nerdy" content, Nerdfighters also self-identify as a community of DIY media producers, specifically part of the YouTube community of video producers (or "YouTubers"; see Lange 2009). As Nerdfighter Theo claimed, "these communities are really based on creating content."

In terms of their participatory politics, Nerdfighters are united by a common—though amorphic—goal: "decreasing world suck." As mentioned before, this broadly defined agenda inspires acts ranging from

REAL QUESTIONS FOR REAL NERDFIGHTERS

1. How long have you been a Nerdfighter?
2. Favorite Hank video & John video?
3. Which charity (or charities) do you support?
4. What do you think your 'famous last words' will be?
5. Best thing about being a nerd/Nerdfighter?
6. Favorite Vlogbrothers punishment(s)?
7. Top THREE favorite Hank Green songs?
8. Tell a 'nerd' joke.
9. Favorite John Green book & why?
10. Give your most creative definition of DFTBA.

Nerdfighter-designed content signaling the community's shared affiliations.

the interpersonal level, such as helping out a friend in need, to collective acts that fit within existing definitions of civic engagement. For example, we mentioned Nerdfighters' activity on Kiva.org, a nonprofit organization that enables individuals to make small loans to people without access to traditional banking systems. Nerdfighters constitute one of the largest communities of lenders on the site, topping groups such as Kiva Christians as well as "atheists, agnostics and skeptics." In comparison to some of the more controversial issues the HPA has taken on (e.g., same-sex marriage), the Nerdfighters generally limit their engagement to charities and nonprofits, pursuing goals that virtually "everyone can agree on." (Of course, this is not always the case. Invisible Children members, too, generally saw themselves as pursuing a goal everyone could agree on, until the backlash against the organization proved otherwise.) This is in a deliberate attempt to create a "big tent," in which all members (ideally) feel welcome—we will later discuss the limits to that notion.

Without relying on a single content world, Nerdfighters still manage to create a vibrant community of fan activists who translate their shared interests, their shared practices, and their sense of community toward real-world action. For example, the Project for Awesome (P4A) is an annual event in which Nerdfighters (and other video creators) are encouraged to create videos about their favorite charities or other nonprofit organizations and simultaneously post them on YouTube. Project for Awesome was one of the first things most Nerdfighters mentioned when asked how Nerdfighteria (the community of Nerdfighters) helps decrease world suck. Jacob explained:

> I think most Nerdfighters realize at least after they've been a Nerdfighter for a while that they're part of a group that is actually actively decreasing world suck in the literal senses. I mean, whenever someone asks me about Nerdfighteria, I instantly list the Project for Awesome . . . because it's just something that you want to say, "Oh, I'm part of this group that every year raises thousands of dollars for charity in an awesome way."

When P4A was launched in 2007, its goal was to somewhat rebelliously "take over" YouTube's front page for one day with videos of charities and nonprofits. Since then, the project has been conducted in explicit partnership with YouTube. In the 2013 P4A, Nerdfighters uploaded hundreds of videos and over 24,000 people donated money to the Foundation to Decrease World Suck, a 501(c)3 charity created by the VlogBrothers, through Indiegogo, a crowdfunding website geared toward nonprofits. The mostly small donations added up to over $850,000, split between the 20 charities whose videos received the most votes by the community.

P4A encourages the mode of expression preferred by many Nerdfighters—video production. The videos uploaded for the project range from ones by semiprofessional "YouTube celebrities" (video artists well known within the YouTube community, though not commonly outside of it), such as "WheezyWaiter," to ones uploaded by young Nerdfighters, who differ widely in terms of their video-production experience. One video, created by two boys in their early teens, was uploaded at a 90-degree angle, with a caption explaining, "I know its sideways but there's no way I'm shooting this again." Exemplifying the inclusive ideals of a participatory culture, Nerdfighters promote creative production by lowering the barriers to expression and encouraging all members to see themselves as potential contributors.

P4A not only encourages Nerdfighters to upload videos, it also supports their creativity through structural features: on projectforawesome.com, one of the ways to pull up videos is by pressing "random video," ensuring that each contribution has an equal chance of being viewed. The website encourages viewers to comment as much as possible on the videos they view, and over 460,000 comments were submitted in response to the 2013 videos. This practice stems from the early days of P4A, when "most-commented" videos would rise to the top of YouTube's browse page, but has been kept "partly out of tradition and partly to help videos by lesser-known YouTubers become more popular in search results." "Comment bombs" are also encouraged through the 48-hour livestream, where the Green brothers and other guests feature P4A videos and, with increasingly silly behavior, comment on them. In 2013, John Green donated one penny for every comment on P4A videos, further encouraging this participatory behavior. Finally, the "perks" offered to those who donate through the Indiegogo website reflect the wide range of content Nerdfighters are fans of, with merchandise related not only to the Green brothers, but also to different YouTube celebrities, as well as art created by the wider Nerdfighter community.

Through P4A and other campaigns, Nerdfighters represent a mode of fan activism that builds on fan practices and a broad shared identity, as well as a wide but shared "universe of taste," while each individual chooses his or her own flavor or point of entry. While the diversity of shared content limits the extent to which the group can count on specific shared references to create a sense of community or an activist commitment,

Nerdfighters may also suggest an additional route to broadening fan activism over time.

The fact that Nerdfighters do not rely on one content world but instead on a wide universe of taste has helped to broaden their base of support. But, while we stress the bottom-up nature of the Nerdfighter community, over time the increasing celebrity status of one of the VlogBrothers—John Green—has significantly contributed to the growth of Nerdfighteria, in sometimes uneven bursts. When John Green started the VlogBrothers project with his brother, Hank, in 2007, he was already an award-winning author of two young adult books. His subsequent books quickly rose to best-selling status, arguably spurred by the growth of the Nerdfighter community. Green's biggest success was *The Fault in Our Stars*, a young adult romance novel about two cancer survivors, that was number one on Amazon six months ahead of its release date and debuted at number one on the *New York Times* best-seller list. The book was inspired by the real story of Esther Earl, a 16-year-old Nerdfighter who found friendship and support in the Nerdfighter community as she was struggling with thyroid cancer. Esther befriended John before succumbing to cancer in 2010, and, in the Nerdfighter community, she became a symbol for warmth, friendship, and courage. When asked by John Green what message she would like to convey to the world, it was "tell the people you love that you love them."

If the existence of the Nerdfighter community was mostly limited to "insiders," this changed in 2014 with the release of the film adaptation of *The Fault in Our Stars*. The modestly budgeted movie broke a record in pre-release ticket sales for a romance, and, in its opening weekend, earned $48 million, topping supposed blockbusters featuring Tom Cruise and Angelina Jolie. The movie's surprising success drew significant media attention not only to John Green, but also to the Nerdfighter community—although it was often discussed as a traditional fan network rather than as a civic movement. Nerdfighters, many of whom relished the sense that their community was a well-kept secret, reacted to this publicity with mixed feelings. At a VlogBrothers meet-up session three weeks after the release of the movie, a young teenager in a Nerdfighter T-shirt asked to read a question she prepared for John and Hank Green: "What do you think is the relationship between the size of the community and the participation of its members?" This question, reflecting the concern of many Nerdfighters over the community's sudden growth, summarizes many of the challenges that Nerdfighters, the HPA, and Imagine Better negotiate, in seeking what makes a community—one that coalesces around popular culture—cohere, and what keeps its members engaged in the pursuit of civic goals.

Before closing, we want to acknowledge some of the limits to the inclusivity of these communities. Nerdfighters strive to be a very open community, with explicitly low "barriers to entry." According to their mantra, "If you want to be a Nerdfighter, you *are* a Nerdfighter." Yet while Nerdfighteria is very large, this group offers the rare opportunity to examine granular data about the demographic makeup of its participants: the VlogBrothers conduct a yearly "Nerdfighteria census." In the 2014 census, over 100,000 Nerdfighters participated—a remarkable response. As this census shows, Nerdfighters are mostly high-school and college age (60 percent of Nerdfighters are between the ages of 16 and 22) and mostly American. Nerdfighters are predominantly female—in the census, 72 percent were female and 26 percent male—while a significant number of community members identify as genderqueer, gender-fluid, or questioning. In terms of race and ethnicity, the group is highly skewed in relation to the racial and ethnic makeup of young Americans in general: 85 percent identify as white, 6.5 percent as Latino, 3.5 percent as East Asian, and only 1.6 percent as black.

The findings of the Nerdfighter census prompt a confrontation with the question of the gender and racial/ethnic makeup of fan communities. Within fan studies, there has long been a discussion around the paucity of people of color participating in the structures of fandom. Jenkins (2014) describes the awkward situation of panels at fan conventions where white fans encircle a handful of minority participants, demanding to know why there aren't more fans of color. As Jenkins points out, the answer goes beyond decisions on the individual level, and may operate "on a systemic or structural level to make it harder for some to speak out as fans" (97). This question is troubling in relation to fandom as an opportunity for pleasure and learning, but it becomes even more pertinent when we think of fan activism as a form of political participation, and of those who may be excluded from it.

One informal, and inadvertent, boundary to participation that may be functioning in the context of the Nerdfighters—as well as the HPA, which acknowledges a similar demographic skew in its membership—may involve cultural distinctions of taste and preference. Based on their shared "nerdy" interests, Nerdfighters can be characterized as a "taste community," referring to a group with a communal preference for certain music, movies, or books (van Dijck 2009). Yet as Antoine Hennion (2007) explains, the allegedly natural affinity of fans toward their objects of passion "is actually socially constructed through the categories employed, the authority of leaders, the imitation of intimates, institutions and frames of appreciation, as well as through the social game of identity making and differentiation" (97). Thus when Nerdfighters say they simply "like the same stuff," this claim may belie the structural determinants of their affinities.

As Jenkins (2014) asserts, fandom mirrors larger forms of segregation in culture at large. Bourdieu's (1984) work on taste politics reminds us that taste is shaped by access to certain experiences, by who is encouraged or discouraged from displaying certain kinds of cultural preferences. And while Bourdieu focuses on class distinctions, we can point to the ways that taste is racialized as well. Using Daniel Dayan's (2005) concept, we may think of Nerdfighters as "taste publics," which are "generally focused on works, texts, or programmes; the performance of these publics is generally 'verdictive' (evaluative)" (54). Dayan also describes such groups as "identity publics" because of the ways they forge common identities around shared interests. While these shared interests constitute a powerful cultural resource for the group to build on as they move into fan activism, those same interests may also serve as an informal means of cultural exclusion—a point that is particularly relevant when we see these groups as the basis for political participation. One way this issue may be addressed is by leaders of these groups overtly taking up racial issues, as when both John and Hank Green repeatedly spoke of racial injustice in the context of the police killings of unarmed black men in 2014. While cultural tastes may limit inclusion, taking an explicit stance in support of racial justice may help young black youth feel more welcome in these communities.

Conclusion

The three case studies described in this chapter all offer successful models of fan activism—mobilizing fan enthusiasm toward participatory politics. Through their different characteristics (focusing on one content world versus moving through multiple content worlds, mobilizing organized fan communities versus attempting to reach individual fans), they help us refine our understanding of fan activism and the ways content worlds may inspire the civic imagination, sketching the boundaries for these terms and testing their limits. This chapter suggests that fan activism can be understood as a continuum between two different modes—fannish civics and cultural acupuncture—that, while closely related, differ in their imagined audience, in the depth of their use of the content world, and in their participatory political outcomes. While the HPA succeeded in mobilizing a highly active fan community into fannish civics, the mode of cultural acupuncture may better serve the group as it seeks to engage other popular texts and reach other potential supporters through Imagine Better.

This chapter also dissects how fan activist groups utilize content worlds. Relying on scholarly examinations of world building as a literary practice, we see that fan activist organizations may benefit from tying into rich, immersive, and expansive worlds, extending their logics to locate almost endless opportunities for real-world connections. Such connections play to the fan community's strength, enabling conversations across ideological and cultural differences. At the same time, content worlds may limit fan activism by the nature of their internal logics, as well as by declines in their popularity over time. Imagine Better presents one possible model to overcome this limitation, shifting to new texts in order to tap cultural pressure points. A different route is suggested by the Nerdfighters, who engage in fan activism based on a wider shared identity as "nerds" with similar cultural tastes. Yet both groups also find that connecting around popular culture content may limit their reach, in often unintended ways.

In the introduction to this chapter, we mentioned Dahlgren's (2003) concept of the civic culture. He explains, "for a functioning democracy, there are certain conditions that reside at the level of lived experiences, resources and subjective dispositions which need to be met" (139). As such, Dahlgren is interested in the sets of cultural norms and practices that enable people to begin to engage as civic agents. He offers a circuit model comprising six dimensions—shared *values*, a sense of *affinity*, *knowledge* and competencies, *practices*, *identities*, and *discussion*—that helps us understand how citizens can use the media in a way that encourages (or hinders) their civic engagement. The groups described here not only provide conditions necessary for their members to participate in the public sphere, they use media engagement as an active way to mobilize their members towards real-world action.

To exemplify how these groups employ the "full circuit" of engagement, we'll examine the most recent campaign that Imagine Better conducted around the release of the third installment in the Hunger Games movie series, *Mockingjay—Part 1* (2014). Again focused on the theme of economic inequality, this campaign includes aspects of awareness raising, expression, and action. To exemplify the links between the Hunger Games narratives and the real world, the campaign calls participants to share how economic inequality has affected their lives. Under the hashtag #MyHungerGames, these stories are shared as a form of broader awareness raising. Yet in this campaign, members are called not only to share their own stories, but to collaborate with a somewhat surprising ally—"Fight for $15," a nationwide protest by fast food workers striking for higher wages and the right to unionize. The oddsinourfavor. org website explains: "These workers struggle with the same issues that workers in the districts face: low pay, bad hours and working conditions, hunger, lack of affordable healthcare, and more." As a specific call for action, members are asked to visit a local McDonald's and hand the manager an information sheet about fair wages and unionization rights. The campaign invites participants to take a selfie of themselves doing the three-finger salute and share it, along with their experiences of the direct action, through #MyHungerGames. It's important to note—a campaign like this definitely demands more than many young participants feel comfortable with. As Andrew Slack admitted in a write-up about the campaign in the *New Yorker*, "some members have expressed social anxiety about doing this" (Wiedeman 2014). The HPA thus attempts to build up its members' confidence, encouraging them to partake in actions they would otherwise be wary of through the inspiration of fictional worlds.

In this campaign, the focus is on equality, a *shared value* that HPA/ Imagine Better identified as one of their key areas of action. The campaign begins by targeting the HPA/Imagine Better membership, tied by an *affinity* building both on the shared content world and shared community structures. In a form of cultural acupuncture, however, the campaign reaches beyond this community, trying to mobilize larger audiences familiar, though not highly engaged with, the Hunger Games narratives. The campaign helps participants to acquire greater *knowledge* regarding economic inequality and fair wages, educating them through the allusions to the fictional narrative coupled with real world labor and income data. Their *identities* as fans, as well as their identification with the protagonists of the Hunger Games, are mobilized toward their engagement. Their action is supported through concrete *practices*— building on the fannish practices they already love engaging in, as well as encouraging them to participate in new activist practices. The #MyHungerGames hashtag and the connection to the Hunger Games content world through both language and visual symbols open opportunities for *discussion* of these issues, with fellow fans and wider audiences familiar with the franchise. The HPA thus not only completes the circuit of the conditions necessary for political engagement, but goes beyond it to harnessing these elements toward real-world change. Moreover, this campaign—through cultural acupuncture—goes far beyond the fan base, to activate and capture the imagination of those with only a superficial familiarity with the Hunger Games. In fact, some union activists report becoming enthusiastic Hunger Games fans through their engagement with the Odds in Our Favor campaign.

Earlier in the chapter we discussed two possible forms of success— success in achieving civic goals, and success in terms of empowering young members to see themselves as civic agents. Based on our conversations with young people, these groups were influential in their development as civic agents, and becoming involved with them was often the precursor to additional civic and political involvement. In terms of their civic goals, these groups have had visible successes in raising funds for charity, in registering and rallying voters, and in increasing public awareness of social issues. The HPA and Imagine Better, in particular, have worked consistently to achieve a range of political goals, while not shying away from more contentious ones, as well.

Fan communities have often been key innovators of new expressive and social practices, often early adopters of new media platforms and practices. This chapter describes ways that fan communities are also pioneering new forms of activism, ones that bridge popular cultural interests and political causes. The achievements of the groups described in this chapter—both in terms of civic goals, and in their civic empowerment of young citizens—did much to inspire us to embark on our broader examination of innovative forms of participatory politics. The examples of fan activism described in this chapter are the most clear manifestations of the ways that the civic imagination may inspire real-world political actions, but we are finding similar logics emerging across all of the case studies we discuss in this book, as more and more youth are using storytelling and media making as tools for promoting political change, for example by employing powerful popular culture symbols like the trope of the superhero (Jenkins et al. forthcoming). In Chapter 4, we will see how American Muslim youth in the post-9/11 era make use of such creative tools, as they negotiate the tension between publicity and privacy.

4

Between Storytelling and Surveillance

The Precarious Public of American Muslim Youth

Sangita Shresthova

The NSA apparently is spying on people by monitoring what apps they're using. Damn son, for all the buildings I've blown up in Angry Birds, I wonder if I'll get interrogated for being a ringleader of Al-Qaeda.
—Aman Ali, January 27, 2014

In a Facebook status update, Aman Ali, an American Muslim comedian and storyteller, connected the popular mobile game Angry Birds to thoughts about surveillance and terrorism. At first glance humorous, Ali's post also succinctly captures a key paradox that surfaced throughout our research on American Muslim youth and participatory politics: young American Muslims' desire to express and connect through creating and sharing stories coexists with a climate increasingly defined by privacy and surveillance concerns. In his post, Ali reveals that like many of his 5,000 largely American Muslim Facebook friends, he is caught in a bind: he constantly juggles his desire to connect with others through social media with the awareness that his posts may be viewed (and possibly misunderstood) by audiences far beyond his intended networks. Acknowledging this reality may, in fact, be a key step toward overcoming its potential to silence voice and expression. Within three days, Ali's Angry Birds Facebook post received 557 likes, while many people left comments on it that poked fun at the underlying situation. One commenter suggested that Ali use a BlackBerry as there are no apps available for the phone, hence (supposedly) safeguarding it from NSA snooping. Another commenter warned that Ali's Facebook post now had so many keywords that it would certainly get flagged for official scrutiny. We might think of this Facebook exchange as a form of informal, collaborative storytelling, shedding light on the situations confronting American Muslims, while producing content that could be circulated across a supportive, yet fragile, network. Together, these humorous comments told a story of storytelling and surveillance.

Drawing on the work of storytellers, civic organizations, and comedians like Aman Ali, this chapter focuses on expressive initiatives by civically engaged American Muslim youth as moderate Muslim voices have struggled to be heard within an increasingly polarized discussion that has characterized American culture in the wake of 9/11. In particular, we highlight media making and storytelling as crucial dimensions of efforts by American Muslim youth to express, poke fun at, network, and mobilize around identity politics. We also point to ongoing in-person and online surveillance as a real obstacle for some young American Muslims, particularly those involved in contentious social justice campaigns. Such surveillance threatens an emergent American Muslim public, which often relies on dark humor as a coping mechanism. Exploring both the possibilities and vulnerabilities of participatory politics in the American Muslim youth context, we argue that these American Muslim youth networks are perhaps best seen as striking a *precarious* balance between vibrancy and fragility, empowerment and risk, and voice and silence, which as our introductory discussion of "precarious publics" in Chapter 1 suggested, relates to the gap between voice and influence.

To be clear, the expressive efforts, projects, and practices we describe here do not map directly onto easily identifiable political objectives. In fact, many of the American Muslim youth efforts we encountered were not conceived as explicitly (or even implicitly) political. Nonetheless, they often assume political meanings as they circulate and reach broader audiences. As filmmaker Bassam Tariq has sadly noted, "things tend to get political" when "Muslims come into the conversation in America." Whether they see themselves as political or not, young American Muslims are often asked to "represent," speak on behalf of, and even defend Islam as a religious practice whose tenets are compatible with the values and ideologies of the United States. Laila Shaikley (2014), one of the creators of the short online video "Mipsterz—Somewhere in America," felt this situation left many American Muslims "wounded, marginalized, reactive, and defensive," circumstances she attributes to the fact that they are "underrepresented and misrepresented in the media." As Shaikley suggests, American Muslim youth operate in an extremely politicized post-9/11 climate where much of what they do *as* American Muslims could potentially be interpreted as having political meaning. In this context, activities (like telling personal stories and faith-based, identity-related expression) that would not necessarily be read as political among other communities do extremely important work in the American Muslim case as they coexist with more established advocacy efforts. Also, cultural efforts that aim to foster more grassroots expression become politically charged, which is why our study of American Muslim communities highlights activities that, at first glance, reside predominantly in cultural realms.

This chapter draws on Sangita Shresthova's two-year research of civically active youth, groups, and networks connected to the Muslim Public Affairs Council (MPAC) and Muslim Youth Group (MYG) of the Islamic Center of Southern California (ICSC). Founded in 1986, the Muslim Public Affairs Council is an advocacy organization that, according to its website, strives for the "integration of Islam into American pluralism, and for a positive, constructive relationship between American Muslims and their representatives." While its agenda often aligns closely with other American Muslim advocacy organizations, MPAC is distinct in its ongoing focus on public opinion and media. Yaida, a young American Muslim woman we interviewed, saw MPAC as "a really press-oriented organization" that "reacts quite quickly to what's going on through social media." MPAC's most prominent youth programs are the annual Young Leaders Summits, which bring together young American Muslims who are, or want to be, involved in journalism, entertainment, and civic engagement. While each summit is thematically specific, they all focus on strengthening participants' abilities to communicate and network effectively. Participants also explore the similarities and differences in their experiences as American Muslims. In doing this, they often connect through a shared knowledge of popular culture as they discuss TV shows, popular religious sites (like suhaibwebb.com), and content created and shared through social networking sites by other American Muslims, including hip hop artist Omar Offendum's latest music video, different ways to tie the hijab featured on hijab-modest-fashion YouTube channels like YaztheSpaz, and the latest comedy video posted on GoatFace Comedy (a youth-run online comedy channel). After the summits end, participants stay in touch through an MPAC-supported Facebook group, webinars, email list, and annual in-person reunions.

An informal space for high-school-aged youth to gather, the mixed-gender Muslim Youth Group resides within the Islamic Center of Southern California in Los Angeles. Founded in the 1970s, ICSC explicitly strives to engage diverse Muslim communities and according to its website promotes a "socially responsible Muslim-American identity." During Shresthova's research, MYG ran weekly meetings that provided high-school youth with social opportunities alongside their spiritual education. The MYG Facebook page, explained Hasina, a 17-year-old youth leader,

> is like the heart of [our] youth group I think. What is the heart of every teenager's life? Our youth group does cater to teenagers. So we have a Facebook page. . . . Some of them [the youth] do not come to youth group anymore, but there are some that can still be in touch with this youth group or there are just kids who have necessarily lived farther away, but they can still know what is going on in the community.

In 2012, MYG discussions often involved media, as the youth discussed news, watched online videos, debated anti-Muslim perspectives, and accessed religious websites during the session.

Both MPAC and MYG were founded through the ICSC, and MPAC staff are closely involved with the programs run by the youth group, whose members in turn help out with MPAC events. Both organizations attribute their ideological underpinnings to Dr. Meher Hathout, a recently deceased physician of Egyptian descent and one of the Islamic Center's founders. Like Dr. Hathout, MPAC and MYG strongly assert that American Muslims need to accept being American as much as they claim their religious beliefs. In Dr. Hathout's words, "Home is not where my grandparents are buried; it is where my grandchildren will live."

In the course of Shresthova's research, she interviewed 30 young people involved with MYG and MPAC activities who came from a range of ethnic backgrounds, including Arab American, South Asian American (Pakistani and Indian), and African American. She attended MYG's weekly meetings for six months, participated in three MPAC Young

Leader Summits in New York, Los Angeles, and Washington, D.C., during the summer of 2012, and conducted 15 expert interviews with American Muslim youth community leaders. Shresthova also connected to American Muslim youth networks online to explore how new media complements, and expands upon, face-to-face encounters.

Post-9/11 American Muslim Youth and Precarious Publics

"I didn't realize it was so big," Walidah, a young American Muslim woman from the Midwest, almost whispered as she circled the noisy construction site at Ground Zero. Walidah had come to Manhattan to participate in MPAC's June 2012 Young Leaders Media Summit. She took several pictures with her cell phone, her expression distraught and pensive. Standing in the atrium of a building newly constructed next to Ground Zero, she discussed how 9/11 had changed American Muslims' lives, what it meant to her in 2001, and what it means more than ten years later. Like Walidah, several MPAC summit participants had not visited Ground Zero before. Their vivid memories of 9/11 were shaped by mediated images and their parents', friends', and teachers' frightened reactions. Despite clear differences in their individual recollections, the youth all agreed that 9/11 had a lasting impact on their lives. For the older youth (in their mid- to late twenties), the aftermath of 9/11 brought the realization that American Muslims were going to need to organize around their faith-based identity in ways that moved beyond the ethnic and sectarian divisions that had dominated Muslim civic communities until then. Other, mostly younger, participants saw 9/11 as the moment when they realized that no matter whether they embraced it or not, they would have to engage with being American and Muslim as an incredibly politicized identity. They also spoke about "fear" as a key dimension of their post-9/11 experience.

Many of the American Muslim youth we interviewed shared experiences of anti-Muslim prejudice growing up in America, which confirmed the findings of other studies of this population. A survey of American Muslim youth conducted by Selcuk R. Sirin and Michelle Fine (2009) found that "88 percent of the participants reported having been subjected to at least one act of discrimination *because they were Muslim*" (87). Reflecting on these realities, Sadia, a young Pakistani

American, sighed and observed, "It's been 11 years since 9/11." Sometimes she felt like "[w]e really moved past that and we made a lot of progress." Other times, she was not so sure. She recounted an incident that happened to her in New York City:

> I was in New York with two other girls. We were walking and there was kind of a crowd and they wanted people to move or whatever and someone called out to us, "You terrorists!" because one of the girls was wearing a headscarf. And I was just like, "Wow. Really? You would stoop that low?" I come from a conservative Texas town so if something like that happens there or in another conservative town, I wouldn't have been as surprised. But seeing as it was New York, I was like, "Really?" Apparently, there are still real problems there and they are really hard to overcome. It's very frustrating when like something like 9/11 happens and there's a few radicals who say, "Yeah, we're Muslims that's why we are doing this," and everyone believe them. Whereas, the guy who flew the plane into a building in Austin because he was mad at the IRS and no one's like, "Wow, Christians are horrible because of that."

According to a 2011 survey conducted by the Pew Research Center, 55 percent of the American Muslim respondents to a 2011 said they felt that living as an American Muslim had become "more difficult" since 9/11. Twenty-five percent reported that their local mosque had been the "target of controversy or outright hostility." Despite the high level of animosity toward American Muslims suggested by these data, the same study found "no indication of increased alienation or anger" among American Muslims toward the United States.

Many analysts attribute the degree of hostility indicated by these surveys to sustained anti-Muslim campaigns by groups affiliated with people such as prominent anti-Islamization campaigner Robert Spencer and Pamela Geller, who argues on her Atlas Shrugs website that "[t]he U. S. Constitution is under attack from Fundamentalist Islam and Shariah, Islamic Religious Law. Fundamentalist Islam wants Shariah to replace the U. S. Constitution and fundamentally transform America." The potential dangers of such extravagant rhetoric and the cultural climate it supports were underscored on December 27, 2012, when Sunando Sen, a man of Indian origin, died after being pushed under a New York City subway train. After she was charged with the crime, Erika Menendez, who is reported to have suffered from mental illness, was quoted as stating , "I pushed a Muslim onto the train tracks because I hate Hindus and Muslims[. E]ver since 2001 when they put down the twin towers I've been beating them up" (Santora 2012). News of the murder spread through American Muslim youth networks and followed on the heels of the debate surrounding a series of "Stop Jihad" ads in subways and on buses paid for by Geller's American Freedom Defense Initiative. Sen's death was often linked in online discussions to other hate crimes like the Sikh temple shooting in Wisconsin and the defacement of nine mosques across the United States that occurred during Ramadan in 2012. The youth shared such news stories, warning their peers to "be careful" and "be safe." Aliyah, a young activist, observed:

> A lot of Muslims, in general, live in a state of fear. . . . Then other people are like, "What are you afraid of?" It just leads to more uncomfortableness and people not being able to relate to each other.

Rubiyah, another young woman we interviewed, concurred with Aliyah. She shared that she lived in "fear" because of the open expressions of hostility she and others had experienced (two men had recently pointed their fingers at her husband, pretending to shoot him, as he walked out of a Sam's Club). News stories of hate crimes in Arizona, where Rubiyah lives, weighed heavily on her every day. Reflecting on this climate of fear, Muin, a high school sophomore, pondered the term "terrorist" during his interview. He paused for a few minutes as he considered where the term originated and how it came to be so linked with American Muslims before concluding it was because of 9/11.

As Sunaina Marr Maira (2003) observes, "9/11 led many youth from Muslim American families to engage with their Muslim identities with a new intensity, with varying trajectories emerging." In one of these trajectories, documented in Nazli Kibria's (2007) study of Bangladeshi youth and Nadine Naber's (2005) research on young Arab Americans, youth are now shifting toward privileging a hyphenated Muslim identity over their ethnic background, leading to what Maira describes as a

"self-conscious production of and engagement with 'Muslim' identity."
In their analysis, Ewing and Hoyler (2008) find that the foundations of
this practice have

> been developing for decades. . . . , many young Muslims link the emer-
> gence of their own intentional identity as a Muslim to the aftermath of
> 9/11 and the war on terror. (82)

In another study, Selcuk R. Sirin and Michelle Fine (2009) argue that
American Muslims experience "hyphenated" identities that are "at once
individual and collective, conscious and unconscious, filled with pride
and shame, politically shared, and wildly personal" (194–195). The youth
we interviewed identified strongly as both American *and* Muslim, referring to themselves as "American Muslim," making a strong claim for a
distinctly American practice of Islam.

As she reflected on the past 11 years during our 2012 interview,
Aliyah, who was a high school sophomore in 2001, suggested that the
security measures, public perceptions, and reactionary attitudes toward
Islam actually "galvanized a really large part of the [American] Muslim
population; the Muslim youth who were in college then provided men-
toring to the people that were in high school." She continued:

> So, you're kind of still seeing that generation and the generations fol-
> lowing it pursuing the code of activism and civic engagement. . . . There
> were definitely people that were active before that but as a whole, the
> community was very insular. . . . [After 9/11,] I feel like that's when our
> community realized like, "Hold on. We need to get active. We need to do
> things because if not, we're screwed."

Maira (2003) proposes that such civic engagement may take several
forms, including "greater involvement in electoral politics," "progressive
activism and grassroots politics," and "outreach to non-Muslim communities." We find that American Muslims take "action" through an
even broader range of activities, many of them situated on the cultural
end of the spectrum of participatory politics. Young American Muslims
use social media to establish and maintain networks. They turn to their

networks to share stories they create and appropriate. At times, they also mobilize these networks to achieve civic goals.

"Precarious publics" may be the right theoretical frame in which to understand this emergent American Muslim movement. We defined a precarious public as "one where there is a considerable gap between voice and influence." In such circumstances, youth have to weigh the perceived benefits of participation against the obstacles and possible risks. Our notion of *precariousness* owes much to Mary Gray's (2009) research on queer and LGBT youth in rural America. Gray harnesses Jurgen Habermas's seminal theorization of the "bourgeois public sphere" as an autonomous space where public opinion can be formed. She also incorporates feminist scholarly critiques of a universalized public sphere. In particular, Gray builds on Nancy Fraser and Michael Warner, who pointedly demonstrated that Habermas's conceptualization overlooked the existence of multiple (counter)publics that have been and will continue to be sites of contention that blur boundaries between what is private and what is public. Extending those critiques, she proposes the notion of "boundary publics," which she defines as "iterative, ephemeral experiences of belonging that circulate across the outskirts and through the center(s) of a more recognized and validated public sphere" (92–93). Through her ethnography of the Highlight Pride Alliance (another HPA), Gray argues "boundary publics" reveal "a complex web of relations that is always playing out the politics and negotiations of identity" (93). As such, they are "at once within and just beyond the reach of conservative elites attempts to" claim control.

Boundary publics, according to Gray, manifest both in everyday face-to-face and online spaces. She recounts the HPA youth "performing drag" in the Springhaven, Kentucky, Walmart, the only business that stays "open 24 hours within an 80-mile radius," as a "rite of passage for those entering the local gay scene" (97). At the same time, she describes an incident at the Walmart where the youth were slandered by a hostile and verbally aggressive peer to the point that they had to leave the store. The rural youth described in Gray's study encountered analogous "opportunities and challenges" online. She finds the internet gave them access to experiences unavailable "in their daily life," but it also brought "risk of exposure" (127–130). As a consequence, they found themselves putting up or removing online content depending on the emotional and political climate in their geographically local communities.

Gray's "boundary publics" are crucial to our analysis of American Muslim networks as precarious publics; her analysis helps us to identify similarities between the conditions faced by American Muslim youth and rural LGBT youth, despite crucial differences in the lived experiences of these communities and networks. For the rural queer youth in Gray's study, "authorized access to public space is fragile" (94–95). The same can be said for American Muslim youth, who struggle to find spaces to connect with other like-minded youth. Whether they are face-to-face or online, these spaces are crucially important to both communities. For the LGBT youth, shutting down such gathering places threatens their emergent community's existence. American Muslim youth negotiate very similar circumstances. On one hand, American Muslim youth recognize the potential of new media to connect to others. They value the open conversations they conduct through these networks. They nourish these connections by creating and circulating media—literally working through "any media" available. At the same time, they weigh these opportunities against the possibility that online expression may attract unwelcome scrutiny, placing them at risk. During the course of our research, the pendulum on these considerations shifted several times in response to current events. For example, we witnessed how the youth decreased their activities when the Associated Press released a Pulitzer Prize–winning report revealing that the New York Police Department authorized and executed widespread surveillance of American Muslim communities and organizations (including campus-based Muslim student associations) in the tri-state area. We saw the pendulum swing the other way when storytelling projects (like 30 Mosques) by young American Muslims inspired the youth in our study to also find ways to communicate about their experiences.

Such shifts indicate these post-9/11 networks are indeed "precarious," as young people weigh concerns around what information, perspectives, and experiences they can (and should) share with others. Some things that might be expressed in an enclosed space become more risky when subject to context collapse. Understanding how young people resolve such issues is key to understanding which youth can deploy the public communication channels that Kahne et al. (2014) see as integral to participatory politics. In *Democracy Remixed*, which focuses on the political lives of "young black people," Cathy Cohen (2010) highlights both "structure and agency" as crucial dimensions that determine the choices and circumstances of young people's (political) lives (11). As she reflects on the surveys and interviews she conducted with black youth, Cohen observes that "the importance of structure in shaping their lives was undeniable, but they never let me discount the control they had over their own lives, however limited" (13).

Similarly, the young American Muslims we interviewed shared their determination to navigate expression in a climate where the odds are often stacked against them. The media these youth created, the networks they fostered, and concerns they articulated have much to teach us about both the opportunities and challenges of participatory politics for an emergent, marginalized American Muslim youth community. For example, American Muslim youth efforts highlight that the ability to contribute to and shape narrative is crucial to the construction of shared identities. These activities also show that access to social networking platforms and media sharing practices is helping to shift control over the construction and circulation of political identities from the few to the many. Much as Cathy Cohen sees black youth "holding a precarious position within our nation" (13), we find that American Muslim youth engagement with participatory politics is fragile, yet significant. The discussion of young American Muslims in this chapter also connects to the obstacles and challenges faced by undocumented youth involved in the DREAM movement discussed in Chapter 5.

Circulation: The Life Force of American Muslim Youth Networks

The young people involved with MPAC and MYG tended to see them as exceptional organizations: both meet American Muslim youth where they are at, rather than asking them to conform to agendas and priorities created for them by community elders. As one respondent bluntly put it, MPAC doesn't "shove religion down your throat." Through their activities, MPAC and MYG also connect youth to a vibrant and dispersed network that shares updates and creative media and stages important and substantive debates about what it means to be Muslim and American.

To be clear, in addition to a large number of Islamic centers around the country, there are also several well established organizations that advocate for American Muslim issues, including the Muslim American Society (MAS), Islamic Circle of North America (ICNA), Islamic Society of North America (ISNA), Council on American-Islamic Relations (CAIR), and Muslim Student Association (MSA) National. Most of these organizations operate on a national level with dispersed regional and local branches. With the exception of MSA National, which is completely youth oriented, these organizations often focus on youth through programs that are fairly conventionally structured, with the central bodies assuming most of the responsibility for organizing and guiding events and activities. Reflecting on this situation, Reyah, a youth activist, saw a disconnect between what young American Muslims want and the programs these organizations offer. She wished that the leaders of these national groups would more often "sit down and have conversations with young people and ask them what it is that interests them" rather than assume that they know what they need. She wanted more programs that are created *by* young people, not just *for* them. She explained that Imams and heads of organizations say, "We need to get our youth to vote, to become informed voters and do all these things," even as "no youth" have a seat "at the table" where this discussion is taking place.

Ahmed Eid's forthcoming *Unmosqued* documentary explores the generational conflict inside American Muslim religious institutions, where older (usually first-generation) immigrants insist on holding on to traditions and values from their past rather than allowing younger people to explore what their faith means to them. In December 2013, another filmmaker, Ali Baluch, described to *Huffington Post* how even prayer can become a site of conflict between younger and older worshippers in American mosques:

> You want to worship and be in a great environment, you're constantly bothered by this religious police who are saying you're not praying the right way. Instead of guiding you the right way, they're just scaring you away. (Hafiz 2013)

Unmosqued grapples with the reality that many young American Muslim youth seem to be drifting away from brick-and-mortar Islamic centers. Imam Shamsi Ali asks: "Where is the young generation?" He then answers his own question: "They are moving away, and they are not coming back."

Our and other research (see Khan 2014) suggests that many young American Muslims are employing new media to find each other, explore their faith, and discuss topics their mosques and other formal American Muslim organizations may not condone. Kadir, a digital media consultant we interviewed, explained that such new media spaces represent "a great alternative to the sort of institutional structure that exists within the Muslim community today." He also noted that online spaces are often where "great intellectual conversations" happen among young American Muslims:

> Anonymity [online] helps because you can have a more open conversation than you would have if you knew this was a person who was part of an institution. . . . In that sense, you can have those uncomfortable conversations that you can't have within an MSA or a mosque, where it may cause reactions and people may get offended and leave.

For some interviewees, this "free for all" atmosphere distinguished online forums from more institutionalized settings with limited opportunities for debating controversial topics (including homosexuality, sexuality, and religion).

Sharing media, with or without political dimensions, was crucial to maintaining these networks. The media youth shared included news reports on current events (like Michelle Bachman's accusations against Huma Abedin and other Muslims in government that surfaced in July 2012), religious materials (motivational quotes from the Qu'ran), faith-based lifestyle topics (photos of food during Ramadan), and popular culture debates (the controversy surrounding whether or not young American Muslims chose to watch *Zero Dark Thirty*; see Hussein 2013). Abu, a young man we interviewed, noted his uses of social media skyrocketed during the "Arab Spring" when he was on Twitter for "almost 15 hours of the day." Leyla, a MYG leader, explained that she often asked people to follow what she posts by saying something like: "Hey, guys, read this article. Check this out!" She also often tried to "spark a debate" around American Muslim issues by posting content with a question like: "Hey, what do you guys think about this?" Circulation of popular culture and news stories thus became an activity that sustained, nourished, and deepened connections within American Muslim youth networks. Such circulation echoes the observations of Henry Jenkins, Sam Ford, and Joshua Green (2013), who describe "the public not as simply consumers of pre-constructed images but as people who are shaping, sharing, reframing, and remixing media content in ways that might not have been previously imagined." Jenkins and his collaborators also stress the importance of "larger communities and networks" that "spread content well beyond their immediate geographic proximity" (2).

American Muslim networks, sustained through ongoing processes of media circulation, have what Ethan Zuckerman (2015) describes as a "latent" capacity for political action. Importantly, "latent" in this case does not imply that these networks are, in any way, dormant. On the contrary, networked American Muslims were able to mobilize *because* they were already actively engaged in largely cultural exchanges. Networks normally sustained through the exchange of funny stories, music videos, and cute cat pictures, Zuckerman suggests, can quickly move into political action when required.

As an activist with experience in both traditional and networked activism, Aliyah confirmed that she is "very invested" in social media "platforms" that help her to "garner support," "mobilize people," and "raise awareness" around issues like humanitarian concerns related to American Muslims and Muslims around the world (in Syria, for example). She referred to suhaibwebb.com (n.d.), known as the "virtual mosque," which—according to its self-description—"seeks to bridge orthodox and contemporary Islamic knowledge, bringing to light issues of cultural, social and political relevance to Muslims in the West" as an example of an online space where "you're educating, you're informing, you're allowing diverse opinions to be shared." Through her description of her efforts as an activist, we can see how Aliyah connects two complementary models of engagement: Ethan Zuckerman's "latent" capacities and Roger Hurwitz's (2004) "monitorial" citizenship. As touched on in Chapter 2, Hurwitz argues that in a world where the ideals of the "informed citizen" are increasingly challenged due to the complexity of issues and the proliferation of news sources, people depend on each other to alert them to topics that require urgent attention (104). Young

American Muslims' ongoing use of new and social media as a way to connect, share, and debate topics that may not be explicitly political builds "latent" capacity to mobilize toward political goals should such a crisis arise. Such circulation *prepares the ground* for those "monitorial" moments when, as Hurwitz explains, "politics comes to life" because of "great dissatisfaction with a current state of affairs and finds expression in ad hoc protest movements." While often organizationally "ephemeral," Hurwitz's monitorial citizenship relies on "volunteers who foresee some national . . . crisis" (108). Functioning as crucial nodes, these volunteers not only "monitor" situations, they are also connected to networks that allow them to respond quickly, often bypassing more established organizational structures.

Building on the work of Foot and Schneider (2002), Jennifer Earl and her research collaborators (Earl et al. 2010) differentiate between scale change and model change paradigms. In the scale change paradigm, the internet "accentuates" or "accelerates" activism, but does not fundamentally change core logics and methods of organizing. The model change approach posits that "some uses of the Internet may actually change the dynamics of activism in important ways" (426–427). American Muslim responses to triggers signal important model-changing dynamics— new media allow activists to work around hierarchical processes that may retard or block grassroots mobilization. In other words, networked communication allows American Muslim youth to bypass complex and historically fragmented organizational structures in moments that call for quick and efficient action around current issues. Such mobilization is enabled through preexisting, but previously politically "latent" networks. Kadir offered a perspective on this "model change":

> The institutions . . . (the mosque and the MSA and the national organizations . . .) have a lot of baggage (cultural, sectarian and ideological). The [American Muslim] community is very fragmented as a result of it. For people who want to get work done, going through institutions is very problematic on certain issues. . . . [For a] very quick response and grassroots organizing, I find it very tempting to resort to new media.

The circulation of media becomes the life force of these new media networks.

Storytelling: Taking Control of the Narratives

In 2009, Bassam Tariq and Aman Ali (the author of this chapter's opening quote), two young American Muslims with a shared faith and curiosity, embarked on a storytelling adventure they called the 30 Mosques project. They visited different mosques in New York City during each night of Ramadan and blogged about their experiences at 30mosques.com. Their journey took them to various parts of the city— from the Masjid Khalifah established by Malcolm X and other Nation of Islam members over 50 years ago in Brooklyn's Bedford-Stuyvesant neighborhood to the recently opened Harlem Islamic Center. Their narratives ranged from the everyday, as they documented what food they ate, to the poignant, as they stood outside a mosque that had burned down due to faulty electrical wiring. As the Ramadan stories accumulated, there emerged a more diverse picture of Muslim experience in New York City. Their blog readership skyrocketed as their stories circulated through social media networks, with the most popular posts receiving more than 9,000 comments. Before Ramadan ended, 30 Mosques had been featured on NPR twice. The stories Ali and Tariq collected contributed to, and also inspired others to join, a growing but dispersed storytelling movement that seeks to counter stereotyped perceptions through the circulation of narratives about the lived experiences of diverse groups of American Muslims.

30 Mosques inspired several similar projects. One of them was Breakfast@Night, a Ramadan photo project launched by MYG youth in 2011 under the guidance of the group's coordinator at the time, Soha Yassine. Jihad Turk (forthcoming), president of the Bayan Claremont graduate school for Muslim scholars, defined Breakfast@Night as a young people's "response to daily bombardment . . . of either negative images about Islam or images that represent Islam as a foreign religion." To Turk, the MYG youth "decided to take the initiative to represent themselves," rather than have others speak on their behalf.

Breakfast@Night, 30 Mosques, and other projects involving participatory storytelling, defined here as a "collective activity in which individuals and groups contribute to the telling, retelling, and remixing of stories [or narratives] through various media platforms" (Brough and

The 30 Mosques visual used during the first year of the project.

Shresthova 2012), are examples of an important mode of expression for American Muslim youth, giving them a voice and the opportunity to share their own experiences. Discussing the importance of storytelling on his blog, Wajahat Ali (2012), a playwright who self-identifies as an "accidental" American Muslim activist, observes:

> The future of Islam in America has to be written by Muslim Americans who boldly grab hold of the conch and become heroes of our own narratives. We can no longer exist in culturally isolated cocoons or bury our heads under the sand waiting for the tide to subside on its own. We must follow the traditions and values of Islam and America by being generous and inviting with our narratives. We must tell stories that are "by us, for everyone," thus accurately reflecting the spectrum of shared common values that exist simultaneously within the Muslim and American spirit.

While the stories that young American Muslims shared at times tapped existing popular culture content worlds, similar to the ones described in our discussion of the Harry Potter Alliance in Chapter 3, they often drew more explicitly on personal experience as a point of entry into narrative creation. In fact, many youth felt that existing mainstream popular culture content worlds failed to adequately reflect their experiences as American Muslims. They turned to storytelling to counter this absence and increase visibility for themselves and others like them. Over time, their projects accumulated a grassroots content world of collected stories that the youth could leverage to talk about shared experiences and imagine other possibilities for their futures. In a climate where the compatibilities and conflicts of an American *and* Muslim identity are actively debated, storytelling assumes two important functions. Firstly, stories articulate diverse American Muslim experiences rather than falling back on the same limited and limiting sets of stereotypes that the youth found pervasive in the content worlds of mainstream media. Instead of being forced into a stereotypical role, these youth shared stories as they imagined a collective, but not homogeneous, identity in American society. Secondly, the circulation and discussion of stories supports and nurtures loosely connected, heterogeneous, yet in some ways cohesive networks that may become a counterpublic that mobilizes civic or political action. American Muslim storytelling does important political work precisely because it evades (or, as in the case of 30 Mosques, intentionally rejects) easy insertion into dominant narratives and existing political frameworks.

Some of the interviewed youth actively contributed American Muslim stories by creating, appropriating, and remixing content. Others were aware of such efforts and had circulated stories across their networks. Whether they told their own stories or shared others', these expressive practices have much to teach us about the ways storytelling bridges cultural experiences and political concerns. As Francesca Polletta (2009) observes: "Activists, like prophets, politicians, and advertising executives, have long recognized the power of a good story to move people to action" (33). Despite its persistence and prevalence, storytelling remains underexplored in social movement literature. When it is addressed, storytelling is often subsumed within what Robert D. Benford and David

A. Snow (2000) characterize as discussions of "framing," or belief processes that "assign meaning to and interpret relevant events and conditions in ways that are intended to mobilize potential adherents and constituents, to garner bystander support, and to demobilize antagonists" (614). While framing focuses on the delivery of "clear, concise, and coherent" messages, the power of stories, as Polletta observes, comes "from their allusiveness, indeed, their ambiguity" (33). Polletta (2006) highlights two analytical tasks relating to understanding storytelling in political contexts: "One is to identify the features of narrative that allow it to achieve certain rhetorical effects. The other is to identify the social conditions in which those rhetorical effects are likely to be politically consequential" (166–167). In the American Muslim case, the political dimensions are often front and center, even if the storytellers themselves do not see their creative projects as political. Even though his stories steer clear of political commentary, Bassam Tariq acknowledges "people tend to get political ideas from the [30 Mosques] blog." As Polletta also observes, stories may affirm the status quo, but they can also disrupt dominant meta-narratives. In the American Muslim context, the stories we encountered challenged mainstream stereotypes that the youth felt almost always connect Islam to terrorism. The youth saw their storytelling efforts as responding to a long history of "Orientalist tropes of Arabs," which, as media scholar Evelyn Alsultany (2012) notes, often conflate Muslims and Arabs "as rich oil sheiks, sultry belly dancers, harem girls, veiled oppressed women, and most notably, terrorists" (7). Building on similar tropes related to Asian American media portrayals, Lori Kido Lopez (2012) argues that analyses of stereotyping should "consider the complicated and nuanced ways in which viewers might read and interact with any kind of imagery, as well as how specific images are being deployed" (56). Ella Shohat and Robert Stam (2007) among others, argue that reducing stereotype analysis to positive and negative portrayals may not address the underlying complexities that drive these representations:

> The focus on "good" and "bad" characters in image analysis confronts racist discourse on that discourses favored ground. It easily elides into moralism, and thus into fruitless debates about the relative virtues of fictive characters . . . and the correctness of their fictional actions. (200–201)

Johanna Blakley and Sheena Nahm (2011), two researchers at the Norman Lear Center, reviewed prime-time dramas that included "War on Terror" themes and found that "sixty-seven percent of terror suspects in these shows were white" and only "fourteen percent were identified as Middle Eastern, Arab or Muslim" (8). Digging deeper into such prime-time narratives, Evelyn Alsultany finds that their creators often attempt to balance negative (i.e., terrorist) portrayals of Muslim characters with more positive representations of Muslims aligned with American ideals and beliefs, even as the plots still pivot around terrorism (18–47). Alsultany concludes that these attempts in the mainstream media to balance representations of good and evil Muslims are a crucial "aspect of the War on Terror" and "deflect attention from the persistence of racist policies post 9/11" (12).

Responding to this tendency, many of the youth-driven storytelling efforts we observed moved away from the "good" versus "bad" Muslim binary to express more complex, diverse, and morally ambiguous (yet still nonthreatening) American Muslim experiences. Bob, an Iranian American film maker who relied on online circulation for his movies, explained:

> I think it's time to tell the story of Muslim-Americans. . . . You should be confident enough in your Muslim identity [that] . . . it should be like, "I'm a filmmaker. I love politics and I'm a Muslim as well . . ." I think that type of integration needs to start happening within the stories that we tell.

Often these storytelling initiatives emerged as young American Muslims invited broader community participation with the goal of evoking a variety of narratives. Sometimes, they were supported by organizations (as in the case of MYG's Breakfast@Night). At other times, they revolved around small, but extremely active groups connected to others through loosely defined networks. Regardless of whether they were supported by organizations or not, all of these storytelling projects took advantage of networks (mostly on social media) to spread the word and garner participation.

These projects we observed were largely nonfictional and focused on participants' lived experiences. For example, Ridwan Adhami's "What Does a Muslim Look Like?" centered on a photo station placed at the

Islamic Society of North America (ISNA) annual conference in 2012. Adhami took photos of passersby, who could decide "how their image would be seen by the world." He then compiled these photos into a collage on Facebook. Adhami encouraged his audiences to "enjoy this gallery, share the images, use them as your own profile photos, tag people you know and that I don't." Many commentators recognized people in the face collage. In fact, many of the photographs were tagged with people's full names and linked to their Facebook accounts, thereby facilitating such recognition.

In another storytelling project, Nura Maznavi and Ayesha Mattu collected romantic stories by Muslim American women for their edited volume, *Love, InshAllah: The Secret Love Lives of American Muslim Women*. Presenting the book at a 2012 reading in West Los Angeles, its young editors stressed the diversity of the narratives in *Love, InshAllah* and the fact that several feature new and social media. In "Punk-Drunk Love," Tanzila Ahmed (2012) confesses that she has always "been a sucker for a man with a mohawk" and describes how a "deep online friendship that consisted of sharing lyrics and MP3s and having GChat conversations about life" spilled into a short-lived love affair with a Muslim punk rocker (58). In another story, Lena Hassan (2012) recalls how the "Internet" became "magic" to her as a "shy and burdened" teenager with a "crippling self-consciousness" who gained little experience with the opposite sex as her life revolved around her gender segregated mosque:

> I didn't have to hide on the Internet. Online, I forgot that I had a thing so unruly and potentially embarrassing as a tongue and body. . . . Paradoxically, in this world divided by barriers and buffers, I opened myself to people and they opened themselves to me. (234–236)

The book sold out on Amazon before it was released. Building on its success, the editors established a Love, InshAllah blog and called for submissions for a *Love, InshAllah* for men, which was published in early 2014.

Love, InshAllah developed out of the Hijabi Monologues, an earlier collective storytelling project inspired by the well-known episodic theater piece *The Vagina Monologues*. Similar in structure, the Hijabi Monologues began as local events at which participants shared personal stories. In 2011, the project's organizers embraced new media when they announced the Hijabi Monologues National Story Contest and invited women to submit their stories through YouTube: "The Hijabi Monologues (2012) is about the power of storytelling. . . . Through sharing stories, strangers touch and connect. Through stories, we are challenged. Through stories, we are humanized."

Some of the projects we looked at were one-off efforts. Others went through several different iterations, changing to respond to shifting interest and network demands. For example, the 30 Mosques project changed every year. In its first year, Bassam Tariq and Aman Ali collected the stories they discovered as they visited different New York City mosques. They also invited participation through their blog's comment section. The following year, Tariq and Ali took their project nationwide. For the next two years, they collected and shared stories from other American Muslims on their website. In 2012, Ali and Tariq revamped the whole project to encourage more direct participation. Using grant funding, they built an interface that allows people to contribute their own Ramadan photos through Flickr, Tumblr, and Twitter. Once approved (Tariq and Ali exercised some curatorial control here), these submissions appeared on 30mosques.com's mosaiclike home page, encouraging visitors to scroll and click through the diverse images and text. Ali offered his perspective on the project's evolution:

> Well, it's just a natural progression. . . . In 2009, it was just a very local venture around New York City. And then it became a cross-country thing in 2010 and 2011. And now it kind of transcends them to become more of a global and more of a virtual kind of project and that's just naturally where it's been going. As more and more people around the world are hearing about it and inspired to do things.

MYG's Breakfast@Night (which later became BF@N) also went through several iterations. In 2011, the project was mostly run over Facebook, as the organizers sent out a call for photographs documenting people's experience of Ramadan through their social media networks. The number of submissions overwhelmed the team. Jihad Turk recalls that news of the project "spread by word of mouth and within two weeks, the site not only got thousands of hits, but American Muslim youth were contributing their own photos from around the country with dozens of states and hundreds of cities being represented."

For their second year, the BF@N organizers took a different approach. They built a separate website rather than using Facebook. The breakfastatnight.com homepage welcomed visitors to "the one and only Ramadan photo project powered by YOU." The team expanded the call for submissions to include other media content. They also launched the BF@N blog, where a team of bloggers, including MYG youth, shared their Ramadan thoughts and experiences.

While diverse in their geographical scope, the other projects inspired by 30 Mosques shared similar goals and methods—all, for instance, used new media to collect and exchange stories of Muslims during the month of Ramadan. These Ramadan storytelling projects endeavored to present a more positive, human, and peaceful image of contemporary Islam, an important message for many American Muslim youth. In various ways, the projects also relied on new media. Aman Ali admits that without new media, "we just don't even have a project." Certainly, some of the projects, like the Hijabi Monologues and *Love, InshAllah* did not depend exclusively on new media, using live performance and print books, respectively. They did, however, benefit from new media in increasing their reach as the editors and directors turned to Facebook and other social media to recruit contributors and circulate what they created.

Crucially, these storytelling projects highlight how, as we have described, American Muslim youth identities are always already political and not simply cultural, as young people seek to define themselves as explicitly both American and Muslim in the context of the post-9/11 world. The significance of these tensions was brought into sharp focus in the days that followed the Boston Marathon bombings in April 2013. As investigators uncovered evidence that the Tsarnaev brothers had used the internet to access materials that supported their shift toward extremism, the debates around "online radicalization" intensified. For example, in an article published by the *New York Times* on April 23 (Cooper et al. 2013), "federal authorities" were said to have speculated that the brothers were "angry and alienated young men, apparently self-trained and unaffiliated with any particular terrorist group, able to use the Internet to learn their lethal craft." Similar statements were made during a debate—"Mining Online for What May Have Radicalized, Informed Tsarnaev Brothers" (2013)—televised on PBS the following day. During this discussion, Dr. Jerrold Post of George Washington University observed that "the phenomenon of radicalization online is really quite alarming. It's been estimated that there's some 4,800 radical Islamist websites. And I am struck that young women and men who are isolated, not feeling they belong, in this way, can belong to a virtual community of hatred."

Responding to the spread of such views, MPAC and the New Media Foundation organized a forum titled "Online Radicalization: Myths and Realities" in Washington, D.C., on May 28, 2013. During this session, one of the panelists, New America Foundation fellow Rabia Chaudry, identified "narrative" as the key to understanding and countering online radicalization. She described how the "You cannot be a good American and a good Muslim" narrative, ironically propagated both by Muslim extremists and anti-Islam advocates, fostered feelings of alienation among American Muslim youth. To counter this, she asked "Western Muslim communities to step up and become engaged and become partners in bringing their voices online to counter these narratives." While Chaudry's statements certainly situate narrative and storytelling as an important component of America's counterterrorism efforts, they also make clear the enormous challenges American Muslim youth face in defining their own terms of engagement through participatory politics. In fact, examining Chaudry's statements from the youth perspective returns us to the notion of "precariousness" raised earlier in this chapter as we pivot our attention to how such projects remain vulnerable to uninvited scrutiny.

Silence and Surveillance

Being a Muslim in America is not easy at all. There are a lot of uncertainties about our role in American narratives because of 9/11. . . . I think this is an issue for people, for Muslims in our community, whose civil liberties are being completely pillaged. You know there are people held without . . . whatever, I don't want to get into that too much.

Selina, a young American Muslim woman and an environmental activist, cut herself off when the conversation she had with Shresthova turned to concerns about civil liberties and privacy. She worried that post-9/11 security measures, such as the Patriot Act, have "pillaged" civil liberties. Selina also hesitated to speak about how surveillance of American Muslim communities had affected her behavior, but explained that she is not very active online even though she recognized that utilizing platforms like Twitter and Facebook would help her spread the word about her environmental causes.

Privacy and surveillance are both fraught concepts often positioned within a dichotomy of private versus public premised on what Helen Nissenbaum (2004) identifies as "the sanctity of certain spaces, or more abstractly, places" (102). While the specifics of the private/public dichotomy certainly merit attention, the American Muslim youth we interviewed articulated privacy in ways that echoed danah boyd and Alice Marwick's (2011) definition, "a sense of control over how and when information flows." American Muslim youth certainly do worry about surveillance that invades traditionally private realms—specifically, systematized monitoring systems put in place by governmental authorities and companies that work with them or may sometimes be obliged to. Such surveillance has, indeed, become a reality for some young American Muslim activists, particularly those involved in contentious social justice campaigns. Even youth who may be less involved in activist campaigns often practice "self-censorship" within what Evgeny Morozov (2012) describes as a "pervasive climate of uncertainty, anxiety, and fear" (145). As they struggle to find a semblance of comfort as they weigh the risks and possibilities of public expression, many young American Muslims strike a constantly shifting balance between finding voice and choosing silence.

During our research, one of the most urgently articulated concerns around the silencing power of surveillance surfaced in connection with what became known as the Irvine11 campaign, supporting a group of University of California, Irvine, students (all members of the Muslim Students' Union) arrested after they disrupted Israeli ambassador Michael Oren's speech on campus on November 8, 2010. Prosecutors used emails and online posts as evidence that the MSU members had planned their disruption of Ambassador Oren's speech well in advance. Tanya, an Irvine11 activist, recalled sitting in the courtroom during the trial and realizing how easily online exchanges could be used against the

Photo published in the *Daily Californian* shows students protesting convictions of students at UC Riverside and UC Irvine.

protesters: "They had every email from the MSU, every single email that anyone had sent out." Reflecting on her own previous involvement with social justice organizations, local nonprofits, and labor unions, Tanya stressed that these groups were "never really active on the internet." She recalled, "None of our communication would be online. None of it." Tanya admitted that she sometimes felt that the groups' avoidance of the internet bordered on paranoia because, "Who really cares about us, right? Who is really watching a bunch of misfit kids doing activism during college?" To her, the Irvine11 case drove home the reality that "they really are!" Someone "is really watching us!"

On the other hand, American Muslim youth also worried about what Alice Marwick (2012) calls "social surveillance" or "ongoing eavesdropping, investigation, gossip and inquiry that constitutes information gathering by people about their peers" (379). Such social surveillance can come from both inside and outside the Muslim community. Muslim peers and elders may dismiss and critique material young American Muslims share online. Hateful anti-Muslim remarks posted in the comments sections of blogs or YouTube videos can hurt youth as they struggle to express their often controversial perspectives. Many worried more about hostile "peer" audiences and "social surveillance" than about government surveillance. Youth who produce public-facing media, like blogs and YouTube channels, were particularly worried about toxic attacks on Islam and Muslims posted by trolls. They also feared harsh comments from other Muslims critical of what they posted online. These concerns often centered on what danah boyd and Alice Marwick (2011) call "context collapse," a concept discussed in Chapter 1, in which a social media user's "imagined audience might be entirely different from the actual readers of a profile, blog post, or tweet" (2). Whether they come from within or outside of Muslim communities, destructive comments have a chilling effect, constantly reminding youth that is impossible to control their content as it travels via social media.

One instance of "context collapse" occurred in December 2012 when MPAC decided to build on its long-term interfaith efforts and held its annual convention at the All Saints Church in Pasadena. The group's choice of venue drew news attention when several anti-Muslim groups pressured the church to withdraw its hospitality. When All Saints refused, they staged a vocal protest outside the church. Arriving convention participants had to walk past anti-Islamic placards. Wardah Khalid (2012), a young American Muslim blogger, reflected on this experience in her blog post after the convention:

> I wasn't quite sure what to expect as I headed to the church that morning, but I guessed I might run into a few protesters there. Sure enough, they were there to greet me when I arrived. Just outside the front doors stood several men holding signs that insulted the Prophet Muhammad (PBUH). They had planted themselves there several hours prior to the start of the convention and were making it quite clear that they were vehemently opposed to Islam and any Christians who associated with its followers.

Khalid's blog inspired much commentary. Most of the responses were positive; a few however, reinforced the protesters' antagonistic stance, effectively bringing the confrontation outside All Saints onto the internet. "Vallie," a particularly insistent commenter, got involved in sharp exchanges: "You guys can call me a bigot and hater all day long, it doesn't bother me one bit, nor am I ashamed. I do in fact hate Islam. It is a death cult."

As discussed earlier, new and social media provide important opportunities for young American Muslims, like Wardah, to express themselves and network with other like-minded young people. But the content they create and share can be manipulated toward very different ends in what Lissa Soep (2012) has called its "digital afterlife" (94; see Chapter 2 for a more detailed discussion of this concept.) The youth who had their own public-facing blogs were aware that there were critics ready to jump on what they posted. Tanisha, a young Pakistani American, observed that "because Muslims are criticized so much in America, a lot of students just don't want to show that they're even Muslim." For some youth, the possibility of negative responses deterred them from making public their religious affiliation, let alone political views related to their faith.

While the American Muslim youth we met certainly thought about top-down surveillance and anti-Muslim sentiment, many more were more worried about "friendly fire" from other, more conservative community members. Some of these critiques came from elders concerned about young people's safety. Others came from youth with very stringent notions of what behavior is acceptable in Islam. The criticism faced by Mo and Nash, known as the HijabiBengaliSisters, is a case in point. Mo and Nash create and post videos on their YouTube channel that playfully address faith-related topics (religious perspectives on dating, fasting during Ramadan) relevant to American Muslim youth. Several of their videos reacted to what they call other Muslim "critiquers" of their channels. In one video, titled "Muslim Critics," Nash says:

> If somebody sends you a message on YouTube attacking you, saying you are the worst representation of Islam, like you are a poor excuse for a hijabi—what do you know about that, really? I don't see you having the courage to get up on YouTube and talk about Islam, because that is a huge thing in itself. Especially being our age, that we are, in our teenage pre-adultish years, you won't see many people on YouTube starting that early. . . . I can see why some people would leave Islam because they are so afraid of the Muslims, of the Muslim critics in this community.

Criticism of the HijabiBengaliSisters escalated in April 2013, when someone used the alias Nashiha Monika to create "The Truth about Hijabibengalisisters" Facebook page dedicated to disparaging them.

The page featured photographs that the sisters had posted on their own Facebook page and comments like "The sisters would have you believe their fame is knowledge. But having over ten thousand followers or a million followers dose [*sic*] not mean you are knowledgeable. FAME IS NOT KNOWLEDGE." The experience of the HijabiBengaliSisters highlights the burden of representation some American Muslim youth bear as they become more publicly visible online. While some, like Mo and Nash, desire to positively "represent" Islam and Muslims, not all youth share this desire, particularly given the harsh criticism to which those with a public presence are often subjected from both within and outside their communities. Selina explained that though her "faith is a big part" of her environmental activism, this is not something she wants to "tell the outside world."

Clearly, privacy and surveillance are urgent concerns for American Muslim youth. They are aware that their communities top the lists of domestic national security concerns. At the same time, these youth worry about privacy more broadly defined. They are concerned about being judged by other Muslims. They also worry about being bullied by "haters." Much like the youth in boyd and Marwick's (2011) study who care about privacy, but with the additional burdens of being Muslim post-9/11, the American Muslim youth negotiate privacy and surveillance concerns alongside their efforts to engage with others within infrastructures they cannot fully control.

Humor over Silence

"I always assume that we're being watched," Wajahat Ali, an American Muslim playwright and journalist, weighed in on surveillance during the "Storytelling and Digital-Age Civics" webinar series that our Media, Activism, and Participatory Politics (MAPP) research team organized in January 2014. He tries to move past such concerns by acknowledging privacy invasion is now a fact of life in all online encounters:

> I sometimes send emails to my friends saying, "Hello NSA" (even in my texts), because I think appreciating the dark humor of it all makes it go down a bit easier and it's a little bit more cathartic. But also it keeps you on your toes to be smarter about how you frame that content.

In explaining how he thinks about surveillance, Ali made a very important point—he identified humor as an important, even "cathartic," strategy for coping with privacy concerns among American Muslims.

Maz Jobrani, an Iranian American comedian, made a similar observation during a performance in 2005. He related how he once had his Hotmail account shut down after he jokingly referenced terrorism in an email to a friend:

> Another friend of mine was at the show, and the next day he emailed me. He said, "Hey, Maz. Had a great time at your show last night. By the way, when is the next terrorist hit going down? Ha ha." So I got on my Hotmail and I was like, I am not being flagged, I can respond, right? So I was like [changes his voice], "Hey, man, I have been talking to Al-Qaeda and the next hit is going down on the lower east side of Iceland. Ha ha." Send. Next day, I try to log onto Hotmail. Account closed. Access denied. . . . It took me weeks, but finally I am back on the internet. But I am freaked out. And you should be too. Don't joke on the internet. . . . Don't send me an email like "Hey, Maz, when is the next terrorist hit going down?" because I will respond like "Fuck you. I am a patriot."

Much like Aman Ali used Angry Birds to ridicule surveillance, as described in this chapter's opening, Wajahat Ali and Maz Jobrani also identified humor as a powerful tool for countering (or at least partially subverting) surveillance's potentially chilling effect. In doing this, they all connected to a larger, and still growing, body of post-9/11 American Muslim comedy.

Ahmed Ahmed, another American Muslim comedian, reflected on the growing role of comedy in the community during an interview that aired as part of a PBS documentary in 2009: "I think the general perception of Islam is so serious that we have a hard time laughing at ourselves or with ourselves. And, if we can't laugh at ourselves or with ourselves, the rest of the world won't." Ahmed spoke from experience. He and Jobrani were founding members of the "Axis of Evil" comedy tour, whose name played off the term that President George Bush introduced during his State of the Union in 2002 to describe Iran, Iraq, and North Korea. Between 2005 and 2011, the group toured extensively in the United States and abroad, and was, at one point, even sponsored by the U.S. Department of State. Numerous other American Muslim comedy tours and shows were organized in the wake of 9/11, including "Allah Made Me Funny" and "The Muslims Are Coming!" In 2007, *Little Mosque on the Prairie,* a CBC sitcom about the travails of a mosque community in a small town in Canada, became a milestone for North American Muslim comedy on mainstream television, running for six seasons. These and other American Muslim post-9/11 comedy projects illustrate the finding of Mucahit Bilici (2010) that there was "an upsurge in ethnic comedy by Muslims in America" in the decade following 9/11 (196).

When we introduced "bridging" and "bonding" as concepts in in Chapter 1, we argued that in-group "bonding" is particularly important for marginalized groups to protect them from hostile outsiders. We saw "bridging" as a closely related set of practices that allow such a group to reach beyond its own in-group borders to build support and deepen connections to other allied communities. Ethnic humor can assume both a "bridging" and "bonding" role for an emergent American Muslim public. Delving more deeply into humor's dual bridging and bonding roles, Bilici observes that these American Muslim comedy projects all humorously highlight, subvert, and "criticize both the majority and their own minority communities" (201). At times, they do this by engaging with particularly tense moments and spaces for American Muslims in the United States, for instance the anxieties of passing through security checks at airports and boarding airplanes. At other times, they turn their attention inward to explore what it is like to live in American Muslim communities, for instance, by highlighting first-to-second generational differences within families. In both instances, they intentionally use humor to move past cultural differences, promote dialogue, and break down dominant stereotypes in ways that release tensions and ease fear. Thus read, such humor does important work by strengthening "bonding" within American Muslim communities, "bridging" to a broader American audience, and desensitizing otherwise taboo topics—like surveillance, dissent within Islam, and Islamophobia.

In *Satire TV: Politics and Comedy in the Post-Network Era,* Jonathan Gray, Jeffrey P. Jones, and Ethan Thompson (2009) argue that "humor allows a relatively open space for critique and reflection, one that is rare in many societies" (11). They quote from the seminal text "Implicit Meanings" by Mary Douglas (2010, 150), who pushes for an even more interventionist perspective on humor when she observes that "jokes have a subversive effect on the dominant structure of ideas," as they challenge accepted social patterns by rendering visible assumptions and biases that may have been previously unapparent. (As they do so, she adds, we must keep in mind that there is only a thin line between certain jokes and insults, suggesting humor can backfire and intensify rather than diminish frictions within or between groups.) Drawing on their review of existing literature on humor, Gray and Thompson similarly conclude that "far from being solely light, frivolous, and wholly apolitical, humor is able to deal powerfully with serious issues and power and politics" (8–11). Amarnath Amarasingam (2010) argues that we should, in fact, think of American Muslim comedians as "a significant social force" in post-9/11 America (464).

American Muslim comedy continues to evolve. In the early post-9/11 years, it was dominated by "stand up" live and eventually televised comedy routines like those created by Maz Jobrani and Ahmed Ahmed, which sought to create a "cultural space" where, Jaclyn Michael (2013) notes, humor was deployed to "engage with the stereotypes and realities of being both Muslim and American." As Michael further observes, American Muslim comedy of this era situated "Muslims in a long history of American minority groups using public humor to address and contest the terms of American social life and national belonging" (130). Such humor often draws on prevalent minority stereotypes, which are, as Mahadev Apte (1985) observes, "crucial to ethnic humor and its appreciation" (114). As he explores the history of black humor in the United States, Lawrence Levine (2007) notes,

> The need to laugh at our enemies, our situation, ourselves, is a common one, but it most often exists the most urgently in those who exert the least power over their immediate environment; in those who have the most objective reasons for feelings of hopelessness. (300)

However momentarily, such humor enables a comic inversion of existing power structures that are stacked against the specific minority community.

Our research suggests that post-9/11 American Muslim humor does such political work and has also, more recently, become more grassroots and participatory, with more reliance on collective storytelling and networked circulation. For example, Bob, a young filmmaker who regularly visited MYG, saw his social media network as his "personal *Daily Show*" that's "wrapped up" in a Twitter feed; he followed members of his American Muslim network, including activist and playwright Wajahat Ali, scholar Reza Aslan, community activist Linda Sarsour, filmmaker Lena Khan, and comedian Asif Ali. Bob chuckled as he explained how this humor works: "Let's say . . . some ridiculous Islamophobic event happens where Mitt Romney said something goofy about Muslims. . . . It's like the jokes and how we're reacting to it. I find those kinds of communication really interesting." As Bob's *Daily Show* analogy suggests, humor plays an important role in shaping the material that circulates through young American Muslim networks.

During our research, we saw how American Muslim youth circulated humor as a form of social commentary, often responding to news-related triggers—two examples illustrate this process. The first, the "Un-Aired Lowe's Commercial for *All-American Muslim*" created by Gregory Bonsignore, Parvesh Cheena, and Rizwan Manji, was produced and circulated as part of the Lowe's boycott, a networked campaign (previously mentioned in Chapter 1) that responded to the home improvement retail company's decision to pull its advertising from the *All-American Muslim* reality TV series. The commercial opens with a group of men, clearly identified as Muslims, going to shop at Lowe's. We see them walking around the store, picking up supplies that suggest they might be building a bomb, an impression intensified by the suspicious looks of other customers. As the tension mounts, we see them assembling something. In the final seconds, they flick the switch . . . to the elaborate Christmas lights they have just installed on their house. Suddenly, the men's demeanor changes and they smile proudly. Superimposed text wishes the viewer "Happy Holidays from everyone at Lowe's."

This advertising parody quickly spread through American Muslim social media networks. One comment on YouTube enthusiastically exclaimed: "OMG I cannot stop_ laughing. . . . I see these as two men as human beings. . . . GREAT VIDEO!!" For others, the "Un-Aired

Lowe's Commercial" signaled more serious concerns. In his comment, rjreeder64 explained:

> lol, I love the humor . . . but what I really hate is when muslims get such dirty looks when in public. . . . I have received similar looks when I wear my koufi in public and people seem to pay me no mind when i go into the same exact store with a fitted cap on.

Reflecting on the Lowe's controversy, Dilshad Ali (2011), a prominent American Muslim journalist, observes that the decision to withdraw advertising "unwittingly inspired a sudden grassroots coalition . . . dedicated to defending American values and fighting back against hate."

The second example is the social media campaign that coalesced in response to the *Newsweek* cover article "Muslim Rage," written by Ayaan Hirsi Ali (2012), an openly atheist Somali Dutch activist and Islam skeptic. In the article, Ali reflected on the violence in Libya that had culminated in the killing of the ambassador and three other staff members at the American embassy in 2012. She argued against sympathy for post-Gaddafi Libyans because they had made a "choice to reject freedom as the West understands it." Though the article inspired an often heated debate, the most visible reaction played out on Twitter when *Newsweek* invited readers to discuss the article under the #MuslimRage hashtag. Soon, the social media platform buzzed with humorous tweets that both questioned Ali's argument and poked fun at the hashtag. For example, Hend commented on the fact that no one notices her hair, because she wears a headscarf, while Hijabi Girl playfully mused on the multiple meanings of Jihad:

Hijabi Girl @HijabiGrlPrblms
You lose your nephew at the airport but you can't yell his name because it's JIHAD. #muslimrage
Expand ← Reply ⟲ Retweet ★ Favorite

Hend @LibyaLiberty
I'm having such a good hair day. No one even knows. #MuslimRage
Retweeted 2198 times

Tweets from Hijabi Girl and Hend.

At last count, Hijabi Girl's one-liner had been retweeted 2,198 times. Many of the #MuslimRage posts explicitly challenged widespread stereotypes about Muslims and Islam, illustrating the creative and civic potential of such networked responses.

Confronting Precariousness?

> The Islam I grew up with in America is not the Islam my children are experiencing. The possibilities for their lives are much more expansive than the possibilities for my life were. The largely comfortable integration and success of American Muslims that sets them apart from their counterparts in Europe also lends space for these possibilities. From tremendously increased participation in American civic and cultural life, to pressing internal demands on religious orthodoxy, another generation or two will see a vastly different American Islam that will likely have an impact on Muslims globally. From marginalized minority, American Muslims are poised to become mainstream leaders and influencers. And it's no small irony that while historians bemoan conquest and Western colonialism as the death knell for Islam's "Golden Age," this new Muslim renaissance is growing out of the West itself.

In an article published in *Time* on April 16, 2014, Rabia Chaudry gave a decidedly positive assessment of the current situation of Muslims living in United States. As she pointed to the significant role that American Muslims play in important current debates around issues like homosexuality and Islam, Chaudry boldly concluded that not only is their situation more stable than it was a decade ago, it is leading towards what she envisions as "a Muslim Renaissance" as American Muslims revisit, contest, or revise religious tenets that no longer serve their needs. Her celebratory tone suggested that American Muslims may now be moving beyond precariousness. Is this really the case? Will the expressive projects described across this chapter eventually transform how their fellow Americans think about these youth and embrace them for their active contributions to participatory politics?

Reflecting on our research, the American Muslim youth we encountered were struggling to balance the benefits and risks of public expression. Determined to tell their stories and challenge existing stereotypes, they have turned to new media platforms and practices as a means to circumvent perceived roadblocks. As traditional advocacy organizations have sought to censor open discussions within the physical space of their local mosques, the youth have sometimes moved these discussions online, forging a potentially supportive peer-to-peer network. As stereotyped portrayals of Islam obstruct the development of a diverse and realistic understanding of their actual lives, American Muslim youth have used digital media tools to collect and share more authentic stories. As concerns over government surveillance have grown, the youth have harnessed humor to acknowledge and ultimately alleviate some of the resulting strain. As more conservative Muslims have slammed young American Muslims for transgressing Islamic norms, the youth have sometimes turned to each other for support. Sometimes. At other times, the youth have withdrawn and chosen silence as their supportive networks faltered under pressure.

Many of the American Muslim youth we interviewed and observed saw new media as crucial tools for exploring issues, expressing their experiences, and connecting with others. They also possessed a heightened awareness of the risks of uninvited scrutiny and surveillance. During our research, we saw the youth networks that connected them teeter several times in response to particular events, which mostly occurred outside the young people's immediate vicinity. For example, many youth went completely silent in the aftermath of the Boston bombings as public discourse turned to "online radicalization." Such networks are thus fragile and precarious, but we might also describe them as liminal and elusive, providing means of escaping the constraints imposed on these youth by various adult authorities. Many of these expressive projects originated outside institutional contexts as formal organizations like MPAC and ICSC played more of a supportive rather than leadership role in their creation and circulation.

For many of the youth included in our study, living in a post-9/11 United States has been defined, at least in part, by their struggles with (and against) antiterrorist security measures. As being a Muslim was perceived as a threat, they had to rally to defend and define their own cultural and spiritual identities while combatting racial profiling and heightened scrutiny. In this context, circulating stories, creating media, acknowledging surveillance, and leveraging humor become crucial practices for an emergent American Muslim counterpublic. As we will see in Chapter 5, the production of "coming out" videos has played a similar role for the DREAMers, undocumented youth struggling for the right to stay in this country and get an education. There, we will get deeper into the affective and psychological consequences of being able to voice your own experiences, as well as the tactical advantages this activist network gained by being able to tap the affordances of social media and participatory culture.

5

DREAMing Citizenship

Undocumented Youth, Coming Out, and Pathways to Participation

Liana Gamber-Thompson and Arely M. Zimmerman

"My name is Mohammad, and I am undocumented," explains a young man speaking directly into the lens of a handheld camera. In a dimly lit room that could belong to almost any 20-something, with magazines stacked on the windowsill and a poster for a popular TV series on the wall, Mohammad tells the story of his parents' migration to the U.S. when he was three years old. He describes the difficulties he has faced as an undocumented student, including revocation of his college acceptance letter when admissions officers realized they had overlooked his undocumented citizenship status. Mohammad recounts how he was rejected from his "dream school" because he did not have a "nine-digit number." Those nine digits, of course, refer to a social security number, which, for most U.S. citizens his age, holds little meaning beyond that little blue card that needs to be fished out of a wallet or filing cabinet now and then. For Mohammad, however, that number means acceptance or rejection.

In his five-minute-long YouTube video—titled, after his onscreen declaration, "My Name Is Mohammad and I Am Undocumented"—he explains how the disappointment of being turned away from college, along with Congress's failure to pass the 2007 DREAM (Development Relief Education for Alien Minors) Act, prompted him to become active in the DREAM movement. He ends the video by encouraging others to rally around the DREAM Act and to pursue higher education. He also stresses the importance of "coming out" as undocumented, both for the cause, but also for the individuals involved, many of whom have felt they had no choice but to conceal their citizenship status.

Mohammad's story is just one of many that were part of the National Coming Out of the Shadows Week campaign in 2011, a youth-organized event in which undocumented youth and their allies uploaded hundreds of video testimonials onto sites like YouTube and Vimeo. This effort, along with those held in more recent years, stemmed from the eponymous one-day event staged on March 10, 2010, in Chicago's Federal Plaza by youth who wanted to come out as "undocumented and unafraid." The Immigrant Youth Justice League now helps groups across the country stage events throughout March for National Coming Out of the Shadows Month, though the production of coming out videos seems to have peaked in 2010 and 2011.

These coming out videos mark a very significant convention—though, as we explain later, an often ephemeral one—for young DREAM activists, or DREAMers as they often call themselves. DREAMers take their name from the acronym for the legislation they are rallying behind, but it's not lost on most participants or those they are seeking to influence that the term has a number of other important connotations. Not only does it speak to the role that dreams play in the civic imagination (dreams of a new future) but also to the nation's political past and present. By calling themselves DREAMers, these young people evoke the American Dream—one that is being rewritten to include not just economic prosperity, but also the affordances of citizenship—and echo Martin Luther King Jr.'s iconic call for racial equality, "I Have a Dream."

Video confessionals like Mohammad's are a central focus of this chapter, which examines a group of youth who have used digital media to build a national movement for immigrant rights against great political, legal, economic, and technological barriers. Specifically, we show how undocumented youth activists have used digital media to meet individual affective/therapeutic ends, create an archive of DREAMer stories and experiences, and engage in movement tactics that lead to and support on-the-ground action.

We point to the ways that DREAMers have used digital media to build on historically situated practices of mobilization and movement building, showing how DREAMers are not completely "reinventing the wheel" when it comes to activism, but making creative use of new media to put a new face on civil rights activism in the 21st century. We argue that DREAMer practices, both affective and tactical, constitute a new repertoire of action to effect change by providing opportunities for members of traditionally marginalized groups to enact citizenship and

DREAMers march. Image courtesy of Immigrant Youth Justice League.

become politically engaged. The case of the DREAMers is illustrative of how the affective and tactical elements of movements are so often blended and symbiotic (Johnson 2009); we want to show how both aspects of the movement are equally important. We examine coming out videos and other "testimonios" to demonstrate how the affective and strategic are not at odds in this movement but, rather, are occurring simultaneously and are mutually reinforcing. Moreover, we argue that these practices of engagement are not necessarily limited to current causes and circumstances, but may represent the shape of new social movements to come.

This chapter draws on data collected by Arely M. Zimmerman in 2010 and 2011; Zimmerman conducted media content analysis, event observations, and 25 semistructured interviews with DREAM activists residing in California, Illinois, Georgia, and Texas (Zimmerman 2012). Only three of the youth interviewed were U.S. citizens. While Mexico was their primary country of origin, some of the youth came from Colombia, Nigeria, El Salvador, Poland, and Chile. Passel and Cohn (2009) estimate that there were 1.7 million undocumented youth between the ages of 18–24 living in the United States in 2008 and that Latinos represented

78 percent of this population. All but three of the youth were enrolled in an institution of higher learning or had completed their bachelor's degree at the time of the interviews. Liana Gamber-Thompson did additional interviews with key DREAMers in 2014 to update our understanding of what has happened to this movement over time.

The Emergence of DREAM Activism

Since 2001, Congress has been considering various versions of the DREAM Act, which would provide an opportunity for undocumented students with "good moral character" who have lived in the U.S. for a certain period to obtain legal status. Due to several compromises to secure bipartisan support, the DREAM Act has undergone significant changes, including the replacement of a community service provision with military service. Over time, these changes, including the lowering of the age limit to 30 years, narrowed the bill's reach and significantly decreased the number of youth who would actually qualify. A 2009 appraisal of the bill estimated that about 2 million unauthorized youth would immediately benefit from the Dream Act, but only 33 percent may benefit from the educational path in the bill (Passel and Cohn 2009). Despite the way its potential effect has been constricted, the DREAM Act has nonetheless sparked unprecedented student and youth activism because it offers one of the few viable pathways to legalization. The DREAM movement, thus, represents the first national youth-led movement for immigrant rights of its kind (Passel and Cohn 2009). While youth have been active in immigrant rights issues historically, the immigrant rights mobilizations of the mid-2000s provided a key structural opening for youth to become more engaged. We refer to the series of massive protests and other actions that took place between the spring of 2006 and 2007 to oppose a draconian immigration bill passed in December 2005 by a Republican majority in the House of Representatives, and to demand comprehensive immigration reform. Nearly 40,000 students staged walkouts in Southern California alone in March 2006, snarling traffic on Los Angeles freeways and thoroughfares with marches to City Hall. These protests mirrored the now famous East L.A. Chicano walkouts of 1968, wherein high school students staged a series of protests against discriminatory educational practices in the

Los Angeles Unified School District. Seven hundred high school students walked out in El Paso, Texas, in late March 2006, as well, with thousands of students also marching in other cities across the country, such as Dallas and San Diego (Gonzalez 2008). These efforts cemented undocumented youth activists' significant place in the broader immigrant rights movement.

Though Congress has yet to pass the DREAM Act, there have been several important national victories since its introduction in 2001. While we refrain from making any causal claims, we speculate that the increased visibility of DREAMers and other young immigrant rights activists in the past decade has had an influence in shifting the national debate on immigration. In June 2012, President Obama announced that his administration would stop deporting young undocumented students that met certain criteria outlined in the legislation. Additionally, in August 2012, U.S. Citizenship and Immigration Services started accepting applications through the Deferred Action for Childhood Arrivals (DACA) program, which enables individuals who immigrated before the age of 16 and who are currently under 31 to apply for deferred removal action should they meet certain criteria such as having a clear criminal record and some history of attending school. DACA does not, however, offer a pathway to citizenship.

DREAMer activism has also drawn attention to other pressing issues, including the Obama administration's deportation policies and the heavily criticized federal program Secure Communities, an information-sharing partnership between the U.S. Immigration and Customs Enforcement (ICE) agency and the Federal Bureau of Investigation (FBI), which effectively turns local law enforcement into de facto Border Patrol agents. DREAMers had little visibility on a national level when the research for this case study began in 2010, but within two years that had changed. Benita Veliz, a young DREAM activist, took the stage at the 2012 Democratic National Convention to tell her story, and President Obama mentioned DREAMers in both his 2012 presidential inauguration speech and his 2013 State of the Union address. One early episode of *Scandal*, the hit TV political drama that debuted in 2012, depicted events that might lead to the passage of the DREAM Act, suggesting its growing hold on the civic imaginations of many Americans.

The emergence of the DREAM movement is particularly impressive given the national and local laws and policies that present serious barriers to political participation by undocumented immigrants, who have been deported at a record-setting rate in recent years. Based on data from the Department of Homeland Security and a 2013 *Bloomberg Businessweek* report, the Obama administration carried out roughly 1.8 million removals from when he first took office in January 2009 through September 7, 2013 (Vicens 2014). At this rate, the Obama administration is poised to surpass the total deportations during George W. Bush's two terms in office (a little over 2 million) by a considerable margin.

New ordinances and laws targeting undocumented immigrants are also being enacted and considered in a number of states and localities. Take, for instance, Arizona SB 1070, signed into law by Governor Jan Brewer in 2010. Perhaps the most aggressive such legislation in the country, the act would have made not carrying immigration papers a misdemeanor (a provision overturned by the U.S. Supreme Court) and requires law enforcement officials to determine the immigration status of those stopped or detained in routine situations like traffic stops.

Other states and localities have recently enacted laws banning undocumented immigrants from renting homes, penalizing employers who hire them, and barring undocumented youth from universities. Meanwhile, for the last four years, the number of states that allow undocumented students to receive in-state tuition has plateaued. As of summer 2014, 18 states now offer in-state tuition to undocumented immigrants, but many states are now looking to roll back in-state tuition or pass laws preventing undocumented immigrants from attending. The most recent punitive measures have been passed in new immigrant destinations such as South Carolina, Georgia, and Alabama, which have banned undocumented youth from universities and state colleges. The criminalization of undocumented immigrant status, institutionalized and reinforced through a complex system of policies and laws enacted over the last 20 years, affects immigrants' everyday lives in multiple ways. Obtaining a driver's license, library card, state identification card, or credit card is contingent on possessing a social security number. While most undocumented youth "pass" as American citizens because of their English-language fluency and social acculturation, they are continuously evading workplace and apartment raids by authorities, challenges to their mobility due to their lack of driver's licenses, and other commonly taken for granted privileges of citizenship. Moreover, many undocumented youth live among families that are struggling with poverty, lack of fixed employment, and other economic stressors.

Despite All Odds: Working around the Participation Gap with New Media

The lack of legal immigration status presents several roadblocks to political participation for DREAMer youth. Most obviously, direct forms of political participation like voting or running for elected office are impossible for DREAMers. But there are other ways that undocumented status impacts the ability to become socially and politically involved. Susana Maria Muñoz (2008, 2013) argues that undocumented status can disengage youth, as they become disaffected, frustrated, and alienated. Furthermore, undocumented youth face an increased threat of deportation, making engagement in politics a high-risk activity. Undocumented youth cope with these circumstances in different ways, including "passing" by not publicly revealing their legal identities to teachers, counselors, or peers. Participants in the DREAM movement have referred to this as "living in the shadows," a condition that makes establishing a sense of community difficult.

Despite these barriers to political empowerment, a sector of undocumented youth has shown a propensity for civic, community, and political engagement. At times, by excelling academically and becoming civically engaged, undocumented youth forge a sense of belonging. Almost counterintuitively, many undocumented youth transform their legal status into a motivation to succeed, rather than viewing it as a roadblock. A recent study by Terriquez and Patler (2012) based on a random sample of undocumented youth in California showed that many undocumented youth activists are excelling academically in high school or college, and are leaders on their campuses and in their communities, despite their low socioeconomic status.

Inequalities in digital media literacy and access to digital technologies have raised concern that the "digital divide" is widening, especially among racial and low-income communities. On the other hand, there is growing evidence that members of marginalized communities—especially youth—are adopting digital media tools and skills to empower themselves, build social movements, and participate politically. The Terriquez survey revealed that undocumented youth activists participate online at high rates, creating their own media, sustaining blogs, and sharing political opinions and news with their peers using social media. In defiance of an expectation of social alienation, these youth are in fact deeply engaged in their civic, social, and cultural communities. Undocumented youth are American in every sense of the word except legal status. An overwhelming majority of undocumented youth migrated before the age of five. Abrego (2006, 2008) observes that undocumented youth are often fluent in English, have been socialized in and graduated from American schools, and view themselves as no different than their peers.

One of the ways that undocumented youth have connected and formed communities despite their legal uncertainty is through their engagement in online participatory cultures. Social and digital media tools have given undocumented youth a way to amplify their voices and connect to others similarly situated. It is in this digital landscape that DREAMers have so successfully harnessed the power of social connection, taking advantage of video sharing, in particular, to tell their stories as undocumented youth and to "come out" of the shadows.

Identity is central to movement building and understanding why people participate, and the case of the DREAMers is no exception. Polletta and Jasper (2001) define collective identity as an individual's cognitive, moral, and emotional connection with a broader community, and argue that collective identity contributes to positive feelings for group members. Such identities involve the perception of a shared status or relation, and are often expressed via cultural resources—names, narratives, symbols, verbal styles, rituals, clothing, and so on (285). Scholars of civic engagement and social movements have acknowledged that the presence of a robust collective identity is a necessary ingredient for sustained political engagement. Activists' efforts to strategically "frame" identities are critical in recruiting participants (291). "Frames" are the interpretive packages that activists develop to mobilize potential adherents and constituents (Snow et al. 1986; Gamson 1988; Snow and Benford 1992; Tarrow 1998).

DREAMers have used new media practices to both create and strengthen movement identity, particularly through storytelling in coming out videos as well as other kinds of testimonials. Community-based organizations regularly use digital media tools to help generate feelings of group identity. Sharing one's story involves high risk, and thus doing so fosters an ethos of trust, mutuality, and reciprocity that contributes to a sense of collective identification both in online and offline spaces.

In his widely cited 2010 takedown of so-called slacktivism, Malcolm Gladwell argues that activism rooted in social media requires no real sacrifice such as that experienced by civil rights activists of the early 1960s who endured concrete threats of arrest, bodily harm, and even death (in part, this is the consequence of Gladwell's view of online activism as totally virtual—not involving real bodies in real space). He argues that, unlike most forms of contemporary social media activism, civic rights activism was high-risk. While the DREAMers also engage in forms of on-the-ground activism of the sort he champions, such as staged "graduations" and confrontation of ICE officials, we argue that the online tactic of producing coming out videos is equally laden with risk. In the case of the DREAMers, the simple, low-bar act of uploading a confessional video recorded in one's own bedroom can become a political grenade when the possible outcome is deportation. In that sense, the DREAMer movement is very much like the counterpublics constructed by American Muslim youth: a group brought together by its members' shared struggles for dignity and acceptance in American society, and one in an often precarious state, given the range of factors that have made it difficult for participants to sustain their efforts or achieve their goals.

It's also important to remember that the online activism Gladwell so laments is often tied to place in very concrete ways. As Erick Huerta, an undocumented activist who has been granted deferred action ("relief from removal" from the U.S. under DACA) and blogs by the name El Random Hero, pointed out in 2014, the act of coming out online can be riskier for some DREAMers than others depending on their geographic locale. He explained:

> So we really have instances here in Los Angeles where we're really progressive. You know it's California, it's a big state, there's a big Latino population. We have that elbow room to be more open and to be more bold and to be more out there as opposed to folks who are in the Midwest or-

ganizing what's a completely different set of issues. It's very hard to navigate those [online] spaces because as somebody who is in California and undocumented, there's so many different privileges that I have and folks that are in other states don't even have and say tuition or access to higher education and issues like that.

Thousands of young people have shared their coming out stories on digital media platforms, pointing to the pivotal role that new media activism has played in mobilizing broader forms of youth participation. In his video, Mohammad declared that coming out does not need to happen in "a press conference or in front of a big audience," but rather can be done effectively in the privacy of your own room with a camera, a point that speaks to the contrast between the networked participation of the DREAMer movement and more hierarchical media strategies of immigrant rights movements that preceded it (such older tactics were bound up with the logics of broadcast media, with talk radio hosts, press conferences, etc. taking on central roles), as well as a shift in media influence, from centralized to decentralized modes. As part of these newer campaigns, undocumented youth became increasingly willing to come out to their peers, teachers, and friends. Using blogs, podcasts, and user-generated video, undocumented youth have declared their legal status openly, many for the first time. Abrego (2013) notes that coming out videos are a radical departure from early organizing in which youth covered their faces with masks or used aliases while giving their testimony. And the prominence of personal blogs used for coming out provides evidence that new media practices have played a key role in the movement's mobilizing strategy.

Coming Out Online

Coming out videos represent an important convention adopted by DREAMers, especially during the early 2010s as DREAM activism ramped up nationwide. Undocumented youth have spread their stories, not only on video sharing sites like YouTube and Vimeo, but across social media platforms, including Tumblr, Facebook, Twitter, and Vine. In 2011, DreamActivist.org, a youth-founded online resource for young DREAMers, housed a section titled "Our Stories" where youth were asked to come out as undocumented. Around the same time, the Illinois Coalition for Immigrant Justice and Refugee Rights asked youth to submit audio recordings of their stories. Sharing these stories is a practice that came to define the organizing repertoires of both individuals and networks (formal and ad hoc) in the early days of the DREAMer movement, and "coming out" remains a central term in its lexicon. It is difficult to trace the exact origin of the coming out video within the DREAMer movement, but it is clear that DREAM activists combined a familiarity with the conventions of the LGBTQ movement with their knowledge of video blogging techniques to publicly claim ownership of their undocumented status and shine a light on their experiences. What's more, as we discuss in greater depth later in this chapter, this seemingly risky move may actually have helped safeguard against detention and deportation in some instances, by building informed and action-ready audiences.

The format used in many coming out videos is a familiar one, echoing the "Hi, my name is ———, and I'm an alcoholic" greeting customarily used in Alcoholics Anonymous meetings since at least the 1940s (Alcoholics Anonymous n.d.) and later in a variety of 12-step programs. Of course, the term "coming out" also has a long history in relation to LGBTQ activism. The phrase, whose origins can be traced to the early 20th century, initially referred to the kind of "coming out" a debutante would engage in upon entering high society; that is, the act of coming out involved entering *into* queerness or the "gay world" (Chauncey 1994). By the 1950s, though, the term took on its contemporary usage, which signifies a coming *out* of hiding, out of the closet, or, as many DREAMers have said, out of the shadows. Chirrey (2003) suggests that the act of coming out is also performative; the declaration is a means by which individuals perform identity, create the self, and form a new reality. By this definition, it's easy to see why the act of coming out carries so much weight for young DREAMers, despite its immense legal ramifications. Unlike the contested practice of "outing" members of the LGBTQ community by journalists and others, a complete breakdown of respect for the sanctity of the closet (Gross 1993), the act of coming out is about agency, power, and control over one's own story.

Zimmerman (forthcoming) notes that coming out narratives have been employed well beyond LGBTQ movements, with members of the fat acceptance and disability rights movements also embracing the concept. Comparative analysis of "coming out" across different movements reveals how cultural narratives travel and how protest strategies can be diffused cross-culturally and applied in different contexts (Saguy and Ward 2011; Chabot and Duyvendak 2002; McAdam and Rucht 1993). This process, in which innovations diffuse from one social movement to another (Soule 2004), is what social movement theorists call a social movement spillover (McAdam in Traugott 1995; Meyer and Whittier 1994), which is most likely to happen when a frame resonates across social settings (Snow et al. 1986) and among movements that have overlapping constituencies (Meyer and Whittier 1994). Saguy and Ward (2011) argue that, insofar as the coming out narrative has become broad and inclusive enough to accommodate a variety of different perspectives and interests beyond the specific social movement where it originated, it could be considered a master frame (Snow et al. 1986), in which people are asserting "their presence openly and without apology to claim the rights of citizenship" (Kitsuse 1980, 8).

Coming out, while important for all DREAMers who choose to reveal their status, takes on an even more complex meaning for those DREAMers who identify as both undocumented *and* queer. In their discussion of post-Stonewall gay rights activism, Chabot and Duyvendak (2002) show how gay identity was framed as a significant component of social, personal, *and* political identity. Within the Gay Liberation Front, for example, coming out was a collective activity and not just a matter of revealing one's sexual identity to one's friends and family. In this way, solidarity and strength through collective action underlined a new sense of well-being, with the promise of a new community. Similarly, in the immigrant rights movement, undocumented youth reimagine their legal status as a political identity by framing their coming out stories within the DREAMer narrative, which emphasizes their work ethic, Americanization, determination, pride, and college aspirations. Coming out as gay or undocumented (or both) can make a compelling case for the "injustice" to which the condition is subjected and the effectiveness of collective "agency" in addressing those wrongs (Chabot and Duyvendak 2002, 291).

The Queer Undocumented Immigrant Project (QUIP), a project of the youth-led United We Dream network, launched the "No More

Closets" campaign in 2013, which urged undocumented LGBTQ youth to come out as "UndocuQueers." Youth participants in the campaign were featured in a YouTube video called the "UndocuQueer Manifesto," which still appears on the United We Dream website. In it, they urge viewers to reject the pressure to separate their queer and undocumented identities and to lobby their communities for support and acceptance, stating that "immigrant rights are queer rights," and "queer rights are immigrant rights." So, the process of coming out as "UndocuQueer" is *simultaneously* about improving the emotional well-being of participants (a "means of survival") and bringing greater visibility to the undocumented experience (both within immigrant communities and without).

This dual function—the creation of both emotional sustenance and strategic visibility—can be seen in DREAMer modes of coming out more generally as well. Using coming out videos and other means of storytelling to share personal experiences serves both an *affective* and a *tactical* function. On the affective side, producing and circulating a coming out video is almost invariably a source of psychic relief; sometimes it is even seen as a means of psychic survival. In our case study of DREAMer activists, we found that, over and over again, participants highlighted the cathartic nature of coming out online. Interviewees often described how the process of getting their stories out helped relieve the huge burden of carrying the secret of being undocumented.

On the tactical side, coming out videos serve as an archive of the struggles of undocumented youth. Stories that, in isolation, seem to document personal difficulties, pain, humiliation, even danger, are revealed to represent shared experiences among undocumented youth that, while varied, hold many commonalities. In short, coming out videos can be therapeutic for their makers, but they also show others that, quite simply, DREAMers exist. Jake, who identifies as queer and undocumented, described the need to publicize the "racial issues and struggles of undocumented students to the community" in his 2010 interview: "For me, it's always been [about] the right to exist. . . . These issues are not going to stop. It's up to us to like keep speaking out and saying, 'Listen, we exist, we're here.'"

We argue that DREAMer coming out stories, which are largely produced and circulated via new media, serve four key functions with regard to participatory politics. These functions constitute various locations on the trajectory from voice to influence, from individual to collective. Coming out stories:

- serve as a psychic survival mechanism, providing an outlet for affective sharing and release on individual and communal levels
- create a visible archive of collective sentiment around the shared struggles and experiences of undocumented youth
- harness the power of collective identity to create vital communities of support for undocumented youth
- help spur involvement in other forms of activism and collective action, even in the face of personal and political risk

This analysis, which directly connects the emotional experiences of DREAMers to their political work, is part of the effort to develop what Jeff Goodwin and others (Jasper 1998; Goodwin, Jasper, and Polletta 2001) have termed an _emotional sociology_: a sociology attuned to the potential causal significance of emotions because they are "constitutive of social relations and action—and not simply as individual, psychological reactions but as intersubjective, collective experiences" (Goodwin, Jasper, and Polletta 2001, 283). As Goodwin and Pfaff (2001) suggest, most of the key causal factors emphasized by analysts of social movements—including such factors as social networks, grievances, collective identities, cultural frames and ideologies, even shifting political opportunity structures—derive much of their causal power from the strong emotions that they embody or evoke among participants (282).

Similarly, in her work on lesbian public cultures and archives of trauma, Ann Cvetkovich (2003) outlines the connection between affective life and citizenship: "It is important to incorporate affective life into our conceptions of citizenship and to recognize that these affective forms of citizenship may fall outside the institutional practices that we customarily associate with the concept of a citizen" (11). While many DREAMers may be fighting for legal status and legitimacy within the eyes of the law, their creation and circulation of coming out videos and other public declarations of undocumented identity constitute an enactment of affective citizenship and group belonging that circumvents the law entirely. In part, DREAMers want legal citizenship status because they *feel* like citizens on a cultural and emotional level, and these affective dimensions are among the strongest arguments behind their cause. In one DreamActivist.org coming out story, a young man from Bangladesh states, "I felt I was an American in every way except where it really mattered: documents. I never told my friends because I didn't know how they would react. After all, it was high school."

Moreover, while many DREAMers have described the process of coming out as individually therapeutic, their collective documenting of experiences can, in and of itself, be viewed as a political act both in terms of building solidarity within the movement and of "giving an account of oneself" to those outside it (Couldry 2010). Cvetkovich (2003) again nudges us toward a "reconsideration of conventional distinctions between political and emotional life as well as between political and therapeutic cultures" and an expanded notion of the category of the therapeutic "beyond the confines of the narrowly medicalized or privatized encounter between clinical professional and client." She explains, "Rather than a model in which privatized affective responses displace collective or political ones, [I propose] a collapsing of these distinctions so that affective life can be seen to pervade public life" (10).

A Sea of Bottles

At its core, the act of coming out is about sharing one's own story and making visible individual experiences. In a 2014 webinar on storytelling and digital-age civics, Erik Huerta underscored the importance of sharing his personal experiences online, which he does via both written texts and videos that range from serious confessionals to vlogs to satirical vignettes. In his recollection of his early blogging experiences on Myspace, where he shared both personal stories and resources for other undocumented youth, he described the process as much like tossing out a "message in a bottle" in hopes that it will reach others:

> So, you know, this kind of like lit this light bulb in me to start putting things out there from my own personal experience. And just kind of like a message in a bottle kind of thing. I'll write it and I put it on the internet, and, you know, hopefully it will come back and it will reach the right folks. And throughout the years it actually has been like one of the best

things I've had and one of the best experiences I've had. This year, 2014, now it will be ten years that I've been doing this—just having an online journal of sorts, sharing my experiences being undocumented.

For Huerta, these messages are just as much about bonding with other undocumented youth—others who have had similar experiences—as they are about bridging with those in positions of political power and influence (see Chapter 1 for a brief introduction to the concept of "bridging social capital"). In fact, they document personal experiences expressly *so* those in power (politicians, journalists, academics) do not misrepresent them. Huerta recalled:

> I wasn't seeing conversations being had about folks that were undocumented and what that meant from a personal perspective. I also didn't want to wait for somebody else to come and find me or somebody else like me and kind of tell our story from their perspective, kind of like from an outsider in.

Since Huerta started blogging almost a decade ago, the number of bottles in the ocean has grown, with DREAMers across the country sharing their experiences online. Over time, as other undocumented youth "opened" bottles washed up on a digital shore, they gathered the courage to share their own stories, creating a flotilla of messages simultaneously familiar and unique. We argue that this proliferation of stories constitutes a public archive. As such, the messages—these coming out stories—are for both the DREAMers themselves (bonding) and for a wider audience (bridging).

We can think of the videos uploaded during the National Coming Out of the Shadows campaign and the coming out videos that have been shared since as a series of intimate utterances, connecting individual DREAMers in a shared conversation that sheds light on a collective struggle. Taken together, they form what Cvetkovich (2003) has called an "archive of feeling" through which DREAMers' personal accounts of their struggles and experiences provide a glimpse into the everyday lives of undocumented youth. In the case of the DREAMers, the benefits of building this archive, this collection of stories, outweighed the potentially catastrophic risks (arrest, deportation, etc.). This is a contrast to the outlook of some of the Nerdfighters interviewed for Chapter 3. For many Nerdfighters, creating videos was seen more as a mode of private communication (even though the videos were uploaded to YouTube and available publicly) than as the production of stories for public consumption.

The DREAMers we interviewed, on the other hand, were keenly aware of the consequences of what they shared online as well as of the power of sharing personal narratives. Despite the fact that coming out can leave DREAMers exposed and politically vulnerable, the creation of this archive has brought with it some added protection in that they have built a community to advocate on their behalf should they encounter legal troubles. A participant in the 2011 DREAMing Out Loud! symposium at USC described how this kind of visibility, in many instances, works to insure their mutual protection, saying that "being in the shadows" is worse than being a public activist because, if he were ever deported, his entire network of activists and allies would know (Zimmerman and Shresthova 2012). Being "out" at least ensures some due process. "Besides," he said,

> activists are well trained prior to doing a direct action. They write their lawyers' phone numbers on the inside of their arms in black marker. They refuse to talk to ICE agents until their immigration lawyers are reached. Prominent activists are more likely to be released. Some activists eventually even qualify for a work permit and a temporary stay in the U.S. Those that are least visible, namely those who are not well connected and cannot access social networks and support, struggle to make people aware of their situation.

In addition to strengthening a (somewhat paradoxical) safety net, adding to this patchwork of online coming out stories sometimes brings with it a sense of pride and can be viewed by participants as the ultimate marker of public visibility. Agustin said,

> There is a video about me on YouTube now telling my story. [When I watch it] I feel proud. I feel something that's a positive feeling, you know, it was a very—I didn't feel ashamed anymore. I feel like I came out and I felt safe to come out. We have to come out of the shadows.

Sharing stories through various social and digital media platforms has allowed youth to challenge and, at times, supplant mass media representations through more locally constructed and participatory forms of messaging. The practice has also given undocumented youth the opportunity to identify and connect with one another online. Given the effects of legal status on youth's social marginalization, isolation, and self-esteem, new media technologies have become an important mechanism of communication and connection. As Zimmerman found in her research on DREAMers, undocumented youth often did not find this kind of connection and support in their local communities, even when they were surrounded by others who faced similar challenges. For example, four of Zimmerman's interview participants were from a local high school where there was no support group for undocumented students, despite the fact that it was located in a majority Latino immigrant neighborhood where close to 30 percent of residents were not citizens. Yet due to the controversy surrounding immigration policy, teachers and administrators were reluctant to raise the issue. Paulita described how she devised ways to identify others, but that shame and stigma often prevent youth from revealing their status:

> I suspected there were people like me, but I never asked. I would just listen: like if they had an accent, or if they weren't involved in stuff, or if they stayed quiet when our teacher would talk about college admissions. I knew by how they acted, if they stayed quiet, they probably didn't have status. But it was hard to find others that would talk about it, and there's a lot of people talking bad about illegals and everything so it's easier to stay quiet.

Storytelling online, meanwhile, can foster feelings of solidarity, trust, and reciprocity among participants in social networks in spite of their not "knowing" one another personally. Take again, for instance, the example of Mohammad, one of the founders of DreamActivist.org. As he explains in his coming out video, through which he aims to speak directly to other undocumented youth, "We've been asking you guys to share so I thought that I should do the same." There is a level of reciprocity and trust—implicit norms between the author of the video and his intended audience. He refers to other undocumented youth who have already made videos, specifically calling them out by their usernames and implicitly referencing the networked online community of DREAMers (which may or may not translate into face to face contacts). Such acts of identification are also consistent with the practices of other video blogging communities and collaboration channels on YouTube.

Mohammad created his video in response to a call for others' stories by Gabriel, another undocumented student who uploaded his own video. Though these two DREAMers had never met face to face (though they later did), they could create a common space by sharing their stories on YouTube. Gabriel's video is an example of how storytelling can help participating youth to shed some of the stigma and shame of being undocumented. Gabriel tells his viewers about coming out as undocumented: "It doesn't roll off your tongue, but every time you say it, it gets easier." He confesses he was once ashamed to say "it." Every time he said "it," he would shake with nerves, he admits. Gabriel continues:

> We have the power to define who we are, as undocumented students, as undocumented immigrants. Unfortunately, we are not using that power. We are letting people like . . . Lou Dobbs and Bill O'Reilly . . . define us. And how can we counteract this? By saying these simple words: "My name is ——, and I am undocumented."

In saying those words, Gabriel affirms, "You're not just coming out, you're shattering the stereotype." As soon as you say this, he tells his audience, "It doesn't define you. By doing that, you're not settling . . . you're not hiding." He ends by inviting others to join the movement: "My name is Gabriel, and I am undocumented, and I invite you to come out."

A Temporal Tradition

While we argue that coming out videos and other forms of coming out online have been crucial for young DREAMers and their movement, today's DREAMers do not seem to be uploading coming out videos en masse as they were in 2010 and 2011. This is not to say that the practice does not still occur, but coming out as undocumented does not seem as pressing a need for those in the movement at the moment we are writing this book. In fact, many of the coming out videos that were online during the period when Zimmerman was conducting research for this case study have been taken down by users or have disappeared in a wave of website updates and platform migrations. So, counter to the popular notion that material shared online (video and photo representations especially) will "last forever," many of the coming out stories shared between 2010 and 2013 are no longer accessible. Additionally, DreamActivist.org, which played such a key role as a meeting place for DREAMers and a forum for sharing coming out videos on its "Our Stories" page, is no longer a live site. While some of the original content has been ported over to the Dream Activist Tumblr page (dreamactivist. tumblr.com), the entire "Our Stories" section is now gone.

So while we still underscore the importance of the DREAMer archive, especially with regard to spurring involvement around the time of its creation, perhaps the very *act* of coming out, not its documentation via video or other means, was the most important part for young participants. For young DREAMers active during that time, new media was a vital tool (one of many in the toolbox), but the primary function of DREAMers' use of new media was never production itself. Rather, it was always rooted in an activist goal. We should also point out that this kind of ephemerality affected all of the MAPP case studies; each researcher found that it was sometimes difficult to track content— from videos to information found on websites prior to redesigns—over time, so the process of internally archiving data via screen captures and downloading became essential, as it was our goal to create a digital archive where readers of this book would be able to engage with the videos we discuss.

For the DREAMers, the tenuousness of their archive is also, in part, related to movement tactics and their temporality more broadly. In those early years of the DREAM movement, the process of documenting personal experiences and encouraging others to do so seemed a vital part of solidifying group identity, building community, and creating affective bonds between participants. But the DREAMer movement is not a static one, and priorities, strategies, and membership change across time. The focus of immigrant rights and youth-focused organizations shift, as do the interests of participants, and as with all movements, sometimes core members burn out. For the DREAMer movement, energy often ebbs and flows around particular victories or legislative efforts (the enactment of DACA, for example).

Many DREAMers who uploaded their coming out stories in those earlier years have moved on to other pursuits. Some have remained involved in activism, with many participants now involved in more established forms of organizing (like labor organizing) and more established organizations associated with the immigrant rights movement. Some have moved on entirely, choosing instead to focus on jobs or college careers (while undocumented students cannot receive federal loans or grants, many institutions admit DREAMers and even provide financial aid). Erick Huerta, interviewed again in 2014, explained (at length):

> One of the analogies that I like [for the DREAMer movement] is your favorite band—nobody knows about them. You can go to a club or a small venue and see them and have like the best time of your life but then eventually they sold out to a record label and their music wasn't as cool as it was.
>
> So for me that's kind of how it went. When I started, I'm meeting all these cool people that do the same work and they're all undocumented and for the first time in my life it felt like I was a part of a community where we have each other and have all these similar experiences, and everybody was a part of that. That was the overall thing, was like the better quality of life for ourselves.
>
> Then as the years progress we started growing as individuals and as a collective being more inclusive, not trying to better ourselves but also better the entire immigrants' community as a whole and then taking it to the next level beyond that—not focusing just on ourselves and not just focusing on Latinos and immigration, we're focusing on social justice overall.

Huerta explained that he didn't feel like the shift toward a more expansive agenda was a bad thing; quite the opposite, as he saw the growing ethnic and national diversity of the movement in which we was involved as very positive. But his analogy helps us understand why some of the founding members might not be as directly involved anymore, and why the collective identity-building and affective-archiving work of the early coming out narratives is not as much of a focus.

Zimmerman (forthcoming) argues that the mediated relationship between individual experience and collective identity in youth's coming out narratives resembles the *testimonio* (testimony), which emerged in the wake of social movements, liberation theology, and other consciousness-raising grassroots movements during the 1960s and 1970s. Unlike an autobiography, which relates an individual life story, a testimonio is the "expression not of a single autonomous account but of a collectively experienced reality." Building on this term, Zimmerman suggests DREAMers have become particularly adept at creating the *transmedia testimonio*, the testimonio that is shared across multiple media platforms, especially in the years since the initial proliferation of online "coming out" stories.

But because the DREAM movement is built around a legislative effort, the work doesn't stop at storytelling. While the American Muslims discussed in Chapter 4 saw storytelling primarily in cultural terms, deploying it to change public perceptions of the group, the DREAMers have understood storytelling in an explicitly political context, deploying it to rally support behind specific pieces of legislation that would materially improve their lives. The movement has, from the beginning, been about highlighting the perspective epitomized by the old feminist adage: the personal is political. The lived experiences of DREAMers are directly linked to structural and legal barriers, and the proliferation of coming out videos was but a first step in overcoming them (but a key one nonetheless). From the beginning, DREAMers have been involved in a range of movement tactics, including more traditional forms of protest as well as innovative, signature actions like staged DREAM graduations. Below, we will provide an account of that history and a discussion of the key role that new media played in moving DREAMers from sharing stories to engaging in on-the-ground action.

Spurring Involvement: New Media as a Bridge to Action

Critics have often depicted young people's expressive activities online as coming at the cost of more traditional kinds of street protest and political lobbying. In the case of the DREAMers, however, we've found that online and offline forms of activism are mutually reinforcing—much as we saw in Chapter 1 that the YPP survey (Cohen and Kahne2012) found that those who engage in participatory politics are much more likely to also engage in institutionalized politics. One interview participant,

Nathan, explained how the personal, affective work of archiving stories online was translated into on-the-ground action:

> Kind of counterintuitively, online is where we really found the ability to personalize the immigrant rights movement. If somebody can see a picture of somebody, hear their story and watch a video of them, they're much more likely to be able to relate to that person and participate with us.

DREAMers have participated widely in more traditional forms of activism, and the formation of online networks and online community building has been key to that kind of "scaling up." Lisa Garcia Bedolla's study of Latino political participation in Los Angeles provides a useful framework to help us understand the role of social networks in activism among underrepresented groups. García Bedolla (2005), who does not look at online networks, but whose points can easily be extended to them, argues that social networks have the potential to be politicized, but also serve as important spaces for group historical memory and sharing collective experiences (15). Social networks are a benefit to individuals because they create feelings of "bounded solidarity" that encourage actors to act altruistically on behalf of their group, sect, or community. Put simply, feelings of attachment and group worthiness are what motivate individuals to act on behalf of the collective. George Lipsitz (2006) makes a similar claim when he looks at the roles that long-standing social networks (again offline) played in giving support (both moral and material) to low-income residents of New Orleans who were displaced by Hurricane Katrina; Lipsitz describes these groups as "resource poor, network rich," suggesting the vital role that strong communication systems play in helping those who are struggling to survive.

Julio, an artist and longtime activist based in Los Angeles, provides another case in point. A few years ago, Julio was an aspiring journalist at a local California university, but, because of his lack of "papers," he could not accept a job at a newspaper. After a few months of battling depression and frustration, he began to upload original drawings to Facebook. His artwork depicted his friends, fellow undocumented youth in everyday scenarios. His colorful, cartoonlike drawings were shared across multiple media platforms and soon Julio became a recognizable spokesperson for undocumented youth across the country. He later formed a media-centered youth

"I Exist," by Julio Salgado.

collective, Dreamers Adrift, which uses digital media to reflect on issues that affect undocumented youth. Importantly, the connections he made on Facebook were what drew him deeper into the movement, much more so than his involvement in campus organizations. Julio explained that participating in some form of movement activism provides him "a sense of community, mutual support, and belonging." He planned to continue contributing to the movement, he said, by using his art on behalf of its goals.

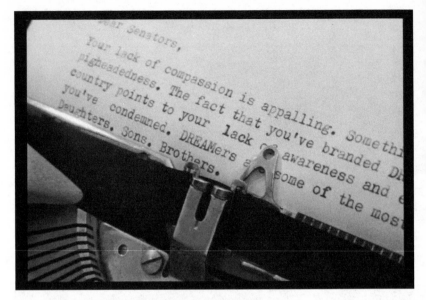

"Dear Senators: DREAM Act 2011," by Dreamers Adrift.

Julio's story demonstrates how undocumented youth have extended new media practices to create and sustain their political community. Online communities and social networks have formed a part of undocumented youth's contextual, cultural, and social capital by creating opportunities for interaction, communication, and connection. While not always explicitly political, these networks have been mobilized in support of DREAM movement actions. The Dreamers Adrift collective of which Julio is a part uses digital media to capture the daily lives of undocumented youth. Not all of their videos are produced as "political" or campaign pieces. Some use humor and irony to capture the challenges youth face on a daily basis because of their status, while others are more explicitly political, directing specific demands or rights claims at elected officials. On the humorous side, Dreamers Adrift members produced a series of "Undocucribs" videos based on the MTV series *Cribs*, in which DREAMers take viewers on a virtual "tour" of their apartments. On the more political end of the spectrum, in another stop-motion-style video, a typewriter seems to type out a letter to U.S. senators on its own explaining the unfairness of their lack of support for the DREAM Act.

Such representations have been important for creating group solidarity and for helping paint a picture of DREAMers' everyday lived experiences, but DREAMers have also been successful in leveraging online networks for actions on the ground. Zimmerman's original case study report describes a number of "offline" actions staged by DREAMers, including the October 2011 sit-in that launched the national E.N.D. (Education Not Deportation) Our Pain campaign, comprising a network of immigrant youth organizations and allies demanding an immediate moratorium on deporting youth eligible for the DREAM Act. In that action, five undocumented youth wearing graduation caps staged a sit-in at the Immigration and Customs Enforcement offices in downtown Los Angeles to urge the Obama administration to stop deporting undocumented youth (Rojas 2011). The action took place on a busy Wednesday morning when most Angelenos were at work and most students were in school. Fearing a low turnout, Dream Team Los Angeles, a local youth-led community group, and their allies used social media to send links of a live broadcast of the action from a free video-streaming site. While 300 people attended, over 4,000 users watched online as the youth entered ICE headquarters and demanded a hearing with officials. The attendees and online audience looked on as handcuffs were placed on the youth. Immediately after the arrests, users were able to make donations and petition for the arrestees' release through another website. The E.N.D. campaign's direct action sought to amplify youth voices by *combining* traditional community organizing with new media strategies. One of those arrested, a leader of a DREAM advocacy group in Los Angeles, explained that a mixed media strategy is key for reaching diverse participants:

> You have to be able to use Facebook and Twitter, but you have to be intentional about it, and strategic. At the same time, you have to also utilize traditional media outlets because our "tios" and "tias" are not using social networking. They are still watching Univision and the nightly news. So you have to engage in both.

During the 2011 DREAMing Out Loud! symposium, Nancy Meza, a prominent DREAM activist, noted, "Anyone can post on Facebook. The key is to have a strategy." Asked to elaborate, she added, "Using social media strategically is to effectively frame and get the message out." Later in the discussion, Meza echoed the other point made by the activist quoted just above: "This is really where social movement and community organizing skills differ among immigrant communities and their allies. Youth may get their news through their social media networks, but their parents still tend to rely on more traditional media. This is why DREAMers need to strategically include both in their communication strategies."

This multipronged approach speaks to the DREAMers' adoption of what Sasha Costanza-Chock (2010) calls *transmedia mobilization,* one of the core concepts we introduced in Chapter 1; this is the process whereby a social movement narrative is dispersed systematically across multiple media platforms, creating a distributed and participatory social movement "world," with multiple entry points for organizing and for strengthening movement identity and outcomes.

DREAMers illustrate how both new and traditional media messaging can be combined to further movement outcomes, but they also show how transmedia mobilization can be employed in the creation of ad hoc movement organizations. Some organizations arise because they do the media bridging work needed by movements, while other media-based groups can evolve into distinct movements that supplant traditional community and movement organizations altogether.

Early on, the student founders of DreamActivist.org, the website that so prominently featured the coming out stories described earlier, came together as a group of youth who met in an MSN chat room. Frustrated by the lack of online resources, they transformed the chat room into a full-fledged blog and website. They initially saw their blog as a resource for activist and undocumented youth, but two years after going "live," DreamActivist.org coordinated a mass public protest in Washington, D.C. The National DREAM Graduation, coordinated under the umbrella of United We Dream, a national coalition for undocumented youth, brought new media based communities like DreamActivist.org together with more locally based organizations and established advocacy groups. It was attended by 500 youth across the country, many of whom had never previously participated in immigrant rights organizing.

DreamActivist.org was no longer just a website that provided tools for organizing; it was now perceived as an organization with a constitu-

DREAM Graduation in Washington, D.C. Photo by Steven Pavey.

ency for whom it "spoke." One of its founders, Kemi, was chosen by her peers to deliver the keynote speech at the National DREAM Graduation, signaling the importance of the organization in the broader movement. For Kemi, the experience was transformative. She reflected on how her involvement with the website was an important stepping stone toward other forms of political activism:

> Well, I guess I was working to set up the website but it was just me back [home] talking virtually with everyone else. I feel isolated quite a bit because I don't have a space to organize locally. So my work with Dream Activist, especially the blog, is where I feel like I can be most effective . . . and, hopefully, through my work there I can motive others to join me here. The national graduation was the first time I immediately saw the impact of our work. And I also felt like, yeah, I'm an activist now.

Kemi was able to interface with political institutions and have an "on the ground" impact through her online organizing. Her first foray into activism was uploading scholarship resources to DreamActivist.org. This experience led her into different modes of activism, including public protest and civil disobedience. Transmedia mobilization and participatory politics thus represent a shift in how one can become politically active, but they do not necessarily displace other forms of community organizing. In fact, they often do support work for street actions.

At the time of Zimmerman's fieldwork, though, participants of DreamActivist.org saw themselves as "different" from nonprofits and immigrant rights organizations, but just as important in representing their constituency. Flavia, a DreamActivist.org volunteer, explained their approach:

> We are grassroots. We are undocumented youth ourselves, so we don't claim to speak *for* anyone but *with* others. We all work in our own ways for the organization but we don't dictate what each of us can do. It is not top-down. But when it comes to taking positions we let our constituent's needs guide us. Like, the military option was controversial no doubt, but we had to take the position of what most of our members wanted—and that was legalization now.

Here, Flavia is referring to the controversial compromise under which military service replaced the community service provision of the original DREAM Act. Flavia's references to her constituency and their membership reflects the ethos of DreamActivist.org. While it was not structured as a traditional movement organization, with top-down leadership, local membership, and professional staff, it became an important representative of youth's voices and interests, and their initial success can be attributed to the combination of digital media and traditional community organizing. The project did not operate in an online-only capacity, but was tightly linked to local campus and community organizations; such linkages are extremely important for the youth described throughout this book, particularly those involved in the American Muslim networks discussed in Chapter 4, and the libertarian youth discussed in Chapter 6.

The case of DreamActivist.org also demonstrates how networked, ad hoc, and horizontal movement formations can, at times, achieve more success than traditional movement organizations that rely on top-down and hierarchical structures. Such networks facilitate new forms of participation and provide alternative entry points for youth who otherwise would not have the opportunity to be "active" in their local spaces. Prerna Lal, one of the organization's founders, recounts:

> We catapulted a failed DREAM Act into a national social movement of undocumented youth using new media tools by building Dream Activist and then creating more spaces for undocumented youth to get involved, share their stories, take action online, scoring victory after victory for immigrant rights.

Like so many of the other young activists we've discussed, the DreamActivist.org participants were willing to use not only any media necessary to further their goals, but a wide range of new and traditional activist tactics to enact national change. Too often, debates about digital activism assume an either-or logic—either online or off, either networked or geographically local, either expressive or tactical; meanwhile, the members of many of the groups discussed herein are finding ways to do it all.

The Future of the Dream

What is the status of the dream today? With partisan gridlock at the center of American politics, efforts toward substantial immigration reform seem futile. As we are writing this chapter, all signs indicate that almost all Republicans, and even some Democrats, want to avoid touching the issue—and no wonder, given former House majority leader Eric Cantor's surprise primary defeat by a little-known Tea Party candidate, Dave Brat, who campaigned against Cantor by painting him as pro-reform.

On November 20, 2014, President Obama announced that the U.S. Department of Homeland Security (DHS) would not deport certain undocumented parents of U.S. citizens and parents of lawful permanent residents (LPRs). The president also announced an expansion of the Deferred Action for Childhood Arrivals program for youth who came to the United States as children. Under a directive from the secretary of DHS, these parents and youth may be granted a type of temporary permission to stay in the U.S. called "deferred action." While these programs are expected to help 4.4 million people, according to the Department of Homeland Security, deportation of immigrants continues. As of

June 2015, pundits were proclaiming that immigration reform was dead, a GOP majority in the House was blocking a vote on a Senate-passed reform bill, and amid increasing media focus on an influx of unaccompanied minors crossing the border, President Obama was vowing to "act alone" as much as possible on immigration reform.

Young DREAMers feel they cannot afford to wait for Congress or Obama, however, and their most recent movement tactics reflect this. On its website, The Dream Is Coming, an undocumented youth initiative that organizes direct actions across the country, explains its recent adoption of more radical approaches: "We are compelled by our frustration and the fierce urgency of our dreams. . . . We have worked for years on a path to legalization. We are at a point in our movement where radical action has become necessary."

In the face of increasing deportations and political stalemates, undocumented youth have used a combination of direct action and media activism to shine a spotlight on immigrant detention and deportation, which has largely remained hidden from public view. They have staged rallies and sit-ins at detention centers and ICE offices; they have even targeted banks that invest in private prisons, directly confronting the institutions that profit from the immigrant detention and deportation system. An important complement to their direct action has been their use of new media and the transmedia testimonio. Utilizing Facebook, Twitter, and microblogging, immigrant youth broadcast the stories of those who are in detention centers and fighting deportation orders. For instance, on the morning that an electronic monitoring device was placed on his ankle, Matias Ramos, an undocumented youth and co-founder of United We Dream, turned to Twitter, posting a photo of himself and announcing that he had been given two weeks to leave the country. Stories like these are transmitted through a broad-based social media network connecting campus organizations, community groups, and allies, providing links to petitions and online donations.

Yet, while the strategies and goals have been adapted in a new political context, the coming out repertoire has maintained its central utility in collective mobilization. For example, during hunger strikes and sit-ins, youth will march and collectively shout, "Undocumented and unafraid! Unapologetic and unashamed!" Many undocumented youth now proudly wear T-shirts, buttons, and other garments that declare their status, especially when they anticipate getting arrested in front of a detention center or ICE facility. In a July 2013 action, youth voluntarily self-deported to Mexico in order to reenter the United States and claim asylum. Updating the youth's status daily and sometimes hourly with the hashtag #bringthemhome, undocumented youth organizers have expanded and complemented the traditional public protest strategies of the immigrant rights movement with social media campaigns.

From Georgia to California, youth of many different national and ethnic backgrounds now record testimonios before engaging in direct action to explain their reasons for risking deportation through acts of civil disobedience against deportation policies. In an example of this type of testimonio, Viridiana, then a 24-year-old member of the North Carolina Dream Team, begins her 2011 video, simply titled "Viridiana Martinez, North Carolina Dream Team," "I am undocumented. If you're watching this video I've been arrested." She states how she is a proud North Carolinian and provides a bit of her background. Yet, soon after, her individual story takes a backseat as she explains things to those who may be unclear about why she took action:

> I am a human being whose dreams have been denied. For those wondering why I am putting my freedom on the line: Why would I risk deportation? Because I've had enough. My people have been criminalized for crossing borders seeking a better life. . . . My community is under attack by laws that strip people of their humanity. Remaining in the shadows is no longer acceptable. Protesting, lobbying, and rallying is not enough anymore.

Her personal testimony is also a call to action. By reframing why action is not only important, but necessary, she asks her audience to also take action: "If you're watching this and have not come out, it's time you come out and declare yourself undocumented and unafraid."

In a video from 2013 called "Bring Them Home: Lizbeth Mateo Checking In from Oaxaca, Mexico," Lizbeth, who chose to "self-deport" knowing that "the U.S. government might not allow [her] to come back," speaks from Oaxaca, urging viewers to take note of the dire consequences of U.S. immigration policies; in Lizbeth's case, she was unable to see her family for 15 years as an undocumented immigrant in the U.S.

and returned to Mexico to be reunited with them. She uses her own experience to illustrate a larger point—that her story is the story of 1.7 million other undocumented immigrants and their families. Lizbeth's use of personal narrative harkens back to the coming out tradition; in this case, it is coupled with a call for continued activism in the form of engaging in public protests and lobbying elected officials.

These calls to action illustrate how, even in the wake of the DREAMers' move toward more radical activism, the coming out narrative is central. We've traced that narrative back to the movement's early days, describing its roots in online coming out campaigns, along with its use for both affective and tactical uses. It seems clear that, no matter the direction of the DREAMer movement, the act of coming out will remain important.

Regardless of shifting strategies and changing membership, young undocumented activists will have to dream as long as politicians refuse to budge on immigration reform. In his 2007 book, *Dream*, on the oft-overlooked relationship between imagination and politics, Stephen Duncombe writes:

> Dreams are powerful. They are repositories of our desire. They animate the entertainment industry and drive consumption. They can blind people to reality and provide cover for political horror. But they also inspire us to imagine that things could be radically different than they are today, and then believe that we can progress toward that imaginary world. (182)

The young activists we highlight in this chapter know better than anyone that the power of dreams can propel a movement and that acts of the civic imagination can inspire direct political action. The next chapter focuses on libertarian youth, who, by and large, come from different communities but embrace some similar practices and ideological beliefs (many of the libertarians we talked to were supportive of immigration reform and sympathetic to the DREAMers and their cause, for instance, and some of them even supported the Occupy movement). Like the DREAMers, young libertarians often use unconventional means and creative practices to influence political debate, but, as we will see, they hold a unique position when it comes to political participation and electoral politics.

6

Bypassing the Ballot Box

How Libertarian Youth Are Reimagining the Political

Liana Gamber-Thompson

In a March 2014 interview with NPR's Don Gonyea, the president and co-founder of Students for Liberty, Alexander McCobin, said, "This is the most libertarian generation that has ever existed. I honestly believe most young people are libertarian. They're socially tolerant. They're fiscally responsible, and they're, in general, noninterventionists on foreign policy."

While it remains to be seen if "the most libertarian generation that has ever existed" will emerge, an increasing number of young people are voicing their displeasure with the political status quo. A spring 2014 survey by the Harvard Institute of Politics (IOP) found that 18–29-year-olds' trust in public institutions such as the Supreme Court and the U.S. military was at a five-year low. In a press release for the study, IOP polling director John Della Volpe said, "There's an erosion of trust in the individuals and institutions that make government work—and now we see the lowest level of interest in any election we've measured since 2000. Young people still care about our country, but we will likely see more volunteerism than voting" ("Low Midterm Turnout Likely" 2014).

This chapter focuses on American youth's frustration with "politics as usual" as explored through a case study of young libertarians, participants in what is often referred to as the Student Liberty Movement. This movement includes those involved in "Big L" libertarian politics, meaning those who have an investment in electoral politics (for this case study, we talked to some supporters of the 2012 Ron Paul campaign—Paul ran as a Republican in the 2012 presidential primaries but holds many libertarian beliefs—and members of the Libertarian Party who supported Gary Johnson's 2012 presidential run). The Liberty Movement also includes "little l" libertarians, who seek to effect social change through educational and discursive means rather than electoral ones—members of this group made up the majority of our case study participants and are the primary focus of this chapter. Libertarianism.com ("The Liberty Movement" n.d.), a libertarian educational website, describes the Liberty Movement as

> the loose association of think tanks, activist organizations, political parties, and individuals who work to promote the ideas of free markets, civil liberties, and limited government across the globe.

First, we discuss the utility of adopting a generational approach to understanding major shifts within social movements and draw on the example of a move toward a "second-wave libertarianism" that focuses more on education and discursive change than an electoral agenda. We then describe how participants in the Student Liberty Movement employ elements of participatory politics and tap popular culture to enact that change, all the while remaining connected to established libertarian institutions and elites. We argue that libertarians utilize a unique blend of participatory and institutional politics to further their goals, and we consider the prospects and paradoxes of such a liminal position. Finally, we examine the current literature on citizenship styles to explore how a marked anti-voting sentiment among our participants reflects fluctuating generational notions of citizenship and social change.

The data from this chapter is taken from fieldwork conducted by Liana Gamber-Thompson in 2011 and 2012. Gamber-Thompson analyzed a range of media artifacts and texts for the case study and conducted participant observation at a regional Students for Liberty (SFL) conference in 2011 and the Students for Liberty International Conference in Washington, D.C., in 2012. The core data comes from her interviews with 30 young libertarians between the ages of 15 and 25 and three expert interviews (for which participants agreed to be identified by name).

Shifting Generations

In 1923, Karl Mannheim wrote, "The problem of generations is important enough to merit serious consideration. It is one of the indispensable guides to an understanding of the structure of social and intellectual movements" (362). Indeed, the "problem" of generations has proven important—indispensable, even—to the study of movements over the past 90 years. Historically, social movement scholars have been interested in showing how generational shifts influence movement dynamics, continuity (Isserman 1993; McAdam 1988, 2009; Reger 2005; Taylor 1989; Weigand 2002), and conflict (Klatch 1999; Henry 2004). We see this work on young libertarians as expanding the literature on political generation, cohorts, and micro-cohorts, particularly because, as it stands, social movement literature tends to lump young libertarians in with young conservatives, although their movements are actually quite distinct (Binder and Wood 2013). Moreover, in the past few years, the Student Liberty Movement has been distancing itself from the libertarianism of the past by focusing on a generational shift within the movement referred to as "second-wave libertarianism."

Since 2012, SFL president McCobin has been publicly discussing this notion; second-wave libertarianism, which explicitly borrows language from the women's movement as a means of distinguishing itself from prior iterations of libertarianism, takes a uniquely "big-tent" approach. In a 2013 blog post on the topic, McCobin states, "No single political party is enough. What we need is for every political party to shift more towards the philosophy of libertarianism. And that will take engaging individuals and institutions across the political spectrum." This strategy marks a significant departure from the one pursued by leaders of the "first wave" of libertarianism in the 1970s and 1980s, who worked very hard to build uniquely libertarian institutions, underscoring the need for a generational approach to shifting social movement dynamics.

More generally, while the repeated and collective identification of each political generation endures, with the movement connecting one wave to the next, different cohorts can have disparate definitions of the movement that serve to reshape it. We see exactly this with young libertarians; while the younger cohort's allegiance to the fundamentals of libertarianism remains, their strategies for effecting social change seem to have largely shifted, with younger members focused more on discursive change than the electoral politics embraced by previous generations. Through an examination of distinct periods within the history of libertarianism, we can also see the growing importance of participatory politics in this age of "digital civics" (Zuckerman 2012b), when new media plays an increasingly important role for young people and is a central part of the story about shifting attitudes around the efficacy of institutional politics.

Along with "ranting" and "hiding within conservatism," McCobin (2013) describes "building Libertarian institutions and ideas" as one of the major strategies employed by the first wave.[1] In his aforementioned blog post, McCobin encourages young libertarians to distance themselves from these strategies. He states:

> By the end of the 20th Century, leaders had emerged and founded the organizations that today are the backbone of the libertarian movement: In public policy, the Cato Institute, Reason Foundation, Competitive Enterprise Institute, and many other libertarian think tanks exist. Students have been supported for decades by the Institute for Humane Studies and Foundation for Economic Education with explicitly libertarian education. Political groups now exist, such as FreedomWorks, the Libertarian Party and various libertarian caucuses within other political parties. And there are countless other nonprofits engaged in other strategies of social reform. (As I've even seen at this convention, there are even a handful of philosophically libertarian politicians.) These institutions formed *the foundations from which the second wave could emerge as a truly independent libertarian movement* [our emphasis].

These foundational ties represent a central focus of this chapter, which also examines the contemporary Student Liberty Movement's relationship to established libertarian institutions like those described above to illustrate the variety of ways in which participatory politics gets enacted. We look at how members of the Liberty Movement are engaged with participatory cultures and involved in a variety of creative, even fannish, pursuits. At the same time, SFL benefits from institutional ties and supports member participation in established libertarian political spheres as represented by the Cato Institute, the Institute for Humane Studies, and other think tanks and policy organizations. We also describe the paradox in this relationship—young libertarians' continued reliance on institutions despite their increasing efforts to gain distance from them.

Later in this chapter, we will explain young libertarians' sometimes fraught relationship with electoral politics, particularly the practice of voting, and how that relates to their philosophical outlook on social change, their belief in a broad repertoire of political action, and their investment in several different levers of change (Zuckerman 2013a) with which to influence institutions and agents of power. This de-emphasis on electoral politics also calls into question changing notions of citizenship, and we describe a few different models of alternative citizenship (Bennett 2008b; Boler 2008; Dalton 2009) wherein young libertarians, who often downplay the importance of national citizenship and emphasize a broader global citizenship, might fit.

The Liberty Movement

The majority of the people interviewed for this study considered themselves part of the Liberty Movement or, as younger members dubbed it, the Student Liberty Movement. As described earlier, the Liberty Movement, which is largely youth driven, includes those involved in "Big L" or electoral-based libertarian politics and "little l" libertarians (who we see as largely adopting the "second-wave" model described above), who seek to effect social change through educational and discursive mechanisms.

The Liberty Movement is a broad one in concept, potentially encompassing anyone interested in furthering the causes of individual and economic liberty regardless of political affiliation. Students for Liberty is the organization at the center of this case study, with most (though not all) participants having some affiliation with it. Students involved with SFL are often self-identified libertarians, though the organization as a whole maintains the broader mission of "advancing liberty," a concept most often used to describe protecting individual freedoms but which can stand in for a wide array of causes. The SFL website (2012) sets forth the organization's commitment to and understanding of liberty:

> Students for Liberty is an organization that supports liberty. SFL does not dictate the foundations upon which individuals justify their belief in liberty. Rather, Students for Liberty embraces the diversity of justifications

for liberty and encourages debate and discourse on the differing philosophies that underlie liberty. What Students for Liberty endorses are the principles that comprise liberty:

- Economic freedom to choose how to provide for one's life;
- Social freedom to choose how to live one's life; and
- Intellectual and academic freedom.

SFL describes its mission as providing a "unified, student-driven forum of support for students and student organizations dedicated to liberty." The following description of the organization's history appeared on the SFL website (2011) before a June 2012 redesign:

> The origins of Students for Liberty can be traced back to the summer of 2007 when several students in the Institute for Humane Studies Koch Summer Fellowship got together on July 24th to hold a roundtable discussion about best practices for student organizations dedicated to liberty. . . . After the successful roundtable Alexander McCobin and Sloane Frost teamed up to take the success of this roundtable to the next level, to create a conference for pro-liberty students to meet and share best practices on organizing for liberty.

Today, Students for Liberty is a 501(c)(3) nonprofit organization whose stated goal is to provide an abundance of activities, programs, and resources to support students interested in liberty. SFL also serves as an umbrella organization for a growing number of affiliated student groups across the country. The Student Liberty Movement more broadly includes participants in other student groups, including Young Americans for Liberty, which grew out of Students for Ron Paul, and those unaffiliated with any particular organization. We found movement members engaging in a range of creative and participatory practices, from the establishment of YouTube channels to the setting up of college campus "free speech walls" on which students are invited to write anything they wish. These practices piqued our interest before we conducted the case study and are well represented by figures like Dorian Electra, a popular video artist within the movement.

On "Hearting Hayek": Libertarians, Fandom and Participatory Cultures

Hey there, Friedrich Hayek, you're lookin' really nice.

Your methodology's oh so precise.

You break down social science to the fundamentals.

Rules and social order are the essentials.

The use of knowledge in society, by each of us we make the economy.

It's not magic that somehow our plans all align,

The result of human action, of human design.

. . .

Sometimes I dream all day 'bout being Mrs. Hayek.

We'd share milkshakes, watch sunsets, and kayak.

We'd work together on that business cycle theory.

Oh, darling, you've been working hard, you must be weary.

Come to my couch, on which you can rest.

I'll make tea and we'll talk credit and interest.

Then I can talk about my interest in you.

Of course, we'll talk about the economy, too.

Just me and you.

Just me and you.

Me and you.

Me and you.

The above lyrics come from then 19-year-old Dorian Electra's 2010 self-produced YouTube video and love song to Austrian economic theorist Friedrich Hayek, "I'm in Love with Friedrich Hayek."

Electra's video represents just one of many examples of young libertarians engaging in participatory cultures.[2] YouTube houses a variety of creative content produced by young libertarians, much of which seeks to make the work of economic and political theorists they esteem (many of whom are disregarded in mainstream education) understandable and enjoyable. On the professional end, there are the hugely popular 2010 and 2011 Keynes versus Hayek rap battles from writer/producer John Papola, which are distributed through the EconStories YouTube channel and depict the two economists dueling for intellectual supremacy. On the

"I'm in Love with Friedrich Hayek," by Dorian Electra.

DIY side, there are the much less polished videos created by Morrakiu, a self-described "atheist, anti-theist and anti-statist libertarian," including the libertarian-themed "Drop It Like It's Hoppe," (2013), which remixes Snoop Dogg's 2004 track "Drop It Like It's Hot" to celebrate German-born Austrian economic theorist Hans-Hermann Hoppe, and "AnCap Black and Yellow" (2011), a tribute to Murray Rothbard set to Wiz Khalifa's 2010 earworm, "Black and Yellow."

Alan McKee (2007) characterizes cultural theory fans (of Foucault, Butler, Žižek, and others) as reaping intellectual as well as emotional benefit from theory:

Theory fans have a passion for Theory that goes beyond a passive acceptance of whatever they are given by publishers and conference organizers. They actively seek out more work by their favorite authors and build strong emotional relationships with it. While some consumers read Theory for purely utilitarian, work-related purposes (for example, to complete a Ph.D., prepare a lecture, or write an article that will be useful on their c.v.), Theory fans will also read it for pleasure. (89)

Libertarian theory fans similarly take great pleasure in mastering (often dense) theory and relish the process of self-learning. But libertarian fandom is also participatory and playful in nature. For example, at any given SFL event, it is common to run into groups of young Rothbardians, devotees of the anarcho-capitalist and Austrian economic theorist Murray Rothbard, all wearing bowties to signify their allegiance (Rothbard himself was known for wearing a bowtie). Still others sport "Hayek Is My Homeboy" T-shirts, or tote "I Heart Hayek" water bottles.

The intellectual canon adopted by today's young libertarians is extremely broad. While libertarianism has historically been associated with Ayn Rand and Objectivism, many other philosophical strands and viewpoints are accepted within the movement, including agorism, anarcho-capitalism, and left-libertarianism. As several interviewees pointed out, Rand is still a key figure for young libertarians, especially those who are just becoming interested in the movement, but a host of other theorists are equally if not more revered by this generation. T.J., a self-described left-libertarian, explained:

I see a lot of times in the media, people think, "Oh, Ayn Rand, libertarian." Yeah, that's like the front porch of libertarianism. Like, "Come into the house. Come upstairs." There are so many more other influences and thoughts in the libertarian movement.

He continued:

The fact that there are libertarians who are starting to buzz about Malcolm X is different. It's going to produce a different kind of libertarian movement because as much as we love Ayn Rand, she's not our saint.

When his interviewer expressed surprise at this mention of Malcolm X, T.J. explained that, these days, many young libertarians are taking inspiration from a wider variety of theorists, even more conventionally progressive ones, as they become increasingly committed to social issues like gay marriage and immigrant rights.

In a follow up conversation, T.J. observed that Malcolm X's 1964 "The Ballot or the Bullet" speech included a passage that summed up an anti-state perspective that he and many of his libertarian peers found inspirational. In this oration, delivered at Cory Methodist Church in Cleveland, Ohio, Malcolm X declared:

> This government has failed us. The government itself has failed us. The white liberals, who have been posing as our friends, have failed us. Once we see that all these other sources to which we've turned have failed, we stop turning to them and turn to ourselves. We need a self-help program, a do it yourself philosophy, a do it right now philosophy, an it's already too late philosophy. This is what you and I need to get with. . . . Black Nationalism is a self-help philosophy . . . this is a philosophy that eliminates the necessity for division and argument.

T.J.'s adoption of this part of Malcolm X's speech seeks to extrapolate the idea of a "self-help" program out of the context of black liberation and map it onto broader ideological concerns about citizenship and democracy. In this case, the "self-help" comes in the form of adherence to radical anti-state, pro-liberty philosophies that, from young libertarians' point of view, will benefit people from all ethnicities, backgrounds, and nations.

With influences running the gamut from Ayn Rand to Malcolm X, the Student Liberty Movement comprises a range of subcultures, each defined around particular tastes and interests, yet connected to each other through a set of common causes (fiscal responsibility, minimal state involvement, etc.). Some participants help both to bridge those subcultures and reach out beyond the movement by working to present the vast, increasingly diverse corpus of thought that informs contemporary libertarianism in ways that are comprehensible, current, and fun. Dorian Electra described her desire to make libertarian theory accessible:

> I want to appeal to people, and even if they disagree, don't understand, or don't care what I'm saying, they will get something out of the video. Because I have this twofold goal with—it's really ambitious, but here, I'm going to try to articulate it. One is to have academic ideas, present it in a more entertaining and accessible format. Accessibility is like what I'm all about, because—I don't know. It's like grandma can understand you, like—I haven't really reached that, but I'm trying. It's not easy.

Electra's objectives are in line with the second-wave emphasis on education over institution building, a more cultural, less top-down approach to change people's behavior and beliefs.

Liesbet van Zoonen (2005) argues that modernist political discourses often frame popular culture and politics as two distinct spheres when, in fact, fan communities and political constituencies have much in common with regard to strategies of performance and community building. Drawing on Jenkins (1992), Van Zoonen explains that academic and popular discourses often hold that fandom is primarily an affective enterprise, while political activities are more rooted in critical cognitive assessments that constitute good citizenship, such as informed knowledge of current events. This line of thinking might have been particularly salient for first-wave libertarians, too, who often relied on a rhetoric of rationality. Both Van Zoonen and Jenkins argue against such a dichotomy, though, offering a range of case studies that demonstrate how fan practices bridge with political and civic activities, in ways that combine rational discourse with more affective expressions. The Harry Potter Alliance (HPA) described in Chapter 3, for instance, encourages its members to become involved in civic and political action campaigns by using metaphors from the Harry Potter narratives. Electra's work also illustrates that fandom and citizenship are far from opposites. She offers her fans a simultaneous experience of entertainment and economics education in her 2012 video "Fa$t Ca$h," which provides a catchy breakdown of the Federal Reserve and what she sees as artificially low interest rates:

"Fa$t Ca$h" promo image, courtesy of Dorian Electra.

The creative productions of young artists/theory fans like Electra and other YouTube stars such as PraxGirl and Token Libertarian Girl, have helped bridge the gap between fandom and politics for a new generation of libertarians. Today's young libertarians have access to a large (and growing) selection of libertarian online communities, social spaces, and platforms, which have been key in defining the contours of the modern Liberty Movement and shaping the tastes of its participants—who consistently characterize themselves as a far cry from those in the first wave of libertarians, whom one interviewee described as "neckbeards" and "computer programmers living in their mom's basement").

The libertarian fandom described here is highly participatory in nature, and the contribution of young people's digital media practices to that ethos is crucial. Given young libertarians' distrust of governmental institutions, it makes sense that their approach to education would emphasize informal, often self-motivated, learning—what we would term connected learning—rather than more formalized instruction, and that they would assume the authority to share insights about theory with their community without regard to academic credentials. Given their emphasis on changing political beliefs through education rather than policies through the ballot box, it also makes sense that much of this generation's activities would be directed toward cultural productions that are intended to inspire and inform others about the theories these young libertarians have embraced. And given their desire to reach out beyond those committed to formal libertarian campaigns, it is unsurprising that they would turn toward general interest platforms such as YouTube and more porous social media such as Twitter to spread their content to diverse audiences who might find them a point of entry into political conversations they might never encounter otherwise. As discussed in Chapter 1, participatory politics depends on consequential connections, often, in this case, where worlds collide—such as when hip hop meets Austrian economic theory.

Participatory Politics and Institutional Ties

Despite SFL's adopted "second-wave" and "little l" stances, today's young libertarians are not seeking to effect change exclusively through cultural modes. They are, in fact, quite savvy at interfacing with established political institutions (though, as we describe later, many maintain an uneasy relationship to institutional politics). James Hay's 2011 account of the Tea Party movement struggles with the degree to which a grassroots movement can rely on support from partisan funders, such as the Koch brothers or FreedomWorks, and benefit from the attention of commercial broadcasters, such as Fox News, and still legitimately claim to be of, by, and for the people. The question is worthwhile, and answering it requires us to consider the hybrid forms that are being taken by some contemporary kinds of political mobilizations. We agree with Hay's conclusion that the Tea Party example illustrates the ways that "grassroots" blogging may be linked to, rather than resistant to, other kinds of political institutions, but we find the SFL example to be balanced a bit more strongly toward participatory rather than top-down models of political change. As we pursued this research, we struggled to identify a more "conservative" case study that would display the kinds of youth-driven participatory mechanisms we have discussed elsewhere. We were often told that the structures of participatory politics were more congenial to progressive rather than conservative movements, but we resisted this conclusion, hoping to identify compelling counterexamples. The Tea Party would not be such an example—all the research on it so far (Skocpol and Williamson 2012) suggests that it skews much older and has not been very receptive to youth participation, let alone youth leadership. Students for Liberty, on the other hand, did meet our criteria, for the most part, since it is youth run, involves the active production and circulation of media by its participants, and deploys less hierarchical and more informal networked structures. Yet it is by no means a pure example of participatory politics at work (nor can libertarianism simply be labeled a conservative movement, given the conscious efforts of the young people we spoke with to straddle partisan and ideological categories). So to reiterate, as we acknowledged up front, the SFL has relationships, of varying degrees of strength, with well-established political groups, think tanks, and policy organizations, as well as with funders like oil magnates Charles and David Koch; the Kochs, in turn, have ties to the Cato Institute and FreedomWorks, both strongly identified with libertarian advocacy, and a range of other conservative groups and causes. These funding sources have been so aggressive at recruiting and supporting young conservatives that it would be hard to find any conservative youth group that does not benefit from their largess. But, like Hay (2011), we are arguing against "binaristic logics" (665) and in favor of a more nuanced reading of the entanglements that shape contemporary political movements.

In their work on conservative college students, Amy Binder and Kate Wood (2013) make the point that well-funded, networked organizations play a key role in mobilizing conservative youth. They give a detailed account of how conservative students benefit from the resources of the

Young America's Foundation, the Leadership Institute, and the Intercollegiate Studies Institute, which were expressly founded for the purpose of "advancing the cause of right-leaning college students" (76). These organizations grant summer fellowships, provide internships, and offer other forms of support for conservative college students and groups, resources that are not always available to students in more left-leaning "grassroots" movements. SFL is very much situated amid institutionalized funding structures like those chronicled by Binder and Wood. Members are encouraged to network with a variety of libertarian organizations like the Institute for Humane Studies (IHS), a prime venue for finding work opportunities, making professional contacts, and taking advantage of fellowships and educational events. This meme, taken from the SFL Facebook page, features a character from the sitcom *Arrested Development*, Tobias Fünke (played by David Cross), pondering such an internship.

SFL, as an organization, also benefits directly from its partnerships with established libertarian organizations. For instance, an SFL staffer indicated that the group's Washington, D.C., headquarters were originally located in free space offered by the Cato Institute. Additionally, SFL partners with the Foundation for Economic Education (FEE), Cato, and the Ayn Rand Institute to provide a variety of free market–oriented books and literature to its members and students at campuses across the country. SFL has collaborated with the Atlas Economic Research Foundation to publish three original books, *After the Welfare State* (2012), *The Morality of Capitalism: What Your Professors Won't Tell You* (2011), and *The Economics of Freedom: What Your Professors Won't Tell You* (2010). As SFL seeks to transform the Liberty Movement into a global phenomenon, Atlas has also sponsored international essay contests for SFL and funded the SFL-affiliated African Liberty Students' Organization, the student arm of Atlas's own AfricanLiberty.org project.

Prominent SFL members have also received direct financial support from conservative sources. Dorian Electra described being contacted directly by the "Koch brothers" and having her travel and registration for the 2012 International Students for Liberty Conference (ISFLC) paid for by them. She said:

> They [the Koch brothers—she does not specify through which channels
> or organization] contacted me saying that they really loved my stuff and

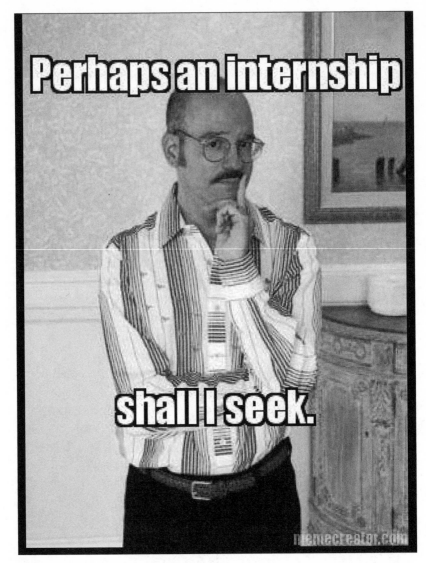

Meme from Students for Liberty Facebook Page.

they wanted to support me however they could. They paid for my plane ticket to go to SFL, which is really nice.

Despite the numerous ways in which SFL and its members are tied to the aforementioned funding streams, SFL characterizes itself as a grassroots network that developed organically after a 2008 roundtable discussion organized by McCobin and his peers at Columbia University—an event which garnered such interest that he says he knew he had to start a national organization. Asked what he thought explained SFL's rapid expansion since its start in 2008, McCobin responded,

> I think there are a couple of reasons why we've grown so quickly. The most important one is that there already was a strong demand for an organization like Students for Liberty among students. There were so many students who wanted something like this, who wanted to run their own groups, who wanted resources like our free books, speakers, networking these conferences. We knew this because we were those students. But no one had successfully done this before. So SFL was able to fill this already existing niche that no one else was doing.
>
> The other thing that I think has been really effective for us is that we've focused on empowering students to run their own organizations and promote liberty as they want to, instead of creating a top-down hierarchical organization that tries to get them to accomplish particular ends determined by an elite who "know best." The groups in our network are incredibly diverse. There are many different issues that students care about, different means of advancing these ideas that different students are more suited towards implementing, even different strands of thought within the Liberty Movement that lead to interesting debates and discussions amongst SFL'ers. We, SFL's leadership at the more national and international level, just exist to empower pro-liberty students to do what they want—providing [them] with leadership training, general resources and even just encouragement and oversight to make sure they're being active instead of giving up or unproductive.

McCobin's explanation of SFL's goals and structure illustrates how the organization is able to balance its participatory and institutional support, though the group's entrenchment with the libertarian elites of D.C. has been emphasized less and less in recent months. Recall McCobin's comments on second-wave libertarianism and the Liberty Movement's need to turn its efforts toward alliance building rather than strengthening and growing libertarian institutions. This makes for a somewhat paradoxical stance given all the institutional support the group has received.

Students for Liberty is in no sense a stealth organization in terms of its relationship to the right-wing funding structure. While McCobin did not address all the assistance he's had from various libertarian organizations in our interview, one can easily locate information about those ties on SFL's website and at its conferences, where representatives from dozens of Liberty Movement–related organizations are invited to conduct sessions and panels and distribute information and literature. Moreover, because SFL is a 501(c)3 organization, it is legally obliged to disclose all financial contributions and prohibited from lobbying.

Everything that McCobin says above appears to be true. SFL *does* take pride in maintaining a horizontal leadership structure and has capitalized on a calculable uptick in youth interest in libertarianism. What's more, SFL has given those young people myriad opportunities to network with important figures in the movement, enhancing their academic and career goals, and, by focusing on education over party politics, has offered students an opportunity to learn about libertarianism in a much less dogmatic manner than one might expect. SFL openly affirms, even celebrates, a wide range of viewpoints, and its emphasis on participatory politics distinguishes it from many conservative groups; Binder and Wood (2013), for instance, argue that while some conservative organizations, like the Young America's Foundation, adeptly employ populist rhetoric, this is more of a tactic than it is the expression of an underlying ideology. At the same time, SFL does not have the same kind of grassroots history as, for instance, the DREAMers chronicled in Chapter 5.

SFL's success and increasing reach has undoubtedly been made possible, at least in part, by McCobin's own networking savvy and political acumen, along with that of his co-founder, Sloane Frost, who was not interviewed for this project. Still, SFL gives its student leaders and members ample autonomy, while it also provides "top-down" forms of support (many participants join SFL's Alumni for Liberty program after graduating college, continue to attend SFL conferences, and often take jobs or internships with libertarian think tanks and policy organizations in the Washington, D.C., area). This combination of approaches has helped shape a movement in which participants remain excited about the project of furthering liberty long-term, even if the goal is sometimes far from tangible.

If we adopt the definition offered by Cohen and Kahne (2012) in the YPP survey report of participatory politics as "interactive, peer-based acts through which individuals and groups seek to exert both voice and influence on issues of public concern" (vi), it is clear that members of Students for Liberty and the Student Liberty Movement are engaged in participatory politics. While SFL has grown tremendously in the past five years, it has remained true to what it calls its grassroots beginnings by resisting top-down leadership models; it still relies primarily on student leaders to implement programs and organize conferences, and the small group of SFL paid staff is composed almost entirely of former student volunteers. Members also engage in a wide range of online participatory practices and modes of creative production, as evidenced by everything from the playful music videos already discussed to the dissemination of memes that critique the political status quo.

While engaging in participatory politics benefits young people in a number of ways, especially germane to young libertarians is how "participatory politics allow[s] individuals to operate with greater independence in the political realm, circumventing traditional gatekeepers of information and influence, such as newspaper editors, political parties, and interest groups" (Cohen and Kahne 2012, vi). Because young libertarians view their opinions as being largely ignored by the mainstream media and major political parties, they feel they must rely on alternative learning networks and forms of communication and circulation. Digital media is central to how young libertarians learn about both the theory that informs the movement and the details of movement-related actions and events. This is especially true for younger participants, many still in high school, who lack the resources to travel to conventions or attend meetings, but have found online discussions and spreadable media to be valuable points of entry into the discussion of ideas they would not have encountered through schools or broadcast media (see Chapter 2 for our account of this dynamic in the case of Invisible Children). Some, who knew of few if any libertarians in their local communities, described the experience of realizing that they were "not crazy" when they discovered others who shared their core ideological commitments online.

Young libertarians also challenge us to broaden the definition of participatory politics. Take, for instance, Cohen and Kahne's assertion that participatory politics navigates around hierarchical institutions and structures of power:

These practices are focused on expression and are peer based, interactive, and nonhierarchical, and they are not guided by deference to elite institutions. The pervasive presence of such practices in the lives of young people is creating an actual culture shift. The participatory skills, norms, and networks that develop when social media is used to socialize with friends or to engage with those who share one's interests can and are being transferred to the political realm. (vi)

Is it possible, in this light, to view young libertarians as engaged in participatory politics? We argue that the answer to that question is "yes," despite SFL's organizational ties. In a 2012 interview ("Youth and Participatory Politics in a Digital Age") released with the survey report, Cathy J. Cohen elaborated on the relationship between participatory politics and institutional politics: "Participatory politics is never meant to displace a focus on institutional politics. We might think of it as a supplemental domain where young people can take part in a dialogue about the issues that matter, think about strategies of mobilization, and do some of that mobilizing collectively online." Instead of saying that libertarians don't effectively disrupt power relations through participatory culture or that their ties to institutions negate their engagement with participatory politics, we can take all their practices, from creative production and meme sharing to networking with political elites, as evidence of their commitment to new modes of engagement. Ironically, some have doubted the political effectiveness of the organizations in our other case studies precisely because they were deemed to be insufficiently engaged with institutionalized politics, political parties, and elected officials.

Implicit in Cohen and Kahne's definition of participatory politics is the question of *who* is exerting political influence via these participatory activities. Scholars such as Nico Carpentier (2011) and Christopher Kelty (2013) have argued that the distribution of decision-making power and governance is the defining trait of what counts as political participation. Under Cohen and Kahne's rubric of participatory practices, the key issue is to what degree the power to influence agendas and tactics resides within individuals and communities (as opposed to voting blocs, special interest groups, lobbyists, media organizations, and political leaders): grassroots decision making dominates participatory politics, while more powerful and elite agents play the decisive role in institutionalized politics.

If we consider that the same influencing practices are deployed in both participatory politics and institutional politics (albeit by differing groups), we can think of young libertarians as utilizing those practices, often with great savvy, in both participatory and institutional politics at different times. Yet members of the Student Liberty Movement and other young libertarians have limited control and *varying degrees of influence* in the realm of institutional politics due to the role of power players and political elites. In the next section, we describe how young libertarians are working to expand their influence in that realm through efforts to reshape traditional civic practices such as voting. While SFL members might be smart about partnering with established institutions, they refuse to accept "politics as usual" (and the various forms of political engagement that go along with it) as their only option.

A Weak Investment: Libertarians and Nonvoting

Over half of the young libertarians we interviewed considered themselves categorical nonvoters. This is not to say that they were uninterested in political issues—quite the opposite. Rather, the nonvoters we talked to felt disaffected by politicians and their empty promises and what they perceived to be a broken system.

Ann, 23, described her ambivalence toward voting: "I just think that my time and energy can be used much better in other ways. . . . I, in no way, I guess, discredit the voting process. It's just not something that is worth it right now for me to engage in." Ann's sense that voting is not "worth it" can be viewed as the result of a kind of cost-benefit analysis of electoral engagement. She suggested that the cost of taking the time to register, educate herself about the candidates, and go to the polls was too high, given that she saw voting as having little benefit to her personally and little impact on the outcome of any election.

This nonvoting stance also surfaced in the media artifacts circulated by Liberty Movement participants. We frequently encountered images and memes related to voting—or rather, not voting—on Facebook and Tumblr. For example, this image of an unknown student was circulated widely on Facebook:

Meme circulated in libertarian Facebook group.

And there was this meme of actor/comedian Drew Carey, who has been a vocal proponent of small government:

Meme circulated in libertarian Facebook group.

While this image, which suggests that the two major political parties are exploiting democracy for their exclusive benefit, seems to question whether voting is a worthwhile endeavor in such an arrangement (with the lamb's vote counting for little to nothing):

DEMOCRACY

TWO WOLVES AND A SHEEP VOTING ON WHAT'S FOR DINNER

Meme circulated in libertarian Facebook group.

Images like these, many of which were circulated widely during the 2012 campaign season, illustrate how the nonvoting stance has become encoded into the movement's iconography. In a blog post on digital civics, Ethan Zuckerman (2012b) suggests that those on the left and the right are increasingly moving away from legislative theories of social change, or the "old civics" model, and adopting a "new digital civics" through which people learn "how to raise attention for causes, how to use distributed populations to propose solutions to problems, and how to synchronize supporters around a strategy." This notion of a new digital civics applies to the young libertarians we interviewed, many of whom described having given up on electoral politics in favor of effecting change through alternative mechanisms, namely educational means.

Charles, 25, explained, "What really matters in terms of making lasting social change is the idea—and specifically kind of the general view of government and power that people have." Similarly, Seth, a 23-year-old from Arizona, said:

> I think most libertarians tend to think of it [libertarianism] as educational. They're introducing ideas to more people. The ways that Americans think about politics tend to be around election time and so they can't see it rather opportunistically perhaps. We don't tend to like the way of solving problems politically. We think the incentives are very bad and they tend to favor people that have the most power at the expense of everyone else.

Interestingly, while many participants felt disillusioned with electoral politics, they often described being supportive of others who might want to get involved in campaigns. Aaron, 21, from Ohio, declared:

> I mean, I'm not going to vote for Ron Paul. I'm not going to vote period. But I don't discourage people from, like, getting involved with it or anything like that. I'll discourage them from voting, but not from actually campaigning and activism; I think that's really valuable.

Notice how Aaron distinguishes voting from other kinds of activism, even campaigning. This stance may seem counterintuitive. However, campaigning (of the sort done by Ron Paul, who knew he had no chance of actually winning the 2008 or 2012 Republican presidential primaries) may be regarded as another form of education and thus congruent with both second-wave libertarianism and Zuckerman's shifting notion of civics. Though their energies are largely focused elsewhere than the ballot box, young libertarians are highly politically knowledgeable, informed, and interested (Gamber-Thompson 2012).

In their account of generational shifts in citizen participation, Zukin et al. (2006, 10) note a generation gap in voter turnout over the past 30-plus years, with younger voter participation on a downward trend and older voter participation stable (though youth voting rates were generally higher in the 2004, 2008, and 2012 elections). Scholars (Putnam 2000; Skocpol 2003) have also noted among young Americans a decline in other types of activities related to public life such as "working for parties and candidates, choosing public service careers, and following public affairs in the news" (Zukin et al. 2006, 10). Young libertarians belie this trend—they are quite active in these more "civic" activities, but they are not as interested in electoral politics. Zukin et al. do find that millennials tend to be more involved in civic activities like volunteering, but they don't often view these activities as politically motivated (195). In contrast, most of the young libertarians with whom we spoke characterized the goals of educating others about liberty and working toward wider acceptance of libertarian ideas as *highly* political, a notion that, again, has been woven into the second-wave ethos (educational, nonelectoral).

Alexander McCobin did not mince words when asked about the value of voting:

I don't think there's going to be any actual reform in the political system in [the] short term. I don't invest my time in the political game because I believe nothing is going to happen there right now. The system is too ingrained for any meaningful change to take place. The older generations have caused the problems we're facing right now, and give little reason to expect their [demonstrating the] capability of offering an alternative.

To McCobin, the most important thing was to

change the general viewpoint of society, which means spreading the philosophy of liberty to more people. I think in 10 and 20 years from now, we're going to be in a very different situation where there are more people who openly endorse libertarianism, who are strong advocates in various positions in the society for these ideas, and who can actually change things. That's what I'm looking toward. Until we have an influential mass though, the only proposals offered will be short-term or marginal at best. Until more people actually embrace the ideas of liberty, spending time on the political system directly is not useful.

McCobin didn't specify his primary source of frustration with the political system, though libertarian critiques often revolve around the extent of lobbying in Washington, D.C., corporate-government collusion, and the rigidness of the two-party system. Rather than taking up the task of fixing an impossibly corrupt system, McCobin and many others in his cohort are betting on shifting public consciousness. He said, "Being an activist doesn't mean you have to support legislation or vote for a candidate. You can be activist for principles and that's what I see myself doing and that's what I see a lot of Students for Liberty [doing] too."

This idea, that one can be an activist for principles, stems, at least in part, from Austrian economist F. A. Hayek's 1949 essay "The Intellectuals and Socialism." Hayek describes the "intellectual" class (he uses the term in a broad sense to describe participants in a number of "learned" fields) as the "professional secondhand dealers in ideas." He argues that the "success" of early-20th-century European socialism was due in large part to intellectuals' influence on public opinion and that those invested in a resurgence of liberalism have much to learn from this model:

> The main lesson which the true liberal must learn from the success of the socialists is that it was their courage to be Utopian which gained them the support of the intellectuals and therefore an influence on public opinion which is daily making possible what only recently seemed utterly remote. (371)

Note that when he talks about the "true liberal," Hayek is referring to classical liberalism. This 19th-century political ideology, which he and Milton Friedman were largely responsible for bringing back into favor, focuses on individual liberties and economic freedom.[3] Hayek encourages his readers to "make the philosophic foundations of a free society once more a living intellectual issue, and its implementation a task which challenges the ingenuity and imagination of our liveliest minds" (384). It is this call to action that McCobin and others at Students for Liberty have taken to heart, choosing to become 21st-century "secondhand dealers in ideas," whether at think tanks and policy organizations like the Institute for Humane Studies or the Cato Institute, the Atlas Foundation or the Foundation for Economic Education, or as aspiring professors, lawyers, and scholars.

While many participants draw their discursive (over electoral) theory of social change from Hayek, public choice theory, a modern school of thought whose adherents apply economic theories to topics traditionally studied by political scientists, also supports a nonvoting stance and is identified by many young libertarians as an influence on their thinking. According to one expression of the public choice theory perspective, public choice scholars

> conclude that voters in democratic elections will tend to be poorly informed about the candidates and issues on the ballot. Voter ignorance is rational because the cost of gathering information about an upcoming election is high relative to the benefits of voting. Why should a voter bother to become informed if his vote has a very small chance of being decisive? Geoffrey Brennan and Loren Lomasky, among others, have suggested that people vote because it is a low-cost way to express their preferences. In this view, voting is no more irrational than cheering for one's favorite sports team. (Shughart 2008)

Another way to think about libertarians' de-emphasis on voting and their parsing out of activism from politics is to think about their embrace of a variety of different "levers of change" (Zuckerman 2013a). In his keynote speech at the 2013 Digital Media and Learning Conference, Zuckerman explains that legislative levers are often considered the "gold standard for progress" but that, in fact, these "legislative levers can be very hard for individuals and for new groups to move, and focusing solely on the legislative lever misses other promising opportunities for change." Sometimes, activists seek to move other levers of power unrelated to politicians passing bills or to voting (examples include influencing authority figures and shifting public opinion). Zuckerman notes that the participants in many online campaigns—such as the one, discussed in Chapter 2, that revolved around Invisible Children's *Kony 2012*—regard shifting public opinion as a valuable lever; similarly, young libertarians see shifting public opinion as an important mechanism for change, if not *the* most important lever.

Toward a Broader Definition of Citizenship

While not all interview participants considered themselves nonvoters, we talked to *no one* who felt that voting was a moral or civic duty. This finding suggests that there is a close relationship between the young libertarians' views of electoral politics and their conceptions of citizenship more broadly. As 24-year-old Rusty put it, "I want to see people get politically uninvolved. I want the politicians to know they are not important. We don't like them, we don't want them around, go away. And citizenship, I don't even know what that's supposed to mean, I don't think of myself as a citizen of anywhere. I'm a human being born on the planet Earth, that's it." This stance is related to the fundamental libertarian position that individual rights are inherent, not contingent on government choices. On citizenship, Seth, a 23-year-old writer and filmmaker, explained:

> The difficult thing for me is that I don't think rights are given to individuals by government. By being a human being, you have certain basic rights that can't be infringed upon by any government whether you're a citizen of that government or not. That's what I care about more than anything else—making sure that those basic human rights are protected. So representation of political system and things like that are to a certain sense secondary to me.

In our interviews with young libertarians, we asked two questions related to citizenship. First: "How would you define citizenship?" And second: "What does a good citizen do?" On the whole, respondents gave answers related to their personal thoughts and feelings toward citizenship *or* descriptions of popular notions of citizenship in their definitions of citizenship. When respondents voiced their own opinions on citizenship, they were often negative. The young libertarians with whom we spoke often described feeling that the concept of national citizenship was too binding and that it was better to seek cooperation on a human level; some, like Rusty, disavowed the concept of national citizenship completely. In their description of what a citizen does according to popular culture, respondents often mentioned political participation and patriotism as core elements of the role. In response to the second question on good citizenship, they reported feeling that there was a disconnect between the ways in which they wanted to enact change (mutual aid, creative entrepreneurship, etc.) and how "good citizens" were supposed to enact change (voting, writing to political representatives, etc.).

These viewpoints are consistent with changing citizenship styles as described in a growing body of literature (Norris 1999; Lichterman 1995,

1996; Youniss et al. 2002; Juris and Pleyers 2009; Zukin et al. 2006; Dalton 2009; Bennett 2008b; Bennett Wells, and Rank 2009; Bennett, Freelon, and Wells 2010; Bennett, Wells, and Freelon 2011, among others). Informing some of this literature is the notion that youth civic engagement is in crisis due to a perceived decline in traditional forms of participation and a growing sense of apathy among youth.

W. Lance Bennett (2008a) argues that citizenship styles are moving from a *dutiful citizen* model, characterized by a sense of obligation to participate in government-centered activities and a belief in voting as the core democratic act, to an *actualizing citizen* model, where government obligation is replaced by a higher sense of individual purpose, and voting is less meaningful than practices like consumerism, volunteering, and transnational activism. The actualizing citizen is also less apt to express her or his interests through political parties, and is distrustful of mass media. Instead of more traditional mechanisms of change such as parties and legislative measures, actualizing citizens favor loose networks like those fostered by digital and online technologies (Bennett 2008a, 14). Young libertarians—who voice distrust not only of the Democratic and Republican parties, but even sometimes of the Libertarian Party—map onto this framework quite easily.

Russell J. Dalton's (2009) account of changing citizenship norms involves an explicit critique of the panics around disengagement. Rather than arguing that alternative citizenship models that focus on civic engagement over political engagement have arisen in recent years, Dalton claims that young people's disillusionment with traditional forms of politics has to do with the fact that "voting is a form of action for those with limited skills, resources and motivations" (67). According to Dalton, as citizens' political skills and acumen grow, they often become dissatisfied with the limited political influence offered by voting and, as an alternative, participate through activities that are citizen initiated, policy oriented, less constrained, and directly linked to government. These are the kinds of activities we address through the concept of participatory politics. While Dalton's claims have not gone uncontested (see Thorson 2010), many young libertarians would agree with his assessment of voting and engagement, which echoes the public choice theory perspective described earlier. As Ann (who said that voting is not "worth it") pointed out in our interview: "I think I view kind of civic engagement and my role in it as more community engagement. So what I do is engaging my peers on issues and topics and stuff like that. And that I think I hope has a bigger impact than I could ever have by just filling in the check box."

Concerning attitudes toward citizenship, it is informative to compare young libertarians with the DREAMers described in Chapter 5. The majority of libertarians with whom we spoke were very supportive of the cause of the DREAMers and of immigration reform efforts. As Andy said, "I think the opposition to immigration is clearly discriminatory. It's not based in economics. It's generally based in bias and racial concerns." Of making immigration policies less restrictive, he said, "It makes economic sense. It's better for individuals to have free motion across borders. It's better for family."

But, as might be expected from young libertarians' view of themselves as "global citizens," their support for immigration reform was often coupled with the downplaying of national identity, which marks a sharp contrast to the DREAMers who call for immigration reform *and* stress the value of citizenship. The libertarian viewpoint on citizenship is also often one of distinct privilege in comparison to the DREAMers; it is easy to take citizenship for granted—and even critique it—when its benefits are assumed. Yet, while young libertarians might not consider citizenship an important part of their own identities, their belief that undocumented immigrants deserve the same rights that they enjoy is undiminished.

The shared concerns of young libertarians and DREAMers speaks to a growing body of scholarship on "DIY citizenship," in which authors and activists like Megan Boler (2008) argue that the "social web," or Web 2.0, allows participants to move toward a "radical democratization of knowledge." In DIY citizenship, the use of web-based media and engagement in practices like citizen journalism can have a direct impact in shaping political and social movements. This space of DIY citizenship is where libertarians make some strange bedfellows. While libertarians and DREAMers may have widely divergent conceptions of national citizenship, they are both engaged in radical efforts to shift the meaning of citizenship and participation, and they do this partly through engagement with the cultural realm and participatory politics. In their efforts to radicalize democracy and expand notions of citizenship through discursive change, young libertarians even built bridges with Occupy protesters, expressing quite a bit of sympathy with them (the case study interviews occurred during the height of the Occupy movement). On Occupy, Benjamin, a 22-year-old college student, recalled, "I went to some of their big marches. It was very fun. It was very exhilarating to see lots of people very angry about injustices and issues that I thought are completely justified to be angry about." Twenty-five-old Charles added:

> Personally, I am very sympathetic [to the OWS movement]. They are equally upset with the status quo as we are, and we identify a lot of the same problems like government being involved with various corporations—very bad. Like the revolving door between Wall Street and K Street—very bad. Like these conflicts of power where you have the same people running a big company also working for the government and giving tons of money to politicians and vice versa. And the bailout. We share these frustrations with them.

Young libertarians' unexpected alliances and complex relationship to the electoral process show us that it is important to continue to refine our working definitions of participatory politics. They illustrate how stronger ties to elite institutions do not necessarily rule out participatory engagement. What's more, they are not alone having connections to elites; we can find examples in all the case studies in this book of participatory groups with elite and institutional ties that are more or less in the spotlight at particular moments.

Of all of the groups we studied, Invisible Children, discussed in Chapter 2, looks and feels the most like a traditional kind of political organization, with top-down leadership, with strong partnerships with mainstream media organizations and celebrities, with guest appearances by elected government officials, and with D.C.-based lobbying initiatives. The HPA, for example, has partnered with established nonprofits such as Oxfam, Partners in Health, and STAND on many of its campaigns. These partnerships enabled the HPA to connect its volunteers' monetary donations as well as their time and effort with the on-the-ground experience and networks of these nonprofits. Regarding the American Muslim youth featured in Chapter 4, both the Young Leaders Summits and MYG reside within the larger institutions of MPAC and

ICSC respectively. Along with the benefits of such affiliations, we also saw the drawbacks, especially when it came to grappling with bureaucracy and the way organizational protocols frustrated young members' attempts to mobilize in a timely manner at key moments. Many campaigns run by the DREAMer youth organizations and collectives are organized in partnership with established immigrant rights groups. For instance, the UCLA Labor Center often acts as an institutional partner, raising money for various DREAMer campaigns, helping affiliated groups develop relationships with foundation partners, and hosting programs like Dream Summer, while the National Day Laborer Organizing Network has teamed up with the youth organization United We Dream. While such institutional partnerships are not often permanent, they are quite common within the movement. In none of these cases, though, would we describe the youth-driven groups as "fronts" for the more established organizations, as has been suggested when we've discussed the Students for Liberty case in some academic settings. We need a more nuanced way to describe the ways that these movements are negotiating between participatory and institutional models as they seek to both expand the number and diversity of voices that get heard and insure that their messages reach those with the power to act upon them.

The Future of Institutional Politics

What, then, is the future of institutional politics in an age of participatory politics? As illustrated by all the case studies in this book, the scenario is not necessarily one in which participatory politics simply supplants institutional politics; the institutional mechanisms by which politics is enacted in this country—sometimes at a grinding pace—are far too ingrained to be superseded in a generation's time. In some cases, our research suggests that engagement in the practices of participatory politics is more likely to increase participation in institutional politics—that these practices serve as an entry point to the traditional political system. Other groups we study, such as the DREAMers, are excluded from participation via voting and some of the other mechanisms for institutional politics, yet they are struggling to gain access to those mechanisms. In still others, young people are turning away from institutional politics as a dead end or time suck and seeking to promote change through other means. Still, we argue that participatory politics is a growing trend with which institutional players must reckon, not only because so many of today's young people have a complex, if not contentious, account of how change occurs, but also because politicians will, quite simply, have a serious youth vote problem on their hands if they choose to ignore it.

A 2014 Pew Report on Millennials found that 50 percent of young people ages 18–33 view neither the Republican Party nor the Democratic Party favorably, and some of those who will campaign for president in 2016 are poised to capitalize on this. Enter Kentucky senator, Tea Party darling, and Republican presidential candidate Rand Paul. Many of his positions, including his highly publicized stands against the use of militarized drones and the National Security Agency's surveillance practices, as well as his isolationist foreign policy, speak to the interests and concerns of American youth, especially libertarian youth, even as they challenge established views within the Republican Party. Paul has also been urging Republicans to do more to reach out to minority voters, refusing to cede them to Democratic candidates.

No doubt, Paul and his supporters are hoping to tap into that millennial independent streak in 2016 (as is Bernie Sanders on the Democratic side) in much the same way his father, Representative Ron Paul, did in 2012, but with an even more successful turnout at the ballot box, a feat our research suggests is less than certain. If sentiment toward the Libertarian Party among our interviewees was tepid, their feelings toward the Republican Party ranged from cool to icy. Rusty said, "I think there is a breakdown with working with conservatives, because we are getting more and more fed up with them and their social views." Ann, a former Young Republican, explained, "That's where I kind of felt uncomfortable with conservatism—when it came to putting things into law with regard to values."

It's easy to see, then, that there may be a mismatch between how Rand Paul wants to effect political change, and the model informing second-wave libertarianism. Unlike the elder Paul, who many in the movement revere for his efforts to bring libertarian ideas into the public debate, his son aims to make a serious bid for the presidency. A January 2014 *New York Times* profile of Rand Paul includes a telling observation by John Samples, a Cato Institute analyst who knows both Pauls. "Unlike his father, he's not interested in educating," said Samples. "He's interested in winning" (Tanenhaus and Rutenberg 2014).

So how will Paul and the Republican Party speak to young voters? We suspect Paul will need to appeal to a wide range of conservative youth voters, including young libertarians, to garner success; our arguments in this chapter suggest that he can rely on libertarian-leaning young people within the party itself, but cannot necessarily count on the burgeoning Student Liberty Movement, whose participants are leery of institutional politics. While Paul has made some effort to appeal to the intellectual sensibilities of those involved in the movement, his conservative personal views on gay marriage, border security, net neutrality, and marijuana legalization are unlikely to play well among its more left-libertarian-leaning ranks.

Young libertarians, like the diverse groups of young people described throughout this book, show us that activism can come in many forms—in their case, often ones articulated as antithetical to the very concepts of electoral politics and national citizenship. For them, the revolution will be won one heart and one mind at a time, and thus only time will tell if young people outside the movement will embrace their efforts to reframe the debate. In our concluding chapter, we return to the concept of participatory politics in an effort to more precisely define the models for political and cultural participation we have described. There, we seek to identify the frameworks that give us the most effective systematic ways to think about how politics is changing, and consider how the participatory forms discussed herein can shift agendas and reshape institutional politics as we know it.

7

"It's Called Giving a Shit!"

What Counts as "Politics"?

Henry Jenkins and Sangita Shresthova

In November 2012, MIT's Futures of Entertainment conference assembled representatives from several of our case study organizations to discuss participatory politics. But, when asked if they identified as activists, each participant distanced themselves from this term. Bassam Tariq of the 30 Mosques project thought it was "awful" that political categories were imposed upon Muslim cultural, social, and religious practices; in his projects he tried to "stay away" from politics in order to focus on "universals," things everyone can "relate to," and ideas that are "more open-ended" rather than "imposing an agenda." Dorian Electra, whose music videos have been widely embraced by Students for Liberty, argued that "being too politicized" might distract from her work's educational and entertainment value. The Harry Potter Alliance's Lauren Bird acknowledged that the group, while nonprofit and thus nonpartisan, was involved in a range of political issues, but Bird stressed that members might have widely divergent perspectives; ultimately the HPA was "more on the side of human rights" rather than a particular political "ideology." In each case, their comments revealed something about the negative ways these youth perceived institutional politics and the ways they define their organizations in opposition to those negative qualities.

As the young panelists expressed their hesitations about situating their work as political, the audience, mostly from a slightly older generation, were expressing, via Twitter, their dissatisfaction with what they characterized as a "backlash" against activism or a denial of the political stakes of these young people's public expression. One audience member summarized the situation as a "wow" moment when "the young panelists . . . knee-jerked away from claiming their work is political."

"Why is activism considered a dirty word?" another audience member asked. "Of course human rights is ideological . . . EVERYthing is political," another vehemently argued. Yet another summed up the collective response, "On the semantics front, it's not called 'activism.' It's called 'giving a shit.'"

These experiences at the Futures of Entertainment conference have haunted us as we have been writing this book, forcing us to continually ask such questions as: What counts as "politics"? Who gets to decide? Throughout this book, we have referred to these youth as activists, because they are seeking to bring about social and political change through their work. Yet some of them adopt other frames for their activity. Who are *we* to identify as "political" activities the participants themselves sometimes understood in different terms—as participation in fan communities, forms of sociability, extensions of their cultural and ethnic identities, tools for education and cultural change, forms of charity and public service, ways to "decrease world suck"? And how do we think about the problematic relationship between these attempts to "change the world" and institutionalized politics?

On their own terms, some of the groups and networks we are discussing provide preconditions for a civic culture, performing such tasks as articulating shared identities or values, fostering greater knowledge and awareness of political issues, encouraging civic conversations, or modeling civic practices, as we saw in relation to the Harry Potter Alliance and the Nerdfighters in Chapter 3. We have argued throughout that fostering a culture of participation—both cultural and political—can be valuable in and of itself, especially for youth, quite apart from the specific outcomes of their efforts. Couldry (2010) discusses such preconditions in terms of the ways young people can develop and deploy their own voices as political agents. Ethan Zuckerman (2015) discusses these preconditions in terms of the latent capacities of some groups to mobilize politically *under the right circumstances*. So what are the right circumstances? We've examined a range of different circumstances that have moved individuals and groups from cultural participation to participatory politics, and yet there's so much more we still have to understand about what kinds of organizational and leadership structures need to be in place to enable such transformations.

Some of the groups' activities can be described as charitable, such as the Harry Potter Alliance campaigns to raise money for disaster relief in Haiti or to provide books for libraries in Africa, Invisible Children's work on the ground in Uganda to counter the consequences of child soldiering, or the efforts of the Nerdfighters to use YouTube to increase the visibility of various nonprofits. Some are conducted in the spirit of "the personal as political" that has motivated previous generations of identity politics movements around race, gender, or sexuality, even as our current understanding of identities is multiple, intersectional, fluid, and contradictory. Consider, for example, the ways the DREAMers' "coming out" videos borrowed practices from the LGBTQ movement and the Latino testimonio tradition, as well as from self-help programs, such as Alcoholics Anonymous. We might want to consider more deeply when "coming out" constitutes a personal statement—asserting greater control over one's own life conditions, claiming a certain kind of identity and agency—and when it addresses institutional politics as a call for immigration reform, though this example makes clear how hard it can be to separate the two. Other activities are explicitly cultural, as in some of the projects in the American Muslim community. Here, the goal is to increase visibility, build community, or challenge stereotypes that block young Muslims' full acceptance into American society. Yet for this particular group, the cultural is always already political. The panelists' comments at MIT suggests that activism is often understood as "politically correct," as embodying the concerns of "special interests," as rigid and uncompromising, whereas these youth are seeking ways to reimagine the civic that allow for diverse voices to be heard and some consensus to be achieved.

Not all of these groups will achieve their civic and political goals. Throughout, we've identified many points where these efforts can break down, including gaps between centralized leadership and dispersed communication or a lack of readiness to engage in contentious politics (as in the case of Invisible Children), struggles to increase diversity (as in the case of Nerdfighters and the Harry Potter Alliance), the chilling effect of surveillance (as in the case of American Muslim youth), the denial of the rights to become citizens or limits to access to communication technologies (as in the case of the DREAMers) or tensions between institutional support and participatory politics (as in the case of Students for Liberty).

We could have pushed further to consider, for example, generational divides in terms of what constitutes appropriate political speech (and thus an inability of those in power to comprehend particular forms of the civic imagination), the impact of systemic forms of exclusion, the many dysfunctions of the American political process, the marginalizing and trivializing representation of these campaigns through news coverage, or the ways that certain topics get proclaimed as the exclusive realm of institutionally sanctioned experts and closed off from popular discourse. We've also discussed in Chapter 2 a series of paradoxes and contradictions—competing pulls and tugs—which these groups must navigate between goals and process, comprehensible and complex stories, activism and entertainment, consensus and contention, spreadable and drillable messages, and top-down and bottom-up approaches. And, as Nico Carpentier might suggest, we also should be attentive to these groups' structures of governance—the ways that they support and sustain their members' active and meaningful participation and, as we saw with IC, the ways they may fall back on minimalist participation structures.

Yet, for each of these groups, there are moments when their activities cross over fully and unambiguously into the political, doing things or addressing concerns that we would understand as political if conducted by any other group—registering people to vote, lobbying elected officials, advocating public policies, mobilizing street protests—and we cannot simply separate these activities from a range of other practices that inspire them. If they are not always activists, they are activists at least some of the time. Pippa Norris (1999) discusses "the new politics:" "[P]olitical activism has been reinvented in recent decades by a diversification in the _agencies_ (the collective organizations structuring political activity), the _repertoires_ (the political actions commonly used for political expression), and the _targets_ (the political actors that participants seek to influence)" (215–216). So we are seeing politics conducted through fan organizations (new agencies), politics conducted through creating and sharing music videos (new repertoires), and politics directed against Lowe's, Warner Brothers, and Lionsgate (new targets) rather than towards elected officials.

Dahlgren (2009) might argue that these groups, organizations, networks, and communities constitute civic cultures, understood as "cultural patterns in which identities of citizenship, and the foundations of civic agency, are embedded" (106). Civic cultures provide the preconditions for political action, and this book has explored some of the ways that those potentials are being realized or thwarted within the current media landscape. What we've called the civic imagination is a fundamental dimension of Dahlgren's civic cultures, shaping the ways people come to think of themselves as political agents, and those civic cultures are, in turn, being shaped by the collective imagining of their participants. In many cases, these imagining communities are addressing classic political questions, such as the DREAMers' focus on what makes someone a citizen or the Students for Liberty's ongoing exploration of the relationship of individuals to government.

As we saw in Chapter 1, there has been an increased need for more precise descriptions of different conditions that get labeled as participation, as a rhetoric of participation engulfs many kinds of contemporary social and cultural activities, from liking someone on Facebook to designing open source software, from contributing to YouTube to organizing a political movement. We might start with the question of what we are participating in—a purely commercial transaction or some form of "community" (itself a vexed word in contemporary commercial discourse) where participants work together to achieve shared goals. We might also ask what features characterize particular kinds of participation and what factors pull a participatory community toward civic engagement and political action. Our assumption here is that these groups have achieved varying degrees of participation (never fully achieving the ideal of maximalist participation), and that we all live in a *more* participatory culture, by which we mean both that more people have the communicative capacities to help shape cultural production and circulation and that more groups are offering members more chances to meaningfully contribute in terms of setting their agendas, defining their tactics, and creating their messages.

Popular Culture as a Civic Pathway

Our book has been mapping some of the "civic pathways" that might enable young people who are active in participatory culture to see themselves as political agents and get involved in practices designed to "change the world." The groups we have discussed often display a complex blending between interest-driven and friendship-based networks. Even with an organization like the Harry Potter Alliance, a textbook example of how an interest-driven network can mobilize its members for political agendas, our research has encountered many people who are participating not because they share a passion for Harry Potter but because they were invited to participate by friends who do. Even in those cases where people are acting on a strong self-interest, such as the DREAMers, we find a social and cultural basis for their involvement—for example, as an extension of their interests in crafts, graphic arts, or video production. And even where groups are formed around a shared political philosophy, as with Students for Liberty, getting involved expands their friendship networks. So all of our cases show a complex interweaving of the cultural, social, and political.

Popular culture offers shared references and resources participants use to help frame their messages and provides platforms through which they can stage their hopes and fears about the world and thus start to exercise the civic imagination. Popular culture facilitates shared affective investments that bond members together, providing a vision of change that is empowering, meaningful, and pleasurable as they conduct the often hard and discouraging work of political activism. Popular culture performs bonding functions within the group and also bridging functions toward a broader public. So, for example, when the DREAMers tap into superhero mythology, this shared reference point allows them to make common cause with Imagine Better, which used the release of *Man of Steel*, a reboot of the Superman saga, for a cultural acupuncture campaign focused on immigrant rights. And beyond this, we have found examples of the use of superhero analogies across all of our case study groups, suggesting many unrealized opportunities for these groups to communicate with each other around shared visions and interests. (Jenkins et. al. forthcoming).

Jonathan Gray (2012) describes the role that signs and costumes drawn from the realm of fandom played among those who organized an extended protest against Wisconsin governor Scott Walker's anti–collective bargaining policies:

> I start with the observation that these signs aided camaraderie. Protest-
> ers came from a wide range of backgrounds, as Madison's Capitol Square

Star Wars iconography used in efforts to oust Wisconsin governor Scott Walker (photograph by Jonathan Gray).

filled with local teachers, graduate students, senior citizens, firefighters, snowplow drivers, high school students, professors, undergraduates from around the state and country, steelworkers, and many, many more, including a wide swath of concerned citizens of Madison. But how do such individuals and such distinct communities come together and work together toward a common goal? How do they create a communal understanding of what is going on and of their role in this?

Star Wars–themed signs, which depicted the governor as an "Imperial Walker," evoked shared cultural experiences and their playful tone dispelled some anxieties that had arisen around the mainstream media's, often hostile, depiction of the protests. Furthermore, they conjured up empowering images of what it meant for these people to stand up against what they saw as entrenched power. Whether or not they were hardcore *Star Wars* fans, they were adopting these images because of their symbolic or mythic value. Their hopes for political transformation (or at least the removal of an unpopular governor from office)

Meme linking Dora the Explorer to the treatment of undocumented immigrants.

were expressed through a shared language drawn from popular culture, which might be deeply valued by some and only superficially appreciated by others.

Gray's example also reminds us of the difference between a fan activist group, such as the Harry Potter Alliance, that grounds its many campaigns in a single content world and other kinds of movements—such as Occupy or the Wisconsin protests—that tap different fictional universes for their rhetorical ends. So for example, we've discussed the DREAMers' use of superhero metaphors, but their media productions display a much broader range of cultural references, as in this graphic, which shows Dora the Explorer, one of the few Latina characters in contemporary children's media, having been subjected to the brutal treatment that border guards sometimes inflict on immigrants.

Some DREAMers are no doubt fans of Superman or Dora the Explorer; for others, these borrowed images are a means to an end, yet few seem as overtly hostile to popular culture as activists of the culture jamming era would have been. The above meme is directed at the INS, not Dora's producers, and it depends on our sympathy for the beloved character.

We are observing a shift in the language of social change from realist to utopian or fantastical modes, from traditional forms of political education to a style of politics that borrows heavily from entertainment. What does it mean, as we've seen in the case of second-wave libertarians, to translate economic theories into a music video or, as we've seen in the case of American Muslims, to turn back a stereotype with a joke? Can we use dance to address horrific conditions in Africa, as Invisible Children tried to do? Richard Dyer (1985) makes the case that entertainment often offers us not a vision for what actual political alternatives might look like but rather a taste of what utopia might feel like, with its values expressed through our sense of empowerment, intensity, and plentitude in contrast to our real-world constraints.

Tapping into the language of popular entertainment may allow participants to bring some of those affective intensities into their work. Here, again, Gray's (2012) discussion of the Wisconsin protests proves helpful: "All of the *Star Wars* signs framed the protests in larger cosmological terms, calling for the protesters to stick around for Episode VI and the celebratory ending. So too did the Harry Potter and *Lord of the Rings* signs invoke grand and grueling battles of good versus evil. They referenced a battle that would be neither quick nor easy, but would reward continued investment, and that was absolutely vital." His comments suggest something else: popular culture provides models for what movements might look like—as in, for example, the ways that the HPA calls itself "Dumbledore's Army for the real world" or Imagine Better has anchored its critiques of economic inequalities to the three-finger salute from *The Hunger Games*. This is at the heart of what the group means by "imagine better," a phrase that takes advantage of two possible interpretations—to do a better job of imagining alternatives to current social conditions, and to imagine a better world and work to achieve it. So-called realist modes often depict problems as overwhelming, conditions as irreversible, thus offering a profoundly disempowering mindset for thinking about politics. Much as earlier civil rights movements discussed their "dreams" or imagined entering the "promised land," these rhetorical and expressive practices increase efficacy as movement participants sought to work around or get past current inequalities and injustices. We shall overcome, indeed.

Zizi A. Papacharissi (2010) talks about a new "civic vernacular," Pippa Norris (2002) about new "repertoires" for civic action, each identifying ways new symbolic resources, new modes of communication, and new rhetorical practices are changing political speech. These new rhetorics impact how we express affiliations with others, how we articulate our political identities, and especially how we deal with those with whom we have significant disagreements. Many of the youth we interviewed experienced the language of American politics as both exclusive and repulsive. Instead, they are creating forms of speech that make sense in their everyday lifeworlds, speaking about politics through channels they already use to connect with their friends. There is much we still need to know about the ways these emerging political rhetorics break down, coming across to those with institutional power as childish rather than engaged, self-involved rather than self-empowering, or escapist rather than pragmatic.

Political Storytelling and Transmedia Mobilization

We've argued that these groups are seeking to bring about social change by any media necessary. In discussing the immigrant rights movement in Los Angeles or, more recently, Occupy Wall Street, Sasha Costanza-Chock (2010, 2012) argues that transmedia mobilization (which he is increasingly calling transformative mobilization) often means a decentering of traditional authorities, so that all participants are seen as having an expressive capacity, free to construct and circulate their own media, framing their message in different languages to reach different audiences. As they do so, these activists reject traditional models of strategic communication that stress the construction of a unified message or stable identity; no one instantiation of the message is likely to reach all potential audiences, while deploying diverse communication practices is likely to accelerate the spread and extend the reach of their shared agenda. Because of the diversity of participants and the lowered stakes of each communication practice, such movements may be highly generative, testing different media platforms or rhetorical practices, as these networks seek new ways to spread their message. These diverse media productions can stimulate more intense discussions, even where individual messages are simplified.

Yet there are also risks that such diffused, decentralized strategies may be more easily co-opted through the broadcast capacity of concentrated media. Michelangelo Signorile (2012), a longtime queer activist and talk show host, discussed the success and limits of a grassroots effort to call out the fast food chain Chick-fil-A for its owner's support of homophobic organizations. Signorile argues that the campaign's participatory approach made it easy to join but difficult to control its messaging: "Our enemies distorted our message and reframed the story. . . . How did we allow it to happen? Because there was no coordinated effort on our side. The controversy was largely driven by blogs, social media and very loosely organized grassroots activists, with no coordinated leadership." For Signorile, the distributed framing of issues is always going to be less coherent than corporate communication strategies that speak with one voice—another reason why the groups we are discussing here constitute "precarious publics."

In a much discussed essay focused on the logics that drive collective and connected action in the digital era, W. Lance Bennett and Alexandra Segerberg (2012) draw a contrast between older movements, which took a long time to develop, but came with shared identities and agendas, and more contemporary movements, which have been able to take shape quickly, often through tapping into the personal narratives and individual experiences of participants, but depend on much looser agreements. The first type is slow to emerge, they argue, while the second struggles with issues of coherence and sustainability. Our focus on groups and networks here prompts us to step back a little from their stress on the personalized or individualistic nature of such political efforts, which they argue, see "politics as an expression of personal hopes, lifestyles, and grievances" (743). However, we share their sense that it is important to identify the mechanisms that enable such movements to solidify around collective concerns and exert sustained pressure on the system to accommodate their demands.

Within this model of transmedia mobilization, youth are encouraged not only to help spread preconstructed messages, but also to "give account of themselves," as Couldry (2010) defines voice, linking their own personal experiences to a larger collective good. Many of the youth discussed across this book have grown up in a world where tools for producing and sharing media were widely accessible. Not surprisingly, their ability to deploy these practices toward civic ends drew them into participatory politics. During one of our webinars on participatory politics, activist Joan Donovan shared a personal trajectory that connected her early involvement with music to her activism around the Occupy movement and highlighted the useful skills she picked up along the way:

As a teenager I was heavily involved in the Boston straight edge hard-core scene. I was introduced to anarchist ideals and began thinking more and more about global politics. Unfortunately, there was no support for feminists or women in that environment, so I started playing in bands to meet more people. Singing in a band put me in touch with many women who felt the same way. Together we formed a collective named "Mosh-trogen" and we put out a zine that focused on women's issues. Many late-night talks and writing sessions solidified our resolve to change the Boston music scene. We did this by holding benefit concerts that featured female musicians and donating the proceeds to local feminist organiza-tions. Some members of Moshtrogen went on to volunteer at those or-ganizations later. For me, the DIY culture of punk and hardcore taught me how to get organized. After learning the basics of booking an event, publishing a zine, and making music, I extrapolated how to build a com-munity and be politically engaged on my own terms.

These youth were not simply stuffing envelopes, as might have been the experience of earlier generations who volunteered with political organi-zations; many of them were expressing why the cause matters to them through the media they created themselves.

Marie Dufrasne and Geoffroy Patriarche (2011) discuss political en-gagement in terms of different genres of participation, with an under-standing of genres less as a set of shared conventions and more as a set of shared practices. A genre, they argue, is "a type of communicative ac-tion recognised by a community (an organisation in this context) as ap-propriate to attain a specific objective." Objectives are "social constructs" and "collective conventions" that reflect member's shared and recurring experiences (65). Drawing inspiration from organizational communica-tion scholars Wanda Orlikowski and JoAnne Yates (1998), Dufrasne and Patriarche describe these genres in terms of how participants address a series of core questions—why, how, what, who/m, when, and where. These genre conventions provide participants' efforts with what Mimi Ito et al. (2015) describe as "shared purpose and practice."

So a project like 30 Mosques offered a template that others could fol-low, a set of basic principles around which shared representations might be constructed. And this model was taken up by a range of individuals and groups, each seeking to change the ways American Muslims were perceived. The focus on Ramadan addressed the when question, while the desire to localize this model gave them more flexibility in terms of where. Focusing on who and why, the DREAMer movement encouraged contributors to start with a simple statement, "My name is X, and I am undocumented." Focusing on how and what, Invisible Children provided workshops to instruct participants how to tell their own IC stories at the Fourth Estate gatherings. Focusing on what and when, the Harry Potter Alliance periodically offers prompts, encouraging members to explore aspects of their personal identities. Neta Kligler-Vilenchik (2013) offers this account of how Nerdfighter practices encourage creative participation:

> Members of collab channels often set a theme for the week (e.g. "the Oscars" or "your first kiss") that solves the problem of deciding what to talk about. Being assigned a regular day means you have a responsibility to the other group members and don't want to disappoint them. Some collab channels even impose playful "punishments" for not creating a video on your day, often consisting of dare-like tasks such as smearing peanut butter on the face while talking. (34)

Such calls for action (whether implicit, as in the case of 30 Mosques modeling, or explicit, as in the case of the HPA's formal prompts) constitute the creation and reaffirmation of genres of participation. By contrast, for many of the youth we interviewed, institutionalized politics offers a narrow set of genres: checking a box on a ballot or signing a petition frustrates those who have grown up within a more participatory culture. Yet even the organizations themselves tend to define success in terms of activities that can be quantified—numbers of views on YouTube, number of retweets on Twitter, number of voters registered, amounts of money raised—and we can anticipate that this tendency to stress quantity over quality of experiences will only increase as we plunge even deeper into an era of big data (for a useful critique of how big data miscounts some forms of civic expression, see Crawford 2013). All of this suggests an even more literal notion of what "counts" as politics.

There is also a tendency for people talking about "storytelling" in politics to focus on the narrative as a product, but we would argue for the value of storytelling as a process. Members of the University of Chicago's Black

Youth Project are dedicated to mobilizing communities of color "beyond electoral politics" in ongoing struggles over freedom and equality. The group was hosting a conference of young black community leaders as the not-guilty verdict was handed down in the case of George Zimmerman, who had been accused of murdering Trayvon Martin, a black teenager on his way home from buying snacks in his father's neighborhood. Devastated by the outcome, BYP participants decided to produce a spoken word response video—"#BYP 100 Responds to George Zimmerman Verdict"— that conveyed their collective concerns. Following another BYP meeting on the Princeton University campus, a car full of participants was pulled over by the cops, allegedly for a broken taillight (which those in the car deny existed). The youth whipped out their video cameras and began recording their conversations with the law enforcement officials; they were able to transform what might have been another example of racial profiling into a teachable moment. They posted the resulting video and called it "BYP 100: Black Youth, Black Police, & Transformative Justice." As one of the BYP members explained, "This is a healthy dialogue that would never have happened if we were individually confronting the police. This is the healthiest dialogue between a public police and young black people that I've ever seen, and that's transformative justice right there, in the flesh." Videos were produced and circulated around both events. The videos reached a wide array of audiences, but the meaning of these events are not reducible to the video content. Working together to create a collective statement or to hold a mediated conversation with the local police created communication contexts that mattered to those participating. The production process helped, in the first case, in bonding and, in the second, bridging across differences.

Circulation and Attention (Wanted or Otherwise)

Some critics have dismissed these new forms of activism as attention seeking, yet traditional demonstrations, focused on getting as many bodies as possible into the streets, also seek to render visible their base of support. There's still some tendency to apply standards of broadcast media in looking at social networking practices. So there is an enormous emphasis on the 100 million people who saw *Kony 2012* in its first week, numbers which, as we've seen, dwarfed hit television series and

Hollywood blockbusters. This extraordinary example of grassroots circulation thrust Invisible Children's cause into the center of a political controversy for which it was poorly prepared. The traffic crashed its site, its staff were overwhelmed, and the group's leaders were emotionally crushed by the backlash's intensity. Invisible Children got more visibility than it could handle.

Thorson et. al's (2013) research on the video-sharing practices of the Occupy movement establishes that many participants' videos were not intended to be seen on such a massive scale; YouTube was often deployed as an archive where media was stored for personal reference or as a means of sharing experiences between different Occupy encampments. Many of the video blogs produced by American Muslim youth or the coming out videos produced by the DREAMers were intended for relatively small audiences, aimed at reaching at most a few hundred viewers, many of them friends or other movement participants. As we discussed in chapters 4 and 5, making these videos allowed their creators to cement their own emerging cultural or political identities and forge ties with others struggling in similar circumstances. And this may explain why many of them have disappeared from larger circulation once they achieved these personal and local purposes.

These communication practices thus serve a range of purposes for participants, some of whom are seeking high degrees of visibility, some of which are actively threatened by unwanted attention. As we saw in Chapter 4, there is a tremendous and justified anxiety about unwanted attention, from government surveillance directed against some American Muslim political organizations to elders in their own communities who disapprove of how youth are practicing Islam or haters directing their anger against them. Such unwelcome and often hostile views are the negative flip side of attention-based activism. So, for example, the DREAMers' coming out videos served an important role in forging collective identities around shared experiences of subordination, marginalization, and oppression, yet they could also expose them to sanctions by Immigration and Customs Enforcement (ICE) or become tools in political struggles close to home. Pedro Ramirez, former student body president at Cal State Fresno, came out as undocumented (Marcum 2010), after a fellow student "outed" him during a battle over campus politics. Consequently, the student ran a persistent social media campaign seeking to get Ramirez removed from office and deported, posting phone numbers for the FBI and ICE and providing instructions to supporters on the best way to put pressure on the university administration to take action against him.

We see our case study groups making different choices, often video by video, in terms of how they negotiate tensions between publicity and privacy. And as Zuckerman (2012b) suggests, these choices are shaped by the network's own models for political change. Those who want to bring about changes on the cultural level through educating the public and shifting popular opinion may need a different degree of visibility than those who seek a more focused exchange with specific government officials who have the capacity to directly alter the policies that impact their lives—the difference, for example, between the wide circulation of *Kony 2012* and the tactics IC adopted in training people to directly lobby their congress members. These groups do not always correctly calibrate the scale of communication, and they do not fully control their digital afterlife (Soep 2012)—far from it! We acknowledge, as skeptics like Jodi Dean (2005) have argued, that there is some risk that expressive politics can sometimes become an end unto itself—an exercise of voice with little or no hope of influence, as circulation displaces rather than encourages mobilization. Many would identify *Kony 2012* as a spectacular example of circulatory politics outstripping real-world impact, though, as we showed in Chapter 2, this story is much more complicated than is often suggested. There are other ways to understand what is taking place at such moments: cultural and social change may be cumulative; campaigns may increase visibility without achieving immediate success; individuals and groups may be acquiring and mastering competencies and resources that they can deploy more effectively in the future. If we consider, for example, the waves of change regarding racialized violence, each protest has brought these issues to the attention of more diverse segments of the population, groups have been quicker to respond to the next catalyst, and there are marked shifts in public opinion over time. Whether such efforts will bring about institutional or systemic change may be a separate issue, but insofar as education and cultural change can have an impact on how people live in relation to each other (including individuals working within larger institutions who may impact how they address such issues), the coupling of expressive politics with traditional kinds of street protest—again, change by any means or media necessary—seems to be reasonably effective.

From Engagement to Participation

Building on earlier work by Amna (2010), Dahlgren (2011) urges us to consider "the subjective predispositions behind participation," identifying four basic kinds of motivation:

- Interest (which he defines as "the perceived potential for satisfaction deriving from everything from basic curiosity, to a drive for knowledge, as well as the seeking of pleasure")
- Efficacy ("a confidence in one's ability and a sense that participation is something amenable, within reach, that can be successfully enacted. At bottom it has to do with a sense of empowerment.")
- Meaningfulness ("the rewards are perceived in rather private, normative, cognitive and/or affective terms")
- Duty ("a sense of obligation, loyalty or solidarity, some kind of social value that resides beyond the self") (96)

We might understand these underlying motivations as helping to move people from engagement to participation: "Engagement refers to subjective states, that is, a mobilized, focused attention on some object. It is in a sense a prerequisite for participation. . . . For engagement to become embodied as participation and therefore give rise to civic agency there must be some connection to practical, do-able activities, where citizens can feel empowered" (Dahlgren 2009, 80–81).

Our research confirms what has been argued by a growing number of political commentators, perhaps most notably W. Lance Bennett (2008a): that the notion of the dutiful citizen is in decline, but that it is being displaced by a stronger emphasis on shared interests. As such, these models push against what many critics have described as the individualizing and personalizing logics of neoliberalism; networked publics depend on social connections among participants and often demand that we care about the plight of others.

Neta Kligler-Vilenchik et al. (2012) discuss the mobilizing structures they identified through their study of Invisible Children and the Harry

Potter Alliance: "shared media experiences" (or what we here call content worlds), "a sense of community," and "the wish to help." The first two, which they see as characteristics of fan communities, might be described in terms of "interest" and "meaningfulness," whereas the later might best fit under Dahlgren's notion of "efficacy." These organizational and rhetorical practices maximize participation by strengthening participants' motivations and directing them toward desired civic outcomes.

The Harry Potter Alliance's Not in Harry's Name Campaign—mentioned briefly in Chapter 3—gives us a rich example of how meaningfulness might inspire political action. The group called out Warner Brothers, the studio that produces the Harry Potter movies, because the chocolate manufacturers the studio had contracted to create chocolate frogs and other confections for their theme park attractions were not certified as deploying Fair Trade practices. The HPA cited an independent report produced by Free2Work that gave the involved chocolate companies an F in human rights, suggesting that there were legitimate concerns regarding their labor policies and practices. The group collected hundreds of thousands of signatures on petitions intended to shame the producers into adopting better labor practices. As Lauren Bird (2013) explained in the video blog *When Our Heroes Fail*, HPA supporters felt directly implicated in these suspect labor practices:

> We chose Harry Potter chocolate because that chocolate comes with a story that is not only near and dear to our hearts but is a story about justice and equal rights. Plus it is chocolate being sold primarily at a theme park for kids. It is pretty disturbing to think that the chocolate these kids are eating at this magical, wonderful place was possibly, coercively made by kids like them in another part of the world. . . . We are Harry Potter fans. That means that this chocolate matters more to us than whether Snickers bars are ethically made. But this also means we're going up against our heroes, the people behind the story.

Bird openly acknowledged the HPA leaders' ambivalence about this campaign, especially their uncertainty about confronting a studio whose good will they depend upon for other work they do. Yet Bird insists that fans have both a right—and an obligation—to question what's being done "in Harry's name." Throughout this campaign, HPA members confronted conflicted loyalties, a tension that also surfaced, as we saw in Chapter 3, when Imagine Better found itself at cross-purposes with Hunger Games fans during its conflicts with Lionsgate. After almost four years of sustained advocacy, the HPA scored a remarkable victory: Warner Brothers announced in January 2015 that they were shifting all of their contracts to Fair Trade companies and publicly thanked the Harry Potter Alliance for its efforts to call these issues to their attention. HPA executive director Matt Maggiacomo wrote a celebratory email to the group's members: "Fan activism has never had a victory like this before. An achievement of this magnitude has required four years, over four hundred thousand signatures, and a lot of help from many passionate and dedicated people."

And, of course, fandom represents only one of the many possible spaces where people come together around their shared passions and interests, any of which are potentially springboards for civic and political participation, as can be seen by research on forms of protest within gamer communities or the ways that craft and maker communities (Ratto and Boler 2014) unite participants with diverse skills that can be tapped for real-world social action. We might position our case studies along this axis: the DREAMers and the American Muslim cases are both more closely aligned with identity politics (though they also are consciously bridging across dividing lines between ethnicities and nationalities); the Nerdfighters and the other fan activists embody what John Hartley (1999) has described as "DIY citizenship," having forged a political identity based around resources borrowed from popular culture; and the Students for Liberty seek to erase notions of identity politics altogether, focusing on a radical notion of the individual who defies demographic categories. This continuum suggests that some youth have greater choice in the range of civic identities they may adopt than others—i.e., those who have the privilege to be relatively unconcerned about the immediacies of their own conditions may be able to perform more playful kinds of political identities than, first things first, those who are fighting for recognition of their basic rights. That said, the continuum breaks down again when we consider how many of those involved in the DREAMer movement or the cultural projects we discussed in the American Muslim case study also selected from and constructed their identities around materials borrowed from popular culture, in part because they wanted to forge strong bonds with others from their generation as they sought to demonstrate why they belonged in the United States, and in part because almost all young people today engage in what Hartley describes as "the practice of putting together an identity from the available choices, patterns, and opportunities on offer in the semiosphere and the mediasphere" (185). Some of these youth have political identities thrust upon them, but their politics emerge from the choices they make in terms of how to respond to those outside suppositions about who they are.

We might similarly distinguish our case studies between those that involve acting in one's own interests (as in the case of the American Muslims and the DREAMers) versus acting from what one perceives as an altruistic stance (as for Invisible Children or the various fan activist projects), though this framing masks the ways that some of the rhetorics associated with these groups stress how "meaningful" it is to participate in a movement to change the world, themes Melissa Brough (2012) emphasized in her discussion of Invisible Children. This distinction breaks down further when we look at HPA members working around LGBT or body image issues, which may impact their own lives more directly. We might also distinguish between efforts motivated by a single goal—the capture of Joseph Kony or the passage of the DREAM Act—that participants pursue through different strategies and tactics (the DREAMers' shift toward a more overtly oppositional stance) and networks that redefine their social agendas to reflect emerging issues, as in the case of the Harry Potter Alliance, Nerdfighters, Imagine Better, and Students for Liberty.

The Social Dimensions of Participatory Politics

We can sum up some of the shifts we are describing as a change from thinking of politics in terms of special events, such as elections, toward understanding political participation as part of a larger lifestyle, one closely integrated into other dimensions of young people's social and cultural lives. Dahlgren (2011) writes, "Participation is fundamentally a social act, based in human communication, and contingent on sociality. All too often analyses ignore the importance of sociality in stimulating and maintaining participation, how interactions with others actually serves to support (or not) participatory activities" (97). We might think about the roles Facebook, YouTube, and other media platforms play in participatory politics not through technological determinism, but rather with the recognition that many key dimensions of young people's social lives get conducted through these various social media platforms: this is where they meet their friends, and thus, it is as natural for them to act politically in this space as it was for participants in earlier civic organizations to forge ties at the local bowling alley, coffee shop, church, or barbershop.

Writers such as Cass Sunstein (2009) argue that the online world has a polarizing effect on political discourse, suggesting that our ability to identify conversation partners based on their ideological alignment forecloses the possibilities of engaging with people with different perspectives. Sunstein's argument rests on the assumption that the most important spaces through which we frame our political perspectives are explicitly political, rather than imagining that communities framed around a range of other interests might also be the site of sociability from which emerge shared ideas about what might constitute a better society. Remember Robert Putnam's bowling leagues were, at the end of the day, focused on bowling, even if they had other civic and political effects. Lana Swartz and Kevin Driscoll (2014), for example, document the kinds of political conversations that occurred on PriceScope, an online site that facilitates conversations among buyers and sellers of expensive jewelry. Participants found that their shared interests in buying, say, wedding rings, cut across differences in ideological perspectives, such as debates around same-sex marriage, and allowed them to reassert their common interests following heated debates: "I hate your politics but love your diamonds." By contrast, Megan Condis (2014) explores how the desire to create an "apolitical" and "disembodied" space of conversation within certain gamer and fan communities (her focus is on *Star Wars: Knights of the Old Republic*) creates a context where certain perspectives, particularly those concerning sexuality and gender, get ruled as disruptive or off topic. Here, the desire to preserve sociability results in the exclusion of some voices, even as it masks the privilege enjoyed by others.

Inserting politics into everyday social interactions has a price, which may involve creating discomfort and disagreement in spaces where one seeks friendship and fellowship. These stakes are often underestimated, as when writers like Malcolm Gladwell (2010) decry the lowered risks of online activism or when critics describe changing your profile picture green (to support the Iranian revolution) or pink (to support marriage equality) as the lowest-cost forms of activism. In fact, as Molly Sauter and Matt Stempeck (2013) note, such activism does involve the risk of social ostracism for youth in communities that do not already support such views, since their profile picture will be seen by parents, teachers, other students, religious leaders, anyone who is part of their social network:

> By going pink, people are standing up as allies and creating the perception of a safe space within their own friendship communities online—spaces where gay people may face stigmas and bullying. . . . But going pink was still, in many individuals' social networks, an act requiring some degree of bravery, because it's a more controversial topic, closer to home, and likely to alienate at least one social contact.

What may seem like a simple, low-cost gesture online may translate into any number of heated and risky exchanges on the ground. Researchers in Harvard's Good Participation project (another part of MacArthur's Youth and Participatory Politics Network) document that many of the youth they interviewed chose not to talk about their political and civic activities in their social media profiles (Weinstein 2013). For some, their volunteer activities are no more a part of their social identities than their after-school job at McDonald's, whereas for others, their political activities are simply understood as an aspect of their lives different from their interactions with their friends on Facebook. And for the members of some of our groups—the DREAMers and the American Muslim youth—the risk that any political speech they engage in online will become the target of surveillance is a serious one.

Concerns that political talk may disrupt everyday social interactions also account for why many participants in our case study groups frame issues in terms of consensus rather than contentious politics or sometimes downplay their own status as activists—the desire to capture and punish an evil warlord is assumed to be something with which few can disagree, and so the goal is to help people understand the stakes, not to debate what actions should be taken. This consensus orientation may account for why many IC supporters were ill prepared to rebut the critiques leveled against the group after the release of *Kony 2012*. By contrast, the young DREAMers and American Muslim youth lack the ability to frame their politics in terms of consensus; they know that they are facing strong opposition not only to their views but to their very existence, and thus, like the Freedom Riders before them, they have trained themselves from the start to face and overcome challenges to their perspectives. In both cases, political solidarity gets formed around shared experiences, values, and visions, yet there is also a heightened awareness of conflicting interests in the surrounding culture.

We can see how sociability and political advocacy get negotiated by looking at the example of Julian Gomez. This college sophomore and regular video blogger for the Harry Potter Alliance drew attention to the DREAMer movement when he came out as undocumented in a video explaining why he would be unable to attend LeakyCon, a popular fan convention. On the one hand, the video reaffirmed his status as a fellow fan by, for instance, its inclusion of personal photographs taken at a previous convention held closer to his home and references to the content world, comparing the plight of the undocumented with Voldemort's attacks on "mudbloods," wizards born to Muggle parents. For fellow fans, Julian was one of them, someone they knew from his previous video blogs, someone who cared about the same things they did. But, at the same time, the video used his desire to attend a convention across the country from where he lived to dramatize the everyday realities of being undocumented: he is unable to get a driver's license, and he lacks even the ID required to take an airplane or an Amtrak train. HPA members were encouraged to share their own reflections about what makes one an American and heated discussions about immigration reform broke out on the HPA's YouTube channel and other fan forums.

However, many fans embraced this issue as a practical problem to be solved. Ultimately, the community found a way to get him to LeakyCon by pooling their resources. In a video produced after the event, Julian explained his mixed feelings:

> I was amazed at how great people were, but I thought they were missing the point. I wanted people to be that passionate about discussing immigration policy flaws, not getting me to LeakyCon. But it turns out that

it is kinda the same thing. People's willingness to help out someone they think deserves the same rights that they do, including being able to attend this conference, shows that they see me the person and not me the undocumented immigrant. They see me the Harry Potter fan. They see me missing out on something I wouldn't have to if I just had the right papers.

Attending LeakyCon also provided another opportunity for Julian to educate Harry Potter fans about immigration reform: immigrant rights activist Jose Antonio Vargas flew in specifically to speak at the gathering and subsequently forged a partnership with Julian and other HPA members to help document the lives of young DREAMers.

Assessing Participatory Politics

Lest we be unclear, the kinds of practices we document in this book, for us, count as politics, though the question remains whether some of these approaches are more productive than others. We have said that we are "cautiously optimistic" about the kinds of participatory politics documented here. On the one hand, we are seeing many examples of how our case study groups, through their mechanisms of translation, are helping young people who might have otherwise fallen through the cracks become more civically engaged and politically empowered. We are seeing young people, who might otherwise have felt excluded from the political system, find their voice and exert some influence on issues that matter to them. Networks (such as the DREAMer movement or #BlackLivesMatter) facilitate collective action; members feel part of something larger than themselves.

Yet many of those whom the Youth and Participatory Politics survey (Cohen and Kahne 2012) identified as having engaged in some forms of participatory political practices did so on their own, within a culture that stresses personal empowerment over collective action, without access to the symbolic resources and infrastructural supports provided by the kinds of organizations our book has discussed. Many of these youth will feel discouraged by their inability to make change, by the fact that their media productions fail to circulate and their messages go unheard, by the hostile reception they receive for their views within their social spheres, and so forth. The kinds of networked publics we are describing are often themselves precarious but individualized actions are even more so. Many lack access to digital technologies; they lack an understanding of how participatory politics works; they do not see themselves as having anything to contribute to larger conversations about politics; they fear that they can not live up to society's impossible ideals about what constitutes an informed citizen; and they lack the social connections to adopt a more monitorial perspective on social change. Lissa Soep (2014) has identified other potential risks of participatory politics:

> Content worlds can feed sensationalization; they can ultimately be unsustainable and thus set up the participants for disappointment, resentment, cynicism, and missed opportunity; they can reveal a kind of saviorism that denies agency to those with direct knowledge and the most to lose; and they can invite slippage to the extent that participants eager to connect with the widest possible audience sometimes obscure the specificity of particular struggles. (71)

Some exceptional individuals will find their ways past such obstacles and engage in tactics that are personally meaningful and politically effective. There are always exceptions, but the kinds of organizations we study increase the effectiveness of their political efforts and, more importantly, provide gateways for youth who would not otherwise have been encouraged to participate politically. In that sense, they provide "consequential connections." Lissa Soep will have more to say about how these practices relate to connected learning in her Afterword.

Dahlgren (2011) discusses such concerns in terms of what he calls "contingencies," factors that "both facilitate and hinder participation" (100). These constraints push potential participations toward the "solo sphere, a politics focused on 'personal identity' rather than 'collectively intervening in the social world and contesting power relations'" (103–104). Many of the platforms deployed for participatory political practices are privately owned, commercially focused, and often adopt policies more attentive to the corporation's desire to profit than by a desire to maximize opportunities for participation (Campbell 2009). Some of the youth we've discussed here are literally disenfranchised—lacking the basic rights as citizens that might traditionally have allowed them to make their voices heard by democratic institutions—and many others may be effectively so, as attempts to restrict voter registration, including a movement away from registering voters through public schools, discourage American youth from participating in elections. Many others are discouraged from political participation by a breakdown of basic trust in government institutions: as of 2014, only 7 percent of Americans felt strong or moderate trust in the U.S. Congress, for example, a crisis point from which it may be very hard to recover (Lightman 2014).

We can see some of the tactics and rhetorics deployed here as politics through other means, politics directed at other targets, politics through other languages. They reflect a desire to disassociate one's self from institutional politics, but not from the idea of social change. We have seen through our research youth who are strongly engaged in political debates, actively participating in change movements, with access to traditional institutions and networks, with a strong sense of empowerment and efficacy, but with little or no motivation to vote. For some of the groups we study, relevant political change may come only through institutional politics—such as the DREAMers' struggle for citizenship—but they still often represent these struggles in terms of their ability to make meaningful choices in the context of their everyday lives—to get scholarships, to go to LeakyCon—and they are still forced to adopt alternative political tactics because they are denied the right of citizens to vote or petition their government.

All of the cases discussed here have some connection with political institutions. We discuss those connections most extensively in considering the relationship between Students for Liberty and a range of conservative think tanks and funders, yet we could also talk about the partnerships that the HPA forges, campaign by campaign, with a range of NGOs and nonprofits, the ways that Invisible Children brought government officials to participate in its Fourth Estate events, the ways that DREAMers measured their success in part based on how their concerns were taken up during highly visible events such as State of the Union addresses and presidential nominating conventions, or the ways that the American Muslim youth groups were funded by government agencies and foundations. Such connections can be understood as valuable ways of translating voice into influence but they also come with institutional entanglements that may threaten more participatory political practices.

Given the general disillusionment with government expressed by many of the young people we encountered, the way the Futures of Entertainment panelists distanced themselves from politics and activism now comes as no surprise. During our research interviews, young people repeatedly resisted labeling their work as explicitly political after having spent the previous one to two hours vividly recounting action they took around civic and social issues. Differences also surfaced across the various cases studies. The DREAMers were the most likely of all the groups to see their work as explicitly political. The American Muslims were the most emphatic in distancing themselves, and their civic work, from formal political and activist categories.

Co-Opting Participatory Politics

If these new kinds of civic cultures are developing a new repertoire of mobilization tactics, communication practices, and rhetorical genres, it should be no surprise that institutional politics is increasingly mimicking their languages, especially the blending of popular culture and political speech. During the 2012 presidential campaign, we saw Samuel L. Jackson tapping into his star persona as a trash-talking action hero eager to rattle the complacency of suburban voters, all in the service of the Obama reelection effort ("Wake the F**K Up"):

> Sorry, my friend, but there's no time to snore
> An out-of-touch millionaire's just declared war
> On schools, the environment, unions, fair pay
> We're all on our own if Romney has his way
> And he's against safety nets
> If you fall, tough luck
> So I strongly suggest that you wake the fuck up

We also saw Joss Whedon, the popular showrunner of fan-favorite series such as *Buffy the Vampire Slayer* and *Firefly*, jokingly endorsing Mitt Romney ("Whedon on Romney") as the candidate best able to prepare America for the impending zombie apocalypse (for more on Whedon and fan activism, see Cochran 2012). Such videos attract attention through their unconventional representations of the political process, their pop culture references, and the ease with which they can be circulated through social media. Both of these videos make the assumption that young voters are culturally and politically savvy, that they are in on the joke, and that they recognize that popular culture metaphors do not fully explain the political process. They speak to a generation whose political education came from *The Daily Show*.

Yet such practices may also patronize young citizens. A series of campaign spots produced by the GOP, for example, speak to a fear of participatory politics. During the 2008 election, John McCain's campaign released "Fan Club 2.0," a spot designed to diminish what pundits had described as the "enthusiasm gap" between the two parties, making fun of young people's passionate embrace of Obama. "Fan Club 2.0" used parody not simply to spoof the candidate but to discourage democratic participation, telling first-time voters who had been excited by the Obama campaign to, in effect, "get a life."

A subsequent GOP advertisement ("The Breakup") depicted young people who wanted to "break up with Obama" as if he was an ill-advised Facebook friend, whose controlling behavior was too big of an imposition: "We met on Facebook. He had me at 'hope and change.' . . . Our parents warned us about this. . . . We're over. You can keep the change." Such rhetoric tries to speak the language of participatory politics, but it also trivializes the political agency of youth. While political media artifacts such as these deploy some of its tactics—depending more on grassroots circulation via video sharing than paid advertising on broadcast media—and its rhetoric—the use of parody and pop culture references—they are designed to delegitimize participatory politics.

Contacts and Exchanges between Our Case Study Groups

While this book's case studies clearly share many similarities when it comes to repertoires of action, imagined outcomes, media-specific practices, and engagement through participatory politics, they are also clearly very different. Our five cases intentionally represent distinct communities facing specific challenges and thus adopting different responses. To state the obvious: context matters when it comes to participatory politics. Clearly, actions and issues relevant to one community may not resonate with the same urgency in another. Different groups have different resources, access to power, networks, and risks.

And yet, we were repeatedly struck by the ways issues that mobilized one case study community were embraced by others. Many of the young libertarians we interviewed, for example, expressed sympathy for DREAMers and their cause. Herman, from Texas, said:

> I think "illegal immigration" is heroic because, frankly, this used to be a land where they said, "Are you tired and poor, and are you yearning to be free?" That was supposed to be our legacy—the ability for anyone to come freely and build a life for themselves. But the way that the government has now progressed . . . if you are somebody who just wants to come and work for a little while, if you need some place to go and get refuge from your foreign government because they are being oppressive. Oh no, man, you might as well just throw a rock against the wall and they are not going to notice. They price people out in immigration by requiring massive amounts of money just to get to the door through paperwork.

Herman explained that his support for immigration reform was primarily related to his belief that open borders made the most *economic* sense, though he also said he felt anti-immigration laws were rooted in xenophobia and racism, as did some other SFL interviewees. The overlap between libertarians and DREAMers on the issue of immigration illustrates how, even though certain groups may be motivated by different beliefs and circumstance, sometimes surprising commonalities exist. Likewise, immigration reform, of tantamount importance to DREAMers, may have been only a tangential concern for many HPA members until they learned that someone in their own community was affected by it.

Another crossover between our cases surfaced when American Muslims became a visible part of the programming at Invisible Children's 2013 Fourth Estate event. Speaking to their youth supporters in UCLA's Royce Auditorium, Jason Russell and Jedidiah Jenkins, the event's moderators and members of IC's leadership team, introduced Linda Sarsour, their American Muslim activist guest speaker:

JASON RUSSELL: Obviously we are all here united under this roof
  because we all believe that all humans no matter where you come

from, no matter what you look like, no matter what your belief is, we are all equal . . .

JEDIDIAH JENKINS: But sometimes it's actually easier to care about someone that's 10,000 miles away than to care for your own community. And sometimes it's even hard to understand the people in your own community that look different from you or maybe you've already decided who and what they are and you don't even know.

Sarsour, who serves as the advocacy and civic engagement coordinator for the National Network for Arab American Communities in New York, came on stage and built on Russell's and Jenkins's comments, sharing personal experiences that both connected her to and separated her from most of IC's youth supporters:

I am here today really to share my story with you and to take you on my own journey. I want my story to be a story that you think about when you see another Arab or Muslim or when you come across people from our community wherever you are in the world. And I also want my story to be a story of an American that comes from a community that might have a different experience than you.

With this introduction, Sarsour took her audience back to September 10, 2001, describing how profoundly her life changed over the next 24 hours as she involuntarily went from being a "mom, college student, daughter, regular person who felt like a New Yorker, and felt like anyone else living in the city" to someone who was seen as an "enemy, a stranger, a foreigner to the very city that I lived in, the country that myself, my family, and my children called home." Sarsour appealed to IC supporters to look past religious and cultural differences and get to know more about people that may follow a different faith. Later, she and other panelists (all of them Christian) participated in a breakout session provocatively titled "Is Religion Destroying the World?"

American Muslims surfaced several more times during the event, for instance when Marium Elarbi, an alumnus of IC's first Fourth Estate, connected her decision to start wearing the hijab to mustering the courage to get involved with IC:

In August 2010, right before starting my senior year in high school, I decided I was going to start wearing hijab (or the headscarf). For so long I had been avoiding doing that. . . . I started to realize that I needed to stop worrying about what everyone else was going to think. . . . [I]n choosing to wear the headscarf, I am now being honest about who I am. Everyday people who will see me will know that I am Muslim. And, I am OK with that. I am proud of that. [applause] In connecting the dots, I realized that deciding to wear the hijab has been part of this entire journey and it gave me the confidence to attend the first Fourth Estate Summit.

Through Sarsour and Elarbi, IC supporters developed a deeper respect for Muslims and Islam as those attending the Fourth Estate event were able to connect their own faith and values to supporting religious freedom in the United States.

As issues spread between our case study communities, they often were reframed to render them relevant to particular contexts. When HPA supporters rallied around Julian's undocumented status, they focused on finding a way to get him to LeakyCon rather than embarking on a campaign for immigration reform. Context gets even more complex when we consider IC youth support for American Muslim youth. As we also discussed in Chapter 4, the American Muslim youth we interviewed generally distanced their faith-related civic engagement from politics and activism as they responded to the already politicized situation they faced on a daily basis as Muslims in the United States. In contrast, IC youth may have learned about the problems confronted by American Muslim youth when they heard Muslim peers speak about their 9/11 experiences at the second Fourth Estate; the IC youth defined acceptance of diverse faiths (including Islam) as an explicitly civic, even political, stance, especially within an organization that historically had strong ties to Christian churches. What one community sees as political, another may declare to be apolitical, even if (and at times precisely because) outsiders disagreed with this categorization. All of this indicates a need for a more nuanced, and culturally inflected, understanding of what constitutes participatory politics.

Is Everybody Happy?

One example of the need for such a nuanced understanding emerged on May 2, 2014, when the Muslim Public Affairs Council (MPAC) released a music video, "American Muslims Get . . . Happy!," set to Pharrell Williams's pop hit "Happy." Initially released in November 2013, Williams's song topped the charts in many countries for weeks in early 2014. The song was originally released alongside "Happy in . . . Los Angeles," a music video shot in 24 hours as a publicity stunt, which featured Williams and other famous and not-so-famous personalities dancing around Los Angeles. Responding to this original music video, more than 1,950 videos were set to this song and uploaded to YouTube from 153 countries around the world. Riding this phenomenon, Julie Fersing and Loïc Fontaine (who are based in France) created the weareahappyfrom.com site in May 2014 to catalogue and map the various "Happy" videos.

Shot in one day in Washington, D.C., the MPAC "Happy" video featured a diverse cast of American Muslims who moved, clapped, lip-synced, and danced to the song's upbeat lyrics. Though the playful video may not—at first glance—appear to have political meaning, the MPAC made two significant statements through its production. First, the video situated American Muslims in dialogue with other local communities around the world who had created and uploaded their own "Happy" videos, signaling that Muslims are just like other people, a theme often expressed by American Muslim youth. Second, MPAC explicitly dedicated the video to Honesty Policy, an anonymous group that had released "Happy British Muslims" a few months earlier and found itself embroiled in a controversy about whether popular music and dance (or movement to rhythm more broadly defined) are appropriate under Islam.

In an analysis of the "Happy" phenomenon and other "georemixed" videos, Ethan Zuckerman (2014) argues that though these videos may not advocate a political party or a cause, they are nonetheless "political":

> When the residents of Toliara, Madagascar make their version of "Happy," they're making a statement that they're part of the same media environment, part of the same culture, part of the same world as Pharrell's LA. . . . Happy in Damman, Saudi Arabia features wonderfully goofy men, but not a single woman. Beijing is happy, but profoundly crowded

and hazy—intentionally or not, the video is a statement about air pollution as well as about a modern, cosmopolitan city.

Two other "Happy" videos, from Tehran and the Armenian capital of Yerevan, are worth considering here for their political relevance. The Tehran version of "Happy," which features young women and men dancing together in ways that are unacceptable under Iranian laws, led to the arrest of six participants. They were later released after they made official statements asserting that they had been coerced into participating in the video's production. In the meantime, #FreeHappyIranians emerged as an expression of protest over the situation. In a different vein, the Yerevan "Happy" video was created with support from the U.S. government and showcased on the YouTube channel of the American embassy in Armenia, featuring alumni of U.S. cultural exchange programs and the U.S. ambassador to Armenia and acknowledging this fact in the final credits. Interestingly, an otherwise identical version of this video, uploaded by Lumen, the production company responsible for it, does not feature these final credits, effectively obscuring the U.S. government's role in the project.

Regarding these, and other, versions of "Happy," Zuckerman (2014) suggests that "perhaps a video that asserts that you and your friends are part of the wider world is political only if your nation has consciously withdrawn from that world. Perhaps it's political any time your city, your country, and your culture are misunderstood or ignored by the rest of the world." Shresthova (2013) makes a similar argument in her analysis of dance specific georemixes. Taking a close look at Bollywood dance–themed flash mob videos uploaded to YouTube, Shresthova identifies a productive tension between how these flash mobs occupy real-world geography and the ways they achieve a broader mobility as their videos are circulated online. Focusing on the CST Bollywood Flashmob, an event staged at Mumbai's central train station, Chhatrapati Shivaji Terminus, which had been devastated by a terrorist attack in 2008, Shresthova argues that the combination of dance, location, music, and circulation through social media allowed the CST flash mob to assume a significance that was intentionally both context specific and politically ambiguous.

Despite their disciplinary differences, Zuckerman and Shresthova both identify geography as a crucial dimension for understanding when and how participatory culture becomes participatory politics. We agree, and see expanding the scope of our case study–based approach beyond the United States as a logical, indeed necessary, next step. When we issued a paper call for submissions to a 2012 special issue of *Transformative Works and Cultures* on fan activism, we were overwhelmed by submissions from all over the world, informing us about everything from the use of political remixes and spoofs in the German elections (Jungherr 2012) to the ways that pop stars in Korea (Jung 2012) and Hong Kong (Li 2012) had succeeded or failed in attempts to politically mobilize their fans.

Researchers working outside the United States describe rich connections between participatory culture and participatory politics. Aswin Punathambekar (2012) argues that the "strong relationship between participatory culture and civic/political engagement would not come as news to anyone in India." Through a study of the third season of *Indian Idol*, the local version of the *Idols* singing competition, he recounts how the show's audience vote became a mechanism that "created the possibility and the space for the renewal of everyday forms of interaction across ethnic, religious, spatial, and linguistic boundaries that had been subdued and rendered difficult, if not impossible, over the decades." In another India-based study, Ritesh Mehta (2012) explores an instance of what he calls real-world "flash activism" inspired by the Bollywood film *Rang De Basanti*, whose plot centrally involves civic action. In this case, as Mehta describes, a cinematic protest inspired one in the real world that emulated the film in both method (both involved sit-ins at the India Gate in Delhi) and cause (both protested high-level government corruption) in ways that actually helped produce tangible results.

These (and other) studies only scratch the surface of an important area for further research. Around the planet, young people are deploying references to popular culture and the infrastructures and practices of participatory culture as gateways into engagement with the core political struggles of their times. In some cases, they are tapping into local forms of popular culture, while in others, they are connecting to forms in global circulation, especially those associated with Hollywood blockbusters (see Jenkins, Ford, and Green 2013 on the various movements inspired by James Cameron's *Avatar*) or popular music ("Happy"). In some cases, they are localizing genres of participation from elsewhere—again, the "Happy" phenomenon, but also the Occupy movement—often because they encountered these tactics through videos shared online. All of these cases involve processes of adaptation and transformation, as participants' actions need to be rendered meaningful to their local communities and effective within the context of local traditions and beliefs. As these processes of localization occur, video traces of the actions involved may also be put into circulation, and in turn may inspire further activities somewhere else on the globe. All of this reflects the remarkable communication capabilities available to many young people, even as many others are blocked from meaningful access to these technologies and to the skills needed to enter into this conversation. Mapping these various forms of participatory politics may help us to better understand what counts as politics in the early 21st century. Identifying the contingencies that block participation (or increase its risks) may illuminate the struggles for basic rights that will need to be waged before we achieve our hopes for a more participatory culture.

A Meeting of Two Generations

Having started this chapter with a cross-generational exchange about what counts as politics, we wanted to end with another such encounter. John Lewis, currently a U.S. representative from Georgia, was speaking in summer 2014 at the Aspen Idea Festival on a panel moderated by *PBS NewsHour* anchor Gwen Ifill. The Aspen audience was thrilled and moved to hear Lewis describe what it was like to be the youngest featured speaker during the March on Washington, to be one of the first hit by police on the Edmund Pettus Bridge, to be with Robert F. Kennedy when he learned about Martin Luther King's assassination. His talk was inspiring, empowering, and grounded in the wisdom of his 60 years as a civil rights advocate.

A young Asian American man asked what advice he would have for young people who wanted to make change, and Lewis began his response by speaking about the role of new technologies:

> You are much better educated, you are better informed, you have all of this new technology. We didn't have a fax machine. We had one of these old mimeograph machines you just turned and turned. You have

an obligation, your generation, young people, have an obligation, a mission, and a mandate to push and pull and not be satisfied and do everything possible. . . . I hear too many people say, "I am not going to participate. That's not my cause." We have to participate. Politics controls everything we do in America, from the time that we are born until the time we die, so you have a moral obligation, a mandate, to push and get out there and do everything you can to leave this little piece of real estate we call America a little greener, a little cleaner, and a little more peaceful for generations yet unborn.

Lewis's shift from technology to notions of participation was a telling one, consistent with our argument across the book: change comes not simply through access to technologies but through structures that support young people's political participation. Lewis has explicitly been using comics to translate lessons he learned in the civil rights movement into a language he hopes will reach young Americans (see Lewis and Aydin 2013). Earlier, he had identified immigration reform and marriage equality as part of the "unfinished business" of the civil rights movement, so he was aligned with these young people in terms of their views of what some of the core issues of the day were.

But the question remained, what counted as political participation? What were the new models for political change? A young African American woman rose from the audience, and asked, "Do you think we'd be better off staying out of office if we are interested in getting something done, insofar as Congress seems to have a hard time with that?" And there was suddenly a gaping generational divide between them. Lewis had fought for voting rights, had struggled to insure that the first African Americans were elected to local, state, and national offices, and had spent two decades in the U.S. House of Representatives. For him, institutional politics was the way through which you could change laws and make a difference. The young woman, by contrast, represented a generation that was politically engaged, socially aware, but deeply skeptical that a deadlocked government was going to act on behalf of its causes. The always eloquent Lewis stammered; Iffil tried to rephrase the question, but the exchange ended with no real answer. Lewis, clearly uncomfortable, restated a call to help elect new people who could change Congress, and then concluded, "I think there are people today who get involved but they do not believe in the political arena. I think there are people who want to tear down rather than to build."

If Lewis had thought back a few decades, he might have remembered a time when it was impossible for African Americans to imagine achieving political success through representative government, might have thought about the progress that was made through social and cultural means, might have thought about the support mechanisms that were offered by the black church or the political roles played by cultural figures such as Ruby Dee or Mahalia Jackson (both of whom were also part of the March on Washington). You could fault this young woman, perhaps, for giving up hope in making the system work again, but you would have to respect the ways that her generation was still fighting for equality and justice, while pursuing politics through other channels.

This book has offered a range of examples of young people working together to try to change the world, some working within "the system" (institutional politics), some working around "the system" (seeking change through other mechanisms) but all imagining politics as something that fits into their everyday lives, something in which they were invited to participate. They had found ways to share their own stories and express their own voices, often through producing and circulating their own media, to set the agenda and frame the message. We cannot understand these practices by bracketing off the cultural from the political: for these youth, the cultural is the gateway into the political. They are seeking political change by any media necessary.

Afterword

Necessary Learning

Elisabeth Soep

Preface

In 2014, I worked with a team of teen designers and adult colleagues at Youth Radio in Oakland to produce an interactive infographic displaying 13 cases in which a police officer shot someone after mistaking an object that person was carrying—a pill bottle, a hairbrush, a water pistol—for a gun. We wrestled with complex questions related to the substance of our reporting: what data to cite, which cases to feature, and how to connect our project with other police shootings including that of 18-year-old Michael Brown (who was unarmed when he was killed) and 12-year-old Tamir Rice (who was playing with a toy gun in a park near his home). There were also technical challenges and design considerations. What combination of fonts, colors, and textures would create the right look and feel? How should we arrange the silhouetted objects on the page? Often, design decisions, like which victim photos to feature, raised digital rights questions and called for ethical judgments, too. The recent hashtag campaign #iftheygunnedmedown censured the press for publishing criminalizing photos in their stories about the killing of young black and brown people, a pattern we by no means wanted to reproduce.

Created by the interactive division of Youth Radio, "Triggered: Mistaken for Guns" was a product of participatory politics as described in this book. Collaborating with peers and adult colleagues, the young people who worked on it were using "any media necessary" to express voice and agency in public spheres. They investigated information, produced and circulated content, sparked dialogue, and contributed to a body of work around which communities all over the country were mobilizing, on- and offline, in support of humanity, racial equity, and freedom.

The makers were also, all along the way, producing a context for learning. "[I]f you have a camera, use that to tell your story. If you don't have that, if you've got a pen and a pad, write your story. If you don't have that, you can literally speak your story," is how youth media educator Tani Ikeda described the approach of her organization, ImMEDIAte Justice, in this book's first chapter. "[T]here's a lack of resources in our communities," Ikeda went on, "so it is really about figuring out how to tell our own stories by any means necessary."

The business of "figuring out" is what I will take up in this Afterword: how and what young people figure out as they produce the kinds of powerful, and sometimes problematic, stories, artifacts, events, and networks described in this book. What does a focus on learning add to the discussion?

Like Ikeda and her colleagues, creative and committed educators operating in all sorts of settings are working across the U.S. to enable young people to tell their civic stories and in the process make a difference for themselves and the people and issues they care about. And yet, too often, in the spheres of public policy and school reform, civic education is reduced to instilling (and testing) knowledge about such facts as the branches of government, or how a bill becomes a law. My discussion here is not meant to minimize the value of mastering basic information related to government structures and electoral politics. I do, though, hope to push thinking in new directions about the relationship between participatory politics, learning, and social justice, drawing on the rich case materials and concepts offered within this book.

I will start by identifying two basic assumptions within the learning theories that are best suited, in my view, to help us understand and promote high-quality participatory politics: that is, approaches that, first, situate learning as a form of participation within communities of practice; and, second, see learning as connected across platforms, settings, and domains of interest and opportunity. Then, bringing in the full range of cases explored within this book—from DREAMers to young libertarians to Invisible Children to American Muslim youth to fans who use popular culture to inspire civic action—I will explore three learning frameworks that I see as especially relevant to digital-age civics: (1) learning through culturally relevant critical pedagogy, (2) learning as transmedia making, and (3) learning as the "release of imagination." Throughout, I will consider both how these learning frameworks advance our understanding of participatory politics and vice versa, how the case studies of participatory politics presented in *By Any Media Necessary* advance our thinking about learning. I will close with some thoughts about what the learning frameworks I have chosen leave undertheorized, and the implications of the book's case studies for the everyday practice of teaching and learning participatory politics.

Like many of you reading this book, tomorrow I head back to work alongside young people as we learn to use digital and social media civically. As senior producer at Youth Radio, I co-founded the organization's Innovation Lab with MIT. We collaborate with teens on broadcast stories and online transmedia projects (like the "Triggered" piece with which I opened) for outlets that include National Public Radio, for which Youth Radio serves as the official Youth Desk. I am also a member of the Youth and Participatory Politics Research Network alongside the authors of this book. Over several years, we have worked with our colleagues to understand what it looks like and what it takes for young people to have a say on issues of public concern and a role in 21st-century democracy (Allen and Light 2015; Cohen and Kahne 2012; DeVoss et. al. 2010; Earl 2013; Gardner and Davis, 2013; Ito et. al. 2015; Jenkins et. al. 2013; Kahne et. al. 2014; Soep 2014; Weinstein et. al. 2015; Zuckerman 2015). My own interests and commitments, then, bridge practice, production, and research. Building from that perspective, my hope is that this discussion provides you with some new questions, strategies, and frameworks for naming and maybe even expanding what you do.

Basic Assumption 1

Learning Is Situated within Communities of Practice

You would think it could go without saying: That learning is more than the acquisition of isolated skills. That assessment of learning needs to do more than test memorization of standardized knowledge. John Dewey made the case back in 1938 that learning is best framed as a "means of attaining ends which make direct vital appeal," and that it relies on "the opportunities of present life" and an "acquaintance with a changing world" (19–20). In Dewey's view, experience is always key, though not always educative; it can be "mis-educative" if it arrests growth by, for example, engendering callousness. If an experience arouses curiosity and enough of a sense of purpose to "carry a person over dead places in the future" (38), that would qualify as one that fuels growth. In the century since Dewey started to frame learning in these ways, educators have built countless curricula, classrooms, and whole institutions grounded in this set of progressive ideals.

And yet, based on the current uneven (to say the least) distribution of opportunities for young people to engage in, and/or get academic credit for, this kind of world-relevant, experience-based learning, it is worth spending a little time highlighting what we know about the ways in which learning operates not as "didactic, decontextualized decoding" (Lee 2012), but as a way of participating in social, cultural, and historical contexts. Knowledge is born of social relations, activities, and encounters with artifacts and other dimensions of our environment (Vygotsky 1978). These relations and encounters form in the context of what learning theorists have called "communities of practice." Theorists working in this participatory tradition explicitly challenge a previously prevailing view that learning happens when teachers transmit information to students, who acquire and internalize skills they can then display on command and transfer to new situations. Instead, a view of learning as a mode of participation connects cognitive development to the transformation of roles and responsibilities. Jean Lave and Etienne Wenger (1991) describe those roles and responsibilities along a trajectory from peripheral to full participation. Both modes of participation are, in these scholars' view, "legitimate" ways to engage in community practice. To start out along the edges, observing, supporting, and carrying out basic tasks, is often to be expected. But for novices to become experts, they need pathways to move progressively toward the center of community practices, driving rather than simply following the action.

The notion of participation is, obviously, central to the framework of participatory politics developed throughout this book and elsewhere (Kahne et. al. 2015; Cohen and Kahne 2012). Increasingly, as Henry Jenkins says in this book's first chapter, "politics requires soliciting participation, getting people to tell their own stories, and also working together to amplify voices that might once have gone unheard." Participation in this sense cultivates the ability to forge a collective voice and the agency required to bring about change. The fans Neta Kligler-Vilenchik describes in Chapter 3 gather on- and offline to talk, make, imagine, and debate. These activities create conditions for them to participate, initially in peripheral ways, and increasingly as experts who bring newcomers into the fold. The framework of "legitimate peripheral participation" derived from learning theory takes on a new charge in the context of the activities of DREAMers and American Muslim youth, for whom what's at stake is legitimacy as full-blown citizens free to live their lives and build communities without fear of government raids or surveillance activities that threaten freedom; peripheral or "precarious" participation is not enough. The young libertarian case study further complicates the concept of participation, by elevating strategic and selective nonparticipation—as in not voting, not aligning with a political party—as a viable form of civic action.

These ethnographic studies highlight some important contributions participatory politics can make to the notion that learning is situated within communities of practice. Kelty is cited previously here on the point that the "rhetoric" of participation can obscure important differences between, for example, liking a photo or slogan on Facebook versus participating in, say, the open software movement, or in state governance. Similarly, not all participation is equally educative, nor does it necessarily unlock opportunities for deeper learning. The *By Any Media Necessary* cases show how difficult it can be for diehards who bond over the mastery of rarified fan knowledge to make their civic-minded activities accessible to and effective at mobilizing those outside the base. As Kligler-Vilenchik argues in Chapter 3, "If the goal is to encourage participatory politics among broader populations of young people, fannish civics can only go so far."

Seen through the lens of learning, achieving "full" participation in any given community of practice does not necessarily prepare someone to expand that community's boundaries, and in this sense learning opportunities can pool around those who already claim membership and acceptance, leaving others out. Finally and perhaps most importantly, there is the gap between participation and critique. What about the cultivation of reflexiveness and critical understanding—a capacity to question the ideological basis or historical origin of conceptual systems we know and use (Gee 1996)? The studies of participatory politics offered here provide concrete examples of the conditions that enable learners to question and rebuild a community's foundations, as well as circumstances like the aftermath of the *Kony 2012* campaign, which exposed the shortcomings of an organizing model that appeared not to give people a lot of practice in anticipating, grappling with, and acting on critique.

Basic Assumption 2

Learning Is Connected across Domains of Interest and Opportunity

The idea that learning is "connected" has been a key building block in the formation of participatory politics as a viable way to frame the development of young people's voice and influence in public spheres. Mimi Ito and her colleagues (Ito et. al. 2013) who are part of the Connected Learning Research Network have carried out basic research, identified design principles, created on-the-ground models, and built infrastructures to support connected learning environments. Those environments have a number of features in common, according to Ito et. al. They are interest driven, meaning they build expertise through pursuits that young people deem relevant and engaging. They are peer supported, in the sense that young people are both teachers and learners, routinely calling upon one another as sources of expertise and mentorship, though not to the exclusion of caring adults. Connected learning contexts are production centered, meaning that participants are actually doing and making something, creating objects, artifacts, and events through iterative cycles and delivering those materials to genuine audiences. These environments are openly networked, giving the young people involved access to supportive technology tools and platforms that lower barriers to widespread participation. Learners come together around a shared purpose and carry out their work across a range of settings and contexts by no means limited to those that the world would identify (or that members would describe) as explicitly "educational." Finally, connected learning environments open pathways to academic and career pursuits.

Starkly evident in this lineup of features are the ways in which connected learning environments stand apart from too many of the educational settings too many young people spend too much of their time in. I am talking about the ones that sideline their interests, demote peers to sources of competition or bad influence, assign rote drills instead of hands-on projects, fracture rather than forge shared purposes among teachers and learners, and fail to unlock equitable opportunities for further academic learning and career pursuits. To be fair, it can be very difficult to create connected learning conditions within complex and underresourced bureaucratic institutions governed by entrenched policies, amid pressures that can derail the best-intentioned reform efforts, and within social conditions that erect obstacles in front of some young people, their families, and allies while easing access and opportunity for others. Educators who have managed to build connected learning opportunities within the context of school settings and other highly bureaucratized places provide proof of concept that this model can thrive inside large public school districts (Kahne 2014) as well as through innovative new cross-sector institutions that organize learning around equitable, digitally enabled, production-centered education (Barron et. al. 2014; Martin and Ito, 2013).

The point is that social supports and an equity agenda are required for young people contending with the biggest institutional obstacles (e.g., low-income youth, black and brown youth, queer youth, rural youth, etc.) to have access to connected learning experiences. It won't just happen automatically, and we need to look beyond the usual institutions for contexts where connected learning thrives. That is where the cases presented here come in. They offer powerful examples of connected learning "in the wild," so to speak—as it forms out of young people's joint efforts to achieve civic and political agency. Through the notion of "connected civics" (Ito et. al. 2015), I have worked with Ito and several of the authors in this volume to draw out the specific relationship between connected learning and participatory politics. Connected civics highlights the shared narratives, practices, and infrastructures that set young people on a path to leverage their deeply felt personal and cultural interests to carry out significant civic and political action. Cases of participatory politics further flesh out the framework of connected learning by adding civics to the other two domains—academics and career pursuits—to which learning needs to connect for it to have maximum positive impact on the young people themselves and the conditions of their social worlds.

So far in this Afterword, I have described some basic assumptions that underlie the kinds of frameworks best suited to expand our understanding of participatory politics as a context for learning. Now I turn to three specific frameworks that view learning as situated and connected, and that are especially well positioned both to expand the relevance of the cases discussed in this book and to benefit from insights derived from these studies of participatory politics.

Culturally Relevant Critical Pedagogy

Revolution is "eminently pedagogical," says Paolo Freire (1989, 54) in *The Pedagogy of the Oppressed*, his iconic treatise on education and social justice. Freire's ideas lay a foundation for "critical pedagogy," through which young people learn to recognize and act on the social, political, and economic contradictions that play out in their lives. In critical pedagogy, inequality is not something that exists in the background of education, nor even something one tries to overcome through education. It is the actual "stuff" of education—the core curriculum itself.

"We knew it was important to encourage students to use words in ways that allowed them to express love for themselves and the many places they came from" is the way one pair of scholar-educators applied critical pedagogy to the design of their curriculum, highlighting the Freirean ideals of dialogue (versus definitive explication) and reciprocity (versus teacher-driven transmission) (Filipiak and Miller 2014, 60). Critical pedagogy calls for the design of "counterspaces" by and with young people. Rather than view young people with suspicion and treat them as deficient (as if they do not know enough, do not care enough, fail to work hard enough, et cetera), in these counterspaces, educators actively work against these pervasive forms of dehumanization. "Any space that dehumanizes young people," say Filipiak and Miller, "becomes disempowering regardless of what tools, teachers, or tests students are given" (64).

This is such an important point with respect to the learning potentially engendered through participatory politics. It doesn't much matter how politically savvy the message or how digitally sophisticated the tools. If young people whose rights and dignity have already been denied are once again cut off from one another as sources of wisdom, collaborators in action, and drivers of social justice, then what they're learning, more than anything else, is a process of dehumanization. This point calls to mind the work of the DREAMers Liana Gamber-Thompson and Arely M. Zimmerman describe in this volume. "We have the power to define who we are, as undocumented students," says one young man they interviewed. By publishing a video in which he states, "I am undocumented, and I invite you to come out," Gabriel starts to build collective momentum by claiming visibility. He speaks for himself and with others, but not on behalf of others. The DREAMers' model is not about telling peers what they can and should do, in part because they, of all people, know that something as seemingly simple as posting a video shot one night in your bedroom can create a political "grenade" if the possible consequence is deportation. This is a very Freirean frame—an insistence that change starts when people with the most at stake "name" the world from their points of view and then are empowered to move from naming to investigating and acting on their own behalf.

This is hardly the framework that comes to mind in the context of learning environments where pedagogy is defined as the transmission of expert information from teachers to students deemed deficient until they "get it," which is partly why contexts for participatory politics provide such important models for what civic education as critical pedagogy can look like. And yet there are very real challenges.

One has to do with the relationship between critical consciousness and academic achievement. In her model of "culturally relevant teaching," Gloria Ladson-Billings (1995, 160) aligns with critical pedagogy in her insistence that education needs to cultivate in students a critical consciousness and prepare them for active citizenship. But she insists that this kind of citizenship development needs to link directly to academic opportunity and performance. Culturally relevant critical pedagogy, in this view, creates conditions that honor marginalized identities and lived experiences while at the same time unlocking academic learning for young people and earning them the credit they need to pursue further opportunity. Jeffrey M. Duncan-Andrade and Ernest Morrell (2008) have developed models along these lines for hip hop pedagogy and critically informed action research; Carol Lee (1993) shows how discourse practices characteristic of African American vernaculars can facilitate classroom-based language arts learning; Kris Gutierrez's notion of "third space" (2008) illuminates the learning that is made possible when teachers and students stop talking past each other or in opposition to each other and instead co-create a shared discourse; Clifford Lee (2012) has described a "critical computational literacy" that brings the principles of critical pedagogy into computer science instruction through the integration of digital storytelling; Angela Valenzuela's (1999) notion of "subtractive schooling" shows what happens when these kinds of efforts are not in place, and young people's social capital and cultural lives are devalued rather than framed as assets. These are all resources for educators and researchers seeking to create robust contexts for participatory politics that are intentionally and undeniably academically relevant.

A second challenge that surfaces when participatory politics is seen through the lens of culturally relevant critical pedagogy centers on risk. In her chapter on American Muslim youth, Sangita Shresthova frames the digital media projects 30 Mosques and Breakfast@Night as responses to the relentless onslaught of negative and dehumanizing images of Islam. And yet by being a part of these projects, young people claim the right to represent themselves from the position of a precarious "in-between." They are always needing to balance the need and right on the one hand to exercise voice, nourish connections, and spark collective action through disclosure and public storytelling, and on the other hand the very real possibility that expression will bring scrutiny, surveillance, and other material dangers. How does one practice culturally relevant teaching that is sensitive to the specter of "context collapse"—the challenge of managing the multiple audiences that accrue around young people's media artifacts as they travel through digital space and time (boyd and Marwick 2011)? Anticipating and preparing for the "digital afterlife" of participatory politics among those with the most to lose is part of what's required for these activities to provide secure and positive learning experiences for the young people involved. Their developmental trajectories and collective well-being need to be key factors in determining civic and political strategy (Soep 2012).

A final insight from this framework for learning revisits Freire's (1989) notion of dehumanization. He says it "marks not only those whose humanity has been stolen, but also . . . those who have stolen it" (28). Critical pedagogy allows that those who have stolen it sometimes aren't aware of the violence they are a part of. They might see themselves as acting on behalf of others who have been silenced, but in the process, they produce a kind of "false charity." The shadow of false charity is always hovering in the background (if not emerging at the center) of discussions of participatory politics if we don't have nuanced ways to account for the involvement of well-intentioned young people who want to "give back" and be a part of something "meaningful," but can be motivated to do so primarily for the sake of personal growth and with a lot of assumptions about what's best for others (Cole 2012). In Chapter 2 of this volume, Sangita Shresthova cites critics of *Kony 2012* and Invisible Children who called out the video for "creating heroic roles for Western activists while denying the agency of Africans working to change their own circumstances." Shresthova suggests that the group's leaders may not have done enough to anticipate counterarguments to their positions or to prepare their network of supporters to form their own opinions and respond. This book's discussion of *Kony 2012* alludes to the possibility that digitally enabled activism can make it "too easy" for young people to take action without ensuring that they "have time to reflect." Learning-rich participatory politics builds the capacity to reflect on one's own role, the space one does and should take up, and the ways in which one might be implicated in or benefit from the conditions that are being critiqued. Critical pedagogy is useful again here, with its insistence that action must always be accompanied by reflection (i.e., praxis), that the goal is not to make it "easy" but to make it thoughtful, and that knowledge emerges through "invention and reinvention" of a reality that is always unfinished and in a process of transformation.

Transmedia Making

One of the "givens" I identified earlier in this chapter is that learning is connected across spheres of interest and opportunity. It is connected in a different way, too. As a result of digital and social media and the proliferation of communication channels, learning increasingly crisscrosses multiple semiotic systems, genres, formats, platforms, and networks. As part of an investigation into any given topic area, learners might review videos, photos, audio clips, archival documents, and posts, each with its own cultural, historical, and aesthetic context and intended audience. They might access these texts through physical documents, mobile devices, public library laptops, and stories exchanged in face-to-face encounters. Each of these "reading" experiences requires specific resources and creates its own social conditions for building comprehension and interpretation. These are just some of the ways that the notion of transmedia storytelling has influenced literacy development and the frameworks required to teach it. And while the sheer number of lists in this paragraph makes for clunky writing, it also reinforces an important point related to transmedia learning. As young people are increasingly called upon to acquire and share knowledge across a dizzying array of dispersed channels, they can benefit from guidance and practice in navigating those channels and forging meaningful connections.

Alper and Herr-Stephenson (2013) define transmedia in terms of both narrative elements (e.g., plot, setting, character) and nonnarrative elements or modes of participation (e.g., ways to contribute to an online community) that cut across platforms. They argue that transmedia contexts are uniquely positioned to build a robust set of literacies. For example, they point to a kind of resourcefulness cultivated through the capacity to discover and juxtapose novel content, the social value of collective interpretation, and a capacity to examine rich texts in pursuit of deeper meanings. These ideas build on earlier frames for literacy that highlight multimodality and intertextuality (Kress 2000) and emphasize not mastery of a fixed set of skills but the negotiation of various dialects, registers, and discourses (Cope and Kalantzis 2000, 14).

I want to connect these frameworks that emerge from studies of transmedia literacies to another, very much related school of thought within learning studies. Researchers and practitioners increasingly frame learning as a process of making. The approach grows out of the burgeoning "maker movement," which has come into public awareness through huge festivals in which artists, engineers, hobbyists, and tinkerers gather to share tools and creations (Sefton-Green 2013). Maker-based education builds curricula around inventing and tinkering using physical materials, often including recycled or repurposed objects, and digital tools (Peppler and Bender 2013). In their review of the existing literature on this approach, Vossoughi and Bevan (2014) highlight the "aesthetic and playful" qualities of making and the various educational outcomes supporters have pinned to it. Maker-based environments are seen by these authors as a way to cultivate learning that is personally relevant, sparked by socially meaningful problems, conducive to novice-expert collaboration, and creatively engaged with the material world. The experience of creating something physical and digital (e.g., a tricked-out bike, a garment stitched together with electronic thread) promotes inquiry and understanding of academically relevant concepts, can expose learners to entrepreneurial opportunities, and can reinvigorate learning in the all-important fields of science, technology, engineering, and math, thereby unlocking pathways into jobs. Making is a kind of transmedia production that moves between the physical and digital worlds.

Both transmedia literacy and maker-based approaches are cross-platform and profoundly interdisciplinary. They recognize a deep relationship between learning and the "everyday," insisting that the kinds of texts and objects young people interact with all the time in their lives deserve prime placement in educational environments. Both cultivate cultures of collaboration and sharing and caution against what in the maker context would be called mere "assembling," which provides no real space for experimenting, breaking, and reinventing (Vossoughi and Bevan 2014). Taken together, an approach to learning framed as a kind of transmedia making gives young people considerable agency over what and how they produce.

This "do it yourself" or "DIY" spirit, which powers transmedia making, is one of the principles that link this framework to participatory politics. Fundamental to the whole concept of participatory politics is a transfer of agency from formal institutions, recognized elites, and sanctioned protocols over to young people who can work in less hierarchical and more decentralized ways to gain attention and bring about change. This process of gaining attention and sparking change is a kind of making in itself, and often requires transmedia storytelling to accomplish.

"To be a member of Invisible Children," says Lana Swartz (2012) (cited in Chapter 2), "means to be a viewer, participant, wearer, reader, listener, commenter of and in the various activities, many mediated, that make up the Movement." The group's tactics unfold as a kind of sprawling, evolving transmedia story, told through T-shirts and accessories; highly produced films; large-scale event-oriented campaigns including policy makers and celebrities, music mixes, print media, and online posts; and face-to-face gatherings of "roadies" and other young supporters dispersed across the United States. This activist toolbox brings to mind the title of this book, *By Any Media Necessary*, which could serve as a rallying cry for the group's cross-platform pursuit of its goals. Certainly Invisible Children's *Kony 2012* campaign provides a striking case of getting runaway global attention for a political point of view and agenda through transmedia making.

This same learning framework contains some clues as to what might have set up the group for the kind of backlash it faced. Though committed to transmedia making, Invisible Children in fact had limited interest in DIY production, according to Shresthova. This was the case before the *Kony 2012* firestorm, and even more so after. Invisible Children "was too centralized, not sufficiently participatory, and knowledge was not adequately dispersed across the network." When the critiques started to overtake enthusiasm for the Invisible Children message, it seems leadership became even more narrowly defined, and the scripting of stories more tightly edited and rehearsed. It's not hard to understand the desire to control what had become a personally and politically chaotic situation. The unintended consequence, though, was to relegate youth increasingly to the role of audience as opposed to participants, leaving them with fewer ways to contribute as makers of an evolving transmedia story that can transform on the basis of critique and sync up with the people who have the most at stake in the story's outcome.

All of the groups described in this book use some form of transmedia making to develop their civic and political stories. Learning unfolds in the production phase and, more unpredictably, through the stories' "digital afterlives," when communities of others start to share, remix, mobilize around, and critique those texts. As described by Gamber-Thompson, young libertarians, identified with the ideology's "second wave," are an especially notable case. "Big L" libertarianism, which characterizes the "first wave," seeks change through electoral politics and party involvement. "Little l" libertarianism, a kind of DIY second-wave version, seeks change through a loose association of groups and individuals advocating for free market ideals, civil liberties, and small government regardless of political affiliation. "Given young libertarians' distrust of governmental institutions," says Gamber-Thompson, "it makes sense that their approach to education would emphasize informal, often self-motivated, learning . . . rather than more formalized instruction, and that they would assume the authority to share insights about theory with their community without regard to academic credentials." As young libertarians turn towards a maker-based approach to transmedia storytelling—whether through the creation of music videos styled around Austrian economic theory or the embrace of a wide variety of theorists, including Malcolm X—they build their case that DIY citizenship and the democratization of knowledge can shape political and social movements.

Taken together, the instances of transmedia making described across this book can but do not necessarily spark the kinds of learning opportunities their designers had in mind, which is why the learning frame is key. It inspires us to ask ourselves all the time: How can we use "any media necessary" to help create conditions for deepening inquiry among the communities we're a part of? What kinds of learning communities are we making when we engage with youth in participatory politics? How are we helping to prepare those communities, when necessary, to remake themselves?

"Releasing the Imagination"

In naming this final framework, I am quoting the philosopher of education Maxine Greene (1995). "Of all our cognitive capacities," Greene argues, "imagination is the one that permits us to give credence to alternative realities. It allows us to break with the taken for granted" (3). Imagination takes us into "as-if" worlds, and educating for the imagination makes it possible for people to conceive of things as if they could be otherwise.

In forming a view of learning as the release of imagination, Greene was making a case for the role of the arts as a core discipline in education. She saw the arts as uniquely suited to bringing about a kind of "wide-awakeness" among learners—an "awareness of what it is to be in the world" and "to reach beyond" (35). Shocks of awareness, in Greene's view, leave us less entrenched in what is and more impelled to wonder and question, to attend to nuance and form our own judgments (Eisner 2002). When learners work through close readings of literature, become someone else in a play, arrange sound and rhythm in an original composition, place pigment on a canvas, or string together lines of computer code to animate an imagined world, they are building "the capacity to look through the windows of the actual, to bring as-ifs into being in experience" (Greene 1995, 140). Greene did not leave politics off the table. In her advocacy for the arts, she described what she considered an "emancipatory" education that dislodged learners from the conditions that reproduce inequality and suffering by calling upon them to question, imagine, and create alternatives to what was being presented to them as the way things are and have to be.

When as-if worlds are defined by the political change young people seek, then Greene's ideas become especially useful as a way to frame the project of learning in and through participatory politics. In his introduction to the concept of civic imagination, Henry Jenkins cites the 2008 Harvard commencement address delivered by Harry Potter's creator, J. K. Rowling, which has strong echoes of Greene's thought. Rowling calls out those who have cut themselves off from empathy: "They choose to remain comfortably within the bounds of their own experience, never troubling to wonder how it would feel to have been born other than they are. They can refuse to hear screams or to peer inside cages; they can close their minds and hearts to any suffering that does not touch them personally; they can refuse to know."

The Harry Potter Alliance, the Imagine Better project, and the other fan-based activisms described here are perhaps the most obvious cases of the cultivation of imagination as a means to learn in and through participatory politics. Young people involved in these communities imagine alternatives to social, political, or economic institutions and problems by mining fiction and pivoting from the private to the public imagination. One HPA member credits literature for creating "a whole new world in our minds. It allows us to experience things we've never experienced before." Neta Kligler-Vilenchik astutely acknowledges that the ability to connect imagined texts to real world issues "may be a learned skill." American Muslim youth use that skill to produce a body of work that is loosely connected, heterogeneous, and in some cases ambiguous, doing "important political work precisely because it evades (or in the case of 30Mosques intentionally rejects) easy insertion into dominant narratives and existing political frameworks." DREAMers use that skill through their creative positioning of comic book superheroes as undocumented immigrants whose epic stories shatter stereotypes and bring to light real-life struggles and rights. Young libertarians use that skill to create videos that delve into and spread dense economic political theory through arch comic characters and winking fan-girl performances.

There are, of course, tensions at the intersection of the as-if and the real. Kligler-Vilenchik points out that the imagined worlds of say, a Harry Potter novel or Hunger Games film provide raw materials fans can use to organize dialogue and action around political issues such as economic injustice or marriage rights. But the "internal logics" that make those worlds function don't necessarily apply to our world, "and making direct comparisons may be problematic." Doing political work at the intersection of art, fiction, and activism raises complex questions related to credibility—a key challenge young people themselves have identified with respect to participatory politics, and an area where they say could use more help from adults (Cohen and Kahne 2012). How do you fact-check a spoken word poem in which a young person enacts the experience of a survivor of child sex trafficking from a first-person point of view that is not necessarily her own? What is the role of data and primary-source reporting in a stage performance drawing attention to labor abuse by transnational corporations? Who has the right to imagine someone else's story, or, put another way, how is that right learned and earned?

Liesbet van Zoonen is quoted in Chapter 1 making the point that "[p]leasure, fantasy, love, immersion, play, or impersonations are not concepts easily reconciled with civic virtues such as knowledge, rationality, detachment, learnedness, or leadership." While it's easy to see that second list of virtues as "old school," the young people whose best work is represented in these pages are always trying to refine knowledge, acquire learnedness, and build leadership (though detachment does seem to show up less as an ideal). Expression, meaning making, and reframing are important outcomes of participatory politics but do not necessarily lead to influence and material change. At the very least, for the civic imagination to be educative, makers need to provide sufficient context so that communities can judge the logic and truthfulness of the as-if world and act accordingly.

It feels good to think about imagination, but we can't forget that young people can imagine and systematically work to create anything—

not only a world that is more humane and just and equitable and free, but also violent dystopias and ways to destroy forces that threaten them. Finally, it can be easier and feel more powerful to conjure the imagined experiences of fictional others than to confront the opinions and intelligence of real people whose real lives challenge your community's reigning approach or point of view. There is nothing automatically "emancipatory" about the imagination, and it is crucial in taking advantage of this imaginative framework in particular that we also account for the notion of critical pedagogy that came before it in this discussion. If education aims to prepare students for active citizenship, as Ladson-Billings has said, we need to make sure that they critically interrogate their own as-if worlds as fully and rigorously as they do the world as it apparently is.

Conclusion

In this Afterword, I have explored insights relevant to participatory politics based on three frameworks for thinking about learning. All three situate learning within communities of practice and see learning as connected across domains of interest and opportunity. Culturally relevant critical pedagogy says the formation of a grounded civic and political consciousness needs to be a driving force in education. Learning as a process of transmedia making highlights the proliferation of channels across which young people produce and share knowledge and makes the case for a "do it yourself" approach whereby learners exercise a great deal of agency over what and how they create. Learning as the release of imagination positions young people to see through the details of their real lives other ways to be and cultivates in them a kind of "wide-awakeness" they'll need to reach beyond the known. Taken together, these frameworks have much to offer as we seek to understand and promote participatory politics as a process and product of learning.

But these three approaches don't satisfactorily address certain important findings from the ethnographic studies of *By Any Media Necessary*. To name a few, first, there are the issues of privacy and surveillance. As I have stated, we don't yet know enough about how to practice culturally relevant critical pedagogy from a precarious position, where self-disclosure, expression, and community inquiry can be high-risk activities, and when "context collapse" can leave makers ill prepared to face life-altering consequences (e.g., deportation) and possible backlash (e.g., waves of cruel online comments). Second, there is the cathartic and therapeutic value of self-expression as a dimension of political becoming. The architects of these learning frameworks were necessarily invested in distancing themselves from prior dominant theories that saw learning as an "in the head" activity and creativity as a mindless release of emotion. Perhaps for that reason, their accounts have a hard time factoring in the domains of desire, pain, trauma, and letting go that show up in moments of participatory politics described here as a matter, sometimes, of "psychic survival." Third, there is the question of credibility I have already raised. If imagination and as-if worlds are key sources for civic and political mobilization, we need a more developed set of strategies and protocols whereby an important thing young people learn by participating in these worlds is how to traffic in truth.

These are worthy challenges for educators in a range of settings who are building contexts for participatory politics. What does a curriculum look like that empowers young people to express voice and achieve influence in public spheres, while enabling them to differentiate productive interest from a sense of entitlement to pursue one's own personal growth on the backs of others? How can models of community-based participatory research, through which young people drive real-time investigations into conditions within their communities, benefit from what we've learned about participatory politics? How can we continue to broaden the range of genres through which young people share their school-sanctioned civic and political knowledge, beyond tests and papers and even briefings, to include community performances and social media conversations and experimental digital displays? Among the many insights in *By Any Media Necessary*, there is the clear mandate to think much more expansively about where and how civic learning happens and who is in a position to shepherd that work forward.

* * *

In small and large ways, we are all civic educators now.

Notes

Chapter 1. Youth Voice, Media, and Political Engagement

1 There is much one could say about Occupy—that Occupy was too fragmented in its agenda despite its efforts to build consensus; that a "leaderless" organization lacked the capacity to negotiate with institutional players; that the Democratic Party held it at a distance in a way that the Republicans have at least sometimes embraced the Tea Party movement—but there's no question that its discursive practices impacted the ways Americans speak about and understand class politics. The 2012 U.S. presidential election can be seen as a battle of percentages, where Occupy's 99 percent versus 1 percent frame competed with the GOP's 47 percent takers versus 53 percent makers language. And at a time of rising class consciousness, even among the young libertarians featured in this book who openly critique "crony capitalism," the Republican Party might as well have nominated the guy on the Monopoly box, a factor in Mitt Romney's defeat. By late 2014, Romney had reemerged, painting himself as a new kind of Republican candidate, defined around his focus on issues of poverty and economic inequality—yet another sign of Occupy's lasting impact on American political discourse.

2 These social media strategies involve what people are increasingly calling "Black Twitter." The term "Black Twitter" is problematic in many ways: creating the illusion of a unified black voice, defining participants primarily or exclusively around their race, and reifying the separation of African-Americans from other citizens of color. What's driven this framing is the reality that while only 14 percent of whites online use Twitter, 26 percent of African American and 19 percent of Latino internet users do. (The Pew Research Center's Internet & American Life Project, unfortunately, does not collect data on Asian American users or other ethnicities.) As a result of this concentration, as well as a growing understanding about how to deploy this platform to foster greater public engagement with race-related issues, Twitter represents an important vehicle for discussing and mobilizing around civil rights and social justice issues (Brock 2012). Yet, in practice, what we are observing are diverse coalitions and networks—sometimes working together, sometimes working apart, sometimes primarily or exclusively black. More often, it is alliances between people of multiple races and ethnicities that have driven conversations around social justice issues. Such grassroots efforts offer a powerful check on governmental action.

3 The use of the term "meme" here is consistent with the ways these practices are discussed by the groups and individuals we researched. Henry Jenkins et al. (2013) challenged the underlying model of viral distribution in their book, *Spreadable*

Media, and we remain somewhat uncomfortable with the ways this term bears traces of the earlier idea of "self-replicating culture" that informed the original meme model, but more recent work by Whitney Phillips (2013) and Limor Shifman (2013) has suggested that the popular understanding of the term has moved beyond these models. As Phillips writes, "Memes spread—that is, they are actively engaged and/or remixed into existence—because something about a given image or phrase or video or whatever lines up with an already-established set of linguistic and cultural norms." Our use of the term "meme" refers here to a set of subcultural practices that are now widespread across the internet, not to a model of cultural transmission that has been largely discredited.

Chapter 6. Bypassing the Ballot Box

1 A note about the first-wave/second-wave terminology: the libertarian "second wave" is really more analogous to the feminist "third wave," if comparisons are to be made. It's also important to note that not all young libertarians are embracing the second-wave model. For example, supporters of Ron Paul's 2012 presidential campaign might be considered adherents of something closer to a "first-wave" libertarian ideology due to their focus on a political campaign/elected office rather than the kind of intellectual social change McCobin is talking about.

2 Electra has, however, distanced herself from the movement in more recent years and does not currently self-identify as libertarian.

3 It should be noted that, while some young libertarians might identify with a so-called neoliberal agenda, which seeks a hands-off approach to economic policy, most participants took a critical stance toward what they viewed as "crony capitalism," characterized by interdependent relationships between entrepreneurs and government officials, and toward unfettered corporate greed that steamrolls individual rights. Libertarians' focus on individual choice and influence over economic policy is also more in line with classical liberalism than with the neoliberalism of the 1980s and beyond.

Bibliography

Abrego, Leisy Janet. 2006. "'I Can't Go to College Because I Don't Have Papers': Incorporation Patterns of Latino Undocumented Youth." *Latino Studies* 4: 212–231.

Abrego, Leisy Janet. 2008. "Barely Subsisting, Surviving, or Thriving: How Parents' Legal Status and Gender Shape the Economic and Emotional Well-Being of Salvadoran Transnational Families." Ph.D. diss., University of California, Los Angeles.

Abrego, Leisy Janet. 2013. "Undocumented Youth Movement." Paper presented at the Fifth Annual Conference of the Unión Salvadoreña de Estudiantes Universitarios (USEU), University of California, Los Angeles. April.

Adelson, Joseph. 1971. "The Political Imagination of the Young Adolescent." *Daedalus* 100(4): 1013–1050.

Ahmed, Tanzila. 2012. "Punk-Drunk Love." In *Love, InshAllah: The Secret Love Lives of American Muslim Women*, ed. Ayesha Mattu and Nura Maznavi. Berkeley, CA: Soft Skull Press.

Alcoholics Anonymous. n.d. "Frequently Asked Questions about A.A. History." http://www.aa.org/pages/en_US/frequently-asked-questions-about-aa-history#dieciseis (accessed September 17, 2015).

Ali, Ayaan Hirsi. 2012. "Muslim Rage & The Last Gasp of Islamic Hate." *Newsweek*, September 7. http://www.thedailybeast.com/newsweek/2012/09/16/ayaan-hirsi-ali-on-the-islamists-final-stand.html (accessed February 13, 2013). Archived at https://web.archive.org/web/20130216040357/http://www.thedailybeast.com/newsweek/2012/09/16/ayaan-hirsi-ali-on-the-islamists-final-stand.html.

Ali, Dilshad. 2011. "Lowes Boycott of TLC's 'All-American Muslim' Has United Muslims, Americans." *Patheos*, December 14. http://www.patheos.com/blogs/allamericanmuslim/2011/12/lowes-boycott-of-tlcs-all-american-muslim-has-united-muslims-americans/.

Ali, Wajahat. 2010. "The Power of Storytelling: Creating a New Future for American Muslims." *Goatmilk Blog*, August 19. http://goatmilkblog.com/2010/08/19/the-power-of-storytelling-creating-a-new-future-for-american-muslims/.

Allen, Danielle. 2006. *Talking to Strangers: Anxieties of Citizenship since Brown v. Board of Education*. Chicago: University of Chicago Press.

Allen, Danielle, and Jennifer S. Light, eds. 2015. *From Voice to Influence: Understanding Citizenship in a Digital Age*. Chicago: University of Chicago Press.

Alper, Meryl, and Rebecca Herr-Stephenson. 2013. "Transmedia Play: Literacy across Media." *Journal of Media Literacy Education* 5(2): 366–369.

Alsultany, Evelyn. 2012. *Arabs and Muslims in the Media Race and Representation after 9/11*. New York: New York University Press.

Amarasingam, Amarnath. 2010. "Laughter the Best Medicine: Muslim Comedians and Social Criticism in Post-9/11 America." *Journal of Muslim Minority Affairs* 30(4): 463–477.

Amna, Erik. 2010. "Active, Passive, or Standby Citizens? Latent and Manifest Political Participation." In *New Forms of Citizen Participation: Normative Implications*, ed. Erik Amna. Baden-Baden: Nomos.

Anderson, Benedict. 1983. *Imagined Communities: Reflections on the Origin and Spread of Nationalism*. London: Verso.

Andrae, Thomas. 1987. "From Menace to Messiah: The History and Historicity of Superman." In *American Media and Mass Culture: Left Perspectives*, ed. Donald Lazare. Berkeley: University of California Press.

Andresen, Katya. 2011. "Why Slactivism Is Underrated." *Mashable*, October 24. http://mashable.com/2011/24/slatctivism-cause-engagement/.

Andrew, J. Dudley. 1984. *Concepts in Film Theory*. New York: Oxford University Press.

Anelli, Melissa. 2008. *Harry, a History: The True Story of a Boy Wizard, His Fans, and Life inside the Harry Potter Phenomenon*. New York: Pocket Books.

Apte, Mahadev. 1985. *Humor and Laughter: An Anthropological Approach*. Cornell, NY: Cornell University Press.

Banaji, Shakuntala, and David Buckingham. 2013. *The Civic Web: Young People, the Internet and Civic Participation*. Cambridge, MA: MIT Press.

Banet-Weiser, Sarah. 2013. *Authentic™: The Politics of Ambivalence in a Brand Culture*. New York: New York University Press.

Barron, Brigid, Kimberley Gomez, Nichole Pinkard, and Caitlin K. Martin. 2014. *The Digital Youth Network*. Cambridge, MA: MIT Press.

Baym, Nancy. 2000. *Tune In, Log On: Soaps, Fandom and Online Community*. Thousand Oaks, CA: Sage.

Benford, Robert D., and David A. Snow. 2000. "Framing Processes and Social Movements: An Overview and Assessment." *Annual Review of Sociology* 26: 611–639.

Bennett, W. Lance. 2008a. "Changing Citizenship in the Digital Age." In *Civic Life Online: Learning How Digital Media Can Engage Youth*, ed. W. Lance Bennett. Cambridge, MA: MIT Press/MacArthur Foundation.

Bennett, W. Lance, ed. 2008b. *Civic Life Online: Learning How Digital Media Can Engage Youth*. Cambridge, MA: MIT Press/MacArthur Foundation.

Bennett, W. Lance, Deen Freelon, and Chris Wells. 2010. "Changing Citizen Identity and the Rise of a Participatory Media Culture." In *Handbook of Research on Civic Engagement in Youth*, ed. Lonnie R. Sherrod, Constance A. Flanagan, and Judith Torney-Purta. New York: Routledge.

Bennett, W. Lance, and Alexandra Segerberg. 2012. "The Logic of Connective Action." *Information, Communication & Society* 15(5): 739–768.

Bennett, W. Lance, Chris Wells, and Deen Freelon. 2011. "Communicating Civic Engagement: Contrasting Models of Citizenship in the Youth Web Sphere." *Journal of Communication* 61: 835–856.

Bennett, W. Lance, Chris Wells, and Allison Rank. 2009. "Young Citizens and Civic Learning: Two Paradigms of Citizenship in the Digital Age." *Citizenship Studies* 13(2): 105–120.

Bilici, Mucahit. 2010. "Muslim Ethnic Comedy: Inversions of Islamophobia." In *Islamophobia/Islamophilia: Beyond the Politics of Enemy and Friend*, ed. Andrew Shryock. Bloomington: Indiana University Press.

Binder, Amy, and Kate Wood. 2013. *Becoming Right: How Campuses Shape Young Conservatives*. Princeton, NJ: Princeton University Press.

Bird, Lauren. 2013. "When Our Heroes Fail." *YouTube* video for Harry Potter Alliance (4:23), January 31. http://www.youtube.com/watch?v=ub6l75MyReo&list=PL1g3MX AZto6J5D9hP3yBE_uN55ayPk1HK.

Blakely, Johanna, and Sheena Nahm. 2011. "Primetime War on Drugs and Terror: An Analysis of Depictions of the War on Terror and the War on Drugs in Popular Primetime Television Programs." Norman Lear Center, September. http://learcenter.org /pdf/Drugs&Terror.pdf.

Bodgroghkozy, Aniko. 2013. *Equal Time: Television and the Civil Rights Movement*. Chicago: University of Illinois Press.

Boler, Megan, ed. 2008. *Digital Media and Democracy: Tactics in Hard Times*. Cambridge, MA: MIT Press.

Bourdieu, Pierre. 1984. *Distinction: A Social Critique of the Judgement of Taste*. Cambridge, MA: Harvard University Press.

boyd, danah. 2008. "How Youth Find Privacy in Interstitial Places." *Apophenia* (blog), March 9. http://www.zephoria.org/thoughts/archives/2008/03/09/how_youth_find .html.

boyd, danah. 2012. "The Power of Youth: How Invisible Children Orchestrated Kony 2012." *Huffington Post*, March 14.http://www.huffingtonpost.com/danah-boyd /post_3126_b_1345782.html.

boyd, danah. 2014. *It's Complicated: The Social Lives of Networked Teens*. New Haven, CT: Yale University Press.

boyd, danah, and Alice Marwick. 2011. "Social Privacy in Networked Publics: Teen's Attitudes, Practices, and Strategies." Paper presented at the Privacy Law Scholars Conference, Berkeley, Calif., June 2.

Break_Fast at Night Project website. 2013.http://breakfastatnightproject.com/.

Brock, André. 2012. "From the Blackhand Side: Twitter as a Cultural Conversation." *Journal of Broadcasting Electronic Media* 56(4): 529–549.

Brough, Melissa. 2012. "Fair Vanity: The Visual Culture of Humanitarianism in the Age of Commodity Activism." In *Commodity Activism: Cultural Resistance in Neoliberal Times*, ed. Roopali Mukherjee and Sarah Banet-Weiser. New York: New York University Press.

Brough, Melissa, and Sangita Shresthova. 2012. "Fandom Meets Activism: Rethinking Civic and Political Participation." *Transformative Works and Cultures* 10. doi:10.3983/twc.2012.0303.

Buckingham, David. 2000. *The Making of Citizens: Young People, News and Politics*. London: Routledge.

Burgess, Jean, and Joshua Green. 2009. *YouTube: Online Video and Participatory Culture*. Cambridge, UK: Polity Press.

Campbell, John Edward. 2009. "From Barbershop to Black Planet: The Construction of Hush Harbors in Cyberspace." Paper presented at the Media in Transition 6 Conference, MIT, Cambridge, Mass., April 5.

Carpentier, Nico. 2011. *Media and Participation*. Bristol, UK: Intellect.

Carson, Clayborne. 1995. *In Struggle: SNCC and the Black Awakening of the 1960s*. Cambridge, MA: Harvard University Press.

Castells, Manuel. 2012. *Networks of Outrage and Hope: Social Movements in the Internet Age*. London: Polity.

Chabot, Sean, and Jan Willem Duyvendak. 2002. "Globalization and Transnational Diffusion between Social Movements: Reconceptualizing the Dissemination of the Gandhian Repertoire and the 'Coming Out' Routine." *Theory and Society* 31: 697–749.

Chaudry, Rabia. 2013. "Online Radicalization: Myths and Realities." Panel at New America Foundation, Washington, D.C., March 28. http://www.mpac.org /programs/government-relations/mpac-tackles-violent-extremism-and-online -radicalization-at-two-dc-events.php#.UhMGQLzEgo4.

Chaudry, Rabia. 2014. "A New Muslim Renaissance Is Here." *Time*, April 16. http:// time.com/65094/look-out-for-the-new-muslim-renaissance/.

Chauncey, George. 1994. *Gay New York: Gender, Urban Culture, and the Making of the Gay Male World, 1890–1940*. New York: Basic Books.

Chirrey, Deborah A. 2003. "'I Hereby Come Out': What Sort of Speech Act Is Coming Out?" *Journal of Sociolinguistics* 7(1): 24–37.

Close, Samantha. Forthcoming. "Graffiti Knitting: A How-To Guide for Participatory Politics." Work in progress.

Cochran, Tanya R. 2012. "'Past the Brink of Tacit Support': Fan Activism and the Whedonverses." *Transformative Works and Cultures* 10. doi:10.3983/twc.2012.0331.

Cohen, Cathy J. 2010. *Democracy Remixed: Black Youth and the Future of American Politics*. Oxford: Oxford University Press.

Cohen, Cathy J., and Joseph Kahne. 2012. "Participatory Politics: New Media and Youth Political Action." MacArthur Foundation Youth and Participatory Politics Research Network, June. http://ypp.dmlcentral.net/sites/default/files/publications /Participatory_Politics_New_Media_and_Youth_Political_Action.2012.pdf.

Cole, Teju. 2012. "The White Savior Industrial Complex." *Atlantic* http://www.theatlantic.com/international/archive/2012/03/ the-white-savior-industrial-complex/254843/.

Condis, Megan. 2014. "No Homosexuals in Star Wars?: Bioware, 'Gamer' Identity, and The Politics of Privilege in a Convergence Culture." *Convergence*, April 4.

Cooper, Michael, Michael S. Schmidt, and Eric Schmitt. 2013. "Boston Suspects Are Seen as Self-Taught and Fueled by Web." *New York Times*, April 23. http://www .nytimes.com/2013/04/24/us/boston-marathon-bombing-developments.html?_r=0.

Cope, Bill, and Mary Kalantzis. 2000. *Multiliteracies: Literacy Learning and the Design of Social Futures.* New York: Routledge.

Coppa, Francesca. 2008. "Women, 'Star Trek,' and the Early Development of Fannish Vidding." *Transformative Works and Cultures* 1. doi:10.3983/twc.2008.0044.

Costanza-Chock, Sasha. 2010. "Se Ve, Se Siente: Transmedia Mobilization in the Los Angeles Immigrant Rights Movement." Ph.D. diss., University of Southern California.

Costanza-Chock, Sasha. 2012. "Mic Check!: Media Cultures and the Occupy Movement." *Social Movement Studies* 11(3–4): 375–385.

Couldry, Nick. 2010. *Why Voice Matters: Culture and Politics after Neoliberalism.* London: Sage.

Crawford, Kate. 2013. "The Hidden Biases in Big Data." *Harvard Business Review*, April 1. https://hbr.org/2013/04/the-hidden-biases-in-big-data/.

Crum, Matt Scott. 2014. "A Global Development Practitioner/Millenial's Thoughts on Invisible Children." *Medium*, December 15. https://medium.com/@mattscottcrum/a-global-development-practioner-millennials-thoughts-on-invisible-children-1f7f6b315da5.

Cvetkovich, Ann. 2003. *An Archive of Feelings: Trauma, Sexuality and Lesbian Public Cultures.* Durham, NC: Duke University Press.

Dahlgren, Peter. 2003. "Reconfiguring Civic Culture in the New Media Milieu." In *Media and the Restyling of Politics: Consumerism, Celebrity and Cynicism*, ed. John Corner. Thousand Oaks, CA: Sage.

Dahlgren, Peter. 2009. *Media and Political Engagement: Citizens, Communication, and Democracy.* Cambridge, UK: Cambridge University Press.

Dahlgren, Peter. 2011. "Parameters of Online Participation: Conceptualising Civic Contingencies." *Communication Management Quarterly* 21: 87–110.

Daley, Patricia. 2013. "Rescuing African Bodies: Celebrities, Consumerism and Neoliberal Humanitarianism." *Review of African Political Economy* 40(137): 375–393.

Dalton, Russell J. 2009. *The Good Citizen: How a Younger Generation is Reshaping American Politics.* Washington, DC: CQ Press.

Dayan, Daniel. 2005. "Mothers, Midwives and Abortionists: Genealogy, Obstetrics, Audiences and Publics." In *Audiences and Publics: When Cultural Engagement Matters for the Public Sphere*, ed. Sonia Livingstone. London: Intellect.

Dean, Jodi. 2005. "Communicative Capitalism: Circulation and the Foreclosure of Politics." *Cultural Politics* 1(1): 51–74.

Delwiche, Aaron. 2013. "The New Left and the Computer Underground: Recovering Political Antecedents of Participatory Culture." In *The Participatory Cultures Handbook*, ed. Aaron Delwiche and Jennifer Jacobs Henderson. New York: Routledge.

Delwiche, Aaron, and Jennifer Jacobs Henderson, eds. 2013. *The Participatory Cultures Handbook.* New York: Routledge.

Denning, Michael. 1998. *The Cultural Front: The Laboring of American Culture in the Twentieth Century.* London: Verso.

Dery, Mark. 1993. "Culture Jamming: Hacking, Slashing and Sniping in the Empire of the Signs." Pamphlet #25, Open Magazine Pamphlet Series. Available at http://markdery.com/?page_id=154.

DeVoss, Danielle Nicole, Elyse Eidman-Aadahl, and Troy Hicks. 2010. *Because Digital Writing Matters: Improving Student Writing in Online and Multimedia Environments*. San Francisco: Joseey-Bass.

Dewey, John. 1938. *Experience and Education*. New York: Free Press.

Douglas, Mary. 2010. *Implicit Meanings*. New York: Routledge.

Drumbl, Mark A. 2012. "Child Soldiers and Clicktivism: Justice, Myths, and Prevention." *Human Rights Practice* 4(3): 481–485.

Dufrasne, Marie, and Geoffroy Patriarche. 2011. "Applying Genre Theory to Citizen Participation in Public Policy Making: Theoretical Perspectives on Participatory Genres." *Communication Management Quarterly* 21: 61–86.

Duncan-Andrade, Jeffrey M., and Ernest Morrell. 2008. *The Art of Critical Pedagogy: Possibilities for Moving from Theory to Practice in Urban Schools*. New York: Peter Lang.

Duncombe, Stephen. 2007. *Dream: Re-Imagining Progressive Politics in an Age of Fantasy*. New York: New Press.

Duncombe, Stephen. 2012a. "Imagining No-place." *Transformative Works and Cultures* 10. doi:10.3983/twc.2012.0350.

Duncombe, Stephen. 2012b. "Principle: Know Your Cultural Terrain." In *Beautiful Trouble: A Toolbox for Revolution*, ed. Andrew Boyd and Dave Oswald Mitchell. New York: OR Books. Available at http://beautifultrouble.org/principle/know -your-cultural-terrain/.

Duncombe, Stephen. 2012c. "Theory: Ethical Spectacle." In *Beautiful Noise: A Toolbox for Revolution*, ed. Andrew Boyd and Dave Oswald Mitchell. New York: OR Books.

Dyer, Richard. 1985. "Entertainment and Utopia." In *Movies and Methods II*, ed. Bill Nichols. Berkeley: University of California Press.

Earl, Jennifer. 2013. "Spreading the Word or Shaping the Conversation: 'Prosumption' in Protest Website." In *Research in Social Movements, Conflicts and Change*, ed. P. G. Coy. Bradford: Emerald Group Publishing.

Earl, Jennifer, and Katrina Kimport. 2009. "Movement Societies and Digital Protest: Fan Activism and Other Nonpolitical Protest Online." *Sociological Theory* 27(3): 220–243.

Earl, Jennifer, and Katrina Kimport. 2011. *Digitally Enabled Social Change: Activism in the Internet Age*. Cambridge, MA: MIT Press.

Earl, Jennifer, Katrina Kimport, Greg Prieto, Carly Rush, and Kimberly Reynoso. 2010. "Changing the World on Webpage at a Time: Conceptualizing and Explaining Internet Activism." *Mobilization: An International Journal* 15(4): 426–427.

Ehrenreich, Barbara, Elizabeth Hess, and Gloria Jacobs. 1997. "Beatlemania: A Sexually Defiant Consumer Subculture?" In *The Subcultures Reader*, ed. Ken Gilder and Sarah Thornton. London: Routledge.

Eisner, Elliot W. 2002. "What Can Education Learn from the Arts about the Practice of Education?" *The Encyclopedia of Informal Education*, at *infed*. http://www.infed.org /biblio/eisner_arts_and_the_practice_of_education.htm.

Eliasoph, Nina. 1998. *Avoiding Politics: How Americans Produce Apathy in Everyday Life*. Cambridge, UK: Cambridge University Press.

Engle, Gary. 1987. "What Makes Superman So Darned American?" In *Superman at Fifty: The Persistence of a Legend*, ed. Dennis Dooley and Gary Engle. Cleveland, OH: Octavia.

Evans, Christina. 2015. "The Nuts and Bolts of Digital Civic Imagination." *DML Central*, March 26. http://dmlcentral.net/blog/christina-evans/nuts-and-bolts-digital-civic -imagination.

Ewing, Katherine Pratt, and Marguerite Hoyler. 2008. "Being Muslim and American: South Asian Muslim Youth and the War on Terror." In *Being and Belonging: Muslims in the United States since 9/11*, ed. Katherine Pratt Ewing. New York: Russell Sage Foundation.

Fellowship of Reconciliation. 1955. *Martin Luther King and the Montgomery Story*. Marietta, GA: Top Shelf.

"Fighting War Crimes, without Leaving the Couch?" 2012. In "Kony 2012 and the Potential of Social Media Activism." *New York Times*, March 9. http://www.nytimes.com /roomfordebate/2012/03/09/kony-2012-and-the-potential-of-social-media-activism /kony-2012-is-not-a-revolution.

Filipiak, Danielle, and Isaac Miller. 2014. "Me and the D.: (Re)Imagining Literacy and Detroit's Future." *English Journal* 103(5): 59–66.

Fish, Adam, Christopher Kelty, Luis F. R. Murillo, Lilly Nyugen, and Aaron Panofsky. 2011. "Birds of the Internet: Towards a Field Guide to the Organization and Governance of Participation." *Journal of Cultural Economy* 4(2): 157–187.

Fiske, John. 1989a [2011]. *Understanding Popular Culture*. New York: Routledge.

Fiske, John. 1989b [2011]. *Reading the Popular*. New York: Routledge.

Fiske, John. 1992. "The Cultural Economy of Fandom." In *The Adoring Audience: Fan Culture and Popular Media*, ed. Lisa L. Lewis. New York: Routledge.

Foot, Kirsten A., and Steven M. Schneider. 2002. "Online Action Campaign 2000: An Exploratory Analysis of the U.S. Political Web Sphere." *Journal of Broadcasting and Electronic Media* 46: 222–244.

"Framework: Public Imagination." 2013. Institute for the Future. http://reconcondev .govfutures.org/?recent_works=frameworks8.

Fraser, Nancy. 1990. "Rethinking the Public Sphere: A Contribution to the Critique of Actually Existing Democracy." *Social Text* 25(26): 56–80.

Freire, Paul. 1989. *Pedagogy of the Oppressed*. New York: Continuum.

Gamber-Thompson, Liana. 2012. "The Cost of Engagement: Politics and Participatory Practices in the U.S. Liberty Movement." Working Paper, December 10. MacArthur Foundation. http://ypp.dmlcentral.net/sites/default/files/publications/The_Cost_of _Engagement.pdf.

Gamson, William A. 1988. "Political Discourse and Collective Action." *International Social Movement Research* 1: 219–246.

Gardner, Howard, and Katie Davis. 2013. *The App Generation*. New Haven, CT: Yale University Press.

García Bedolla, Lisa. 2005. *Fluid Borders: Latino Identity, Community and Politics in Los Angeles*. Berkeley: University of California Press.

Gatson, Sarah N., and Robin Anne Reid. 2012. "Race and Ethnicity in Fandom." *Transformative Works and Cultures* 8. doi:10.3983/twc.2012.0392.

Gee, James Paul. 1996. "Vygotsky and Current Debates in Education." In *Discourse, Learning, and Schooling*, ed. Deborah Hicks. New York: Cambridge University Press.

Geller, Pamela. 2013. "Pamela Geller to Speak at Liberty Counsel's Awakening 2013." *Atlas Shrugs* (blog), March 21. http://atlasshrugs2000.typepad.com/atlas_shrugs /2013/03/pamela-geller-to-speak-at-liberty-counsels-awakening-2013.html.

Gibson, Cynthia. 2003. "The Civic Mission of Schools." Report from Carnegie Foundation and CIRCLE: The Center for Information and Research on Civic Learning and Engagement. http://www.civicmissionofschools.org/site/campaign/cms_report.html.

Giroux, Henry. 2010. *Zombie Politics and Culture in the Age of Casino Capitalism*. New York: Peter Lange.

Gladwell, Malcolm. 2010. "Small Change: Why the Revolution Will Not Be Tweeted." *New Yorker*, October 4. http://www.newyorker.com/reporting/2010/10/04/101004fa _fact_gladwell.

Gomez, Julian. 2013. "Immigrants Are the American Way." *Huffington Post*, July 16. http://www.huffingtonpost.com/julian-gomez/superman-is-an-immigrant_b _3606264.html.

Gonyea, Don. 2014. "Sen. Rand Paul to Address Annual CPAC Meeting." *National Public Radio*, March 7. http://www.npr.org/2014/03/07/287117290/sen-rand-paul-to -address-annual-cpac-meeting.

Gonzalez, Roberto. 2008. "Left Out but Not Shut Down: Political Activism and the Undocumented Student Movement." *Northwestern Journal of Law and Social Policy* 3: 219–245.

Goodwin, Jeff, James M. Jasper, and Francesca Polletta, eds. 2001. *Passionate Politics: Emotions and Social Movements*. Chicago: University of Chicago Press.

Goodwin, Jeff, and Steven Pfaff. 2001. "Emotion Work in High-Risk Social Movements: Managing Fear in the U.S. and East German Civil Rights Movements." In *Passionate Politics: Emotions and Social Movements*, ed. Jeff Goodwin, James M. Jasper, and Francesca Polletta. Chicago: University of Chicago Press.

Gray, Jonathan. 2012. "Of Snowspeeders and Imperial Walkers: Fannish Play at the Wisconsin Protests." *Transformative Works and Cultures* 10. doi:10.3983/twc.2012 .0353.Gray, Jonathan, Cornel Sandvoss, and C. Lee Harrington. 2007. *Fandom: Identities and Communities in a Mediated World*. New York: New York University Press.

Gray, Jonathan, Jeffrey P. Jones, and Ethan Thompson. 2009. *Satire TV: Politics and Comedy in the Post-Network Era*. New York: New York University Press.

Gray, Mary L. 2009. *Out in the Country: Youth, Media, and Queer Visibility in Rural America*. New York: New York University Press.

Greene, Maxine. 1995. *Releasing the Imagination*. San Francisco: Jossey Bass.

Gross, Larry. 1993. *Contested Closets: The Politics and Ethics of Outing*. Minneapolis: University of Minnesota Press.

Gutierrez, Kris. 2008. "Developing a Sociocritical Literacy in the Third Space." *Reading Research Quarterly* 43(2): 148–164.

Hafiz, Yasmin. 2013. "'Unmosqued' Debate: Muslim Millennials Explore the Problem with American Mosques." *Huffington Post*, December 9. http://www.huffingtonpost .com/2013/12/09/unmosqued-muslim-millenials_n_4394588.html.

Hanisch, Carol. 1970. "The Personal Is Political." In *Notes from the Second Year: Women's Liberation: Major Writings of the Radical Feminists*, ed. Shulamith Firestone and Anne Koedt. New York: Radical Feminism.

Harris-Lacewell, Melissa Victoria. 2006. *Barbershops, Bibles, and BET: Everyday Talk and Black Political Thought*. Princeton, NJ: Princeton University Press.

Hartley, John. 1999. *Uses of Television*. London: Routledge.

Hartley, John. 2006. *Television Truths: Forms of Knowledge in Popular Culture*. London: Wiley-Blackwell.

Hassan, Lena. 2012. "Cyberlove." In *Love, InshAllah: The Secret Love Lives of American Muslim Women*, ed. Ayesha Mattu and Nura Maznavi. Berkeley, CA: Soft Skull Press.

Hay, James. 2011. "'Popular Culture' in a Critique of the New Political Reason." *Cultural Studies* 25(4–5): 659–684.

Hayek, F. A. 1949 [1960]. "The Intellectuals and Socialism." In *The Intellectuals: A Controversial Portrait*, ed. George Bernard de Huszar. Glencoe, IL: Free Press. Available at http://mises.org/document/1019.

Hellekson, Karen, and Kristina Busse, eds. 2006. *Fan Fiction and Fan Communities in the Age of the Internet*. Jefferson, NC: McFarland & Company.

Hennion, Antoine. 2007. "Those Things That Hold Us Together: Taste and Sociology." *Cultural Sociology* 1: 97–114.

Henry, Astrid. 2004. *Not My Mother's Sister: Generational Conflict and Third-Wave Feminism*. Bloomington: Indiana University Press.

Herrera, Linda. 2012. "Youth and Citizenship in the Digital Age: A View from Egypt." *Harvard Educational Review* 82(3): 333–352.

Hijabi Monologues. n.d. *Facebook*. http://www.facebook.com/hijabi.monologues .3?ref=ts&fref=ts (accessed January 15, 2012).

Hills, Matt. 2002. *Fan Cultures*. London: Routledge.

Hinck, Ashley. 2012. "Theorizing a Public Engagement Keystone: Seeing Fandom's Integral Connection to Civic Engagement through the Case of the Harry Potter Alliance." *Transformative Works and Cultures* 10. doi:10.3983/twc.2012.0311.

Howe, Neil, and William Strauss. 2000. *Millennials Rising: The Next Great Generation*. Vintage: New York.

Hunting, Kyra. 2012. "'Queer as Folk' and the Trouble with Slash." *Transformative Works and Cultures* 11. doi:10.3983/twc.2012.0415.

Hurwitz, Roger. 2004. "Who Needs Politics? Who Needs People? The Ironies of Democracy in Cyberspace." In *Democracy and New Media*, ed. Henry Jenkins and David Thorburn. Cambridge, UK: MIT Press.

Hussein, Yasmin. 2013. "Why I Won't Be Watching 'Zero Dark Thirty.'" *Huffington Post*, January 11. http://www.huffingtonpost.com/yasmin-hussein/why-i-wont-be -watching-ze_b_2458999.html.

ImMEDIAte Justice. n.d. "About Us: Our Mission." http://immediatejusticeproductions .org/our-mission/ (accessed October 16, 2015).

Isserman, Maurice. 1993. *If I Had a Hammer . . . The Death of the Old Left and the Birth of the New Left*. Champaign-Urbana: University of Illinois Press.

Ito, Mizuko, Sonja Baumer, Matteo Bittanti, danah boyd, Rachel Cody, Becky Herr Stephenson, Heather A. Horst, Patricia G. Lange, Dilan Mahendran, Katynka Z. Martinez, C. J. Pascoe, Dan Perkel, Laura Robinson Christo Sims, and Lisa Tripp. 2009. *Hanging Out, Messing Around and Geeking Out: Kids Living and Learning with New Media*. Cambridge, MA: MIT Press.

Ito, Mizuko, Kris Gutierrez, Sonia Livingstone, Bill Penuel, Jean Rhodes, Katie Salen, Juliet Schor, Julian Sefton-Green, and S. Craig Watkins. 2012. "Connected Learning: An Agenda for Research and Design." Report, December 31. MacArthur Foundation. http://dmlhub.net/publications/connected-learning-agenda-research-and-design.

Ito, Mizuko, Elisabeth Soep, Sangita Shresthova, Neta Kligler-Vilenchik, Liana Gamber-Thompson, and Arely Zimmerman. 2015. "Learning Connected Civics." *Curriculum Inquiry* 45(1): 10–29.

Jasper, James M. 1998. "The Emotions of Protest: Affective and Reactive Emotions in and around Social Movements." *Sociological Forum* 13(3): 397–424.

Jenkins, Henry. 1992. *Textual Poachers: Television Fans and Participatory Culture*. New York: Routledge.

Jenkins, Henry. 2006. *Convergence Culture: Where Old and New Media Collide*. New York: New York University Press.

Jenkins, Henry. 2009. "How 'Dumbledore's Army' Is Changing Our World: A Conversation with the HP Alliance's Andrew Slack." *Confessions of an Aca-Fan* (blog), July 23. http://henryjenkins.org/2009/07/how_dumbledores_army_is_transf .html.

Jenkins, Henry. 2011. "Acafandom and Beyond Conversation Series." *Confessions of an Aca-Fan* (blog), October 22. http://henryjenkins.org/2011/10/acafandom_and_beyond _will_broo_1.html.

Jenkins, Henry. 2012a. "'Cultural Acupuncture': Fan Activism and the Harry Potter Alliance." *Transformative Works and Cultures* 10. doi:10.3983/twc.2012.0305.

Jenkins, Henry. 2012b. "Participatory Politics: New Media and Youth Political Action: Interview with Cathy J. Cohen." *Confessions of an Aca-Fan* (blog), July 20. http:// henryjenkins.org/2012/07/participatory_politics_new_med.html.

Jenkins, Henry. 2014. "Fandom Studies as I See It." *Journal of Fandom Studies* 2(2). doi: http://dx.doi.org/10.1386/jfs.2.2.89_1.

Jenkins, Henry. Forthcoming. "From Culture Jamming to Cultural Acupuncture."

Jenkins, Henry, and Nico Carpentier. 2013. "Theorizing Participatory Intensities: A Conversation about Participation and Politics." *Convergence* 19(3): 265–286.

Jenkins, Henry, Katie Clinton, Ravi Purushotma, Alice J. Robison, and Margaret Weigel. 2006. *Confronting the Challenges of Participatory Culture: Media Education for the 21st Century*. Cambridge, MA: MacArthur Foundation.

Jenkins, Henry, Sam Ford, and Joshua Green. 2013. *Spreadable Media: Creating Meaning and Value in a Networked Culture*. New York: New York University Press.

Jenkins, Henry, Sangita Shresthova, Liana Gamber-Thompson, and Neta Kligler-Vilenchik. Forthcoming. "Superpowers to the People!: How Young Activists Are Tapping the Civic Imagination." In *Civic Media: Technology, Design, Practice*, ed. Eric Gordon and Paul Mihailidis. Cambridge, MA: MIT Press.

Johnston, Hank. 2009. *Culture, Social Movements, and Protest*. Burlington, VT: Ashgate.

Jung, Sun. 2012. "Fan Activism, Cybervigilantism, and Othering Mechanisms in K-pop Fandom." *Transformative Works and Cultures* 10. doi:10.3983/twc.2012.0300.

Jungherr, Andreas. 2012. "The German Federal Election of 2009: The Challenge of Participatory Cultures in Political Campaigns." *Transformative Works and Cultures* 10. doi:10.3983/twc.2012.0310.

Juris, Jeffrey Schott, and Geoffrey Henri Pleyers. 2009. "Alter-Activism: Emerging Cultures of Participation among Young Global Justice Activists." *Journal of Youth Studies* 12(1): 57–75.

Kahne, Joseph. 2014. "Why Getting Kids College and Career Ready Isn't Enough." *Washington Post*, October 20. http://www.washingtonpost.com/blogs/answer-sheet /wp/2014/10/20/why-getting-kids-college-and-career-ready-isnt-enough/.

Kahne, Joseph, Erica Hodgin, and Elyse Eidman-Aadahl. Forthcoming. "Redesigning Civic Education for the Digital Age: In Pursuit of Equitable and Impactful Democratic Engagement." *Theory and Research in Social Education*.

Kahne, Joseph, Nam-Jin Lee, and Jessica Timpany Feezell. 2011. "The Civic and Political Significance of Online Participatory Cultures among Youth Transitioning to Adulthood." DML Central Working Paper, February 5. http://dmlcentral.net/wp-content /uploads/files/OnlineParticipatoryCultures.WORKINGPAPERS.pdf.

Kahne, Joseph, Ellen Middaugh, and Danielle Allen. 2014. "Youth, New Media, and the Rise of Participatory Politics." Working Paper, March 31. http://dmlhub.net/publica tions/youth-new-media-and-rise-participatory-politics/.

Kahne, Joseph, Ellen Middaugh, and Danielle Allen. 2015. "Youth, New Media, and the Rise of Participatory Politics." In *From Voice to Influence: Understanding Citizenship in a Digital Age*, ed. Danielle Allen and Jennifer S. Light. Chicago: University of Chicago Press.

Karlin, Beth, Crystal Murphy, and Kehau Ahu. Forthcoming. "Exploring a New Model of Global Citizenship: An Evaluation of the Fourth Estate Leadership Summit." Grant Report for Gates Foundation.

Kedhar, Anusha. 2014. "'Hands Up! Don't Shoot!': Gesture, Choreography and Protest in Ferguson." *Feminist Wire*, October 6. http://thefeministwire.com/2014/10 /protest-in-ferguson/.

Kelty, Christopher M. 2013. "From Participation to Power." In *The Participatory Cultures Handbook*, ed. Aaron Delwiche and Jennifer Jacobs Henderson. New York: Routledge.

Khalid, Wardah. 2012. "A Muslim Convention in a Church? You Better Believe It." *Huffington Post Religion Blog*, December 19. http://blog.chron.com/youngameri canmuslim/2012/12/a-muslim-convention-in-a-church-you-better-believe-it/# comments.

Khan, Nadia. 2014. "American Muslims in the Age of New Media." In *The Oxford Handbook of American Islam*, ed. Yvonne Y. Haddad and Jane I. Smith. New York: Oxford University Press.

Kirshner, Ben. 2006. "The Social Formation of Youth Leadership." In *Proceedings of the 7th International Conference of the Learning Sciences*, ed. S. Barab, K. Hay, and D. Hickey. Mahwah, NJ: Erlbaum.

Kirshner, Ben. 2008. "Guided Participation in Three Youth Activism Organizations: Facilitation, Apprenticeship, and Joint Work." *Journal of the Learning Sciences*, 17(1): 60–101.

Kibria, Nazli. 2007. "The 'New Islam' and Bangladeshi Youth in Britain and the U.S." *Ethnic and Racial Studies* 31(2): 243–266.

Kitsuse, John I. 1980. "Coming Out All Over: Deviants and the Politics of Social Problems." *Social Problems* 28(1): 1–13.

Klatch, Rebecca E. 1999. *A Generation Divided: The New Left, the New Right and the 1960s*. Berkeley: University of California Press.

Kligler-Vilenchik, Neta. 2013a. "'Decreasing World Suck': Fan Communities, Mechanisms of Translation, and Participatory Politics." Working Paper, June 1. MacArthur Foundation. http://dmlhub.net/publications/decreasing-world-suck-fan-communities -mechanisms-translation-and-participatory-politics.

Kligler-Vilenchik, Neta. 2013b. "Mobilized Communities: Reconstructing Alternative Citizenship Models through Participant Observation." Paper presented at the National Communication Association Conference, Washington, D.C., November 21–24.

Kligler-Vilenchik, Neta. 2014. "Decreasing World Suck: Diversity and Equality in Nerdfighteria." Paper presented at the Digital Media & Learning Conference, Boston, Mass., March 6–8.

Kligler-Vilenchik, Neta. 2015. "From Wizards and House-Elves to Real-World Issues: Political Talk in Fan Spaces." *International Journal of Communication* 9: 2027–2046.

Kligler-Vilenchik Neta, Joshua McVeigh-Schultz, Christine Weitbrecht, and Christopher Tokuhama. 2012. "Experiencing Fan Activism: Understanding the Power of Fan Activist Organizations through Members' Narratives." *Transformative Works and Cultures* 10. doi:10.3983/twc.2012.0322.

Kligler-Vilenchik, Neta, and Sangita Shresthova. 2012. "Learning through Practice: Participatory Culture Civics." Youth and Participatory Politics Research Network Working Paper, September 30. MacArthur Foundation. http://dmlhub.net/publica tions/learning-through-practice-participatory-culture-practices/.

Kligler-Vilenchik, Neta, and Sangita Shresthova. 2013. "The Harry Potter Alliance: Connecting Fan Interests and Civic Action" In *Connected Learning: An Agenda for Research and Design*, ed. Mizuko Ito, Krist Gutierrez, Sonia Livingstone, Bill Penuel, Jean Rhodes, Katie Salen, Juliet Schor, Julian Sefton-Green, and S. Craig Watkins. Report, December 31. MacArthur Foundation. http://dmlhub.net/publications/connec ted-learning-agenda-for-research-and-design/.

Kligler-Vilenchik, Neta, and Sangita Shresthova. 2014. "'Feel That You Are Doing Something': Participatory Culture Civics." *Conjunctions* 1(1). http://www.conjunctions -tjcp.com/article/view/18604/16266.

Kligler-Vilenchik, Neta, and Kjerstin Thorson. 2015. "Good Citizenship as a Frame Contest: Kony2012, Memes, and Critiques of the Networked Citizen." *New Media & Society*, March. doi: 10.1177/1461444815575311.

Klein, Naomi. 2000. *No Logo*. New York: St. Martin's Press.

Kress, Gunther. 2000. "Multimodality: Challenges to Thinking about Language." *TESOL Quarterly* 34(2): 337–340.

Ladson-Billings, Gloria. 1995. "But That's Just Good Teaching! The Case for Culturally Relevant Pedagogy." *Theory into Practice* 34(3): 159–165.

Lange, Patricia. 2014. *Kids on YouTube: Technical Identities and Digital Literacies*. Walnut Creek, CA: Left Coast Press.

Lange, Patricia, and Mizuko Ito. 2009. "Creative Production." In *Hanging Out, Messing Around and Geeking Out: Kids Living and Learning with New Media*, ed. Mizuko Ito et al. Cambridge, MA: MIT Press.

Lave, Jean, and Etienne Wenger. 1991. *Situated Learning*. Cambridge, UK: Cambridge University Press.

Lee, Carol D. 1993. *Signifying as a Scaffold for Literary Interpretation: The Pedagogical Implications of an African American Discourse Genre*. NCTE Research Report No. 25. Urbana, IL: National Council of Teachers of English.

Lee, Clifford. 2012. "Re-mastering the Master's Tools: Recognizing and Affirming the Life Experiences and Cultural Practices of Urban Youth in Critical Computational Literacy through a Video Game Project." Ph.D. diss., University of California, Los Angeles.

Levine, Lawrence W. 2007. *Black Culture and Black Consciousness: Afro-American Folk Thought from Slavery to Freedom*. Oxford: Oxford University Press.

Levine, Peter. 2006. Response to Question #1: Changing Political Orientations of Young Citizens. *MacArthur Online Discussions on Civic Engagement*, September 29–October 13. http://ccce.com.washington.edu/about/assets/Civic_Engagement -Online_Discussions06.pdf.

Levine, Peter. 2007. *The Future of Democracy: Developing the Next Generation of American Citizens*. Medford, MA: Tufts University Press.

Lewis, John, and Andrew Aydin. 2013. *The March: Book One*. Marietta, GA: Top Shelf.

Li, Cheuk Yin. 2012. "The Absence of Fan Activism in the Queer Fandom of Ho Denise Wan See (HOCC) in Hong Kong." *Transformative Works and Cultures* 10. doi:10.3983/twc.2012.0325.

"The Liberty Movement." n.d. *Libertarianism.com*. http://www.libertarianism.com /content/the-liberty-movement/lib_mov (accessed June 20, 2012). Archived at https://web.archive.org/web/20120404183633/http://www.libertarianism.com /content/the-liberty-movement/lib_mov.

Lichterman, Paul. 1995. "Beyond the Seesaw Model: Public Commitment in a Culture of Self-Fulfillment." *Sociological Theory* 13(3): 275–300.

Lichterman, Paul. 1996. *The Search for Political Community: American Activists Reinventing Commitment*. Cambridge, MA: Cambridge University Press.

Light, Jennifer S. 2015. "Putting Our Conversation in Context: Youth, Old Media, and Political Participation, 1800–1971." In *From Voice to Influence: Understanding Citizenship in a Digital Age*, ed. Danielle Allen and Jennifer S. Light. Chicago: University of Chicago Press.

Lightman, David. 2014. "Americans' Confidence in Government Down as 7 Percent Now Have Trust in Congress." McClattchy DC Blog, June 30. http://www.mc clatchydc.com/2014/06/30/231889/americans-confidence-in-government.html.

Lipsitz, George. 2006. "Learning from New Orleans: The Social Warrant of Hostile Privatism and Competitive Consumer Citizenship." *Cultural Anthropology* 21(3): 451–468.

Livingstone, Sonia. 2005. "On the Relation between Audiences and Publics." In *Audiences and Publics: When Cultural Engagement Matters for the Public Sphere*, ed. Sonia Livingstone. Bristol, UK: Intellect.

Lopez, Lori Kido. 2011. "Fan Activists and the Politics of Race in *The Last Airbender*." *International Journal of Cultural Studies* 15(5): 431–445.

Lopez, Lori Kido. 2012. "Asian American Media Activism: Past, Present and Digital Futures." Ph.D. diss., University of Southern California.

Lotan, Gilad. 2012. "KONY2012: See How Invisible Networks Helped A Campaign Capture the World's Attention." *SocialFlow*, March 14. http://blog.socialflow.com /post/7120244932/data-viz-kony2012-see-how-invisible-networks-helped -a-campaign-capture-the-worlds-attention.

"Low Midterm Turnout Likely, Conservatives More Enthusiastic, Harvard Youth Poll Finds." 2014. *Harvard University Institute of Politics*. http://www.iop.harvard.edu /Spring-2014-HarvardIOP-Survey?utm_source=homepage&utm_medium=hero&utm _campaign=2014SurveyRelease.

Lyon, David. 2007. *Surveillance Studies: An Overview*. Cambridge, MA: Polity.

Maira, Sunaina. 2003. "Youth Culture and Youth Movements: United States of America." *Encyclopedia of Women & Islamic Cultures* (ed. Joseph Suad and Afsaneh Najmabadi) at *BrillOnline Reference Works*. http://referenceworks.brillonline.com/entries /encyclopedia-of-women-and-islamic-cultures/youth-culture-and-youth -movements-united-states-of-america-EWICCOM_0709.

Malcolm X. 1964a. "The Ballot or the Bullet." Speech at Cory Methodist Church, Cleveland, Ohio, April 3. *EdChange*. http://www.edchange.org/multicultural/speeches /malcolm_x_ballot.html.

Malcolm X. 1964b. "By Any Means Necessary." *History Genius*. http://history.genius .com/Malcolm-x-by-any-means-necessary-annotated.Malitz, Zack. 2012.

"Détournement/Culture Jamming." In *Beautiful Trouble: A Toolbox for Revolution*, ed. Andrew Boyd and Dave Oswald Mitchell. New York: OR Books. Accessible online at http://beautifultrouble.org/tactic/detournementculture -jamming/.

Mannheim, Karl. 1923 [1993]. "The Problem of Generations." In *From Karl Mannheim*, ed. Kurt H. Wolff. New Brunswick, NJ: Transaction Publishers.

Marcum, Diana. 2010. "He's the Cal State Fresno Student Body President—and an Illegal Immigrant." *Los Angeles Times*, November 18.

Margon, Sarah. 2012. "Awareness Can Translate into Action." *New York Times*, March 10. http://www.nytimes.com/roomfordebate/2012/03/09/kony-2012-and-the -potential-of-social-media-activism/awareness-can-translate-into-action.

Martin, C. E. 2012a. "From Young Adult Book Fans to Wizards of Change." *New York Times*, March 21. http://opinionator.blogs.nytimes.com/2012/03/21/from-young -adult-book-fans-to-wizards-of-change/

Martin, C. E. 2012b. "Fan Power: Hunger Is Not a Game Revisited." *New York Times*, March 31. http://opinionator.blogs.nytimes.com/2012/03/31/fan-power-hunger-is -not-a-game-revisited/.

Martin, Crystle, and Mizuko Ito. 2013. "Connected Learning and the Future of Libraries." *Young Adult Library Services* 12(1): 29–32.

Marwick, Alice. 2012. "The Public Domain: Social Surveillance in Everyday Life." *Surveillance and Society* 9(4): 379.

Marwick, Alice, and danah boyd. 2010. "I Tweet Honestly, I Tweet Passionately: Twitter Users, Context Collapse, and the Imagined Audience." *New Media Society* 2, July 7. http://nms.sagepub.com/content/early/2010/06/22/1461444810365313.

McAdam, Doug. 1988. *Freedom Summer*. New York: Oxford University Press.

McAdam, Doug. 2009. "Assessing the Effects of Voluntary Youth Service: The Case of Teach for America." *Social Forces* 88(2): 945–969.

McAdam, Doug, and Dieter Rucht. 1993. "The Cross-National Diffusion of Movement Ideas." *Annals of the American Academy of Political and Social Science* 528(59): 56–74.

McCobin, Alexander. 2013. "Second Wave Libertarianism." *Students for Liberty* (blog), March 5. http://studentsforliberty.org/blog/second-wave-libertarianism/.

McGuigan, Jim. 1992. *Cultural Populism*. London: Routledge.

McIntosh, Jonathan. 2011. "Right-Wing Radio Duck Hits the Net." *Al Jazeera*, March 7. http://www.aljazeera.com/indepth/opinion/2011/03/20113685813934602.html.

McKee, Alan. 2007. "The Fans of Cultural Theory." In *Fandom: Identities and Communities in a Mediated World*, ed. Jonathan Gray, Cornel Sandvoss, and C. Lee Harrington. New York: New York University Press.

Mehta, Ritesh. 2012. "Flash Activism: How a Bollywood Film Catalyzed Civic Justice toward a Murder Trial." *Transformative Works and Cultures* 10. doi:10.3983/twc .2012.0345.

Merrick, Helen. 2009. *The Secret Feminist Cabal: A Cultural History of Science Fiction Feminism*. Seattle, WA: Aqueduct Press.

Meyer, David S., and Nancy Whittier. 1994. "Social Movement Spillover." *Social Problems* 41: 277–298.

Michael, Jaclyn. 2013. "American Muslims Stand Up and Speak Out: Trajectories of Humor in Muslim American Comedy." *Contemporary Islam* 7: 129–153.

"Mining Online History for What May Have Radicalized, Information, Tsarnaev Brothers." 2013. *PBS Newshour*, April 24. http://www.pbs.org/newshour/bb /terrorism-jan-june13-bostonupdate_04-24/.

Mittell, Jason. 2013. "Forensic Fandom and the Drillable Text." In *Spreadable Media: Creating Value and Meaning in a Networked Culture*, ed. Henry Jenkins, Sam Ford, and Joshua Green (web-exclusive essay). http://spreadablemedia.org/essays/mittell/.

Mochocki, Michael. 2013. "Participatory Poland (Part Three): Historical Reenactment in Poland—Where Grassroots and Institutions Collide." *Confessions of an Aca-Fan* (blog), November 27. http://henryjenkins.org/2013/11/participatory-poland-part-three -historical-reenactment-in-poland-where-grassroots-and-institutions-collide.html.

Morozov, Evgeny. 2012. "Why the KGB Wants You to Join Facebook." In *The Net Delusion: The Dark Side of Internet Freedom*, ed. Evgeny Morozov. New York: PublicAffairs.

Mukherjee, Roopali, and Sarah Banet-Weiser, eds. 2012. *Commodity Activism: Cultural Resistance in Neoliberal Times*. New York: New York University Press.

Muñoz, S. M. 2008. "Understanding Issues of College Persistence for Undocumented Mexican Immigrant Women from the New Latino Diaspora: A Case Study." Ph.D. diss., Iowa State University.

Muñoz, S. M. 2013. "'I Just Can't Stand Being Like This [Undocumented] Anymore': Dilemmas, Stressors, and Motivators for Undocumented Mexican Women in Higher Education." *Journal of Student Affairs Research and Practice* 50(3): 233–249.

Mutz, Diana. 2006. *Hearing the Other Side: Deliberative versus Participatory Democracy*. Cambridge, MA: Cambridge University Press.

Naber, Nadine. 2005. "Muslim First, Arab Second: A Strategic Politics of Race and Gender." *Muslim World* 95: 479–495.

"'A Needed Response' Might Be the Simplest, Best Reaction to the Stubbenville Rape Case." 2013. *Huffington Post*, March 26. http://www.huffingtonpost.com/2013/03/26 /a-needed-response-steubenville-video_n_2952246.html.

Nissenbaum, Helen. 2004. "Privacy as Contextual Integrity." *Washington Law Review* 79: 102.

Norris, Pippa. 1999. *Critical Citizens: Global Support for Democratic Government*. New York: Oxford University Press.

Norris, Pippa. 2002. *Democratic Phoenix: Reinventing Political Activism*. Cambridge, UK: Cambridge University Press.

"Opting out of Voting." 2012. *Huffington Post* video (4:43), July 26. http://www.huffing tonpost.com/2012/07/09/latest-conversations-opti_n_1659981.html.

Orlikowski, Wanda, and JoAnne Yates. 1998. "Genre Systems: Structuring Interaction through Communicative Norms." CCS Working Paper 205. Sloan Working Paper 4030. Cambridge, MA: MIT. http://ccs.mit.edu/ papers/CCSWP205/.

Panth, Sabina. 2010. "Bonding vs. Bridging." World Bank, June 3. http://blogs.world bank.org/publicsphere/bonding-and-bridging.

Papacharissi, Zizi A. 2010. *A Private Sphere: Democracy in the Digital Age.* London: Polity Press.

Passel, Jeffrey S., and D'Vera Cohn. 2009. "Unauthorized Immigrant Population: National and State Trends, 2010." Pew Research Hispanic Trends Project, February 1. http://www.pewhispanic.org/2011/02/01/unauthorized-immigrant -population-brnational-and-state-trends-2010/.

Patel, Eboo. 2007. *Acts of Faith: The Story of an American Muslim, the Struggle for the Soul of a Generation.* Boston: Beacon Press.

Peppler, Kylie, and Sophia Bender. 2013. "Maker Movement Spreads Innovation One Project at a Time." *Phi Delta Kappan,* November.

Perez, William, Roberta Espinoza, Karina Ramos, Heidi M. Coronado, and Richard Cortes. 2010. "Civic Engagement Patterns of Undocumented Mexican Students." *Journal of Hispanic Higher Education* 9(3): 245–265.

Pew Research Center. 2011. "Muslim Americans: No Signs of Growth in Alienation or Support for Extremism." August 30. http://www.people-press.org/2011/08/30 /muslim-americans-no-signs-of-growth-in-alienation-or-support-for-extremism/.

Pew Research Center. 2014. "Millennials in Adulthood." March 7. http://www.pew socialtrends.org/2014/03/07/millennials-in-adulthood/.

Pfister, Rachel Cody. 2014. "Hats for House Elves: Connected Learning and Civic Engagement in Hogwarts at Ravelry." Connected Learning Working Papers, May 15. Digital Media and Learning Research Hub.

Phillips, Forrest. 2013. "Captain America and Fandom's Political Activity." *Transformative Works and Cultures* 13. doi:10.3983/twc.2013.0441.

Phillips, Whitney, 2013. "In Defense of Memes." In *Spreadable Media: Creating Value and Meaning in a Networked Culture,* ed. Henry Jenkins, Sam Ford, and Joshua Green (web-exclusive essay). http://spreadablemedia.org/essays/phillips/#.VfR3r UuEjhg.

Polletta, Francesca. 2006. *It Was Like a Fever: Storytelling in Protest and Politics.* Chicago: University of Chicago Press.

Polletta, Francesca. 2009. "Storytelling in Social Movements." In *Social Movements and Culture,* ed. Hank Johnston. New York: Routledge.

Polletta, Francesca, and James Jasper. 2001. "Collective Identity in Social Movements." *Annual Review of Sociology* 27: 283–305.

Potok, Mark. 2012. "FBI: Anti-Muslim Hate Crimes Still Up." *Salon.com,* December 10. http://www.salon.com/2012/12/10/fbi_anti_muslim_hate_crimes_still_up/.

Pratt Ewing, Katherine, and Marguerite Hoyler. 2008. "Being Muslim and American: South Asian Muslim Youth and the War on Terror." In *Being and Belonging: Muslims in the United States since 9/11,* ed. Katherin Pratt Ewing. New York: Russell Sage Foundation.

"Public Choice Theory." n.d. *Wikipedia.* http://en.wikipedia.org/wiki/Public_choice _theory (accessed August 8, 2012).

Punathambekar, Aswin. 2012. "On the Ordinariness of Participatory Culture." *Transformative Works and Cultures* 10. doi:10.3983/twc.2012.0378.

Putnam, Robert D. 1995. "Tuning In, Tuning Out: The Strange Disappearance of Social Capital in America." *Political Science & Politics* 28(4): 664–683.

Putnam, Robert D. 2000. *Bowling Alone: The Collapse and Revival of American Community*. New York: Simon & Schuster.

Quinnipiac University Poll (Colorado). 2014. "Economy, Healthcare Hurt Udall in Colorado Race, Quinnipiac University Poll Finds; Sen. Rand Paul Leads 2016 Presidential Pack." April 24. http://www.quinnipiac.edu/news-and-events /quinnipiac-university-poll/colorado/release-detail?ReleaseID=2034.

Ratto, Matt, and Megan Boler, eds. 2014. *DIY Citizenship: Critical Making and Social Media*. Cambridge, MA: MIT Press.

Reger, Jo, ed. 2005. *Different Wavelengths: Studies of the Contemporary Women's Movement*. New York: Routledge.

Rojas, Leslie Berestein. 2011. "Undocumented Student Activists in LA Get Audience with Federal Officials, Get Arrested." *MultiAmerican*, October 12. http://multi american.scpr.org/2011/10/undocumented- student-protesters-get-audience-with -federal-officials-get-arrested/.

Rosanvallon, Pierre. 2008. *Counter-Democracy: Politics in an Age of Distrust*. Cambridge, UK: Cambridge University Press.

Ross, Andrew. 1991. *Strange Weather: Culture, Science and Technology in the Age of Limits*. London: Verso.

Rowling, J. K. 2008. "The Fringe Benefits of Failure, and the Importance of Imagination." *Harvard Gazette*, June 5. http://news.harvard.edu/gazette/story/2008/06 /text-of-j-k-rowling-speech/.

Ruge, TMS. 2012a. "A Peace of My Mind: Respect My Agency 2012!" *TMS Ruge* (blog), March 8. http://tmsruge.com/respect-my-agency-2012/.

Ruge, TMS. 2012b. "Opinion: Why Kony 2012 Created the Wrong Buzz." *CNN.com*, March 14. http://www.cnn.com/2012/03/12/world/africa/kony-2012-tms-ruge -opinion/index.html?iref=allsearch.

Rundle, Margaret, Carrie James, and Emily Weinstein. Forthcoming. "Doing Civics in the Digital Age: Casual, Purposeful, and Strategic Approaches to Participatory Politics." Youth and Participatory Politics Working Paper Series.

Saguy, Abigail, and Anna Ward. 2011. "Coming Out as Fat: Rethinking Stigma." *Social Psychology Quarterly* 74(1): 1–23.

Saler, Michael. 2012. *As If: Modern Enchantment and the Literary Prehistory of Virtual Reality*. New York: Oxford University Press.

Salgado, Julio. 2011. "Queer, Undocumented, and Unafraid: Sexuality Meets Immigration Politics in a Youth-Led Movement for Immigrant Rights." *Briarpatch*, May/June 2011.

Sandvoss, Cornel. 2005. *Fans: The Mirror of Consumption*. Malden: Polity Press.

Santora, Mark. 2012. "Woman Is Charged with Murder as a Hate Crime in a Fatal Subway Push." *New York Times*, December 29. http://www.nytimes.com/2012/12/30

/nyregion/woman-is-held-in-death-of-man-pushed-onto-subway-tracks-in-queens
.html?_r=1&.

Sauter, Molly, and Matt Stempeck. 2013. "Green vs Pink: Change Your Picture, Change the World." *MIT Center for Civic Media*, March 28. http://civic.mit.edu/blog/nate matias/green-vs-pink-change-your-picture-change-the-world.

Scardaville, Melissa. 2005. "Accidental Activists: Fan Activism in the Soap Opera Community." *American Behavioral Scientist* 48: 881–901.

Schudson, Michael. 1999. *The Good Citizen: A History of American Civic Life*. Cambridge, MA: Harvard University Press.

Schulzke, Marcus. 2012. "Fan Action and Political Participation on 'The Colbert Report.'" *Transformative Works and Cultures* 10. doi:10.3983/twc.2012.0316.

Scott, Suzanne. 2010. "Revenge of the Fanboy: Convergence Culture and the Politics of Incorporation." Ph.D. diss., University of Southern California.

Sefton-Green, Julian. 2013. *Mapping Digital Makers: A State of the Art Review*. http://www.julianseftongreen.net/wp-content/uploads/2013/03/NT-SoA-6-FINAL.pdf.

Servai, Shanoor. 2012. "Confessions of a Kony 2012 Action Kit Purchaser." *Identities. Mic*, April 23. http://www.policymic.com/articles/7368/confessions-of-a-kony-2012 -action-kit-purchaser.

Shaikley, Layla. 2014. "The Surprising Lessons of the 'Muslim Hipsters' Backlash." *Atlantic*, March 13. http://www.theatlantic.com/entertainment/archive/2014/03 /the-surprising-lessons-of-the-muslim-hipsters-backlash/284298/.

Shifman, Limor. 2013. *Memes in Digital Culture*. Cambridge, MA: MIT Press.

Shohat, Ella, and Robert Stam. 2007. *Unthinking Eurocentrism: Multiculturalism and the Media*. New York: Routledge.

Shresthova, Sangita. 2013. "Bollywood Dance as Political Participation? On Flash Mobs, New Media, and Political Potential." *Convergence* 19(3): 311–317.

Shughart, William F., II. 2008. "Public Choice." *The Concise Encyclopedia of Economics*, at *Library of Economics and Liberty*. http://www.econlib.org/library/Enc/Public Choice.html.

Signorile, Michelangelo. 2012. "Chick-fil-A: Were the Protests a Big Fail? And Where Do We Go from Here?" *Huffington Post*, August 6. http://www.huffingtonpost.com /michelangelo-signorile/chick-fil-a-were-the-prot_b_1746382.html.

Sirin, Selcuk R., and Michelle Fine. 2009. *Muslim American Youth: Understanding Hyphenated Identities through Multiple Methods*. New York: New York University Press.

Skocpol, Theda. 2003. *Diminished Democracy: From Membership to Management in American Civic Life*. Norman: University of Oklahoma Press.

Skocpol, Theda, and Vanessa Williamson. 2012. *The Tea Party and the Remaking of Republican Conservatism*. Oxford: Oxford University Press.

Slack, Andrew. 2010. "Cultural Acupuncture and a Future for Social Change." *Huffington Post*, July 2. http://www.huffingtonpost.com/andrew-slack/cultural -acupuncture-and_b_633824.html.

Slack, Andrew. 2013. "Ad Campaign (Lip) Glosses over 'Hunger Games' Message." *Los Angeles Times*, November 25. http://articles.latimes.com/2013/nov/25/opinion/la-oe -1125-slack-hunger-games-covergirl-capitol-20131125.

Smith, Aaron. 2013. "Civic Engagement in the Digital Age." Pew Research Center, April 25. http://pewinternet.org/Reports/2013/Civic-Engagement.aspx.

Smith, David. 2007. "Dumbledore Was Gay, JK Tells Amazed Fans." *Guardian*, October 20. http://www.theguardian.com/uk/2007/oct/21/film.books.

Snow, David A., and Robert D. Benford. 1992. "Master Frames and Cycles of Protest." In *Frontiers in Social Movement Theory*, ed. A. D. Morris and C. M. Mueller. New Haven, CT: Yale University Press.

Snow, David A., and Robert D. Benford. 1999. "Alternative Types of Cross-national Diffusion in the Social Movement Arena." In *Social Movements in a Globalizing World*, ed. Donatella della Porta, Hanspeter Kriesi, and Dieter Rucht. London: MacMillan.

Snow, David A., R. Burke Rochford Jr., Steven K. Worden, and Robert D. Benford. 1986. "Frame Alignment Processes, Micromobilization, and Movement Participation." *American Sociological Review* 51: 464–481.

Soep, Elisabeth. 2012. "The Digital Afterlife of Youth-Made Media: Implications for Media Literacy Education." *Comunicar Scientific Journal of Media Education* 38(19): 93–100.

Soep, Elisabeth. 2014. *Participatory Politics: Next Generation Tactics to Remake Public Spheres*. Cambridge, MA: MIT Press.

Soule, Sarah A. 2004. "Diffusion Processes within and across Movements." In *Blackwell Companion to Social Movements*, ed. Sarah A. Soule, David A. Snow, and Hanspeter Kriesi. Malden, MA: Blackwell Publishing.

Srivastava, Lina. n.d. "About" and "Basic Framework." *Transmedia Activism*. http://transmedia-activism.com/.

Students for Liberty. 2011. "History." http://www.studentsforliberty.org (accessed June 30, 2011).

Students for Liberty. 2012. "Students for Liberty FAQ." http://studentsforliberty.org/faq/ (accessed August 8, 2012).

Suhaibwebb. n.d. "About." http://www.suhaibwebb.com/about (accessed June 20, 2013).

Sunstein, Cass. 2009. *Republic.Com 2.0*. Princeton, NJ: Princeton University Press.

Swartz, Lana. 2012. "Invisible Children: Transmedia, Storytelling, Mobilization." Working paper, Civic Paths research team, University of Southern California. http://civicpaths.uscannenberg.org/wp-content/uploads/2012/03/Swartz_InvisibleChildren _WorkingPaper.pdf.

Swartz, Lana, and Kevin Driscoll. 2014. "'I Hate Your Politics but I Love Your Diamonds': Citizenship and the Off-Topic Message Board Subforum." In *DIY Citizenship: Critical Making and Social Media*, ed. Matt Ratto and Megan Boler. Cambridge: MIT Press.

Tanenhaus, Sam, and Jim Rutenberg. 2014. "Rand Paul's Mixed Inheritance." *New York Times*, January 25. http://www.nytimes.com/2014/01/26/us/politics/rand-pauls -mixed-inheritance.html?_r=0.

Tarrow, Sidney. 1998. *Power in Movement: Social Movements and Contentious Politics.* Cambridge, MA: Cambridge University Press.

Taylor, Verta. 1989. "Social Movement Continuity: The Women's Movement in Abeyance." *American Sociological Review* 54(5): 761–775.

Terriquez, Veronica, and Caitlin Patler. 2012. "Aspiring Americans: Undocumented Youth Leaders in California." Los Angeles: USC Center for the Study of Immigrant Integration (CSII). http://csii.usc.edu/documents/AspiringAmericans_web.pdf.

Testa, Jessica. 2014. "Two Years after KONY 2012, Has Invisible Children Grown Up?" *Buzzfeed*, March 14. http://www.buzzfeed.com/jtes/two-years-after-kony-2012-has -invisible-children-grown-up.

"Thomas Jefferson and 'the Boisterous Sea of Liberty.'" n.d. *Monticello.org.* http://www .monticello.org/site/visit/thomas-jefferson-and-boisterous-sea-liberty.

Thorson, Kjerstin. 2010. "Finding Gaps and Building Bridges: Mapping Youth Citizenship." Ph.D. diss., University of Wisconsin–Madison.

Thorson, Kjerstin, Kevin Driscoll, Brian Ekdale, Stephanie Edgerly, Liana Gamber Thompson, Andrew Schrock, Lana Swartz, Emily K. Vraga, and Chris Wells. 2013. "YouTube, Twitter, and the Occupy Movement: Connecting Content and Circulation Practices." *Information, Communication & Society* 16(3): 421–451.

Tilly, Charles. 1983. "Speaking Your Mind without Elections, Surveys or Social Movements." *Public Opinion Quarterly* 47: 461–478.

Trope, Alison, and Lana Swartz. 2011. "The Visual Culture of the Occupation: Month One and Counting." *Civic Paths* (blog), October 26. http://civicpaths.uscannenberg .org/2011/10/the-visual-culture-of-the-occupation-month-one-and-counting/.

Traugott, Mark, ed. 1995. *Repertoires and Cycles of Collective Action.* Durham, NC: Duke University Press.

Turk, Jihad. Forthcoming. "Social Media, Social Change, and Interfaith Relations: An American-Muslim Perspective."

Turner, Fred. 2008. *From Counterculture to Cyberculture: Stewart Brand, the Whole Earth Movement, and the Rise of Digital Utopianism.* Chicago: University of Chicago Press.

Valenzuela, Angela. 1999. *Subtractive Schooling.* Albany: SUNY Press.

van Dijck, José. 2009. "Users Like You? Theorizing Agency in User-Generated Content." *Media, Culture & Society* 31(1): 41–58.

van Zoonen, Liesbet. 2005. *Entertaining the Citizen: When Politics and Popular Culture Converge.* New York: Rowman & Littlefield.

Vicens, AJ. 2014. "The Obama Administration's 2 Million Deportations, Explained." *Mother Jones*, April 4. http://www.motherjones.com/politics/2014/04/obama -administration-record-deportations.

Vossoughi Shirin, and Bronwyn Bevan. 2014. "Making and Tinkering: A Review of the Literature." White Paper. National Research Council Committee on Out of School Time STEM.

Vygotsky, L. S. 1978. *Mind in Society: The Development of Higher Psychological Processes.* Cambridge, MA: Harvard University Press.

Wattenberg, Martin P. 2008. *Is Voting for Young People?* New York: Pearson Longman.

Weigand, Kate. 2002. *Red Feminism: American Communism and the Making of Women's Liberation.* Baltimore: Johns Hopkins University Press.

Weinstein, Emily. 2013. "Beyond Kim Kardashian on the Middle East: Patterns of Social Engagement among Civically-Oriented Youth." *Good Project* (blog), February. http://www.thegoodproject.org/beyond-kim-kardashian-on-the-middle-east -patterns-of-social-engagement-among-civically-oriented-youth/.

Weinstein, Emily, Margaret Rundle, and Carrie James. 2015. "A Hush Falls over the Crowd?" *International Journal of Communication* 9: 84–105.

Weintraub, Jeff. 1997. "Public/Private: The Limitations of a Grand Dichotomy." *Responsive Community* 7(2): 13–24.

Wesch, Michael. 2008. "Context Collapse." *Digital Ethnography* (blog), July 31. http://mediatedcultures.net/projects/youtube/context-collapse/.

White, Micah. 2010. "Clicktivism Is Ruining Leftist Activism." *Guardian*, August 12. http://www.theguardian.com/commentisfree/2010/aug/12/clicktivism-ruining -leftist-activism.

Whiteman, Natasha, and Joanne Metivier. 2013. "From Post-Object to 'Zombie' Fandoms: The 'Deaths' of Online Fan Communities and What They Say about Us." *Participations* 10(1): 270–298.

Wiedeman, Reeves. 2014. "#Activism." *New Yorker*, December 22. http://www.new yorker.com/magazine/2014/12/22/activism.

Williams, Raymond. 1977. *Marxism and Literature.* Oxford: Oxford University Press.

Williams, Rebecca. 2011. "'This Is the Night TV Died': Television Post-Object Fandom and the Demise of The West Wing." *Popular Communication* 9(4): 266–279.

Wills, Emily R. 2013. "Fannish Discourse Communities and the Construction of Gender in 'The X-Files.'" *Transformative Works and Cultures* 14. doi:10.3983 /twc.2013.0410.

Wolf, Mark J. P. 2012. *Building Imaginary Worlds: The Theory and History of Subcreation.* New York: Routledge.

Woo, Benjamin. 2012. "Understanding Understandings of Comics: Reading and Collecting as Media-Oriented Practices." *Participations* 9(2): 180–199.

Wuthnow, Robert. 2002. "The United States: Bridging the Privileged and the Marginalized?" In *Democracies in Flux*, ed. Robert Putnam. New York: Oxford University Press.

Yockey, Matt. 2012. "Wonder Woman for a Day: Affect, Agency, and Amazons." *Transformative Works and Cultures* 10. doi:10.3983/twc.2012.0318.

Youniss, James, Susan Bales, Verona Christmas-Best, Marcelo Diversi, Milbrey McLaughlin, and Rainer Silbereisen. 2002. "Youth Civic Engagement in the Twenty-First Century." *Journal of Research on Adolescence* 12(1): 121–148.

"Youth and Participatory Politics in a Digital Age: A Few Moments with Joseph Kahne and Cathy Cohen." 2012. *DML Central.* http://dml2011.dmlhub.net/newsletter /06/2012/youth-and-participatory-politics-digital-age-few-moments-joseph-kahne -and-cathy.html.

Zimmerman, Arely M. 2011. "Dreams Detained: Undocumented Latino Youth and the DREAM Movement." NACLA Report on the Americas. https://nacla.org/sites /default/files/A04406016_5.pdf.

Zimmerman, Arely M. 2012. "Documenting Dreams: New Media, Undocumented Youth and the Immigrant Rights Movement." Working Paper, June 6. MacArthur Foundation. http://ypp.dmlcentral.net/sites/all/files/publications/Documenting%20 DREAMs%20-%20Working%20Paper-MAPP%20-%20June%206%202012.pdf.

Zimmerman, Arely M. Forthcoming. "Transmedia Testimonio as Syncretic Repertoire: Digital Media, Coming Out, and Undocumented Youth Activism." New Media and Society.

Zimmerman, Arely M., and Sangita Shresthova. 2012. "DREAMing Out Loud!: Youth Activists Spoke about Their Fight for Education, Immigrant Rights and Justice through Media and Art." Confessions of an Aca-Fan, January 4. http://henryjenkins .org/2012/01/dreaming_out_loud_youth_activi.html.

Zuckerman, Ethan. 2012a. "Unpacking Kony 2012." My Heart's in Accra (blog), March 8. http://www.ethanzuckerman.com/blog/2012/03/08/unpacking-kony-2012/.

Zuckerman, Ethan. 2012b. "Understanding Digital Civics." My Heart's in Accra (blog), August 30. http://www.ethanzuckerman.com/blog/2012/08/30/understanding -digital-civics/.

Zuckerman, Ethan. 2013a. "'Beyond the Crisis in Civics'—Notes from My 2013 DML Talk." My Heart's in Accra (blog), March 26. http://www.ethanzuckerman.com/blog /2013/03/26/beyond-the-crisis-in-civics-notes-from-my-2013-dml-talk/.

Zuckerman, Ethan. 2013b. "New Media, New Civics?: My Bellweather Lecture at the Oxford Internet Institute." My Heart's in Accra (blog), December 6. http://www .ethanzuckerman.com/blog/2013/12/06/new-media-new-civics-my-bellweather -lecture-at-the-oxford-internet-institute/.

Zuckerman, Ethan. 2013c. Digital Cosmopolitans: Why We Think the Internet Connects Us, Why It Doesn't and How to Rewire It. New York: W. W. Norton.

Zuckerman, Ethan. 2014. "YouTube Parody as Politics: How the World Made Pharrell Cry." Atlantic, May 21. http://www.theatlantic.com/technology/archive/2014/05 /youtube-parody-as-politics-how-the-world-made-pharrell-cry/371380/.

Zuckerman, Ethan. 2015. "Cute Cats to the Rescue?: Participatory Media and Political Expression." In From Voice to Influence: Understanding Citizenship in a Digital Age, ed. Danielle Allen and Jennifer S. Light. Chicago: University of Chicago Press.

Zuckerman, Ethan. Forthcoming. "Talking about Civic Media: Towards a Language of Civic Efficacy." In Civic Media: Technology, Design, Practice, ed. Eric Gordon and Paul Mihailidis. Cambridge, MA: MIT Press.

Zukin, Cliff, Scott Keeter, Molly Andolina, Krista Jenkins, and Michael X. Delli Carpini. 2006. A New Engagement? Political Participation, Civic Life, and the Changing American Citizen. New York: Oxford University Press.

Index

#BlackLivesMatter, 6, 276
#FreeHappyIranians, 285
#iftheygunnedmendown, 5, 290
#LetNoorShine, 34
9/11, 150–151, 153–154, 156, 158, 168, 172–173, 179, 180–181, 184, 283–284
30 Mosques, 158, 164–167, 170–171, 253, 264, 305

A Needed Response, 18
American Broadcasting Company, 34, 35
Abedin, Huma, 161
Abrego, Leisy Janet, 193–194
Access, 42
Adbusters, 2
Adhami, Ridwan, 168–169
Adorable Care Act, 38
Affiliation, 107
African Liberty Students' Organization, 233
After the Welfare State, 233
Agenda setting, 62
Ahmed, Ahmed, 178, 180
Ahmed, Tanzila, 169
Ajtai, Peter, 69
Al-Qaeda, 149
Alcoholics Anonymous, 196, 255
Ali, Aman, 149–150, 164, 170–171
Ali, Asif, 181
Ali, Dilshad, 182
Ali, Imam Shamsi, 161
Ali, Wajahat, 165, 177–178
Ali, Ayaan Hirsi, 182
All-American Muslim, 19–20, 181
Allen, Danielle, 11, 36, 42
Alper, Meryl, 301
Alsultany, Evelyn, 167–168

Amarasingam, Amarnath, 180
American Freedom Defense Initiative, 155
American Idol, 87
American Museum of Natural History, 138
American Muslims, 10, 13–14, 19, 20, 22, 27, 34, 36, 42, 148, 149–185, 194, 207, 214, 264, 275, 281, 284, 291, 299; and defining identity, 57–58
"American Muslims Get . . . Happy!," 284
Amna, Erik, 269
Anderson, Benedict, 36–37
Angry Birds, 149, 178
Apprenticeship, 47
Apte, Mahadev, 180
Arab Spring, 3, 23, 101, 161
Arrested Development, 233
Aslan, Reza, 181
Aspen Idea Festival, 287
Atlas Economic Research Foundation, 233
Atlas Shrugs, 154
Attention-driven activism, 62
Audiences vs. publics, 97
Avatar, 129, 286
"Axis of Evil" tour, 178
Ayn Rand Institute, 233

Bachman, Michelle, 161
Bailey, Bobby, 73
Baluchi, Ali, 160
Banet-Weiser, Sarah, 89
Bansi, Shakuntala, 30
Batman, 137
Beautiful Trouble, 87, 88
Beck, Glenn, 22–23
Bedolla, Lisa Garcia, 208
Bell, Kristen, 80, 96, 128–129

Benford, Robert D., 166
Bennett, W. Lance, 9, 247, 263, 269
Bevan, Bronwyn, 301
Big data, 265
Bilici, Mucahit, 179
Bilson, Rachel, 85
Binder, Amy, 232, 233
Bird, Lauren (Jackson), 48–50, 108, 126–127, 253, 270
Black Youth Project, 266; "BYP 100: Black Youth, Black Police, & Transformative Justice" video, 266; "#BYP 100 Responds to George Zimmerman's Verdict," 266
Blakley, Johanna, 168
Bloomberg Businessweek, 191
Bodgroghkozy, Aniko, 24
Boler, Megan, 248
Bonding vs. bridging, 26, 55, 179, 201, 212
Bonsignore, Gregory, 181
Boston Marathon bombings, 171, 184
"Bounded solidarity," 208
Bourdieu, Pierre, 144
Bower, Ben, 44
Bowling Alone, 107
boyd, danah, 10, 26, 75, 173, 175, 177
Breakfast@Night, 164, 168, 170–171
Brewer, Jan, 191
British Broadcasting Company, 94
Brough, Melissa, 8, 73, 86, 129, 164, 272
Brown, Michael, 5, 6, 290
Buckingham, David, 30
Buffy the Vampire Slayer, 22, 279
Burges, Jean, 128
The Buried Life, 85
Bush, George W., 178, 191
Bush, Sophia, 85, 96
"By any media/means necessary," 15, 16, 24, 289, 292, 307–308

Cameron, James, 129, 286
Cantor, Eric, 215
Capra, Frank, 1

Captain America, 33
Captain EO, 88
Carey, Gordon, 90
Carnegie Corporation, 48
Carpentier, Nico, 40–41, 52, 238, 256
Castells, Manuel, 3, 9
Cato Institute, 222, 232–233, 244
Cats, 138
Celebrity, 96, 141
Chabot, Sean, 197
Charity, 140
Chattrapati Shivaji Terminus, 285
Chaudry, Rabia, 172, 183
Chauncy, George, 196
Cheena, Parvesh, 181
Chick-fil-A, 262
Chirrey, Deborah A., 196
Chu, Jon, 80, 96
Citizenship, 68, 132, 199–200, 246–248; good, 246; dutiful, 269; informed, 68, 131, 162; monitorial, 68–69, 162–163; actualizing, 247
Civic culture, 55, 103, 145–146; affinity, 55, 145–146; discussion, 55, 145, 147; identity, 55, 145, 147, 184, 193, 197, 199, 271; knowledge, 55, 145, 147; practices, 55, 145, 147; values, 55, 145, 146
Civic imagination, 17, 28–33, 37–39, 55, 59, 107, 109, 114–115, 145, 218; and public imagination, 30–31, 33, 37; political imagination, 30; releasing imagination, 304, 306
Civic media, 5
Civic Mission of Schools, 48
Civic Paths, 106, 113
Civic pathways, 257
Civil Wars storyline, 32
Clicktivism, 9, 65–66, 68–69, 71, 74
Cohen, Cathy J., 11, 42, 44–45, 92, 159, 207, 236–238
Cohn, D'Vera, 188–189
The Colbert Report, 113
Collective action, 276

Collins, Suzanne, 121, 136
Comic-Con, 85
"Coming out," 14, 58, 135, 186–187, 195–207, 216–218
Communities of practice, 292–294
Compassion fatigue, 68
Condis, Megan, 273
Congress of Racial Equality (CORE), 89–90
Connected learning, 17, 47, 49, 50–51, 56, 59, 108, 231, 295–296
Connected Learning Research Network, 295
Consequential connections, 277
Conservative youth, 232–233
Content worlds, 13–14, 31, 57, 83, 102, 106–107, 109, 112, 127–138, 140, 142, 145–146, 166, 277
Context collapse, 26–27, 75, 175, 299, 308
Cooper, Anderson, 34
Copeland, Aaron, 1
Cory Methodist Church, 228
Costanza-Chock, Sasha, 25, 28, 212, 262
Couldry, Nick, 20–22, 63–64, 200, 254, 263
Council on American-Islamic Relations (CAIR), 20, 160
Counterculture, 2, 40
Counter-Democracy, 4
Counter-narratives, 88
Counterpublics, 26, 37
Cribs, 210
Critical literacy skills, 294
Critical pedagogy, 297, 299–300, 307
Crum, Matt Scott, 100
CST Bollywood Flashmob, 285
Cultural acupuncture, 31, 57, 119–121, 125–130, 134, 136, 145, 147
Culture jamming, 2, 17, 18, 87
Curation, 170
Cvetkovich, Ann, 199, 200–201

Dahlgren, Peter, 37–38, 40, 55, 103–104, 145, 256–257, 269, 272, 277; and duty,

269; and efficacy, 269, 270; and interest, 269; and meaningfulness, 269; and motivation, 269
The Daily Show, 20, 181, 280
Daley, Patricia, 86–87
Dalton, Russell, 247
Darfur, 119
Dayan, Daniel, 97, 144
Dean, Jodi, 41
Dee, Ruby, 289
Deferred Action for Childhood Arrivals (DACA) program, 190, 194, 205, 215
Delwiche, Aaron, 2, 40
Democracy Remixed, 159
Democratic Party, 247, 251
Dery, Mark, 17
Détournement, 87
Dewey, John, 292
Digital afterlife, 76, 176, 303
Digital civics, 15, 222, 241
Digital divide, 192
Digital Media and Learning Conference, 245
Digital natives, 10
Disney, 62
DIY aesthetic, 127
DIY citizenship, 248, 271
Doctor Who, 137–138
Donald Duck, 22–23, 31
Donovan, Joan, 263
Dora the Explorer, 260
Douglas, Mary, 180
Doyle, Arthur Conan, 111
DREAMers, 12–14, 22, 24, 25–26, 28, 32, 42, 58, 159, 185, 236, 248, 250, 255, 257, 265–267, 271, 275–276, 278–279, 281, 291, 305; define American, 135; Dream Act provisions, 189–192; DreamActivist.org, 195, 200, 203, 205, 212–215; "Dear Senators . . . 2011," 210; DREAMing Out Loud!, 202; The Dream Is Coming, 216; Dreamers Adrift, 209–210; Dream Team LA, 211;

DREAMers (*cont.*)
"My Name is Mohammad . . ."
186–188, 195, 203–204; National Coming Out of the Shadows Week, 186–187,
201; National DREAM Graduation,
212–213; "No More Closets" campaign,
198; Queer Undocumented Immigrant
Project (QUIP), 197; "Undocribs" videos, 210; "Undocuqueers," 198; United
We Dream network, 197–198, 212, 216
DREAMers' stories archive, 187, 198,
201, 208; affective, 199, 200; fragile,
205–206
Drew, Carey, 240
Driscoll, Kevin, 273
"Drop It Like It's Hoppe," 226
"Drop It Like It's Hot," 226
Drumbl, Mark A., 68, 86
Dufrasne, Marie, 264
Duncan-Andrade, Jeffrey M., 298
Duncombe, Stephen, 29, 33–34, 87–88,
116, 218; *Dream*, 218
Duyvendak, Jan Willem, 197
Dyer, Richard, 261

Earl, Esther, 142
Earl, Jennifer, 11, 163
*The Economics of Freedom: What Your
Professors Won't Tell You*, 233
EconStories, 225
Edmund Pettus Bridge, 287
Education Not Deportation, 211
Egypt, 46, 152
Eid, Ahmed, 160
Eidman-Aadahl, Elyse, 11
El Random Hero, 194
Elarbi, Marium, 282–283
Electra, Dorian, 224–225, 229, 233, 253;
"Fa$t Ca$h" video, 229; "I'm in Love
with Friedrich HYWK," 225
Eliasoph, Nina, 54
Emotional sociology, 199
Entertaining the Citizen, 113

Ethical spectacle, 34
Evans, Christina, 39
Ewing, Katherine Pratt, 156
Exclusion, 55
Expressive politics, 268

Facebook, 6, 17–18, 23, 40, 61–62, 70, 93,
96, 100–101, 124, 149, 152, 169, 170–171,
173, 176–177, 195, 208–209, 211, 216, 234,
239, 240–241, 257, 273–274, 280, 294
Fair Trade, 270–271
Faith, 283
Fan activism, 14, 33–34, 57, 106–109, 113,
115, 116, 119, 127–131, 134, 141, 144–145,
148, 256, 271, 286
"Fan Club 2.0," 280
Fannish civics, 57, 115–117, 119, 121–125,
128–130, 134, 136, 145
Fannish practices, 39, 47, 50, 102, 109,
111–112, 114, 137, 145, 147
Fawkes, Guy, 9
Federal Bureau of Investigation, 190, 268
Federal Reserve, 229
Feezell, Jessica Timpany, 72
Feminism, third-wave, 110, 207
Ferguson, 5, 6
Fersing, Julie, 284
Filipiak, Danielle, 297
Fine, Michelle, 153, 156
Firefly, 279
Fiske, John, 109–110, 131
Flash activism, 286
Flickr, 170
Florida Family Association (FFA), 19
Fontaine, Loïc, 284
Foot, Kristen A., 163
Ford, Sam, 17, 93, 108, 129, 162
Foundation for Economic Development,
233, 244
Fox News, 23, 231
Framing, 167, 193
Frazier, Nancy, 157
Free Software, 40

Freedom Riders, 23, 89–90, 275
Freedom Works, 232
Freire, Paolo, 297–298, 299
Friedman, Milton, 244
Frost, Sloane, 236
Fukuyama, Francis, 26
Fünke, Tobias, 233
Futures of Entertainment conference, 253–254, 279

Gamber-Thompson, Liana, 188, 219, 220, 298, 303
Gardner, Howard, 11
Garner, Eric, 6
Gay Liberation Front, 197
Geller, Pamela, 154–155
Generational approach, 221, 253, 287–288
Giving Keys, 100
Gladwell, Malcolm, 23–24, 68, 70, 194, 274
GoatFace Comedy, 151
Gomez, Julian, 135, 275
Good Participation project, 44, 274
Goodwin, Jeff, 199
Google, 19, 52
Gordon-Leavitt, Joseph, 59
Gray, Jonathan, 113, 179–180, 258, 260–261
Gray, Mary, 157–158
Green, John and Hank, 49, 105–106, 138, 142, 144; Crash Course channel, 105; The Fault in Our Stars, 142; Sci Show channel, 105; as VlogBrothers, 105–106, 138, 141–142
Green, Joshua, 17, 93, 108, 128–129, 162
Greene, Maxine, 304–305
Ground Zero, 153
Gutierrez, Kris, 298

Habermas, Jurgen, 157
"Happy" videos, 284–285; "Happy British Muslims," 284
Harlem Islamic Center, 164
Harry Potter Alliance, 12–14, 29, 31, 47–49, 55–56, 89, 102–106, 108, 111–128, 130–133, 135, 137, 140–147, 166, 229, 249–255, 258, 260–261, 265, 269–270, 305; "Fight for $15" protest, 146; Helping Haiti Heal, 49, 104, 108; "The Hunger Games Are Real," 126–127, 128; Hunger Is Not a Game campaign, 121–123, 125; Not in Harry's Name campaign, 49, 270; Odds In Our Favor campaign, 125, 127, 136, 147; "Orphans vs. Empires" talk, 137; When Our Heroes Fail video blog, 270; Wrock4Equality campaign,103
Harry Potter Education Fanon (HPEF) 121
Harry Potter franchise, 29, 31, 48, 50, 102, 114–116, 119–127, 131–133, 135, 138, 305–306; Sirius Black, 117–118; Death Eaters, 117; Dumbledore's Army, 117–118, 136–137; Hogwarts, 103; House Cup, 103; Order of the Phoenix, 118; school's houses, 103; Voldemort, 118, 275
Hartley, John, 87, 271–272; mediasphere and semiosphere, 272; plebiscite entertainment, 87
Harvard Institute of Politics (IOP), 219
Hassan, Lena, 169
Hathout, Meher, 152
Hay, James, 45–46, 231–232
Hayek, Friedrich, 225, 227, 244,
Henderson, Jennifer, 40
Hennion, Antoine, 144
Herrera, Linda, 46
Herrington, Lee, 113
Herr-Stephenson, 301
High School Musical, 62–63
Highland Pride Alliance, 157
Hijabi Girl, 182–183
Hijabi Monologues, 169, 170–171
HijabiBengaliSisters, 176–177
Hills, Matt, 133
Hinck, Ashley, 132
HitRecord, 59
Hogwarts at Ravelry, 50, 52
Honesty Policy, 284

Hoppe, Hans-Hermann, 226
Hotmail, 178
Howe, Neil, 81
Hoyler, Marguerite, 156
Huerta, Erick, 32–33, 194–195, 200–201, 206
Humor, 178–183, 184
Hunger Games franchise, 12, 49, 62, 122, 125, 133, 136–137, 146–147, 261, 271, 306; Capital, 121, 126–127; *Catching Fire*, 125; Cover Girl, 126; Katniss Everdeen, 121, 123–124, 126; *Mockingjay Part One*, 146; Panem, 121, 126; Coriolanus Snow, 126; Three Finger Salute, 136
Hurowitz, Roger, 68, 162–163
Hyperdiegesis, 133

Ifill, Gwen, 287
Ikeda, Tani, 15, 16, 291
Illinois Coalition for Immigrant Justice and Refuge Rights, 196
Imagine Better, 12–14, 29, 33, 56, 103, 105–106, 113, 120–127, 130–131, 133–137, 143, 146–147, 261, 271, 305; Superman is an Immigrant campaign, 135
Imagined/imagining community, 36–37
ImMEDIAte Justice, 15, 16, 291
Immigrant Youth Justice League, 187
"Implicit Meanings," 180
Indian Idol, 286
Indignadas, 3
Influence, 157
Institute for Humane Studies, 222, 233, 244
Institute for the Future, 30–31
Institutional politics, 4, 8, 14, 39–40, 42, 53, 64, 70–71, 76, 220, 238, 239, 250–251, 278
Institutional supports, 233, 250, 289
Intercollegiate Studies Institute, 233
Interest-based vs. friendship-based networks, 47, 54, 72
International Criminal Court, 82
International Crisis Group, 104

International Students for Liberty Conference (ISFLC), 233
Invisible Children, 12–14, 22, 27, 28, 46, 56, 61–101, 102–103, 127, 140, 237, 245, 249, 255, 267, 269, 275, 281, 283, 291, 300–303; blog, 90; Cover the Night initiative; 76–77; Fourth Estate, 71, 78, 80–84, 92, 95–96, 99, 100, 265, 278, 281–282; Global Night Commute, 63; *Invisible Children Musical*, 63, 88; *Kony 2012* campaign, 10, 27, 28, 42, 56, 61–101, 245, 266, 275, 291, 295, 300, 303; LRA Crisis Tracker, 94; *Move*, 66; My IC Story, 95–96; *Rough Cut*, 73, 76, 84–86; shutting down, 99; *Tony*, 76; ZeroLRA campaign, 85
Irvine11 campaign, 173–174
Islamic Center of Southern California, 12, 152, 184, 250
Islamic Circle of North America, 160
Islamic Society of North America, 160, 169
Ito, Mimi, 49, 72, 264, 295–296

Jackass, 85
Jackson, Mahalia, 289
Jackson, Michael, 88
Jackson, Samuel L., 279
Jasper, James M., 193, 199
Jenkins, Henry, 17, 40–42, 74, 93, 108, 129, 131, 143–144, 148, 162, 229, 293
Jenkins, Jedidiah, 79, 281–282
Jobrani, Maz, 178, 180
Johnson, Gary, 219
Jones, Jeffrey P., 179
Justice League, 32

Kahne, Joseph, 11, 42, 44–45, 47, 72, 92, 158, 207, 236–238
Kedhar, Anusha, 5, 30
Kelty, Christopher, 40–41, 238, 294
Kennedy, Robert F., 287
Khalid, Wardah, 175

Khalifa, Wiz, 226
Khan, Lena, 181
Kibria, Nazli, 155
King, Martin Luther, 23–24, 187, 287
Kiva.org, 105, 139
Kligler-Vilenchik, Neta, 47, 54, 64, 68–69,
    72, 79, 106, 109, 114–115, 130, 265, 269,
    294, 305–306
Koch, Charles and David, 231–232
Kony, Joseph, 61, 73, 76, 78–79, 82–85,
    89, 94
Krypton, 135

Ladson-Billings, Gloria, 298, 307
Lady Gaga, 85
Lal, Prerna, 215
Latent capacities, 162–163
Lave, Jean, 293
Lawrence, Jennifer, 124
Leadership Academy, 233
Leaky Cauldron, 104, 127
LeakyCon, 120–121, 275–276, 278, 283
Learning Channel, 19
Lee, Carol, 298
Lee, Clifford, 72
Legion of Extraordinary Dancers
    (LXD), 85
Lego, 138
Levers of change, 5, 63, 245
Levine, Lawrence, 180
Levine, Peter, 8
Lewis, John, 287–289
LGBTQ, 255, 272
Liberalism, 244
Libertarians, 28, 46, 214, 218, 303; party,
    247; second-wave, 38, 58, 261
Liberty Movement, 230, 235, 237, 242
Light, Jennifer S., 42
Ling, Lisa, 34
The Lion King, 137
Lionsgate Entertainment, 124–126,
    256, 271
Lipsitz, George, 208

Little Mosque on the Prairie, 179
Livingstone, Sonia, 97
Lobbying, 71, 99
Lobogo, Sanyu, 90
Lopez, Lori Kido, 167
Lord of the Rings, 137, 261
Lord's Resistance Army (LRA), 61, 64, 70,
    78–79, 83–84, 94–95, 98
Lotan, Gilad, 74–75, 96
Love, InshAllah: The Secret Love Lives of
    American Muslim Women, 169, 171
Lovecraft, H. P., 111
Lowe's (store chain), 19–20, 181–182, 256

MacArthur Foundation, 11, 92
Madonna, 109–110
Maggiacomo, Matt, 271
Maira, Sunaina Marr, 155–156
Maker Movement, 301
Malcolm X, 16, 23, 164, 227–228, 304
Malitz, Zack, 87
Man of Steel, 135, 258
Mandvi, Aasif, 20
Manji, Rizwan, 181
Mannheim, Karl, 220
March on Washington, 287
Martin, Treyvon, 6
Martinez, Viridiana, 217
Marvel Comics, 32
Marwick, Alice, 173–175, 177
Masjid Khalifah, 164
Mastery, 119, 123–125, 129, 131
Mateo, Lizabeth, 217
Mattu, Ayesha, 169
Maznavi, Nura, 169
McCain, John, 280
McCobin, Alexander, 219, 221–222,
    235, 244
McDonald's, 67, 119, 146
McIntosh, Jonathan, 22–23, 31; "Buffy
    vs. Edward," 22; "Right Wing Radio
    Duck," 22–23
McKee, Alan, 226–227

Measuring success, 103–104
Mechanisms of translation, 109, 276
Media, Activism, and Participatory
    Politics (MADD) research group, 12,
    21, 62, 177
Media literacy, 42, 92, 192
Media sphere, 272
Mehta, Ritesh, 286
Meme, 66–69
Mendez, Erika, 155
Merchant, Joshua, 21, 34
Merrick, Helen, 112
Meza, Nancy, 211–212
Michael, Jaclyn, 180
Middaugh, Ellen, 43
Millennials, 80–81, 100
Millennials Rising, 81
Miller, Isaac, 297
Minimum wage, 146
"Mipsterz—Somewhere In America," 150
Mittell, Jason, 93, 129
Model change, 163
Modern Family, 61–62
*The Morality of Capitalism: What Your
    Professors Won't Tell You*, 233
Morell, Ernest, 298
Morozov, Evgeny, 173
Morrakiu, 226
Moshtrogen, 264
Motivation, 269
MTV, 85, 210
Munoz, Maria, 192
Muslim American Society, 160
Muslim Public Affairs Council, 12, 20,
    151–152, 159, 172, 175, 184, 249, 284
Muslim rage, 182–183
Muslim Student Association (MSA)
    National, 160
Muslim Students Union, 173–174
Muslim Youth Group, 12, 15, 152, 159, 161,
    164, 168, 170–171, 181
MySpace, 200

Naber, Nadine, 155
Nahm, Sheena, 168
Naidoo, Jay, 85
National Association of Media Literacy
    Educators, 60
National Day Laborer Organizing Net-
    work, 250
National Network for Arab American
    Communities, 282
National Public Radio, 164, 219, 292
National Security Agency, 149, 177, 251
National Writing Project, 60
Nerdfighters, 12–14, 47, 49, 54–56, 89, 91,
    103, 105, 106, 112–113, 131–145, 254–255,
    265, 271; demographics, 143; Founda-
    tion to Decrease World Suck, 105, 140;
    Nerdfighteria, 140, 142
Netflix, 85
Networked publics, 269, 276
New Media Foundation, 172
New York Police Department, 158
New York Times, 20, 67, 124, 142, 146,
    171, 251
Newsweek, 182
Nike, 119
Nissenbaum, Helen, 173
Nomadic, 137
Norris, Pippa, 256, 261

Obama, Barack, 23, 38, 44, 50, 76, 190–
    191, 211, 215–216, 280
Objectivism, 227
Ocampo, Luis Moreno, 82
Occupy Wall Street, 1–3, 9, 10, 23, 31, 52,
    218, 249, 260, 262–263, 267, 287
Offendum, Omar, 151
Okot, Jolie Grace, 84
Olympics, 50
Once Upon a Time, 137
Online activism, 274
O'Reilly, Bill, 23
Oren, Michael, 173

Orientalism, 167
Orlikowski, Wanda, 264
OxFam, 121, 124, 249
Oyston, Grant, 90, 91

Panth, Sabina, 26
Papacharissi, Zizi A., 261
Papola, John, 225
Paradoxes of participatory politics, 56,
    61, 65, 77–98, 256; activism/entertain-
    ment, 56, 85–89; bottom-up/top-down
    approaches, 56, 65, 95–98; complex
    vs. comprehensible stories, 64, 82–85;
    consensus/contention, 56, 65, 89–93;
    goals/process, 78–82; spreadability/
    drillability, 56, 74, 93–95, 129–130, 256
Participant media, 59
Participation: boundaries, 143, 287, 144;
    degrees of, 70, 257, 293; genres, 264;
    minimalist vs. maximalist, 41, 52; gap,
    45, 192; peripheral, 294; rhetoric of,
    53; resistance vs. in/through, 51–52;
    scaffolding, 71
Participatory culture, 2, 14, 17, 39–42, 46,
    56, 110, 143, 286
Participatory politics, 2, 14, 17, 25, 39–46,
    50, 53–54, 56–57, 59, 61, 64, 82, 97–98,
    102, 105, 109, 115, 138, 143–145, 148,
    150, 156, 199, 214, 231–232, 236–238,
    273, 276–278, 280, 283, 292–295, 300,
    306, 308; dialogue and feedback, 43;
    investigation, 44; mobilization, 44;
    production, 44
Participatory storytelling, 164
Partners in Health, 249
Passel, Jeffrey S., 188
Patler, Caitlin, 192
Patriarche, Geoffroy, 264
Patriot Act, 173
Paul, Rand, 251–252
Paul, Ron, 219, 224, 242, 251
PBS NewsHour, 287

Peabody Awards, 18, 21
Pendergast, John, 104
Performance, 63
Pew Research Center, 154
Pfaff, Steven, 199
Pfister, Rachel Cody, 50
Philanthropy, 86, 87
Policy Mic, 77
Polletta, Francesca, 166–167, 193, 199
Poole, Lauren, 73, 101
Popular culture, 107, 109–110, 120,
    128–129, 145, 148, 162, 166, 258
Post, Jerrold, 172
Post-object fandom, 120"
Power, Samantha, 80, 82
PraxGirl, 230
Precarious publics, 42, 149, 150, 157–159,
    183–184
PriceScope, 273
Privacy/publicity, 14, 42, 148, 173, 177–178
Project for Awesome (P4A), 140–141
Proposition, 34, 117
Public Broadcasting System, 178
Public engagement keystone, 132
Public spheres of the imagination, 57,
    112, 133
Publics, 157; boundary publics, 157–158;
    identity publics, 144
Pulitzer Prize, 158
Punathambekar, Aswin, 286
"Punk-Drunk Love," 169
Putnam, Robert, 26, 54, 103, 107, 116, 273

Qu'ran, 161

Race and ethnicity, 45, 54, 143–144
Ramadan, 155, 161, 164–165, 170–171, 265
Ramirez, Pedro, 267–268
Ramos, Matias, 216
Rand, Ayn, 227–228
Rang De Basanti, 286
Reciprocity, 52, 203

Remix, 22, 98
Republican Party, 247, 251, 280
Resolve, 99
Resource poor, network rich, 208
Rice, Tamir, 290
Riot Grrrls, 110
Rockwell, Norman, 1
Romney, Mitt, 181, 279
Room for Debate (*New York Times*), 67
Rosanvallon, Pierre, 4
Ross, Andrew, 112
Rothbard, Murray, 226–227
Rowling, J. K., 28–29, 102, 110, 115–117,
    119–120, 305
Ruge, TMS, 66
Russell, Jason, 27, 61, 65–66, 73, 76, 84–85,
    88, 101, 281, 282

Saguy, Abigail, 197
Saler, Michael, 111–112, 133
Salgado, Julio, 208–210
Sam's Club, 155
Samples, John, 251
Sanders, Bernie, 251
Sandvoss, Cornel, 113–114
Sarsour, Linda, 181, 281–283
Sartre, Jean-Paul, 16
Satire TV, 179
Sauter, Molly, 274
Scale change, 163
Scaling up, 208
Scandal, 190
Schneider, Steven M., 163
Schudson, Michael, 68
Secondary/primary worlds, 133
Second-wave libertarianism, 220–223, 229
Secure Communities, 190
Segerberg, Alexandra, 263
Self-deportation, 217
Sense of community, 72, 116, 270
Servai, Shanoor, 77
Sesame Street, 10
Sexuality, 103, 143

Shadyac, Tom, 96
Shaikley, Laila, 150
Shared media experiences, 72, 270
Shariah, 154
Shohat, Ella, 167
Shresthova, Sangita, 8, 47, 79, 106, 129–
    130, 151–152, 165, 172–173, 202, 285, 299,
    300, 303
Shughart, 245
Shum, Harry, Jr., 85, 96
signon.org, 19
Signorile, Michelangelo, 262–263
Sikh, 155
Sirin, Selcuk R., 153, 156
Slack, Andrew, 31, 102, 104, 117, 119–124,
    126, 137, 146
Slacktivision, 69, 194
Snoop Dogg, 226
Snow, David A., 167
Social Flow, 74–75
Social surveillance, 174–176, 274, 307
Sociality, 89
Soep, Lissa, 11, 49, 59, 76, 176, 277
Soulstein, Seth, 102
South by Southwest, 85
Spectacle, 97
Spencer, Robert, 154
Spider-Man, 32
Spreadable Media, 17
Srivastava, Lina, 25
Stam, Robert, 167
STAND, 249
Star Wars, 137–138, 259, 261; *Knights of the
    Old Republic*, 273
State of the Union, 278
Stempeck, Matt, 274
Stendal, Samantha, 18
Stereotypes, 166, 168, 179, 183, 204
Stewart, Jon, 20
Stigma, 204
Storytelling, 13–15, 21, 56, 82–84, 149–150,
    165–172, 184, 193–194, 203, 207, 263,
    302, 304

Strategic nonvoters, 58, 239–243
Strauss, William, 81
Steubenville rape case, 18
Students for Liberty (SFL), 12–14, 42, 50–51, 58, 219–222, 228, 220–224, 233–236, 248, 250, 253, 255, 257, 265, 271, 278
Sunstein, Cass, 273
Superman, 12, 32, 33, 133, 135–137, 258
Surveillance, 14, 42, 57, 149–150, 172–173, 177, 184
Swartz, Lana, 73, 84, 93, 273, 302

Tagouri, Noor, 34–36
Tariq, Bassam, 150, 164, 167, 170, 253
Taste, 137, 141–142, 145; taste communities and taste publics, 144
Tea Party, 23, 45–46, 215, 231–232, 251
Technological determinism, 273
TEDx-Youth conference, 137
Terriquez, Veronica, 192, 193
Testimonios, 188, 207, 217
Theory fans, 226
Thick vs. thin engagement, 130
Third space, 299
Thompson, Ethan, 179–180
Thorson, Kjerstin, 64, 68–69, 132, 267
Time, 80–81, 85
To Write Love on Her Arms, 100
Tocqueville, Alexis de, 107
Token Libertarian Girl, 230
Tolkien, J. R. R., 111
Transformative works and cultures, 113
Transmedia Hollywood, 22
Transmedia mobilization, 17, 24–25, 27, 55, 58–59, 63, 207, 212–215, 262–263, 291
"Triggered: Mistaken for Guns," 290
Trust, 203; making, 300, 302, 304, 307
Tsarnaev Brothers, 171–172
Tumblr, 51, 66, 99, 135, 195, 239
Turk, Jihad, 164, 170
Turner, Fred, 2
Twilight, 22

Twitter, 17, 23, 43, 62, 68, 70, 161, 170, 173, 182, 195, 211, 216, 231, 253

UCLA Labor Center, 250
Uganda, 61, 66, 73, 76, 78, 84, 85, 90, 92, 94, 95, 101
United to End Genocide, 86
University of Chicago, 265
Univision, 211
Unmosqued, 160
U.S. Census Bureau, 45
U.S. Congress, 278
U.S. Customs and Immigration Services, 190
U.S. Department of Homeland Security, 191, 215
U.S. House of Representatives, 288
U.S. Immigration and Customs Enforcement, 190, 194, 202, 211, 216–217, 267–268
U.S. Immigration and Naturalization Service, 260
U.S. Supreme Court, 191

V for Vendetta, 9
The Vagina Monologues, 169
Valenzuela, Angela, 299
Van Zoonen, Liesbet, 29, 87, 113, 229, 306
Vargas, Jose Antonio, 135, 276
Veliz, Benita, 190
Veronica Mars, 128–129
Vimeo, 187, 195
Vine, 195
Voice, 15, 17, 20–22, 40, 42, 55, 63–64, 82, 157
Vossoughi, Shirin, 301
Voting, 278

"Wake the F**K Up," 279
Walker, Scott, 258
Walmart, 114, 157
Ward, Anna, 197
Warner, Michael, 157

Warner Brothers (Warner Communications), 116, 125, 256, 270–271
Washington, D.C., 220, 284
Washington Square Park, 2
Weareahappyfrom.com, 284
Weintraub, Jeff, 89
Wenger, Etienne, 293
Wesch, Michael, 26
West Bank, 129
The West Wing, 120
West, Noelle, 66, 98
Whedon, Joss, 279
Why Voice Matters, 20, 63
Williams, Pharrell, 284
Williams, Rebecca, 120
Wilson, Joseph C., 104
Winfrey, Oprah, 34, 96
Wisconsin, 258
Wish to Help, 72, 270
The Wizard of Oz, 137
Wizard Rock, 102, 104, 111, 115, 131
Wolf, Mark J. P., 133
Wolverine, 32
Wonder Woman, 33
Woo, Benjamin, 115
Wood, Kate, 232–233

X-Men, 32

Yarnbombing, 19
Yassine, Soha, 164
Yates, JoAnna, 264
YaztheSpaz, 151
Yerevan, Armenia, 285
Young America's Foundation, 233, 236
Young Leaders Summit, 151, 152
Youth and Participatory Politics Network, 11–12, 39, 43, 54, 92, 207, 274, 276, 292;
Youth, 7–8
Youth Radio, 59, 290
YouTube, 18, 32, 34, 52, 58, 66, 99, 102, 105, 126–128, 138, 141, 151, 170, 174–176, 181, 186–187, 195, 198, 202, 204, 224–225, 230–231, 255, 257, 265, 267, 273, 275, 284–285

Zero Dark 30, 161
Zimmerman, Arely, 24, 28, 32, 188, 196, 202–204, 206, 211, 214, 298
Zombie fandom, 120
Zombiecon, 1
Zuckerman, Ethan, 5, 11, 37, 53, 54, 62, 83, 108, 130, 162, 207, 222–223, 241–242, 245
Zukin, Cliff, 242–243, 254, 284, 285

About the Authors

Henry Jenkins is Provost's Professor of Communication, Journalism, Cinematic Arts and Education at the University of Southern California. His previous books include *Convergence Culture: Where Old and New Media Collide* and *Spreadable Media: Creating Meaning and Value in a Networked Society* (with Sam Ford and Joshua Green).

Sangita Shresthova is Director of Henry Jenkins's Media, Activism & Participatory Politics (MAPP) project based at USC. She is also the author of *Is It All about Hips? Around the World with Bollywood Dance* (2011).

Liana Gamber-Thompson is Program Associate at the National Writing Project and Community Manager for Connected Learning TV.

Neta Kligler-Vilenchik is Assistant Professor of Communication at the Hebrew University of Jerusalem.

Arely M. Zimmerman is Assistant Professor of Ethnic Studies at Mills College in Oakland, California.

Elisabeth Soep is Senior Producer and Research Director at Youth Radio, where she founded the Innovation Lab with MIT in 2013. Youth Radio's Peabody Award–winning newsroom serves as National Public Radio's youth desk.